Library of
Davidson College

THE CARD CATALOG: CURRENT ISSUES

READINGS AND SELECTED BIBLIOGRAPHY

Edited by
CYNTHIA C. RYANS

The Scarecrow Press, Inc.
Metuchen, N.J., & London
1981

025.3
C266

Library of Congress Cataloging in Publication Data
Main entry under title:

The Card catalog, current issues.

Includes index.
1. Catalogs, Card--Addresses, essays, lectures.
2. Library catalogs--Addresses, essays, lectures.
3. Libraries--Automation--Addresses, essays, lectures.
I. Ryans, Cynthia C., 1933-
Z710.C3   025.3'1   81-720
ISBN 0-8108-1417-X   AACR2

Copyright © 1981 by Cynthia C. Ryans

Manufactured in the United States of America

For

John

CONTENTS

Preface ix

Part I. THE FUTURE OF THE CARD CATALOG 1

1. Ten Ways to Profit From a Long Engagement
JAMES THOMPSON 7

2. Alas, Poor Card Catalog
CAROLYN DUSENBURY 17

3. The Assumption of Automation or: The Card Catalog Is Dead! Long Live the Card Catalog!
DAN C. HAZEN 30

4. A New Code! A New Catalog?
FRANKLYN F. BRIGHT 35

5. New Catalog for UW-Madison
FRANKLYN F. BRIGHT 38

6. Problems With the Card Catalogs: Present and Prospective
GAIL KENNEDY 42

7. Where Will Your Card Catalog Be in 1980?
ROCHELL CROW 47

8. Opening a Library Catalog
MAURICE J. FREEDMAN 51

9. Adopting AACR 2: The Case for Not Closing the Catalog
JOE A. HEWITT and DAVID E. GLEIM 59

10. Closing the Card Catalog, or Two Years Before the Blast
MARY B. HENRY 67

11. Close the Card Catalog?
JEFFREY T. SCHWEDES 71

12. Catalog "Closings" and Serials
JEAN S. DECKER 74

13.	Closing the Card Catalog ANN EKSTROM	84
14.	Closing the Card Catalog BILL CADDELL	87
15.	Living Amid Closed Catalogs SANFORD BERMAN	89

Bibliography 94

Part II. ALTERNATIVES TO THE CARD CATALOG 99

16.	Of Catalogs, Computers, and Communication LIZ DICKINSON	103
17.	Automated Network Catalog Products and Services MAURICE J. FREEDMAN	115
18.	Alternatives to the Conventional Card Catalog from the User Point of View STANLEY McELDERRY	126
19.	Alternative Physical Forms of Catalogues in Large Research Libraries H. D. L. VERVLIET	132
20.	Card Catalog to COM JOHN NORTH	140
21.	Computer Output Microfiche Catalogs: Some Practical Considerations RICHARD W. MEYER and BONNIE JUERGENS	147
22.	Public Response to an Academic Library Microcatalog JAMES R. DWYER	155
23.	The Use and Economics of Computer-Generated Microfiche Catalogs WILLIAM C. HORNER	175
24.	On-Line Computer Terminal Versus COM Systems FRANK J. MALABARBA and WILLIAM D. McCULLOUGH	179

Bibliography 189

Part III.	PREPARING FOR AN ALTERNATIVE FORM OF BIBLIOGRAPHIC ACCESS	197
25.	Thinking About Automation? Consider These Factors in Making a Decision JAMES KRIKELAS	206
26.	Card Catalogue to On-Line Catalogue--The Transitional Process CAROLE WEISS	205
27.	Automation--Planning to Implementation; The Problems En Route IRWIN H. PIZER	214
28.	Financial Considerations Involved in Closing the Catalog KAZUKO M. DAILEY	219
29.	Planning for the Catalogs: A Managerial Perspective JOSEPH A. ROSENTHAL	227
30.	Automation and the Library Administrator ELEANOR MONTAGUE	242
31.	The Effects of Automation on Library Administration GÜNTER PFLUG	255
32.	The Retrospective Conversion Project at the University of Utah Marriott Library YASUKO KAO	266
33.	Converting a Card Catalogue to Microfiche PHILLIP WATSON	273
34.	Freezing the Library of Congress Catalogs	277
Bibliography		283
Part IV.	CASE STUDIES	287
35.	Computer-Produced Book Catalogue for New Brunswick Public Library System AGNEZ HALL	291
36.	Computer Output Microfilm: Stout Uses a New Library Tool PHILIP SCHWARZ	296

37.	COM Comes to the Chicago Public Library PATRICK M. O'BRIEN	299
38.	RMIT COM Catalogue Study Results ELIZABETH STECHER MORRISON	308
39.	600 Users Meet the COM Catalog BRIAN AVENEY and MARY FISCHER GHIKAS	315
40.	COM Catalog vs. Card Catalog: The Experience of the University of Oregon Law Library DENNIS RAY HYATT	320

Bibliography 328

Index 331

PREFACE

One of the most topical issues in the library world today is the question of whether or not to close the card catalog. This has been brought about by several factors: the continued growth of library holdings which creates a need for the expansion of the card catalog; the physical deterioration of the card catalog through constant use; the advancement in the library field of the use of computers and machine readable data; and finally, the planned acceptance and the adoption of the revised edition of the Anglo American Cataloguing Rules (AACR 2) by the Library of Congress and consequently by libraries across the country.

For many decades, the card catalog has been the traditional bibliographic record of a library's collection. It has continued to provide the identification, the description, and the location of the library's many holdings. However, the card catalog is becoming obsolescent for a number of reasons: the increasingly large number of titles being added to library collections generates more cards for the card catalog, thus causing a space problem; the increasing drain on the library budget for catalog maintenance (one of the larger expenditures in the library budget); and the time lapse which often occurs in getting cards into the catalog after new titles have been processed.

The Library of Congress has announced that on January 2, 1981 it will begin cataloging by AACR 2 and at that time, will freeze its current card catalog. This means it will no longer add cards to its present card catalog and will rely on automated data to provide access to its collections. One reason for this decision is that the new cataloging rules will create problems in interfiling new entries into the existing catalog; the new rules not only change access points but also create different forms of headings.

Although the size of the library's collection, as well as library policy, are important factors in determining the decision regarding the present library catalog, the Library of Congress often simply sets the pace for the actions of libraries in this country. Many libraries may feel that it is best to follow the Library of Congress' decision. This decision will naturally have an effect on libraries throughout the country, even if they choose not to follow the Library of Congress' lead to freeze its catalogs. For those who decide not to freeze their card catalogs, or even for those who prefer to delay the decision, the issue should perhaps be viewed in greater depth.

With more advanced technology continually being pursued, there are several alternatives that have been developed to the card catalog. Thus, the question arises: Is the card catalog the most efficient and economic form of bibliographic access to a library's collection? The mark of a good bibliographic access system (in whatever form) is that it is designed to answer questions concerning what books are in the library. These books should be searchable by author, title, subject, etc., and these searches should be made possible with the greatest of ease and for the least cost.

The objective of this book is to furnish the reader, through a series of readings and a comprehensive bibliography, with an over-all view of the steps necessary in determining the future of the card catalog. The compiler has tried to select a wide range of readings, some of which will answer questions for many different sizes and types of libraries. A general background on this topic will help to make the reader cognizant of the factors involved in making decisions of this type.

The readings included in this book were selected from hundreds of articles in order to provide an in-depth coverage. I hope that this compilation will aid librarians in the decision-making process and will stimulate a continued interest/dialogue in the field. The book is intended to contain the most significant and recent articles on the future of the card catalog.

Some libraries (mainly smaller and mid-sized libraries) have replaced their card catalogs with book catalogs as long ago as the early 1960's. In addition, some planning regarding alternative forms of bibliographic access has been in progress for many years. This book, however, deals only with material of a more current nature-- that published since 1975.

The book is organized to provide the reader a sequential look at the processes necessary for them to determine the most advantageous decision on the future of the library and catalog. A general introduction is given to each section to familiarize the reader with an over-all view of the card catalog and its future (Part I) and the factors involved in the decision-making process.

There are several factors which should be taken into consideration before a library reaches a decision on what to do about its card catalog. For example, what are the alternatives to the traditional card catalog that best fit the needs of the library? These include: the Computer Output Microform (COM) catalog, the book catalog, and a completely on-line catalog. A fourth possibility is to employ a combination of one of these alternatives with the existing card catalog. In order to determine if the card catalog should be closed, these options should be studied. Part II of this book covers such alternatives.

The cost factor is very important in the determination of an alternative form of bibliographic access. This involves a study of

Preface

the costs of maintaining the present card catalog and of converting existing records to a machine system, as well as the projected cost of maintaining the new system. The costs involved include not only hardware and software, but also expenditures for staff time, planning, and development.

Further, effects on the administration must be taken into consideration when decisions are being made on the form of bibliographic access for a library collection. In addition, it is important to involve the library staff at all levels in the planning process; the form of catalog and organization produces varied working conditions.

The decision maker should be cognizant of the needs and use patterns of the library's clientele. Only then can he or she determine what form of bibliographic access would best serve the patron, while at the same time be efficient and economical for the library.

Part III covers these points and gives some examples on how library management is involved in these decisions and the effects these changes will have on the entire library and library personnel as well as the user.

The final part (Part IV) includes readings and citations of "case histories" of libraries that have changed from a card catalog to some other form of bibliographic access. Some libraries find that the change is a positive step, while others find it less advantageous than they had hoped. Perhaps one of the best ways of preparing for such a change is to read and study what other libraries have done. Much can be gained and many hours saved by not having to "reinvent the wheel." As can be seen in the readings included in this book, there is a great deal of preparation and study needed before such an important decision as closing the card catalog is made by any library, regardless of its size.

In acknowledging those who made this book possible, the author must first express her gratitude to the many authors and publishers of the included readings. A special thanks goes to Mr. James Thompson of the Milton S. Eisenhower Library at Johns Hopkins University in Baltimore, Maryland for his suggestions and for supplying extra bibliographies for the author to study. I would also like to thank the staff of the Interlibrary Loan Department at the Kent State University Library for their assistance in obtaining copies of many of the articles that the author needed. In addition, the author would like to thank Janet Gifford for the hours spent handling the typing as well as the other necessary tasks needed in a project such as this. I would like to thank Nancee Collis and Jenny and Amy Davidson for their help with the proofreading. Most important, the author would like to thank her husband, Dr. John K. Ryans, Jr. for his many editorial suggestions and his assistance in reading the drafts, as well as his continued encouragement throughout this project.

PART I. THE FUTURE OF THE CARD CATALOG

The term "bibliographic control" refers to various means of retrieving library materials, the most common of which has been a card or a printed catalog, and more recently an on-line catalog. This catalog, in whatever form the library chooses to use, should be designed to tell the library user what materials are in the library and where they can be found.

The type of bibliographic control that a library chooses is determined by a number of factors. Perhaps the most prominent one for many libraries is cost or financial considerations. User needs is another important factor to be considered. These, of course, can vary in different types of libraries. Many library users are accustomed to using the card catalog and find it difficult to change to any other form of bibliographic control. Naturally, this can be just a matter of preference, since they do not know how to use another technique or are afraid to change.

In order to have an effective system of bibliographic access, regardless of the technique used, the system should provide the types and the quality of information needed by its patrons. The most important access points include author, title, subject, and perhaps series information. For certain types of libraries, such as research libraries and special libraries, even more detailed access points are necessary.

The adoption of the revised edition of the Anglo American Cataloguing Rules (AACR 2) and the future of the card catalog are two decisions which face library administrators. Regardless of the decision made on closing the card catalog, the use of AACR 2 will have a great impact on the future of the card catalog.

Advent of AACR 2

The Library of Congress (LC) has announced that they will adopt AACR 2 and begin cataloging using these new rules on January 2, 1981 and in addition, they will freeze their card catalogs at that time. Since most libraries throughout the country are linked to LC through the use of LC printed cards, LC proofslips, MARC tapes, or the National Union Catalog, this decision by LC will affect these libraries in one way or another.

Under AACR 2, there will be some changes in access points and headings which will cause filing problems if cards produced under

The Card Catalog

AACR 2 cataloging are interfiled with those using former cataloging rules. For example, AACR 2 uses the direct form of entry, i.e., University of .... rather than entering under place first, followed by University of. As can be seen, titles cataloged using the old rules would be filed in an entirely different place in the card catalog from those using AACR 2. This is just one illustration of the changes that will occur when using AACR 2.

Card Catalog Adequacy

Although the card catalog has been the standard form of bibliographic access for many years, its adequacy is now called into question because of a number of factors. Perhaps one of the most important is the size. More and more books are being added to library collections, thus generating more cards to be filed into an existing card catalog. This growth requires staff time to file the cards and of course requires more space as more catalog drawers are needed. In addition, cards tend to wear out with constant use and so need continuous replacement.

As in many other fields, libraries are beginning to use computers. For example, in 1971 the Ohio College Library Center (OCLC), a computerized data base for library catalog records, went on-line. In addition, there are a number of similar regional systems throughout the country.

With the advent of computer technology and its application to libraries, the question arises as to the validity of continuing to maintain the card catalog manually when a machine-assisted form of bibliographic access is feasible. There are several types of bibliographic access that can be used in libraries. For example, the book catalog was perhaps the first type used in libraries. One of the new forms of machine-assisted catalogs is the Computer Output Microform (COM) and an even more sophisticated form is an on-line system. Any one of these systems can be used alone (with the proper preparations, such as conversion of the library's existing records), or they can be used in combination with one another. Another alternative is to use a machine-assisted catalog in concert with the existing card catalog.

Which is Best?

But what system is best for your library? The answer can only be determined by a thorough study of the library itself, its staff and user needs, along with a study of the various options available to the library.

When studying user needs, several points must be considered such as use patterns, user likes and dislikes, staff work patterns, reference search techniques, etc. In addition, terminal location or location of COM readers, user orientation and education, and public relations programs should be investigated.

The Future of the Card Catalog 3

If the decision is made to change to an automated system, plans must be made to familiarize the user as well as the staff with the intricacies of the new system. Planners should consider not only immediate needs but longer range concerns and objectives. The main goal of all libraries is to have a catalog that provides access and is economical to operate, both now and in the future. While it is wise for libraries to look at all the options that have been developed, one must also keep in mind that in some cases, the present form of the card catalog may be the best form of bibliographic access.

LC Decision Implications

Since LC cataloging data forms the basis for much of the cataloging in libraries throughout the country, it is necessary to understand the impact of LC decisions and options of AACR 2.

If a library does choose to maintain its existing card catalog and interfile the cards for new acquisitions into this file, there are several options that can be used. For example, cross reference cards can be made from the old form of entry to the new form of entry. The existing form for headings which have already been established by the library can be retained, using AACR 2 rules for those entries new to the library's catalog. This is in effect maintaining two catalogs within one physical entity.

A second option is to change the existing cards in the catalog according to the new rules and refile them. In cases where there are a large number of cards under one heading, it might be best to refile the cards into the new position without physically changing each card. Further, in any option, the fate of serial records and multi-volume monographs must be considered.

Linking

The question of links arises in a situation of two catalogs or interfiling into one catalog. One way to handle this is through the LC authority file (now available through OCLC). Another way is through user demand, or as the need arises.

Serials probably create the largest problem demanding links. They are perhaps the most difficult category to handle when preparing to change to some alternative to the card catalog. Successive changes in titles and changes in name of issuing body in current titles can cause many problems. As more libraries study this dilemma, more possibilities for integrating AACR 2 headings into existing catalogs will evolve.

If none of the above options are suitable for a particular library, another choice is to freeze or close the card catalog. Under this option, the library can choose not to file any more cards into the present card catalog after a certain date (using either imprint date, cataloging date, or an arbitrary cut-off). Books cataloged after this date will be included in the bibliographic access system. This can take the form of a new card catalog, one of the machine-assisted forms of bibliographic control, such as a COM catalog, a book catalog, or an on-line catalog.

If a library is to go to a totally on-line system, all existing records must be converted to machine readable form. This is also true of the COM catalog and the book catalog. The cost of conversion must be considered. In addition to cost of staff, the cost of equipment (hardware and software) as well as the cost of start-up procedures must be studied when changing to an alternative catalog format. However, it is quite possible that when a significant number of libraries convert to some alternative to the card catalog, they will do so cooperatively in order to reduce development and operation costs. Many will not even have their own hardware and software systems.

If your library does decide to introduce an alternative to the card catalog, it is imperative that all staff be involved. Library planners should always keep the user in mind in the decision-making process and it is the staff that must answer to the user and that knows user needs. Compromises may sometimes have to be adopted.

Once a form of bibliographic access has been adopted, the library users must be educated as well as the entire library staff. This may take quite a bit of planning. A careful and detailed explanation of why the change has been made is often very helpful in gaining user acceptance.

The Selected Readings

The articles selected for this section give a general overview of the future of the card catalog. For example, in "Ten Ways to Profit from a Long Engagement" Thompson discusses the arguments in favor of the Library of Congress' decision to delay the adoption of AACR 2 for one year. He lists 10 projects which can greatly ease the transition to the alternative forms of the library catalog, and points out the advantage of this year's delay to libraries in planning for their future and the effects AACR 2 will have on their individual libraries. In addition, a brief glossary of terms is included.

Dusenbury, in "Alas, Poor Card Catalog," gives some advantages of an automated catalog and indicates client needs within the library. She also points out some problems that can arise with an automated catalog, using a COM catalog as an example. The article concludes with a list of strategies to be used in the planning and implementation stages of an alternative form of catalog.

In Hazen's article, "Assumption of Automation: or, The Card

The Future of the Card Catalog 5

Catalog Is Dead! Long Live the Card Catalog!," he reports on a task force study at Cornell University Library on automation and the future of its card catalog. He lists several facts that point to the inevitability of automation within the library. As pointed out in other articles, however, a lot of time and planning must go into this change to automation. Some arguments for and against the continuation of the card catalog are examined. He outlines several reasons why, since most libraries depend upon LC's decision, they should wait on these final decisions by LC before any change is made in the local library.

In "A New Code! A New Catalog?," Bright presents his views on how the adoption of AACR 2 will affect the card catalog and offers four ways to cope with this situation. In an update of this article, "New Catalog for UW-Madison," he describes how the University of Wisconsin-Madison has been working with the problems connected with improved bibliographic access. He also outlines several proposals that UW-Madison will accept in connection with AACR 2 and concludes the article with seven problems that he believes must be resolved.

Kennedy, in "Problems With the Card Catalogs: Present and Prospective," touches on some problems with existing card catalogs and those that can occur with the adoption of AACR 2 and the effects that the freezing of the Library of Congress card catalogs will have on other libraries.

In addition, in "Where Will Your Card Catalog Be in 1980?" Crow raises the question of accessibility of LC printed cards for the library not cataloging on-line. Many libraries have come to rely on the LC printed cards and accept LC cataloging except for adding some local notes. A few pros and cons of changing access points and subject headings in the on-line catalog and the card catalog (or on the LC printed cards) are discussed.

In his article "Opening a Library Catalog," Freedman points out the basic problems of the card catalog, but gives several ways that current technology has eliminated some of these problems through machine-assisted bibliographic control. He lists several areas of concern to both librarian and patron in dealing with a closed catalog, such as local information, the integration of technical reports, journal literature, etc.

Although many articles in the current literature take the approach that it is perhaps best to close the card catalog and adopt an alternative form of bibliographic access based on machine-readable records when using AACR 2, Hewitt and Gleim, in "The Case for Not Closing the Catalog," discuss the merits of the integration of cards based on AACR 2 into existing card catalogs. They present the advantages of continuing to maintain the existing card catalog. Cost factors in closing the card catalog are mentioned along with some suggestions on handling entries under AACR 2 that are incompatible with existing records. The authors also outline some advantages to delaying the transition from a card catalog to some alternative form of catalog.

In her article "Closing the Card Catalog, or Two Years Before the Blast," Mary B. Henry gives a brief description of closing the card catalog and its alternatives, along with several reasons for libraries to choose to close their card catalogs. Several points to consider in implementation of an automated file are mentioned.

In his article "Close the Card Catalog?," Schwedes reports the results of a survey by ACRL on AACR 2 and the future of the catalog. Along with the answers as to whether respondents would accept AACR 2 and close their catalogs or not, a number of reasons for these responses were given. In addition, brief explanations of how libraries would cope with AACR 2 and the card catalog are discussed.

Decker, in "Catalog 'Closings' and Serials," presents and analyzes some of the problems that affect serials when a library closes its card catalog. Some discussion is made of the problems with access points in AACR 2 and how these will affect serial entries and the location of serials by the patrons, with some speculations on how the user will respond to an alternate form of the card catalog and the new AACR 2 entries. Other problems involved with serials such as check-in, holdings, payment, bindery records, etc., are discussed in connection with closing the card catalog and conversion. Five options are given for handling the card catalog in conjunction with using AACR 2, along with the effect each option will have on serials.

In her article on "Closing the Card Catalog" Ekstrom relates the OCLC plan for providing full system support for participating libraries. In his article with the same title, Caddell looks at closing the card catalog from the point of view of the small public librarian. He gives six reasons why he feels that these libraries cannot justify a change in bibliographic access.

In the final article in this section, "Living Amid Closed Catalogs," Berman suggests ways libraries can use AACR 2 without closing their card catalogs or changing to an alternative form of bibliographic access.

1. Ten Ways to Profit from a Long Engagement*

by James Thompson

As reported last month in American Libraries (p. 450), representatives of key library agencies have persuaded the Library of Congress to put off its Jan. 1, 1980, D-day for massive and far-reaching changes in its cataloging practices and catalogs. Shortly after an Aug. 3 meeting in Chicago between these representatives and LC officers, LC agreed to postpone:

● Adoption of the Anglo-American Cataloging Rules, 2nd edition;
● Abandonment of "superimposition" (systematic exceptions to AACR 1); and
● The "freezing" of its catalogs (separation of pre-AACR 2 card catalogs from post-AACR 2 automated catalogs).

Led in the United States by the Association of Research Libraries, several influential library groups had insisted on a year's delay. At the Aug. 3 meeting, LC agreed, but demanded and got a second resolution calling for the Library to go ahead with the changes on Jan. 1, 1981, and to do so without further debate. Both resolutions were approved unanimously.

The decision has been made, albeit with a different date, and some of its previous opponents are now on record as supporting it.

The Politics of Postponement

Pressure for a postponement had grown through the spring, culminating in resolutions at meetings of the Canadian Association of Research Libraries, the Association of Research Libraries, and, finally, the American Library Association. At the forefront of this concerted effort to force LC to delay its decision were the directors of a number of major library systems, for the projected changes are expected to cause problems for many libraries and will require considerable immediate, and some prolonged, adjustment. The changeover will be particularly difficult for large research libraries with multi-branch systems and heavy non-Roman acquisitions.

Among the arguments advanced in favor of the one-year delay

---
*Reprinted by permission of the author from American Libraries, 9 (October 1978), p. 538-42.

were these:

- Libraries, now with no alternative but to freeze their own catalog, could not afford the expense;
- Libraries could not afford the increased costs of catalog maintenance if they did not freeze;
- Publication of the new rules had been delayed, so that libraries had been unable to prepare adequately for the change;
- Library technology was not yet capable of handling the closing of card catalogs, but soon would be;
- A delay of a year or so would make no real difference to LC or anyone else;
- There was no evidence the new rules would provide significant benefits to library users or, in the phrasing of OCLC's Fred Kilgour, slow the rate of rise in per-unit costs.

These reasons are interrelated, if not wholly compatible with one another, and deserve continued debate. But they do not address the main incentive for postponement: that the research libraries, the libraries most actively concerned with the impact of AACR 2 and desuperimposition, simply are not ready to respond effectively to LC's promised--or threatened--catalog freezing.

Although LC has made its intentions known since the mid-60s, most library directors have taken a wait-and-see approach in the hope that technological advances would provide easier solutions to the problem (or, in some cases, in the hope that the problem would go away). LC's unequivocal announcements in the Nov. 4, 1977, Information Bulletin and at the 1978 ALA Midwinter Meeting came as a shock to many librarians. But the message is now clear, and at the Aug. 3 meeting some ARL librarians acknowledged their failure to take the issue seriously enough. At the same time, the ARL forswore any further hindrance of LC's freezing and committed itself to productive use of the extra year.

The Perils of Delay

Perhaps one source of nervousness about the automation of card catalogs has been the recognition, felt though not always expressed, that what is approaching is not simply the adoption of another new cataloging code, but a basic change in the nature of library use and of scholarship itself.

The card catalog has been recognized for some time as inherently inefficient, overly expensive, and backward. It is obsolete as a means of bibliographic control in LC's and other large collections. The abandonment of card catalogs will be a major undertaking requiring the reallocation of financial commitments. It will mean administrative and political involvement cutting across the whole spectrum of library activity. A change of this magnitude will be more readily accomplished if its various elements are undertaken jointly, and it is no accident that AACR 2, desuperimposition, LC's catalog freezing, national network development, and international standardization have been developed simultaneously, along parallel paths.

The one-year delay has been forced upon LC at the risk of fragmenting the changeover to alternative forms of bibliographic control. One immediate cost is that of adding to the national data base another year's worth of MARC records which will have to be revised and edited before they can be used in the AACR-2-based catalogs of 1981 and thereafter.

We librarians owe it to ourselves to make the most effective use of the now-extended time before we must face the reality of catalog automation. We have a deadline--a rare experience for those in a nonprofit profession with no visible product--and, with little more than two years remaining, the ordinary processes by which our profession plans for innovation will not suffice. The library research community alone cannot solve the many problems which must be overcome before 1981; nor can we depend for leadership on the small number of grant-supported research libraries undertaking comprehensive library automation projects.

The key questions to be answered must be approached by dedicated task forces selected from the most appropriate elements of the library community, with the ALA and related bodies providing active coordination of these efforts and prompt dissemination of their results. In addition, a number of projects involving persuasion or marketing will be necessary, and here again, coordination and cooperation among all interested library factions will be crucial, given the limited time available.

Which are the areas requiring greatest effort, and who is best equipped to take on this work? Below, I offer 10 projects which, if undertaken cooperatively, could greatly facilitate the transition to alternative forms of library catalogs.

How to Use the Extra Time

1. Establish an effective medium for communication.

Library planners must communicate fast and thoroughly to avoid widespread duplication of effort and to keep tabs on successes and failures in a highly experimental field. The existing library journals are neither fast nor comprehensive enough to disseminate the voluminous and quickly outdated documentation task forces and networks will be producing.

The issues involved in the freezing of card catalogs cross all type-of-library and type-of-activity boundaries, but the general-interest journals cannot deal with the technical aspects of the question in sufficient detail. The specialized journals, such as Library Resources & Technical Services, appear too slowly to meet this need. ERIC/IR currently has a substantial backlog. Certainly the institutions originating research cannot be expected to reproduce and distribute innumerable copies of their internal reports. The Alternative Catalog Newsletter is fast and cheap, but on its low budget must continue to appear in microfiche, an inferior medium for circulation to staff and for referral in discussion.

Whatever the choice, there should be a primary, coordinated avenue for communication, preferably centralized through ALA (the Office for Research was suggested at the Aug. 3 meeting), since the future of the card catalog concerns the entire profession.

    2. Determine the true impact of developments at the Library of Congress on other American libraries.

It has been assumed widely that research libraries will have to freeze their card catalogs when LC takes this step, but this assumption has yet to be proven. No thorough study has been published on how AACR 2 and desuperimposition would affect the cataloging of a particular library. The difference between entry under AACR 1 and AACR 2, for the overall LC output, changes from one day to the next, with LC announcing lower and lower percentages with every new decision on rule options. How will the effects of AACR 2-with-options vary by type and size of library?

Most of the analysis and planning has been performed by the research libraries and their representatives such as the ARL. Small college and public librarians (the latter not represented at the August 3 meeting) have too often assumed that their limited size would mitigate the problem. Because smaller libraries tend to interfile all records, however, including many of those which will be most heavily affected in 1981 (e.g., government publications entered under corporate author or by place), the proportionate burden may be greater on them than upon the large research collections with separate and maintainable card catalogs for documents, non-Roman scripts, serials, and so forth. As suggested on Aug. 3, ALA coordination of research methodology will promote consistency and facilitate replications by other institutions.

    3. Gather better information on the potential uses of COM and online catalogs.

There have been a number of excellent catalog-use studies[1] in recent years, but most have been assumed a card format. Wide distribution of copies of a COM catalog, or of terminals linked to an online catalog, would substantially invalidate these use studies. The early work of Palmer,[2,3] Cooper,[4] and others should be repeated with reference to the most likely possibilities for computerized catalogs in the 1980s.

In particular, we need much better evidence to support what

may be the most critical question between now and 1981: What elements of the full MARC bibliographic record should be immediately available in the catalog, and which (if any) can be relegated to a nonautomated or low-priority form of access? This question has enormous implications for systems design and funding. The library research community is best prepared to delineate and evaluate the options here.

4. Accelerate the education of American catalogers in the use of the new rules.

ALA, LC, CLENE, and the library schools must coordinate this stepped-up activity. It is becoming increasingly clear that the details of AACR 2 will affect more than the cataloging of particular titles. The final version of the rules, along with LC's preferred options, will do much to determine (a) which other libraries must also close their catalogs, and (b) how the workflow and therefore the personnel structures of cataloging departments will have to be altered in the early years of AACR 2 implementation. A thorough understanding of the new rules is a prerequisite for impact studies now being considered, and, since all else awaits confirmation of the expected effects of the new rules, analysis of their content and application should begin now.

5. Promote the new catalogs among users and decisionmakers.

The initiation of a new form of catalog will have immediate, sometimes traumatic effects on library staffs and constituencies. The transition can be eased through thoughtful marketing to library users and friendly persuasion of institutional administrators.

AACR 2 impact studies must be completed as the first step in this presentation; but we would do well to base this effort on evidence of the advantages of alternative catalogs, instead of trying to fix the blame on LC for forcing them upon us. The library community must stand together and present, to those who hold the purse strings, a consistent and reasonable program of development which will deflect charges of extravagance in a time of adversity.

The application of marketing theory to library service is a new phenomenon, and, so far, communication in this area has been confined largely to an "invisible college" with few members. This topic would be suitable for a colloquium sponsored by a library school or a regional association, or for an ALA program meeting or preconference.

6. Standardize COM equipment.

The most common format for new catalogs will almost certainly be

COM (computer output microform). COM catalogs now in use are having mixed success, and libraries working together could do much to overcome some of the problems they are encountering with current COM hardware. Motorized cassette microfilm readers require continual maintenance and offer poor images which deteriorate rapidly with use. One manufacturer of such machines professes the ability to offer a superior reader for a few hundred dollars more, but claims that librarians would be too penny-pinching to support it. Let us hope the more affluent spenders of the library world will soon create a market for quality products. In the meantime, we can move forward on standardization.

One of the chief arguments for COM catalogs is the ease and economy of wide distribution of copies, particularly of the increasingly popular microfiche variety. But distribution will be difficult without standardization of COM reader specifications and of display format. Without a cutback on the options already available, libraries will be unable to make effective use of one anothers' catalogs. They will continue to be plagued by the present confusion of brands, sizes, reductions, page formats, modes, matrices, grids, etc.

This standardization is a job for ALA and ANSI, in conjunction with the major COM catalog vendors. An agreement on the part of these organizations and even a few vendors would quickly reduce the available options to manageable proportions. ALA should take the lead in proposing such cooperation.

7. Develop COM self-sufficiency.

Even more critical is the imminent overload on the COM service industry, as more and more libraries turn to COM catalogs. Provision of COM production from MARC records is complicated by the nature of the MARC record and by the limitations inherent in the tape format of the major bibliographic utility, OCLC, Inc. Existing COM catalog service bureaus are beginning to report waiting lines, and there appears to be little likelihood that they will be able to serve more than a fraction of the libraries currently planning to bring up COM catalogs in the next few years.

Libraries should encourage their bibliographic utilities and regional cataloging brokers to undertake the maintenance of local data bases and the production of COM catalogs, even if it must be at the expense of other projects which can be postponed more easily (such as interlibrary-loan networks and serial or monograph acquisitions systems).

8. Develop replicable systems for online catalogs.

Institutions with ready access to computer services, or with the cash to purchase hardware, will consider producing their own COM catalogs or going directly to online systems. But should they reinvent the wheel?

A number of major libraries are already heavily involved in systems development, and in most cases they are going it alone. A few institutions have spent recent years designing integrated library processing systems, but these systems have not, for the most part, been conceived with public online access in mind. They have been supported with grant funds; they are poorly documented and hardware-specific; and they are behind schedule.

Hardware incompatibility severely limits the transferability of programs. The relatively small market keeps the computer giants away, and the turnkey vendors are showing little interest in catalogs. To avoid having to reinvent the wheel in every online library, we need transportable systems specifications oriented toward the several common computer configurations capable of handling an online catalog: IBM, Amdahl, and Digital Equipment mainframes, for example, and some of the large minicomputers. The impetus for this sort of cooperation can best come from the potential users themselves, through brand-name users groups.

It would be highly appropriate for funding agencies which have generously financed the as-yet uncompleted development of integrated systems to lend support to the design and documentation of replicable specifications for basic, single-function, public-access online catalogs. A comparable effort should be made to develop transportable software for the production and maintenance of COM catalogs through local computer systems.

9. Develop appropriate authority control.

The need for authority control is much greater in computer-based files (whether displayed online or as COM) than in manual catalogs, owing to the inability of automated filing and retrieval methods to accommodate slight differences in forms of headings, or to apply common sense. Before alternatives to card catalogs can be established, authority data bases must be defined, and, in institutions with large collections, their use should be automated. The experiences of institutions already relying on machine-readable data bases, such as the New York Public Library, bear this out.

Authority control with provision for automatic updating will become all the more important when changes in name and subject headings accelerate after Jan. 1, 1980. In addition to the cooperative development and replication of automated authority systems, two lobbying efforts are called for:

● Support for LC's role. The Library of Congress is, for most libraries, the sole authority for subject headings, and a major source of name authority information. The ability of LC to update and distribute authority records in machine-readable form is ham-

pered by restrictions on the funding of its automation projects.
LC's solicitations of response from the library community regarding
the need for authority distribution have met with little response,
owing primarily to the rudimentary state of deliberation on this
problem in most libraries. We need to make clear to LC and to
Congress the vital role authority control will play once our catalog
data bases begin to reside on disks rather than cards. The message should come from a wide spectrum of individual libraries, and
through ALA Council and Board.

● Pressure on bibliographic utilities. Bibliographic utilities
are taking a variety of approaches to authority control, ranging
from the Washington Library Network's complete and mandatory participation, to OCLC's insistence on its superfluousness.

OCLC is the country's largest cataloging support system,
and its failure to prepare for the inconsistencies caused by AACR 2
and desuperimposition promises to add an unnecessary obstacle to
libraries' adaptation to the new cataloging practices. What if OCLC
should make good on its threat not to require the use of AACR 2, [5]
and at the same time provide no automatic linkage between different
headings for the same authors? (As for subject links, that's another
story; OCLC has no subject access. The searching function on
OCLC would become unreliable, and its usefulness as a base for
automated catalogs would be substantially reduced. [6])

Libraries using the services of bibliographic support systems
such as OCLC must take the necessary steps to see that the priorities of these utilities are in accordance with their own. The OCLC
Users Council (and its equivalents) must undertake this task, backed
by member-library pressure on OCLC and its regional networks.

10. Seek necessary funding.

Finally, financial support will be needed for some of the items
mentioned above. It is to be hoped that the Council on Library Resources will play as effective a role in the development of cardless
catalogs as it has in other recent progress. ALA support of education and communication is clearly appropriate.

Time to Shake and Move

The next three years will not be easy ones for the catalogers who
have to implement new types of catalogs and cope with several
substantial changes in the nature of the standard cataloging record.
It should, however, be a rewarding experience when library users
are introduced to the first truly up-to-date catalog format they've
ever known. It is now up to the shakers and movers in libraries
and library-related associations to make this transition possible
through such concerted and decisive actions as those itemized
here.

Speaking Desuperimposition: A Brief Glossary

Anglo-American Cataloging Rules: The standard rules for bibliographic description and establishment of name headings for libraries in English-speaking countries. The first edition (AACR 1) was published in 1967 and departed substantially from previous codes; the second edition (AACR 2, 1978) will be adopted by the Library of Congress and ALA in January 1981.

Authority control: The process by which use of an authority file (q.v.) enables the library to: (1) provide consistency of headings for the subjects and names entered in the catalog; (2) provide references to these headings from forms not used (see references); and (3) provide references from headings used to other related headings used (see also references).

Authority file: A file of authority records (q.v.). There are two basic types of authority file structures: (1) A full authority file contains a record for each heading used in the catalog, and for each variant not used from which the catalog contains a cross reference. See also references are included; (2) A partial authority file contains only the headings used. Terms not appearing in the catalog as headings are indicated only within the authority records for headings used.

Authority record: A record indicating the form (and sometimes the choice) of a heading used in the catalog; or a reference from a heading which is not used to a related term which is used. See Authority file.

Desuperimposition: The implementation of the decision by the Library of Congress to abandon the policy of superimposition (q.v.); this is scheduled for Day 1 (January 1, 1981).

Editing: The process of evaluating and altering cataloging copy to conform to local specifications, e.g., by altering the call number.

Freezing (of a catalog): (Also referred to as "closing.") The termination of addition to a card catalog, with records for a new works being entered in another catalog, in whatever form. The frozen card file would still serve as the catalog for books cataloged before the date of freezing (or, a less common alternative, for books published before the date of freezing). The frozen, retrospective catalog can be retained indefinitely and corrected as necessary; it can be photographed or otherwise preserved in a fixed state; or it can be converted to machine-readable form and merged with the newer catalog.

Index/register file: A file in which the full bibliographic record appears under only one heading, with abbreviated records under other appropriate headings. The file of full records is the register; the abbreviated file, the index. The register is usually a serial-order file, i.e., records are added at the end of the file as they are created, and are accessible through serial numbers indicated in the index records. In this way the full-record register need not be refiled along with the index file as new works are cataloged.

Menu: In an online interactive system, a display of a list of options from which the user chooses the next step in the interaction; e.g., a list of available files which can be searched.

Search key: An indexing element for a bibliographic or authority record, consisting of a few bits of information derived from the record and which are specific enough to refer only to that record or a small number of other records. For example, the OCLC search key for the Johns Hopkins, Milton S. Eisenhower Library is MILT, S, E. The OCLC data base contains over four million records, but only four are retrieved by this key.

Superimposition: The policy, adopted in 1967 by the Library of Congress, not to revise author headings already in the LC catalog in spite of changes required by the Anglo-American Cataloging Rules, 1st ed.

Tree: A sequence of increasingly specific menus (q.v.) leading to the retrieval of the desired record or set of records.

Notes

1. For an excellent summary, see F. W. Lancaster, The Measurement and Evaluation of Library Services (Washington, D.C., Information Resources Press, 1977), pp. 19-72: "Studies of Catalog Use."
2. Richard P. Palmer, "User Requirements of a University Library Card Catalog." Doctoral Thesis, University of Michigan, 1970.
3. Computerizing the Card Catalog in the University Library: a Survey of User Requirements (Littleton, Colo., Libraries Unlimited, Inc., 1972).
4. William S. Cooper, "The Potential Usefulness of Catalog Access Points Other than Author, Title, and Subject." Journal of the American Society for Information Science, 21 (March-April 1970), pp. 112-27.
5. Statement of Frederick G. Kilgour as quoted in The Chronicle of Higher Education, 16 (April 3, 1978), p. 13; follow-up American Libraries, 9 (May 1978), p. 254 and (July/August 1978), p. 412.
6. OCLC has taken the position that its system never provides more than 32 "hits" in any given search, but the growing list of unsearchable dead-end keys disproves this claim. And after the adoption of AACR 2, many entries will become fugitive to searches which now retrieve them (for example, while the search key WELL, H, G will retrieve the works of H. G. Wells as nicely as those of Herbert George Wells, DODG, CHA, L will not retrieve works entered under Lewis Carroll). See Frederick G. Kilgour, "New Concepts in Librarianship," in On-Line Library and Network System. Symposium held at Dortmund University, March 22-24, 1976 (Frankfurt am Main, Vittorio Klostermann, 1977), pp. 84-93.

2. Alas, Poor Card Catalog*

by Carolyn Dusenbury

How does the future of the card catalog strike you? Is it the adventure of a major breakthrough in library technology? the subject producing exasperation, boredom and endless debate? the inevitable? a yawn? a sinking feeling in the pit of your stomach? No show of hands necessary.

I would venture a guess that most librarians react as I reacted when asked to discourse about the catalog today. First, knees shake. Impending doom. The great unknown. Second, knee jerk. Crisis. Need to make up my mind. Need immediate solution. Don't know enough. The third phase is, essentially, one of calming down, looking at the nature of the beast, doing some reading and some thinking. When the smoke clears one finds that the sky is not falling and that the card catalog and its possible futures present a rather unique opportunity for librarians to think seriously about their environment, their clientele and their needs.

First, let me tell you what I am not going to do: talk about AACR 2, talk about the eccentricities of the Library of Congress, authority control, closing versus freezing, the salvation of networking, anything in depth. I will attempt an overview of some of the major issues facing public service librarians in relation to future catalog alternatives as I perceive them: the impact on the librarian and, more importantly, the user. More questions may be asked than answered, and if it seems to you that I explore more peaks than valleys, and probably miss a few peaks too, you are correct.

What follows is, briefly, some thoughts on the symbol of the card catalog, the catalyst for change, the behavior of the user, plusses and "nonplusses" of catalog futures, change strategies, and options.

Card Catalog as Metaphor

Perhaps the most fundamental obstacle we as librarians face in contemplating the future of the card catalog is our psychological attachment to the traditional format. Not only to ourselves, but to many

---
*Reprinted by permission of the author and publisher from Utah Libraries, 22 (Spring 1979), p. 30-38.

of our patrons, a library is as much symbolized by the card catalog as by shelves of books. Indeed, the very words "card" and "catalog" seem to be as inextricable as "death" and "taxes". While this is not necessarily a logical association, the symbolic equation of library and card catalog and the accompanying feeling that we stand somehow on a foundation of 3x5 cards cannot be disregarded.

What accounts for this irrational attachment? I certainly have no conclusive answer. It may be tradition, it may be a tactile response, it may be habit, and to a greater or lesser degree, it may be prejudice. How many times, when the future of the card catalog is discussed, are we able to articulate our anxiety in any specific manner? We just don't like machines or microforms or computers, we don't understand them, they break, they are hard to use. Putting technology in the hands of users is like putting it in a cage of chimpanzees. We are able to envision countless doomsday scenarios, the upshot of which is that someone is tampering with something fundamental in our concept of ourselves, our profession, and our environment.

The card catalog then, is more to us than a tool to indicate library holdings. S. A. Cramer sums it up in his observation:

> Various claims have been made by the library catalogue describing its role as the backbone of the library, its central record, the intellectual heart of its operation and interpreting the library to the reader. Such ringing phrases may have elements of truth in them, but are too generalised and lofty to facilitate close, analytical examination. Other generalised claims have been made, but the only one which bears close examination is that summarized in the <u>Report of the Committee on University Libraries,</u> Oxford, University, 1966 which states, 'the question should be asked, is a library catalogue to be regarded as a series of irreproachable bibliographical documents, or as a means of finding books? We take, without hesitation, the second view.[1]'

Cramer is, no doubt, correct. To us the card catalog is the product of generations of debate about the intricacies of main entry, subject access, and other issues completely arcane to our clientele, who take the direct, unsubtle, and irreverent position that the catalog is the means to the end of finding a book. Our attempts to train "the great unwashed" about corporate entries, uniform titles, filing rules, and so on may well be futile and frustrating for both parties.

In sum, if we are indeed performing open-heart surgery on the heart of the library, it is major change and one that merits the most serious evaluation, the least of which may be a reorientation from "how to use the card catalog" to "how to find a book."

The Catalyst for Change and the Public Service Response

Another cause for our anxiety in public service is that the future of the card catalog appears to be out of our hands. An automated catalog is foisted on us by an administration mostly concerned with the escalating costs of card catalogs and a fervent desire to be in the vanguard of au courant trends. They don't know what the public needs, they don't work with them day to day. These isolates see everything on a balance sheet and the patron, to say nothing of ourselves, be damned. If that doesn't work we have an alternate villain in technical services. It is more convenient for them to automate the catalog, it's cheaper for them if the catalog is automated, they don't know what the public needs, we spend enough of our time interpreting their work already, it will only get worse. Where are our priorities? Failing the first two, or more creatively combining all three into a truly diabolical menage à trois is the looming "day-one" at the Library of Congress when they close their catalog and adopt AACR 2. Somehow, life as we know it will never be the same.

This, it is hoped, is an obvious overstatement, but burying our heads in the sand is no solution either. Clearly the intent of the Library of Congress, the adoption of AACR 2, the cost of generating bibliographic records, and maintaining of a card catalog cannot and should not be ignored.

Public service librarians, then, have two choices. They may, figuratively, be raped or seduced. The former could be characterized as allowing the decision to be made by others and then having to accept the inevitable in suitable martyred fashion. The latter is to ask, and failing that, to demand to be a part of the decision making process, to help make the choices, to accept responsibility for result and take our lumps. This is not as easy a decision to make as it appears: "it is infinitely worse to be seduced than to be raped; the latter is an unfortunate occurrence, while the former signifies that you were a party to your own downfall."[2] While this presents something of an occupational hazard, it is imperative that all affected areas of the library be involved in planning and implementing of the future of the card catalog.

Client Needs

Before we attempt to design any new system, it is important to assess user needs and behavior. We need some clues about how they go about a catalog search, what information they need, and what their level of expertise is. Academic libraries have categories of users in a range from sophisticated faculty members (a few anyway) to those who have never previously seen a catalog, or if they have seen one are not awfully skilled in its use. The system design must be equal to the needs of all levels. User studies in the specific area of card catalog use are not numerous, but those which do exist show some very interesting characteristics and patterns of use.

Frederick Lancaster has compiled the existing studies on the behavior of users in chapter two of his book, The Measurement and Evaluation of Library Services, and notes the following general patterns:

- Users avoid using the card catalog if they can.
- They have little knowledge of the structure of the catalog.
- Few users have complete bibliographic data, written information is highly unreliable, often no more accurate than memorized information.
- Users look for titles more frequently than authors, and often know only key words in titles.
- Most searches are for known items, many subject searchers start with a known item.
- Most users do not persevere in their search, 50% try only one entry and then stop regardless of their success. They do not use "see" or cross references.
- 74% of users use less than 10 cards. [3]

Findings of a user study at the University of Toronto were very similar to Lancaster's results: 60% wanted a specific work, 29% asked by author, and 33% by title in in-person requests. Telephone requests were almost always for specific items, 42% requested by author, 53% by title. It is interesting to note that user's perceptions of their needs were quite different. In answer to a questionnaire, 77% were looking for a specific item, but 85% claimed they would look under author, few thought they would look under title. [4]

From my empirical evidence as a reference librarian, these findings are fairly generalizable. Those who lose sleep worrying about closing the card catalog by imprint date or date cataloged are far too optimistic about the sophistication of catalog use. Without much fear of contradiction, I can say flatly that imprint date is not of much concern to users until they prepare their final bibliography, at which time (usually late at night) they call the library to obtain the imprint they neglected to copy down when they first consulted the catalog.

What, then, are user needs? From the information above we can surmise that title, author, call number, and to a lesser degree, subject headings are used routinely. Pagination and imprint are in most cases not vital at all access points. Experience at the Marriott Library indicates that our initial trepidation about tracings appearing only on main entry cards has not been noticed or missed by the vast majority of our users. Again, their fundamental desire is to find a book.

Advantages of an Automated Catalog

For the public services librarian there are clear advantages in an alternative format catalog. A complete list is not feasible here, but some of the major advantages are:

1) Access--Alternative formats such as microfilm, microfiche or on-line allow for better access to cataloged materials than we have presently. A union catalog can be available in many locations, giving branch libraries and academic departments access to holdings.
2) Display--The user can see several records at once, and could copy entries on a printer if one were available.
3) Holdings--Presently many large libraries do not include the contents of major microform sets, serials, books in process, or other types of information in their catalogs. An alternative format may allow (when the bibliographic records are available on-line through a network like OCLC) for more of the library's holdings to be included in the catalog. My particular concern here is microfilm sets that are not fully analyzed and suffer "format discrimination" because they have good, but little used indexes. As libraries move toward the microformat alternative it will be necessary to upgrade the second-class citizenship of these materials.
4) A "cleaner" catalog--An alternative format makes it much more economical to change location symbols on catalog records. Many special designations become outdated, but the process of changing the card catalog records is costly for technical services. Public service librarians also spend time explaining outdated locations, and the ability of an automated format to make these changes would free time for other duties. Similarly, changes in subject headings become drastically easier.
5) An on-line catalog opens the possibility of a non linear "free text" search. Key words could be used as points of access. The inflexibility of the present form of subject headings might be ameliorated by the ability to combine search terms in new ways to make subject searches easier for the user.

Cost is often listed as an advantage, but I think this may be misleading. The cost of cataloging and the catalog itself may decrease over time, but any system that is designed primarily on cost-saving criteria is an inadequate catalog from a public service point of view for reasons that will be discussed later.

Problems and Challenges

One would like to take a positive approach here and believe that there are only challenges, but, in fact, real problems do exist in the consideration of various catalog futures. As an illustration, the focus here will be on the COM catalog either as a bridge to another format or as the end result. A discussion of the COM concept raises many of the issues that will need to be considered in any alternative. Again, a comprehensive list is not necessary, but the following need to be considered.

A library catalog does not change format overnight. Almost all libraries are closing their present card catalogs as of a given date and henceforth producing records for public use in an alternative format. It is a process of many steps and accompanying frustrations for public service librarians. In most cases the card catalog is superseded by a COM format on microfilm or microfiche. It is important to note that the public service librarian is, at this point, not teaching the same tool in a different format, but is, in fact, confronted with two tools that are substantially different in physical format. The University of Toronto COM catalog is a good illustration.

Toronto uses a COM format in both microfilm and microfiche. The COM catalog consists of four separate files: full bibliographic entry listed in call number sequence; author, subject, and title are each in a different file organized alphabetically. In the microfilm format the entire catalog consists of five readers: two dedicated to the full record and one each for the author, subject, and title (the complete set is called, affectionately, the FAST catalog).

As you can see from the example of an entry from the title catalog, the information included is rather different from the familiar card.

TITLE INDEX

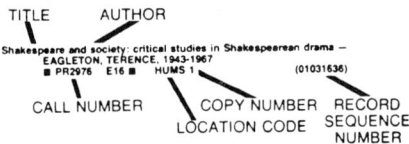

The placement of the elements is changed and the user must consult the full record for the imprint and collation as well as subject headings because the author, subject and title files are abbreviated.

In addition, computers are no more capable of understanding filing rules than the average user. The filing arrangement at Toronto is strictly alphabetic: numerics file according to their numerical value; Roman numerals file by their alphabetic value; and abbreviations file as written rather than spoken, as you can see in Table 1. [6] I am definitely not taking the position that LC filing rules are superior, I have been known to utter a few epithets myself when dealing with the Bible, and the experience at Toronto indicates that users have less trouble filing like the computer. The larger issue is that while the library has two catalogs in operation they are used differently in substantial ways that have an obvious impact on public service staff.

A second major problem/challenge is the appearance of the records. Any large library is dealing with a lot of film or fiche in a COM format. Again using Toronto, "the initial COM catalogue required the cumulation of approximately 1.2 million records, with 5.4

million access points. Physically, this represents 514 fiche in 48x reduction, or 5 reels of ... film ... each approximately 700 feet long."7 The first edition of the microcatalogue provided a space between entries, but because there were only 700 feet of film available, as the number of records grew, the second edition eliminated the space between entries. It seems clear that this presents a real disadvantage to the user, and it is unfortunate that user convenience was sacrificed because of the number of feet available on a roll of film or the number of fiche that can be accommodated by the chosen binder. The "mashing" together of information in the entries themselves is a similar issue, but I think that is enough said.

Table 1
COM Filing Rules: Examples

Card Catalogues	Microform Indexes
A mes amis Gaullistes	13th century Cyrillic Gospel fragment
AEI Hoover policy studies. 1	40 (i.e. quaranta) sonetti di Shakespear
Adams, Alexander	A mes amis Gaullistes
Adams, Henry	Adams, Alexander
Adams Federalists	Adams Federalists
France, Peter	Adams, Henry
France, Parlement	AEI Hoover policy studies, I
London, Kurt	France, Parlement
London-Brown, Mary	France, Peter
London, County Council	London-Brown, Mary
London College of Speech Therapists	London College of Speech Therapists
Moses, Bernard	London, County Council
Moses Ben Miamon	London, Kurt
40 (i.e. quaranta) sonetti di Shakespeare	Moses Ben Maimon
13th century Cyrillic Gospel fragment	Moses, Bernard
Aesthetics	Aesthetics
Aesthetics — Bibliography	Aesthetics — Bibliography
Aesthetics — Early works to 1800	Aesthetics, British
Aesthetics, British	Aesthetics — Early works to 1800
Aesthetics, Japanese	Aesthetics, Japenese
France — History	France — History
France — Intellectual Life	France in literature
France — Military policy	France — Intellectual life
France — Politics and government	France, Marine
France, Marine	France — Military policy
France, Ministere des affaires entrangeres	France, Ministere des affaires etrangeres
France in literature	France — Politics and government

Because of the findings of the user study at Toronto indicating low use of cross references, there are none in the COM catalog and no linkages from one catalog to another. They claim that it works, but I am quite honestly baffled at this omission. Another reason for the elimination of linkages and cross-references is probably available space, which leads to the larger issue of the future necessity of truncating or deleting items like added entries and multiple subject headings to conform to space restrictions. 8 Any COM alternative with these limitations would be a less than ideal solution, and that is _very_ politely stated.

To pick again on the COM format and the Toronto experience,

the currency of the microcatalogue is another major consideration. Toronto issues the microcatalogue in "editions" on film and fiche with supplements on fiche. By their admission the fiche supplements are rarely used because there are now three places to look for the desired title and this seems to cross the threshold that most users deem reasonable. I rather agree with them. Many libraries note this phenomenon and have in mind a better system of quarterly or bi-annual complete cumulations. But there is a catch here also. It seems that it will take about 4 months to process these cumulations. The chain of events goes something like this: cumulations are done quarterly, assume a March, June, September, December schedule. In January a book is cataloged and put in a quarterly supplement to be added to the March cumulation, in March it is "sent away" for 4 months until the cumulation is received. This means that the title will appear in the COM catalog in July. Until that time the user uses the current cumulation and the first quarter, possibly even the second quarter supplement to gain access to the title. Even with laudable intentions the problem persists.

A lesser issue it seems to me is alternative format itself. Some alarmists among those of us in public service are worried about a much simpler matter: patron response to the alternative format. I honestly believe that this is a greatly exaggerated issue. We stand ready for hand-to-hand combat with users, we wait (anxiously?) for tons of complaints, we don't like machines remember. While I do not for a moment suggest that the patron education involved will be easy, that it will not be time consuming, that it won't have its moments in many ways, I think that the attitude of the librarian can, almost entirely, ameliorate the presumed hostility. If we tell them it is a bore and a waste of time they will probably agree with us. Some of them will certainly make that determination on their own, but in a perverse sort of way today's student seems to think machines are fun, they are used to them. At Toronto, a user survey taken after installation of the COM catalog indicated that most respondents even felt that there was some cachet in being so avant garde.

Many of the problems/challenges above are not such pressing issues with an on-line catalog. But the cost of an on-line system is assumed to be expensive, approaching prohibitive, and most of the discussion centers on COM as the next likely step upon closing the card catalog. Suffice it to say that we generate a catalog for the user and any solution which does not have the user as its focus can only be met with the most qualified optimism.

Is There Life After the COM Catalog

The LITA Institute on Closing the Card Catalog, held one month ago in San Francisco, is the most recent and comprehensive overview of the ultimate direction of the future catalog. Most of my remarks here are taken from this conference.

The consensus of opinion is that most libraries will have to generate some response to the action by the Library of Congress in 1981, and that this date has presented a "deadline" for libraries to consider catalog alternatives. For most libraries, this response will be the closing of their present catalog coincident with "day one" at LC and the beginning of the transition process to an automated catalog. This transition process has as its ultimate goal an on-line fully retrospective catalog, with a COM format as an interim step to an on-line catalog of new materials, followed by a retrospective conversion of the card catalog to the on-line system. The end result of returning to one catalog in an on-line format with an acceptable backup to provide access during "down time" is clearly the best future imaginable, given the present state of the art. No one should be deluded into thinking that this process will be easy, fast, or cheap. The planning alone will be time consuming and therefore expensive. The public service librarian has to consider user education and orientation at each stage of development. Given the present financial condition of most libraries, this will have to be done without additional public service staff and limited additional funds for orientation materials. The possibilities of the on-line catalog are sufficiently attractive that many libraries will want to include extra features not contained in the present card catalog, and if this is the prevailing view any anticipated cost savings may be diverted into additional catalog holdings or access, creating a "better" but more expensive tool than the card catalog. The importance of detailed planning at the earliest possible date cannot be over-emphasized and will be discussed shortly.

A Rush to Judgement

The assumption of the COM catalog as an interim step came under serious question at the LITA Conference. There are concerns that COM will, because of cost factors of the on-line catalog and retrospective conversion, become the ultimate solution and libraries face the possibility of having two catalogs in perpetuity. I believe it was Seymour Lubetsky who stated at the conference that a "scarred card catalog is better than a dismembered catalog"; reflecting the views of some that there are other alternatives that can be considered as interim steps:

1) Do not close the card catalog. The March 1979 American Libraries contains an article by Hewitt & Gleim entitled "A Case for Not Closing the Catalog,"[9] suggesting that AACR 2 can find happiness in your current catalog.
2) Close the card catalog and begin a new card catalog for public use, but also generate the records in machine readable format until the library goes on-line at which point the second catalog is discarded.
3) Retain the present card catalog and change the essential records that are at a great variance with AACR 2 so that the entire catalog reflects the new code.
4) Close the card catalog and go to a COM catalog as discussed above.

There are various permutations and combinations of these four, but the upshot of the new debate is that we have not fully considered all of the possibilities and arrived at the best solution for our particular library. Libraries in general, and public service libraries in particular, have a responsibility to keep user needs as the first priority in considering and designing alternative futures. The library as a whole must take a systemic view and evaluate all consequences in the total scheme of things. As an example, a decision to alter the catalog because of the cost of generating, filing, and maintaining catalog cards in isolation from all salient impacts is short-sighted and ill-conceived.

Change Strategies: Planning and Implementation

For the public services librarian, the process of user education and orientation to the "new" catalog may seem absolutely horrendous. In the cautious optimism department, I would strongly recommend that all of those who will be even tangentially involved read some of the excellent material available on the subject: the ARL Spec Kit #46: Planning for the Future of the Card Catalog; Linda Beaupre et al., "Future of the Card Catalog: Public and Staff Relations"; and Valentina de Bruin's article, "Sometimes Dirty Things are seen on the Screen," are just a few of the many available. The proceedings of the "LITA Conference," when published, will be another valuable source.[10] These discussions deal in depth with the four major tasks involved: planning, training, implementation, and evaluation. Each of these is treated in detail in the literature so I would like instead to focus on a basic change model used in organizational development and apply it to catalog implementation specifically. The model was developed by J. Richard Hackman of Yale University and discussed in Hackman & Suttle in Improving Life at Work, Chapter 3 "Work Design."[11]

1) Diagnose the system prior to change. In making any decision on the future of the catalog all affected groups should be involved in the decision-making process. Usually this is accomplished by the formation of an "umbrella" task force, with a series of implementation teams in the various affected areas: the distribution and format of the catalog, the technical services procedures, costs/benefit comparisons, public service implications, etc.

The public service team needs to ascertain the following:

a) Patterns of use and convenience:
   Which access point is most frequently used?
   Do planned indexes contain sufficient information most
     of the time for all categories of user?
   Should all indexes contain the same information?
      Use of full bibliographic record?
      The inclusion of untraced series and titles.
b) Format of entry.
c) Appearance of catalog.

d) How to deal with the supplement problem.
e) Filing arrangement.
f) Orientation and training:
Do users know what is contained in the new catalog, the correct access points and what is not included. Logical steps in training of users. Appropriate sequence of orientation and instruction, preparation of materials, nature and location of training sessions.
g) Feedback and evaluation.[12]

The time sequence for Berkeley might serve as a model of the tasks and time frame (Fig. 1).[13] This model gives some interesting guidelines: 1) Working papers are prepared first and the total planning and implementation decision is reached. 2) Preparation of materials begins over a year before implementation date. 3) The user is forewarned of the change to prevent "day one panic." 4) Feedback and revision also begin prior to implementation and is an ongoing activity. The model gives 2 years of planning time before implementation.

2) <u>Keep the focus on the task itself</u>. This may seem deceptively simple, but often other concerns (real or imagined) can impinge on the immediate task. This is not the time to rethink the diagnosis, cast recriminations, conclude that the whole endeavor is hopeless, or worry about the great unknown.

3) <u>Prepare ahead of time for unexpected problems</u>. Try to anticipate and be prepared, do not wait to react to a crisis. One successful method that has been used is to do a trial run with all library staff before you turn your system loose on the public. All library employees should be knowledgeable about the system in any event, and they will constitute a fairly critical audience. It gives everyone an opportunity to comment on the change, which may alleviate the feeling of not being involved in major decision making. Selected campus populations could be enlisted for the same reasons.

4) <u>Evaluate continuously</u>. We cannot be so optimistic as to assume that we will get everything right on the first attempt. One of the advantages of computer technology is the ability to make changes relatively easily. Evaluation should be open-ended and not designed toward eliciting desired responses. One major library reports that 90% of their users are very positive toward the new format. This may be a completely gratuitous finding: they feel "positively" relative to what? the card catalog? since there is no alternative, this is OK? relative to no access at all, it is terrific? While it may be true that the new format is a <u>fait accompli</u>, we still need to elicit rather specific information on the effectiveness of the new system initially and over time as modifications are made.

5) <u>Confront the difficult problems early</u>. We cannot assume that the tough issues will resolve themselves. If some major issues cannot be resolved to the satisfaction of the affected population, this

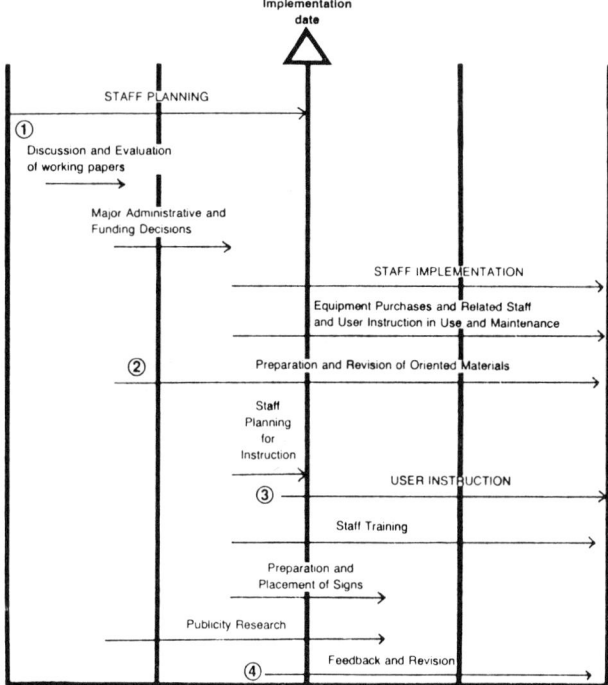

Figure 1. Future of the Catalogs--Sequence of Events

may say something very basic about our fundamental construct. Early recognition of these issues may mean a few trips back to the drawing board but may prevent even more costly mistakes in the future.

6) Design change processes that fit with change objectives. For the fifth or sixth time, I reiterate that the focus of the change and our major objective is to utilize the best means available to provide the user with the material(s) he wants. All means to the end ought to have this focus in mind. The primary consideration is not cost, existence of networks, AACR 2, a deadline precipitated by the Library of Congress, or technological superiority. Our separate institutions may have differing clientele and needs requiring differing catalog futures, but it all boils down to the ability of our users to find things.

Conclusion

So. How does the future of the card catalog strike you? Perhaps the sinking feeling is still in order, we face a big job, but I am confident that it can be done. Public services librarians are going to be in the front lines, but they do not have to be battle lines.

I had not planned to end with any platitude about how we are entering the new era, a crisis in the profession, the 21st century of librarianship, and the rest of the stuff of fanfare but, I do think it is an interesting and complex phenomenon that will summon our collective wits and shake loose our individual and collective cobwebs. But I did find a sentence that was so appealing in this vein that out of respect for tradition let me quote: "The credibility of librarianship, and perhaps the future of the profession, will depend partially on our meeting this challenge in a professional and user-oriented manner, with a minimum of panic and rancor."[14]

That sounds OK to me, especially the part about panic and rancor.

Notes

1. S. A. Cramer, "The Computerized Catalog in a University Library," Libri 26 no. 1 (1976): pp. 38-9.
2. Frederick Herzberg, "One More Time: How Do You Motivate Employees," Harvard Business Review 46 no. 1 (1968): p. 54.
3. Frederick M. Lancaster, The Measurement and Evaluation of Library Services. (Washington, D.C.: Information Resources Press, 1977), Chap. 2.
4. Carole Weiss, "Card Catalogue to On-Line Catalog--The Transitional Process," in ARL Spec Kit #46: Planning for the Future Card Catalog (Washington, D.C.: Association of Research Libraries, 1978), p. 112.
5. Valentina de Bruin, "Sometimes Dirty Things Are Seen on the Screen," Journal of Academic Librarianship 3 no 5 (1977): p. 258.
6. Ibid., p. 260.
7. Ibid., p. 260.
8. Ellen Altman, "Reactions to a COM Catalog," Journal of Academic Librarianship 3 no 5 (1977): p. 268.
9. Joe A. Hewitt and David E. Gleim, "The Case for Not Closing the Card Catalog," American Libraries 10 no 3 (1979): pp. 118-121.
10. American Library Association Library Information and Technology Association. "Institute on Closing the Card Catalog." San Francisco, 1979. (Tape recorded)
11. J. Richard Hackman, "Work Design," in Improving Life at Work, J. Richard Hackman and J. Lloyd Suttle (Santa Monica, Ca: Goodyear, 1977), pp. 96-162.
12. De Bruin, p. 260.
13. Linda Beaupre, Charles Martell and Gail Nichols, "Future of the Card Catalog: Public and Staff Relations," in Future of the General Library Catalogs. Phase IV Reports. University of California, Berkeley, Library (Berkeley: University of California, Library, 1978), p. 8.
14. Hewitt and Gleim, p. 121.

3. The Assumption of Automation

   or: The Card Catalog Is Dead! Long Live the Card Catalog!*

by Dan C. Hazen

Academic libraries throughout the land are abuzz with deliberation over the future of their card catalogs. Cornell is no exception. Our initial response, the report by the Task Force on the Future of the CUL Card Catalogs, constitutes an impressive effort to confront the imponderables of the future, and merits our applause for both the energy and the spirit with which it was compiled. The report demonstrates the extreme complexity of the issues at hand, and exhaustively documents actual and potential costs of existing systems.

Nonetheless, the Task Force report fails to convince in its general recommendations that immediate movement toward automation comprises our only viable alternative. While we would all doubtless agree that our principal goal lies in meeting the information needs of Cornell's scholarly community, it is less obvious that mechanization now affords the most satisfactory means to this end. The Task Force's conclusion derives from several clusters of suppositions which, unfortunately, are both untested and in large measure untestable.

It is far from obvious that a chain of reasoning founded on unsubstantiated assumptions can constitute a compelling case for library automation: the edifice may be sound, but it may also only be a house of cards. The assumptions which have not been explicitly justified may well be correct and susceptible to proof. Alternatively, other reasons may exist to support the Task Force's recommendations. The purpose of this note is to stimulate the commentaries and data which would so indicate.

Four sets of suppositions underlie the conclusion that we must immediately mobilize for systemic automation:

1) Library automation is inevitable;
2) The card catalog is on the verge of collapsing under its own weight, a delicate condition which only automation can remedy;
3) The Library of Congress is and will remain the model for

---

*Reprinted by permission of the author and publisher from Cornell University Library Bulletin, No. 207 (January 1978), p. 1-5.

library practice and procedure, and drastic transformations will occur in each of these after 1980;
4) Cornell will lose status as a vanguard automator if we are not among the pioneers of integrated on-line systems.

Though none of these assumptions can be absolutely disproved, their substantiation is equally problematic. By accepting these hypotheses as postulates, we have been encouraged to accept a scenario by which automation is our only hope. If the hypotheses are faulty, so may be the predictions based upon them.

A first Task Force assumption, and one apparently general throughout the profession, is that library automation is imminent. Computerized systems do have the data manipulation capabilities required in information systems as complex as libraries, and this technical capacity far outstrips that of any manual system. Were theoretical plausibility the only relevant consideration, immediate commitment to automation would clearly be in order, and librarians could be faulted for any hesitation or delay. In the unhappy realm of reality, though, the theorist's benign vision of an efficient and all-encompassing computerized system confronts a wide range of limitations and constraints. The Task Force itself has declared that "... technology cannot yet offer an affordable substitute equal to the present card catalog" (p. 4). The means exist in theory, but remain beyond our practical grasp. Moreover, even if economically attractive and programatically adequate hardware and software were readily available, the resources required to load the resultant system would be phenomenal. Adoption of new technology may be inevitable, but the timing of this inevitability must remain cost-dependent.

A corollary to the inevitability of automation maintains that an automated system must naturally move toward appropriation of all compatible library functions (e.g. acquisitions, serials control, cataloging, circulation, reserve, accounting, access to on-line data bases, etc.). Once again, we are assured that the computer's theoretical capability to control such operations constitutes adequate grounds for embracing a mechanized approach. In some ways, one can find a parallel with the early days of urban renewal: city planners drew on new theories of urbanization and changing construction technology to plan vast redevelopment schemes. Their Brave New Urb proved far more elusive than anticipated, in large part because their plans failed to account adequately for the imponderables of human responses. Some of the same overreliance on technology seems to typify our headlong rush toward library automation.

Although assumptions regarding the short-term inevitability of library mechanization remain unproven, cybernetic trends do make economically feasible technology appear to be an eventual certainty. The question is when, rather than whether.

The second cluster of Task Force hypotheses appears less clear-cut. The existing card catalog is depicted as an information monster, which only automation can tame. At least two elements contribute to this supposition: that access more or less as provided in the card catalog constitutes the most efficient mode for conveying bibliographic information; and that automation will restore this mode to an acceptable level of efficiency.

The catalog card, and the card catalog, were created for particular reasons at a certain point in time. They are human and historical products, neither of which embodies ultimate wisdom or Truth. Beyond short-term convenience, there are no inherent reasons to justify this system's mechanical replication. Particularly for subject access, new techniques of key-word indexing, as well as more adequate thesauri, are now on the horizon. While the Task Force report acknowledges such potentials, it also argues that increased rates of changes in LC subject headings--which will be facilitated by automation in Washington--will overwhelm any manual system. The implication is that subject access will continue to depend on lists of standardized headings. In other words, our real options remain traditional. We may have the ability to automate a dinosaur, but it's not entirely clear why we should want to.

Perhaps more to the point, much of the argumentation for automation reflects an apparent capitulation before the card catalog's immense size and complexity. Statistical evidence of the most arcane sort (some students have even documented the distances paced by card filers in large libraries) is employed to hammer away at the card catalog. We are then, for instance, assured that search times in an automated file will be significantly shorter than those exacted by a large card file. Unfortunately, no evidence is provided. (In fact, the limitations on author searches via OCLC once again suggest that technical capability in no way guarantees actual accessibility. Even were such searches possible on a regular basis, staring at screen after screen of "Smiths" might well prove no more satisfying than thumbing through card after card in the union catalog.)

Assertions that we must automate because the card catalog has finally defeated us by virtue of its superior cost and complexity can only become convincing when complemented with hard evidence on the cost and utility of available alternatives. The obvious fact that it costs money to sustain a large card catalog has been, in general, too cavalierly presented as an argument sufficient unto itself for justifying an automated world of effortless access to a bibliographic record equal or superior to that now available. If it is uncertain whether automation will be most fruitfully applied to information reducible to, or derived from, the catalog card format, it is no less uncertain that an automated system would in fact compete favorably with the card catalog, in terms of either economics or service.

Once again, a parallel might be drawn with the ideology of urban renewal. Card catalog blight--extending even to such details as the deteriorating physical condition of catalog drawers and card stock--is eroding the academic library. Technological solutions, long gospel for our cities, and for which total costs were unknown and probably unknowable, are being incanted to reverse our once creeping and now rampant bibliothecal affliction. However, as the lesson of our cities may suggest, caution is in order.

The clusters of untested assumptions involving the inevitability of automation, and the futility of even attempting to sustain the card catalog, provide a general mandate for automation. They do not, however, convey any time urgency. Two other arguments have been adduced to provide this dimension. The first anticipates developments at the Library of Congress; the second appeals to staff loyalty and local pride.

Early automation is largely urged upon us on the basis of expectations, or fears, of what the Library of Congress may do. We are told to expect changes both instantaneous and drastic when LC closes its card catalog in 1980. The effects of AACR II, and even more those of desuperimposition and new subject headings, are presented as impending realities which will simply overwhelm any manual system. It is impossible to disprove such pessimistic forecasts. On the other hand, it is clear that this prognosis at once accepts a total systemic dependency on LC practice, and assumes that LC will initiate intense and immediate changes in that practice.

In fact, even though the Library of Congress retains its goals of automation, it appears to be retrenching on its time-table. Plans to generate machine-readable alphabets for non-Roman scripts continue to suffer delays, and the Library recently revealed its "contingency plans" for initiating new card files in 1980 in case its automated system is not then ready (Library of Congress Information Bulletin, March 3, 1978). The very existence of such plans suggests that the automation effort is behind schedule. The implications of the mystery clauses of AACR II, desuperimposition, and new subject headings may be drastic, but the logistical and technical problems which are plaguing LC in these and other efforts may dilute the impact. Moreover, if LC's innovations are forced through without adequate planning and trial at that institution, with all of its resources, it would indeed be folly for one of its poor cousins to blindly follow suit.

Related to the last point is the continuing and facile assumption that LC is a library leviathan which inexorably compels total conformity from any and all creatures within its grasp. Many libraries, both locally and abroad, appear to have survived in the absence of absolute adherence to LC initiatives. Particularly if subject access in future LC systems relies on only a revised list of subject headings, the Library of Congress will itself be in danger of archaistic automation. We must not assume that following along will always be our best option.

A final, emotional argument which has been cited to prod us toward early automation maintains that Cornell was a leader among library automators in the late 1960's, but that financial cutbacks in the 1970's have undermined our once-enviable position.

Quite apart from mechanization's theoretical and practical dimensions, support for innovation is implicitly tied to loyalty to Cornell. In fact, the Task Force's references to such activities as CONSER, ISIS, SPINDEX, etc., suggest that we have not entirely dropped out of the library automation picture. More important, the appropriate question is not whether new systems will boost the image of Cornell, but rather whether they will best serve the Library and its users. Returning to the urban renewal parallel, technocratic appeals to local pride were often employed to quell the cautious and to divert attention from substantive issues. Any tactical parallels would be unacceptable here.

To this observer, the arguments presented for immediate movement toward closing and automating Cornell's card catalogs are far less compelling than a quick perusal of the Task Force report might suggest. It is uncertain that library automation is either possible or inevitable in the short term (say, the next five years). It is uncertain that the information afforded by the catalog card, or the card catalog itself, provides an ultimately efficient mode of bibliographic access and control. It is uncertain that practicable technological alternatives to the card catalog can be either less expensive or more flexible than the card catalog. It is uncertain that, beginning in 1980, the Library of Congress will overwhelm the profession with new practices and procedures. It is uncertain that LC must forever remain the sole arbiter of cataloging practice and subject access. And it is uncertain that Cornell's reputation will suffer if we are not among the pioneers of new structures.

These doubts do not justify passivity or inaction--they only suggest that the consequences of failure to automate by 1980 are far from clear-cut. Experience and information are sadly lacking. In this situation, we might most profitably build incrementally on existing activities and experience, rather than hoping to generate a new and comprehensive system from scratch. If automation does become both technically and economically feasible, we should be prepared to innovate. But the existing arguments for automation, to the extent that they derive from the assumptions herein described, are inadequate.

There may be other good reasons for immediate automation, and there may be data available to substantiate some of the assumptions which now seem uncertain. The purpose of this essay is to provoke the responses which would so indicate, and to appeal for their dissemination in future issues of the Bulletin. An innovation as sweeping and exciting as widespread mechanization should be undertaken in a spirit of cooperative enterprise and mutual understanding. By substantiating our assumptions and expectations, such consensus should become possible.

4. A New Code! A New Catalog?*

Library of Congress Changes Are Planned for 1981

by Franklyn F. Bright

Over the past few months many catalogers have been spending a good deal of their time trying to evaluate the impact the revised edition of the Anglo-American cataloging rules, scheduled to be published this fall, will have on the catalogs they administer. Because there has been an extremely tight security policy, very few persons other than those directly involved with preparing or approving the revised edition have been permitted to see a final draft of the rules. The official position is that the code will be published and available to everyone more than a full year before it is scheduled to be implemented by the Library of Congress, adequate time, in the Committee's view, to permit thorough and careful planning. However, an increasing number of people feel that it is not enough lead time for libraries to prepare for what is expected to be for many libraries a time of basic change in the catalog.

The most reliable estimates of the impact of adopting the new code are the announcements that have been made by the Library of Congress. Last January, after a preliminary study, it announced that under the revised code 37 percent of the entries used on all MARC (machine readable LC cataloging) records, affecting 49 percent of the records, would have a different form of entry. This announcement caused many administrators to worry, and it should be no surprise that the number of persons to speak out for a delay in implementing the new rules increased sharply. Five months later, at the Annual Conference of the American Library Association in June, the Library of Congress announced that further study which had taken into account the most favorable of the options offered at various places in the new code, one rule change made since January, and a decision not to implement certain minor changes in form of entry that would not affect filing, the new code would require a different form for 17 percent of the entries, affecting 22 percent of the records. (The decision mentioned smacks suspiciously of the discredited policy of superimposition, adopting the new form of name without changing the form previously used.) Further, they point out that more than half of these changes are not caused by the revised edition, but result from the failure to implement fully the first edition of AACR, the "superimposition" decision.

---

*Reprinted by permission of the author and publisher from Wisconsin Library Bulletin, 74 (Nov.-Dec. 1978), p. 278-79.

The Library of Congress has announced that when it implements the revised edition of the cataloging rules on January 2, 1981, it will establish a new catalog with new authority files, based on machine-readable records, that will contain all new cataloging done under the new code and discontinue editorial work on records in its old catalog.

No matter what one thinks of the revised cataloging rules or LC's decision to close its catalog, it is clear the impact will be substantial for all libraries. Even using the most favorable of the estimates, the University of Wisconsin--Madison Library, for example, will have over 700,000 records in its catalog on which one or more entries will require a change.

How will libraries of various types and sizes cope with this very serious problem? Because almost every library uses cataloging done at the Library of Congress, one governing principle must be that after 1981 we all must be able to continue to use LC cataloging as efficiently as in the past. There are four basic ways a library can choose to handle new cataloging and each can have a number of variations.

Option 1. Change all new LC cataloging back to old form of entry and file it into the present catalog, thus maintaining the unity and consistency of the present catalog. This option is really a decision not to adopt the revised rules. Because it will require changes to much LC cataloging, it will increase cataloging costs indefinitely into the future and put the library that elects it out of consistency with national standards and most other libraries, thus making cooperative programs with other libraries extremely difficult.

Option 2. Accept all new LC cataloging and file it into the present catalog, linking conflicting forms of old and new style entries by "see also" references when they occur. This decision accepts more inconsistency in the catalog than the policy of superimposition, which has already been found to be confusing to library users. This option is undeniably inexpensive, but it can only lead to degraded library service.

Option 3. File all new LC cataloging into the present catalog and whenever a conflict in form of entry occurs, change all existing records in the old form of entry to the new. Further, begin immediately a systematic program to change all existing entries to the new form when the revised rules call for a change. This option will produce a single catalog, consistent with current national cataloging practice. Unfortunately it is also the most expensive of the options and logistically impossible for the larger library.

Option 4. Establish a new catalog based on machine-readable records, which will include only new cataloging done under the revised edition of the AACR. Close the old catalog and discontinue further editorial work on it. This is the option that most larger libraries will choose.

As libraries grow larger and age, card catalogs become increasingly ineffective. Today they contain a serious level of inconsistency that is the result of successive generations of catalogers working under at least four different cataloging codes. Filing errors also multiply as catalogs grow and become more complex--certainly going beyond the two percent normal human error rate. The physical condition of the card stock and the print image is also deteriorating in many catalogs.

For these reasons, but even more importantly, because there is no known way that the card catalog can provide any new type of access to the collections beyond what it is now doing, many libraries will choose Option 4.

Under Option 4 display of the resources of the collection is based on machine-readable records. This opens the prospect of greatly improved search capability and expanded points of access as the power of the computer is used more and more effectively in bibliographic control.

The convergence of the bibliographic crisis and the demonstrated potential of library data management systems to improve library service, coming at the beginning of the age of networking, offers librarians a great challenge and surely the greatest opportunity to develop improved bibliographic access since the advent of the card catalog.

5. New Catalog for UW--Madison*

Work of the steering committee on bibliographic control

by Franklyn F. Bright

In an article published in the November-December 1978 issue of the Wisconsin library bulletin, we wrote about the impact adopting the revised edition of the Anglo-American cataloging rules (AACR-2) will have on library catalogs. Since that article was written, a few new proposals have been suggested by the Library of Congress. These proposals, which will not affect filing order, will reduce the percent of entries that will be in a different form under the new code from the level reported in the earlier article to the range of 11-17 percent. This is still a serious level of inconsistency to handle. When the problem of inconsistency is considered in combination with the fact that computer-based systems of bibliographic control are maturing rapidly, and that a plan for a national bibliographic network with computerized regional networks as the key operational unit is also just now emerging, the argument that the time is right to make a major change to a system of bibliographic control that has the power to provide users with improved access to library resources in the decades ahead becomes most convincing.

In the earlier article it was suggested that a library could choose one of four possible ways of handling new AACR-2 cataloging from the Library of Congress:

 1. Change new entries back to old and file in the present catalog.

 2. Interfile new entries with old in the present catalog. Link entries with conflicting forms by cross references.

 3. Interfile new entries with old in the present catalog. Change old to new whenever a conflict occurs. Begin a systematic program to edit all old form entries to new.

 4. Establish a new catalog based on machine-readable records and include only entries in AACR-2 form. Close the old catalog and discontinue further editorial work on it.

The University of Wisconsin--Madison Libraries have been

*Reprinted by permission of the author and publisher from Wisconsin Library Bulletin, 75 (May-June 1979), p. 129-30; 132.

working on the problems associated with improved bibliographic access for a year and a half now. This article is a report of the progress that has been made to date.

In July 1977 Joseph H. Treyz, Director of Libraries, appointed a six-member Steering Committee on Bibliographic Control with three representatives from public service departments and three from technical service departments. He invited the other libraries which contribute their cataloging to the Madison Campus Union Catalog to appoint representatives to the Steering Committee. The Health Sciences Library, Historical Society Library, Law Library and the Library School Library all responded. The Campus Special Libraries Group, which is not presently recorded in the Union Catalog, has also sent a representative to meetings of that Steering Committee.

Mr. Treyz gave the Steering Committee three premises derived from earlier studies done on other campuses and directed that Madison Campus planning should build on these.

1. Wisconsin should be recording all current cataloging in machine-readable form by 1981.

2. Wisconsin should close its catalog at the same time as the Library of Congress closes its catalog, which has been announced for January 1, 1981. At the time the catalog is closed we will also adopt the second edition of the Anglo-American cataloging rules and abandon superimposition.

3. Wisconsin should create a unified bibliographic data base in which all records are in full conformity with national standards.

Starting from these premises, the Steering Committee has reached several fundamental agreements for the Madison Campus Union Catalog. These include the following:

1. All current cataloging in roman alphabet languages will be in machine-readable form by 1981.

2. All libraries that contribute their cataloging to the Madison Campus Union Catalog will adopt AACR-2 when the Library of Congress does in 1981.

3. A new bibliographic data base comprised of machine-readable records that are in AACR-2 form will be established and the card catalog will be closed.

4. All cataloging libraries agree to use a common authority file.

5. All libraries agree that we will establish an on-line catalog as quickly as developing technology and our resources will permit.

6. Until the on-line catalog is ready, the new catalog will be displayed on an interim basis, as a microfiche/microfilm catalog rather than as a card catalog.

As a result of the early work of the Steering Committee, six Subcommittees have been set up to deal with specific problems:

1. Reserve Book Collection. To make recommendations concerning the active and inactive Reserve Book Collection, at the present time not recorded in the Union Catalog. How can we effectively preserve and continue the best features of the Reserve Book System but convert the record format to MARC (Machine Readable Cataloging)? Should the Reserve Book Collection be recorded in the new data base?

2. Locally cataloged material. To identify all material that is cataloged locally and not recorded in the Union Catalog. To make recommendations as to whether each category should continue in that status or be included in the new bibliographic data base.

3. Music. To consider whether music scores and sound recordings, now cataloged in the Music Library and not recorded in the Union Catalog, should be included in the new bibliographic data base.

4. Non-roman scripts. Because we will not have the technology or equipment to handle non-roman scripts in a computer-based catalog by 1981, we need to review the problems associated with representing these records in romanized form and to recommend which should be included in the new data base.

5. Authority control. To review all the problems associated with authority control when multiple cataloging sources contribute to a union catalog, and to make recommendations for an authority control system that will ensure consistency of entry in the new data base.

6. Education of users. To study the problem of preparing students, faculty and library staff to accept and to use the computer-based catalog, to prepare all necessary publicity and to write the user manuals.

The Steering Committee is now engaged in the process of writing the specifications for the new bibliographic data base. We hope to complete the specifications, have them carefully reviewed by all concerned campus groups and negotiate the contract by January 1980. This will give us one full year to test the system in pilot mode before we put our full reliance on it starting in January 1981.

There are still many problems that must be resolved. Some of the more pressing ones are:

1. How can we convert approximately 200,000 existing ma-

chine-readable records in AACR-1 cataloging to AACR-2 form so that they can be included in the new data base?

2. Should any other old cataloging be upgraded to AACR-2 form and converted to machine-readable form for inclusion in the new data base? How should the more heavily used material be treated: the College Library, the Reserve Book Collection, the Reference Collection, Serials?

3. How should the cost of maintaining the new data base be apportioned among the participating libraries?

4. What shall we do with material that cannot be recorded in machine-readable form by 1981? In addition to non-roman scripts, how can the temporary records for uncataloged material be handled?

5. How can we develop an authority control system by 1981?

6. When can we reasonably expect to have the on-line catalog ready?

7. What shall we do with the old card catalog?

Although the Steering Committee has made good progress, there is a great deal more to be done. The process of making the change from a card catalog to a computer-based catalog is an awesome and challenging task, but it offers the greatest hope, perhaps the only hope, for improved bibliographic access to the resources of our libraries in the years ahead.

6. Problems with the Card Catalog

Present and Prospective*

by Gail Kennedy

In reading accounts of what various libraries in the United States and Canada have planned for the future of their card catalogs, I am impressed by the depth to which librarians at Berkeley, UCLA, the University of British Columbia, the Library of Congress, and so on, have examined the problem and weighed the various available alternatives to a catalog in card format. At the same time, I am increasingly concerned that we at King Library, University of Kentucky, have not made similar investigations. We do not have a catalog planning committee. In truth, we have not as yet really addressed ourselves to the question of what will we do with our card catalog in the next ten years.

I do not feel, however, that we are alone in our non-attention to the catalog situation. In fact, of 49 libraries with over 250,000 titles (each interviewed in a recent survey for the Council on Library Resources), only slightly over half had formal committees looking into alternatives (in this case specifically automated alternatives) to the card catalog.[1] It stands to reason that if 50+ percent of medium to large sized libraries have engaged in investigation of the card catalog then perhaps an even smaller percentage of small libraries have done so. And I do believe that size is the chief reason libraries are propelled into urgent consideration of the feasibility of maintaining the card catalog. If our collection reaches the gargantuan proportions of those at LC, UCLA or New York Public, we will not have a long-range option to close or not to close. I am thankful then that we have not reached that point and that we have a card catalog which we believe is sufficiently healthy--both physically and intellectually--to support our collection for the next few years.

The key phrase here is "the next few years." There are problems with the catalog, though not formally stated, that are apparent to us all and are growing and compounding all the time. The reality of these problems leads to the conclusion that given the grace of a few years, we cannot plan for the future beyond that time and include the card catalog as we now know it.

I would like to touch briefly on a few of the most prominent

---
*Reprinted by permission of the author and publisher from Kentucky Library Association Bulletin, 41 (Spring 1977), p. 10-14.

problems we are encountering at UK. At least a few of these no doubt are problems shared by all libraries, large or small, who currently maintain card catalogs.

The first and perhaps most obvious problem I would mention is the size of the card catalog itself. John Rather described the card catalog as a living organism--and as a living organism, it is subject to growth, change, and deterioration.[2] Carrying that analogy further, the growth of this organism--the card catalog--tends to resemble the growth of weeds in the garden--rapid and relatively uncontrollable.

Research library growth studies have indicated that collections grow at an exponential rate and tend to double in size every 16 years.[3] New titles added to the collection require new cards in the catalog and if quality cataloging is carried out, we have little control over the number of cards each new title will generate. If an average of 5 cards per title is arbitrarily estimated in our collection, King Library's catalog could grow 150,000 cards fatter next year from new titles alone. This does not include all the cards that will be added as a result of cross references, main entries from cooperating libraries, etc. Our policy of filing full sets of cards for every title in each branch library means that we often have several sets of identical cards in the catalog differentiated only by the location designation above the call number. This practice has proven quite effective for catalog users but it tends to expand the catalog quickly.

Rapid growth and expansion of the card catalog naturally translates into space problems. Many libraries are in the same predicament we are in at UK. Real estate in the library is at a premium and we are under constant pressure to make room for more people, more tables, chairs, and study carrels. What we least want to see is our valuable floor space eaten up by more card catalog cabinets. Even though no one denies the necessity of the public catalog, I fear our public would be unsympathetic to our appropriation of their study space for catalog cabinets. But the catalog will grow and cabinets will have to be added as long as there are cards to be filed.

At this time the King Library catalog occupies 51 cabinets of 72 drawers each. The 51 cabinets themselves cover a little over 265 square feet of floor space. The surrounding aisle and table space requires another 800 or so square feet. If the growth rate 150,000 cards per year is used to estimate, then we might need to add between 2 and 3 cabinets per year to our card catalog bank in order to house the increase.[4]

New headings by the thousands require distinctions of increasing subtlety. Browsing through the catalog becomes more difficult as entries pile up in various headings. As an example: 19 different John Smiths are included in the 42 entries in our author/title catalog under that name. The distinguishing terms consist of a variety of birth and/or death dates as well as phrases such as "dealer in pictures," "writer on finance," and "clock maker."

A conglomeration of headings such as this make filing as well as retrieving in the catalog most difficult. Alas, another problem rears its head. Complex card catalogs are highly susceptible to human error. The process of adding, withdrawing, revising and returning cards to the catalog is risky business. The intricate and highly technical nature of the catalog maintenance job is a problem itself. Herculean stamina is required to work with catalog cards for hours at a time and the margin of error increases concurrently with time on the job.

We have a staff or six part time filers whose sole responsibility it is to file in and revise the public catalog. The six filers work four hours a day--from 9:00 a.m. to 1:00 p.m. This system has worked better than any we have had previously and still the errors occur.

Deterioration of some of the "antique" cards in our catalog is becoming a problem for us. There is no systematic yet simple way of replacing cards that either become so soiled, smudged, or worn that they are illegible. In the same vein, there is no systematic approach to the identification and correction of the inconsistencies in the catalog which crop up almost daily. Our current policy is to correct errors and inconsistencies as they are found--usually by the filers or reference librarians. What worries us is the notion that surely undiscovered errors have confused and misled catalog users over the years.

We know of a couple of specific areas in the catalog that are deficient right now but corrections would be costly in terms of staff time. So, frankly, they are not priority projects at this time. The deficiencies I refer to are the result of what might be termed "division hangover."

In 1973 we divided our dictionary catalog into author/title and subject divisions--a move, by the way, which has proved to be a wise one for us. The initial splitting was engineered by an excellent committee and went very smoothly. Unfortunately separating the author and title entries from the subject entries was not all there was to it--and of course the remainder of the job, truly the dirty work, was left to the Cataloging Department.

These little remainders included relabeling all 51 cabinets and 3,672 drawers and adding cross references throughout the subject catalog where they were needed to refer from proper names which had been used as subject headings as well as main or added entries. The title entries which had been left out of the dictionary catalog because they duplicated subject headings were given up as a lost cause.

Currently we still have some temporary labels on drawers and many subject cross references have not been added. We know there must be a great number of missing title entries but the task of generating them now is not feasible. Hence our division project, as worthwhile as it was, has left us with areas of concern in the catalog and has proved the theory that anytime you mess around with the cards you are going to have some problems.

OCLC--undeniably a positive addition to our Cataloging Department--has presented us with a few problems in catalog control. I hasten to add that it is our manipulation of the data from the system, not the system itself, that presents the problems.

Now that we receive large batches of ready-to-file catalog cards daily from the Center in Columbus, it is most expedient to file them as soon as possible. Consequently, our filers get batches of cards to file which have been neither processed nor fully examined in house. We do check the shelf list pack against our own temporary cataloging slips but sorting through an average of 400-500 additional cards a day would be impractical, if not impossible. Obviously though, we cannot be sure that every card in every set is actually present and accounted for. Sporadic reports of missing cards in the OCLC format indicate there is some cause for concern and possibly we should be checking more closely.

We have made it a practice, for the sake of speed, to try to accept all OCLC 100 fields (main entries) whether they're MARC or member-input. The non-MARC records we accept and print cards from present some confusing variations at the point of filing in the catalog. Again it is our manipulation of the data, in this case not checking for authority, which causes the problem. Yet if we are to get the most from our network participation we must try to avoid as much time consuming verification as possible. It all boils down to the fact that fitting a printed card into a manually maintained catalog is the real problem we are up against.

One other major concern to us--and to virtually all libraries --is the decision that the Library of Congress will make about their catalog and how these decisions will ultimately affect us. When will the impending closing of LC's catalog occur? When will the planned move to desuperimposition at LC take place? How extensive are subject heading revisions going to be? All of these are questions which we feel must be answered to some degree before we can intelligently plan our own course of action.

With closing of the catalog at LC tentatively set for 1979 or 1980, the time in which we have to plan for the impact of that change is set at no more than 3 years.

The actual physical closing of LC's catalog will mean very little to us since we will have access to MARC records either online or through LC's continued card distribution service. The real impact will be the changes LC can freely make after closing their old catalog and starting a fresh one aided by the flexibility of the computer.

The old policy of superimposition (or maintaining established headings regardless of new rules in AACR) will be the first burden

LC can easily cast off. A new catalog can begin with all new rules. Machine readable cataloging can be manipulated and altered with ease. Therefore, with on-line authority controls, new rule changes can be incorporated by tapping a few keys. The same holds true for subject heading changes if they are machine readable and the authority is on-line.

But what is to become of us who do not close our catalogs and start out fresh ones along with LC? We are likely to be plagued with inconsistent LC entries, new subject headings which bear no relation to old ones, possible changes in LC filing rules ... In short, all the benefits LC will derive from closing its card catalog might be potential headaches to those of us out in the hinterlands.

There are many problems with card catalogs I have not mentioned. But even the major ones: size and growth, complexity, inconsistency and error and LC changes are enough to make us wonder how effective any card catalog can ever be--and how much it would cost to maintain a thoroughly monitored, revised and updated one!

The alternatives to card catalogs are varied but most of them center around first the closing and possibly freezing of the old card catalog. A new catalog, whether it is book format, computer output microform or on-line is the only real solution to the problems endemic to card catalogs.

I said earlier that we feel our card catalog at UK is basically healthy. In spite of the negative points raised, our overall impression of our catalog is that it has a few good years left. We are grateful that we are not in a critical state at this time. We have the leeway to review our position and learn from the experiments of others. But it is high time for us, and all other libraries who have not yet done so, to extract our heads from the sand and start planning the future of our catalogs.

Sources

1. K. J. Bierman, "Automated Alternatives to Card Catalogs; the Current State of Planning and Implementation," Journal of Library Automation, vol. 8, no. 4 (Dec., 1975), 284.
2. Association of Research Libraries. The Future of Card Catalogs, (Report of a Program Sponsored by ARL, Jan. 18, 1975), Washington, D.C., ARL, 1975, 11.
3. Fremont Rider. The Scholar and the Future of the Research Library: A Problem and Its Solution. (New York: Hadham Press, 1944), p. 3.
4. Based on the formula: 100 cards = 1 inch, Ten inches of cards in each drawer (or 720 inches of cards per cabinet).

7. Where Will Your Card Catalog Be in 1980?*

by Rochell Crow

1980 will mark a major milestone in the history of libraries. This is the date that has been projected for closing the Main Catalog at the Library of Congress. By that date it is expected that the catalog records for all current material will be converted to MARC with on-line access to those records. Some libraries have already announced their intention of doing the same. Those libraries are making plans. But what are the libraries doing if they cannot convert to an on-line system by 1980, or any other year within the foreseeable future? Every library using LC cataloging will be affected in several ways. Nothing will be accomplished by lamenting the inevitable. We must look at the problems this change will create in our own libraries and make plans to cope with them.

Following the appointment of Herbert Putnam as Librarian in 1899, the Library of Congress began a card service, printing and distributing copies of its own catalog cards. This was in response to a long expressed need for a central cataloging source. Through the years changes have been made in and information added to the LC cards for the sole benefit of subscribers to the card service, i.e., Dewey classification and alternate classifications. Libraries have become dependent on this service, with over seventy million cards now being distributed annually. Even libraries buying cards from commercial firms are using LC cataloging copy via MARC tape.

In the past it has not been possible for a library to deviate too much from LC cataloging practice. Because it has not been economically feasible to edit every LC card to conform to local cataloging decisions, the card service has had the side effect of hastening uniformity in cataloging. It is more economical to use the cards as printed than to maintain local variations. Changes now are usually nothing more than adding local notes, or adding or deleting tracings.

From the very beginning the card service has received complaints about the slow service. Complaints covered not only the length of time it took to fill a card order but also the length of time it took to catalog a book after it had been published. As a

---

*Reprinted by permission of the author and publisher from Alabama Librarian, 28 (September 1977), p. 12-14.

result of these complaints, Library of Congress changed to machine-readable card orders, MARC tapes, CIP, and faster printing methods. At the same time that LC is responding to the needs of other libraries, it is looking for ways to cut its own costs. The card catalog is, admittedly, an expensive behemoth, but many a librarian was stunned by the announcement that the card catalog at Library of Congress would close in 1980. Did this mean an end to the card service? Would a library need computer facilities to make use of LC cataloging in the future? Just what do we face?

Whatever might have been the intention when the announcement was made, librarians have effectively conveyed their alarm to the decision-makers at the Library of Congress. Whenever a representative of LC has spoken to a professional meeting, the question of card service has been raised. At a conference in New York in 1975, William J. Wel[s]h told his audience that Library of Congress would continue to provide printed cards, even after it closed its own catalog. In the Fall of 1976, there is a statement in Cataloging Service, Bulletin 119 reaffirming LC's intention to distribute catalog cards "as long as there is sufficient demand for them to support the distribution service financially."[1] The same statement affirms the intent to continue publishing book-form catalogs.

The June 10, 1977, issue of Library of Congress Information Bulletin[2] reports on a system called CARDS to be acquired next spring. CARDS will print catalog cards from MARC on demand, hopefully at a savings to LC. The key to the question of card service is self-support. This service is required to pay for itself.

In the final analysis our problem will not be with acquiring a printed card but with what is on that card. It has been impractical to revise existing entries in the card catalog every time a change in the form of the entry is made. LC has long been criticized for failing to keep up with current forms of subjects, but until now there seemed to be no way to keep up with changes. The expense of changing cards already in the catalog has effectively limited changes in the past. Now, with on-line cataloging it is possible in one step to change all records from an outmoded subject to one in current use.

Closing the Main Catalog means just that. Those records will remain as they are without change. There will be no attempt to relate subjects in the Main Catalog with subjects in the data base. If a subject in the data base changes, the same subject in the Main Catalog remains unchanged. The same is true of other entries. Names, corporate or personal, can be changed as needed in the data base but remain unchanged in the Main Catalog.

Now, the problem should be apparent. For those libraries not cataloging on-line, what can be done? LC has already begun making extensive changes. The change from "aeroplane" to "airplane" has long been needed and was a welcome change, but what does this mean in terms of staff and time?

Decisions should be made now for handling this. Every library probably has a policy now, even if the policy is to do nothing. Will the existing policy be sufficient after 1980? Several choices are obvious. 1) File a "see also" card every time an entry changes. This could lead to a treasure hunt through the subjects with new terminology in a state of flux. 2) Change all existing entries to the new entry. This is expensive even with cards produced in-house. 3) Accept changes selectively. This is a choice for those who want to maintain an authority file of deviations. Except for doing nothing, any policy will be more expensive in the future than it has been in the past.

Another problem will be that faced by the cataloger. Any cataloger doing original cataloging will have to be up-to-date with the latest subjects and names. If the cataloging is on-line to a network, there will be a lot of other catalogers checking up. Who wants to be one of those catalogers talked about derisively whenever network catalogers gather?

It looks as though LC cards will be in our future for some time to come, but the problems to be faced once the cards are received by the purchasing library will be there also.

Will there be help in finding solutions? Help comes through the concerted efforts of involved librarians. Card service from the Library of Congress evolved through the efforts of earlier librarians to avoid the repeated cataloging of a single item. Small, large, public school, academic, and special libraries have benefited. One day there will be a way to accommodate the "card catalog" needs of these same varied types of libraries. Libraries on networks have records on tape which can be Manipulated. Solinews volume 5 number 6, July/August, 1977, contains the announcement that MIDLNET is going to provide service to a for-profit corporation. Perhaps the answer will come from this direction. Perhaps in the not-too-distant future a modernized non-card catalog will be a reality for all libraries. Think about it and speak out. Take part in planning your library's future.

References

1. "Distribution of Catalog Cards," Cataloging Service, Bulletin, 119:25-26 (Fall 1976).
2. "New Card Printing System to Be Acquired," Library of Congress Information Bulletin, 36:371, 389 (June 10, 1977).

* * *

Goodrum, Charles A., "What Librarians Can Expect from Congress' Library," Wilson Library Bulletin, 48:405-411 (January, 1974).
Krieger, Tillie, "Catalogs and Catalogers: Evolution Through Revolution," Journal of Academic Librarianship, 2:172-179 (September, 1976).

Rather, John C., "The Future of Catalog Control in the Library of Congress," Journal of Academic Librarianship, 2:4-7 (May, 1975).

8. Opening a Library Catalog*

by Maurice J. Freedman

The Library Catalog has been the traditional means of access to the library's collection, but it has proven to be a barrier, as well, to reaching the library's information resources. For the last 75 years or more, the card catalog has been the almost exclusive form of catalog in American libraries.

The basic principles governing the catalog in United States libraries were defined by Charles Cutter in 1876, and elucidated upon and amplified by Seymour Lubetzky in the 1950's and 1960's. Fundamentally, these greatest American theoreticians of cataloging posited that the catalog had the following fundamental functions:

1. "To enable a person to find a book of which either the author, the title or the subject is known." (Charles A. Cutter, Rules for a Dictionary Catalog, 4th ed., rewritten, GPO, Washington, D.C., 1904, p. 12.)
2. "... be an efficient instrument for ascertaining ... which works by a particular author and which editions of a particular work are in the library." (Statement of Principles Adopted by the International Conference on Cataloguing Principles, Paris, October 1961, annotated ed., IFLA, Sevenoaks, England, 1966, page facing p. 3.) One can extend this to include which works under a given subject are in the library. Note that "book" and "work" should be taken as including information in all of its physical manifestations, i.e., all editions, translations, media formats, etc.

A basic problem of the card catalog is its inertness and lack of flexibility. As the library's card catalog grows over time, it becomes harder to use for a variety of reasons:

1. Sheer size: As the number of cards increases, there is a larger file to be queried; this becomes even more difficult as large files of cards accumulate under a given author or subject. One must examine each card, in many cases, to conclude a search, and there is no way to obviate the need to handle each card.

2. Resistance to change: Because so many cards accumulate

---

*Reprinted by permission of the author and publisher from Library Journal, 104 (Nov. 1, 1979), p. 2277-80. Published by R. R. Bowker Co. (a Xerox company). Copyright © 1979 by Xerox Corporation.

under a given heading, it can become too costly to change that heading, even if the manner of referring to it is different, has changed, or the area covered by a topic has been redefined. For example, the Library of Congress (LC) would have to shift many drawers of cards if it wanted to change the anachronistic name "Motor trucks" to "Trucks." Consequently, LC is retaining the antiquated form. As a result of this inflexibility many anachronistic, insensitive, and otherwise objectionable terms have been retained in library card catalogs; it is just too costly to change them.

Technological alternatives

Present technology has eliminated or ameliorated some of these problems of the card catalog and facilitates a more open view of the catalog as a medium of access to all forms of information. There are three technological considerations bearing on the role of the catalog at this time:

1. Because of the existence of such huge data bases as OCLC's (presently, over 4,000,000 catalog records), the costs of converting a card catalog to machine-readable form are as little as one-third to one-half as expensive as they were ten years ago. (If one includes a factor for inflation, the costs are even more dramatically reduced.) This means that libraries can now have all of their catalog information in the computer for a far more manageable price than ever before. This cost can be offset by the elimination of the continued maintenance cost of the individual library's card catalog in many instances. It has now become economically viable for many libraries to convert their card catalogs to machine-readable form.

2. Automated authority control, pioneered by the New York Public Library (NYPL), allows the library to make the change described above, "Motor trucks" to "Trucks," simply and quickly, whether there are one, 1000, or 10,000 entries under "Motor trucks." Earlier in the decade, NYPL was virtually alone in the development of automated catalog control facility, but now, apparently, all major library network agencies are in the process of developing this capacity.

3. The development of computer-output microform (COM) as a catalog medium allows for the complete regeneration, cumulation, and duplication of the catalog (on reel microfilm COM or microfiche COM) quickly and cheaply. This avoids the expensive terminal, telecommunication line, and computer charges associated with the online catalog while still dramatically improving upon the costliness and diminishing the inflexibility of the card catalog.

Opening the catalog

Without belaboring points made elsewhere by many writers on the subject, many of the LC subject headings and name entries are neither timely, relevant, nor sensitive to the constituencies served by vast numbers, if not all, of American libraries, and the overwhelming majority of libraries LC purportedly serves insofar as it claims to be the de facto national library. Whereas in the card-based past a single form of entry, in effect a single standard record, seemed the only economically sound alternative, the machine-based present allows for a master machine record which can contain alternate forms suitable to the needs of different library publics. The National Library of Canada's machine controlled dual entries (i.e., English and French equivalents of a heading) and LC's provision of the National Library of Medicine's MESH headings, as well as juvenile headings, are, in effect, examples showing that a multiplicity of forms are possible with respect to a given bibliographic entry.

The catalog can thus be opened to meeting the needs of disparate publics through the dissemination of machine-readable records which carry alternate forms of headings suited to those publics. Because of the efficacy of machine-based authority control systems, the new forms of headings usually can be integrated into a master authority file, and through the cost efficiency and timeliness of COM, updated reaccumulated versions of the whole catalog can be published. (Whether LC is either capable of or interested in such an alternate service is only partially relevant; what is critical is that the technology now makes such a service possible.)

The abandonment of the card catalog now permits libraries to drop the undesirable forms of entries and headings used in that catalog, and initiate terms which promote rather than hinder access to the library's collection. Of course, many of the LC changes needed will well serve both public and research libraries, but many others will entail dual or alternate forms--a manageable problem with a machine-based authority controlled catalog. Further, some of the entries will not involve one-to-one differences. For example, a book on eight famous black leaders held by an American public library would be much better cataloged by having added subject entries for each of the leaders described, whereas a collective biographical heading has been viewed by LC as meeting the needs of a U.S. research library.

Integrating formats

In both of these cases, a national cataloging distribution center would open up the service range of the nonresearch library's catalog through such an enriched standardized record. Although not specifically tailoring the service to a single library, it would come a lot closer to meeting the needs of the clientele of the nonresearch library than the single heading service which is based solely on LC's own research library needs.

Librarians have tended to discriminate against nonprint media.

Public libraries are probably the worst offenders in view of their
frequent practice of segregating catalog files by media format.
There is usually a separate sound recording catalog and a separate
film catalog. When there are media forms other than film and
sound recordings, there is limited if any cataloging for them at all.
If the Cutter/Lubetzky principles are to be taken seriously: that
is, the requirement that all materials by a given author or on a
given topic be brought together in a single place, then it is mandatory that an open catalog integrate all of the materials on "pollution"
or by Maurice Sendak, irrespective of their format. The library user
should not be forced to look in several catalogs to satisfy an information need. Or worse yet, having looked in the catalog for print
materials, think that all of the library's holdings on Picasso have
been displayed, thus hiding, in effect, a fine documentary film interview or a slide-tape presentation on Picasso's blue period. Of
course, machine-readability does allow, as appropriate, for the display of information by medium and does not preclude the generation
of a separate film catalog. One cannot deny that the adult education
instructor who wants a series of films to supplement a course being
taught, will find it far more efficient to select from a catalog containing just films.

It is especially true of research libraries that the catalog has
been closed all too long to their users in the area of government
documents, technical reports, and journal literature. The technology
discussed has less bearing on those areas, but nonetheless these materials must be included in any discussions of opening the catalog
and providing access to all of the library's holdings. A major step
forward was the production and dissemination of the Monthly Catalog
in the MARC format, no small feat. It is particularly important
that valuable information contained in documents be brought to the
attention of the reader, much in the same collocative way discussed
in reference to nonprint materials. An excellent government pamphlet on home repair, child-rearing, farming, or first aid may
satisfy the information need of the library user, but because it is
not referred to in the catalog, it is not accessible. Commendably,
many libraries do catalog especially worthy documents and thus make
them available with the library's book materials.

As to technical reports and the journal literature, these are
still far away from integration into library machine-readable cataloging files. However, the first and necessary step is being taken
with the procurement of data base services by libraries so that access to these materials is greatly enhanced. It is absolutely critical
that individuals using these services not be personally charged for
that use. One is not talking about "free" access; nothing is free.
But people currently do not pay special fees for the printed bibliographies and indexes which libraries provide at great expense,
Chemical Abstracts, for example, or for that matter, the card
catalog, the most expensive tool in the library. One sees no compelling reason why an individual should be separately charged for
the same information in machine-readable form that can be obtained
without added charge in print form. The catalog is the instrument

through which access is gained to the full variety of materials held by the library. Materials such as technical reports and journal literature should at least be considered in our future thinking regarding organized access to all of the library's holdings.

Local information

Another major area of concern--in effect, another place in which the catalog has been closed--has been the absence of access to local information resources. It is not surprising that network planning and automation development have been focused almost exclusively on bibliographical and material delivery systems which will meet the needs of scholars at Harvard, HEW, the Rand Corporation, and the rare public or academic library user who effectively emulates those researchers. But what of the information needs of the local community? Of the people who want to know which city agency will help them with the landlord who's turned off the heat, or where to get redress when a merchant will not take back defective merchandise, or where to take their children for free inoculations, or where the nearest private tennis club is located. These are all examples of community information needs that are not met through traditional card catalogs, and do not seem to be the concern of those planning America's bibliographical networks or, for that matter, local catalogs. But is it not reasonable that, if someone is looking up "methadone" in a local library catalog, in addition to print and nonprint materials on methadone held by the library a citation be given for the local methadone clinic, certainly a place where a great deal of information is available on the subject? The notion here is to integrate all information resources into the catalog, and indirectly break down the fortress-like setting traditionally provided for it by the library. We can now see the library as being not just a custodian for the materials it houses internally, but a more aggressive referral agent. Getting these local information resources into machine-readable form and disseminated locally is a local information network problem which must be addressed and provided for. The national context of discussions should at least take cognizance of the development requirements involved in the integration of local information resources into the local library's data files. For example, there is no MARC format for community agencies--that is, no subfield code for phone number, address, eligibility requirements, etc. Recognition of the value of this kind of information, and its standardization and appropriate thesauri and service protocols, must be focused upon and developed. Each library should not have to create its own information and referral format.

How the information resources of one community will relate to those of another requires further thought, but one can see potential uses made both by scholars and nonscholars. The head of a NOW chapter might want to find out the names of all of the women related organizations in nearby counties. On the other hand, a university professor might conceivably want a list of all of the local consumer advocate offices in a given region of the country, or perhaps throughout the country. Thus the inclusion of local information resources opens the catalog to a wider and more integrated variety of information.

Special catalogs

Another major area of enriched access to library collections would be the production of special purpose catalogs. These would not have been practically feasible prior to automated systems. An innovative application was the use of NYPL's automated system, created originally to meet the needs of its Research Libraries, to produce a special book catalog for a media center created in the George Bruce Branch in Harlem. Enough copies of this catalog were printed so that each teacher in the branch's four neighborhood schools had available in each classroom, a wholly integrated catalog of all of the specially acquired media materials and all of the print and nonprint items held by the branch serving the neighborhoods of those schools. It is through the machine manipulability of a data base that such special products or services are possible. Obviously, the catalog, at least in this instance, is a tool which is actively promoting library service by going where the students and the teachers are, as opposed to waiting for them to show up at the library.

This leads back to the more general points about opening the catalog through the use of machine-based products. The COM catalog is readily reproducible and usable in as many places as there are COM readers. The Georgia Institute of Technology put COM copies of its catalog in dormitories, faculty and department offices, libraries, etc. at relatively little cost in the early 1970's. The University of Toronto COM catalog has been widely discussed at meetings and in the literature. This dissemination of the catalog is a major advance in research library bibliographic or catalog service.

ISBD

The International Standard Bibliographic Description (ISBD) is probably of usefulness to national libraries, and conceivably to some of the large research libraries. It performed a valuable service by prescribing a standard sequence of descriptive elements. However, the value of the prescribed punctuation and Latin and other abbreviations required by ISBD, especially for public and school libraries is totally unconvincing. In addition, the necessary repetition of the author statement when it is identical to the main entry, violates any principle of reason or economy. The 1946 <u>Report of the Advisory Committee on Descriptive Cataloging of the Librarian of Congress</u> (p. 5) stated: "The omission of author statements that are identical with author headings is a clear gain in the catalog entry." One hastens to point out that machine-readability makes it possible for the library to exercise the option of deleting the relatively useless and obligatory ISBD punctuation from its own catalog records through local program-

Freedman

ming or the programming of their bibliographic utility. For nonresearch libraries, it has been proposed that a format be developed which actively promotes recognition or understanding by the layperson; i.e., those who have not been exposed to the meaning of religious symbols of revised Chapter 6 of The Anglo American Cataloging Rules. The creation of such a descriptive format would attempt to foster the immediate comprehension of the data elements of the catalog record. Marvin Scilken has offered one alternative, having the words author, title, subject, appear immediately adjacent to the appropriate headings to which they refer. In this light, one study which should be considered is the development of an optimum nonresearch library catalog record display format. Such an alternative standard display could then be made available to libraries and library processors in the commercial and noncommercial area. In the process preceding the adoption of ALA of ISBD, no use studies were conducted. This alternative standard should include empirical investigation.

Lest one think that this notion of opening the catalog is "bluesky" or impractical, a brief description is offered of a place where much of this has been done. Using NYPL's automated authority control system to its fullest potential, the Hennepin County Library (HCL) of Minnesota converted its shelflist to MARC in 1972. HCL produced a computer typeset book catalog widely available in all of its facilities as well as some nonlibrary agencies such as the county government building and a local police station (the branch head wanted her community to have 24-hour bibliographic access). HCL wholly revised antiquated and otherwise deficient LC headings in a simple and relatively painless way from a cost and time standpoint, integrated all of its nonprint media into the catalog, and even lists several community information resources as well as most of the government documents it acquires under appropriate headings in the catalog. In addition, HCL refers the catalog user to the vertical file via a public catalog note under the appropriate subject heading when pamphlet, ephemeral, or other noncataloged material is available on that topic. The HCL also routinely and automatically strips ISBD punctuation from LC/MARC records entering Hennepin's data base. In 1973 it closed all of its card catalogs and eventually removed them from its branches. Some of the work of HCL was described in the author's "Cataloging systems: application status 1973," in Library Automation: State of the Art II, ALA, 1973. It has since been elaborated upon in the writings of Sanford Berman in the Hennepin County Library Cataloging Bulletin, of which he was editor, and in his paper in the forthcoming Closing the Catalog, edited by Kaye Gapen and Bonnie Juergens, to be published by Oryx Press.*

Opportunity in closing

Librarians can insure that the closing of the card catalog is an op-

---

*Reprinted in this volume, No. 15.

portunity to truly open the library catalog and promote the satisfaction of all user information needs. To do so they cannot follow, lemming-like, the de facto national library's practices nor countenance a bibliographic utility's practices if neither meet the local library's needs. When LC or OCLC or any other agency does not do the job local library users need, librarians should lobby for change and the services those users deserve. If neither LC nor one's bibliographic utility can meet the information users' information needs, try to satisfy them locally or in concert with similar libraries. Work to make the information resources of your library and your community as accessible to the library users as is within your power.

In that way bibliographic service can be enhanced, greater access to more information will be provided, and, ultimately, the user will be better served.

9. The Case for Not Closing the Catalog*

by Joe A. Hewitt and David E. Gleim

The decision of the Library of Congress to adopt AACR 2 and to automate its catalogs in 1981 has been perceived by many members of the research library community as a crisis of considerable proportions. Librarians are compellingly preoccupied with the possibility of closing card catalogs. Reporting the results of an informal survey by the Association of Research Libraries, Richard Dougherty stated that "the majority of respondents see no alternative to closing card catalogs and adopting AACR 2 in concert with the Library of Congress."[1]

This inability to perceive other alternatives no doubt reflects the reaction to LC's plans announced at ALA's Midwinter Meeting in 1978. Then LC estimated the combined effects of adopting AACR 2 and desuperimposing would change 37 percent of existing MARC headings and 49 percent of existing MARC records.[2] Later decisions by LC have moderated this impact considerably. The alternative of continuing existing card catalogs for after 1981 now appears to be a viable approach to code adoption, and may be the best approach.

Until recently the suggestion that adopting AACR 2 need not require the closing of card catalogs in research libraries has not been treated as a serious alternative in the literature. Workshops and institutes since LC's decision seem to be focused exclusively on catalog closure. The documents receiving wide notice and distribution come from libraries which have decided to close their catalogs. There is little evidence that the techniques, costs, and probable results of integrating AACR 2 into existing catalogs have been investigated thoroughly. Indeed, some writers indicate the idea of not closing in concert with LC is a rather tainted and backward view.

We believe the integration of AACR 2 into existing catalogs is a reasonable and legitimate approach. We do not intend to debate the merits of card catalogs as compared to other forms. We do not doubt the superiority of COM and online catalogs in the modern research library environment. However, the role of AACR 2 as a catalyst for closing card catalogs and moving to computer-based catalogs before a library is fully prepared is questionable.

Some research libraries may be in a position to make an or-

---

*Reprinted by permission of the authors from American Libraries, 10 (March 1979), p. 118-21.

derly conversion to COM catalogs in 1981. Many libraries, however, will not be ready in terms of budget, bibliographic, and systems planning. Libraries committed to the concept of closing may well face the need to begin an add-on card catalog. Continuing present card catalogs, while at the same time planning for their eventual replacement by COM or online, may be the best alternative.

In order to adhere to national standards, research libraries should use AACR 2 for all original cataloging performed after 1981. AACR 2 records and cataloging copy formed under earlier codes could continue to be added to the local catalog. This could be accomplished by a combination of interfiling, changing headings, and creating split files, depending upon various factors related to each heading.

Several commentators have mistakingly associated this approach with the opprobrious term "superimposition." However, it differs fundamentally from LC's practice in adopting AACR 1 in 1967, when headings formed under an obsolete code continued to be used on new works. In the alternative proposed here, superseded headings on pre-1981 LC cataloging would continue to be added to the local catalog under certain conditions, but the practice would have local impact only and would not result in the creation of new records with obsolete headings. In general, this pragmatic approach respects both operational and budgetary realities, as well as the need for standards.

Is Closing Feasible?

Closing the card catalog and continuing it by COM supplements is technically a simple matter for any library capable of producing all its current cataloging in machine-readable form. Any library using OCLC or a similar system has this potential. But in reality, how many research libraries can afford to put into machine-readable form all the records now being added to its card catalog?

A number of libraries can produce machine-readable records for all current monographic and serial cataloging performed by centralized units. Typically, however, this cataloging constitutes only a portion of the new records being added to a research library's central catalog. Other records may include main entries from autonomous campus libraries such as law and medicine, purchased cards for microform sets, and cards prepared for special collections, pamphlets, arrearage titles, and materials in non-Roman alphabets. Few libraries will be able to render all such bibliographic information into machine-readable form in 1981. Closing the card catalog will mean many libraries which hope to produce COM catalogs in 1981 will have to abandon the concept of the main catalog as a union catalog. If this concept is abandoned, considerable planning would be required to provide equivalent access in other forms.

In the library press, writers imply that the transition to

COM catalogs requires an abrupt break. COM would contain all the cataloging produced after a certain date and no newly cataloged materials would be added to the card catalog. For libraries maintaining a comprehensive catalog for all materials in the system, this appears to be an unrealistic scenario, perhaps based on an unjustifiable use of LC's "day one" deadline. A more realistic projection would be a gradual supplanting of the card catalog by COM, including a period when some new records would be added to COM and others to the card catalog, but not to both. The complete transition could take a number of years. In order to avoid a fragmented combination of old card catalog, add-on card catalog, and COM catalog, it would be preferable to maintain a single card catalog after 1981.

Can Libraries Afford to Close?

Commentators frequently assert that research libraries cannot afford to continue their card catalogs. In the long run, card catalog maintenance will become an excessive burden for large research libraries. An eventual transition to some form of computer-based catalog is inevitable. But the staggering costs of catalog maintenance should not obscure the fact that AACR 2 adoption will increase the cost of producing records for local catalogs even if the card catalog is closed. Purely in terms of the transition to AACR 2, it is also fair to raise the question, "Can research libraries afford to close their catalogs?"

Closing the catalog involves operating costs above and beyond the cost of producing COM and equipping user stations. If COM itself is not to be subject to the same inconsistencies as an integrated card catalog, all entries in an add-on COM or card catalog will have to be validated in conformity with AACR 2. Since it is unlikely that the major retrospective data bases from which libraries draw their information will be converted to AACR 2 by 1981, or even soon thereafter, the manner in which this cataloging copy is used in research libraries will be changed greatly.

The warning that a research library must close its catalog simultaneously with LC in order to remain cost effective is perhaps based on an inappropriate comparison between LC and other research libraries. Most research libraries depend heavily on cataloging information produced elsewhere and gear their operations to the use of outside records more than to the production of original cataloging. Any library, like LC, which is engaged mainly in producing original cataloging records would probably find it more cost effective to start a new catalog upon the adoption of AACR 2. Libraries making extensive use of the existing store of bibliographic records may not find this necessary.

The high production "mass" operations based on acceptance of LC, often without authority verification at the point of cataloging, will grind more slowly and in all probability require more competent staff. Establishing adequate links between the old and the new catalogs will involve essentially the same authority work as changing headings or creating split files in an existing catalog. While beginning a new catalog will reduce the cost of filing and other maintenance activities, the cost of creating local records based on data from outside sources will increase. Library administrators must be made aware that either approach will involve temporary cost increases. The individual library must study the cost trade-offs before making a decision.

The most important factor affecting the cost of implementing the code is the number of heading changes. LC's latest estimate is an 11 percent incompatibility rate between AACR 2 and the MARC data base, affecting 15 percent of existing MARC records.[3] These estimates probably represent the maximum rate of conflict for research libraries with card catalogs constructed on ALA and AACR 1 rules. The wisdom of the decisions acting to moderate the impact of AACR 2 is debatable. Some "acceptable exceptions," for example, might have been handled locally while LC aimed at a purer implementation. The extreme pressure on LC to moderate the impact was due partially to the fact so few libraries had thoroughly evaluated their capacity to change, abetted by the rather careless rhetoric discussing the issue.

Automation does create a truly alarming potential for LC to change subject headings, but the existence of this potential does not mean that it will be used fully. With a few notable exceptions, LC has done a reasonably good job in updating its terminology over the past several years. Since most of the frustration over the inadequacy of subject access results from the limitations of LC's concept rather than its terminology, fewer terms may require changing than one might suppose. In any case, the computer cannot accelerate the intellectual decision that one term represents a topic better than another. Mary K. Pietris, chief of LC's Subject Cataloging Division, has indicated there will be no massive increase in the rate of change to subject headings.[4]

Taken together, an 11-percent rate of heading incompatibility and a moderate increase in subject heading change do not portend a sizeable rise in catalog maintenance costs in the short range, provided librarians take a cost-conscious approach. Such an approach will involve some compromises, but will not add perceptibly to the already complex and confusing nature of research library catalogs.

Techniques of Continuing the Catalog

No single technique need be adopted for integrating AACR 2 headings into existing catalogs. Rather, a pragmatic combination of methods must be devised based upon factors such as the number of headings in the file and the degree of incompatibility. Many catalog maintenance staffs are already familiar with these techniques since they are widely used to keep up with normal heading changes. Before taking the drastic action of freezing the catalog, these suggestions should be considered carefully:

1. Changing obsolete headings when their number is limited. (In doing so, it might also be worth ignoring some of our cosmetic standards, since the catalog's days are numbered.)
2. Interfiling superseded headings with new ones without change when the differences are inconsequential.
3. Establishing split files between old and new headings when large files of superseded headings exist.
4. Changing large files of superseded headings by photographic techniques and shifting files in conjunction with already scheduled shifts or expansions. (Photographic methods for making such changes are now under investigation at the University of North Carolina/Chapel Hill.)

Some librarians argue that these techniques will result in a "catalog within a catalog." They do reflect to some extent the abandonment of the collocation principle. On the other hand, closing the catalog creates a total split when up to 90 percent of new catalog records might easily file with older records. Although the number of headings requiring split files is not yet known, the total should be substantially less than LC's 11-percent incompatibility rate.

Advocates of the separate catalog for post-1981 LC records note that the reference structure needed to integrate old and new headings in a single catalog will be complex and expensive. On the other hand, the structure required to link variant headings in separate catalogs is equally complex and expensive, perhaps more so. Offering limited or no linkages between old and new catalogs is not a solution, but a surrendering of important services.

A single catalog conceived as a transitional measure and integrated by the methods suggested above would appear to provide better service than separate card catalogs. To automatically require everyone to search a separate file for all headings, rather than for a small subset of changes, would be an imposition on users and staff alike. The same union catalog coverage could be continued until it can be replaced by a machine-readable system. Since the old card catalog will be a significant presence in the library system for some time to come, and some users may be weaned from this familiar form only gradually, a degree of overlap between the card catalog and its COM replacement could be useful.

The Advantages of Delay

If a library does find its best option is to retain a single card catalog through the AACR 2 transition, it should also begin planning for its eventual replacement by COM or other forms of the computerized catalog. The continued maintenance of a serviceable, integrated catalog will allow time for a deliberate and well planned transition. There may also be other advantages:

First, if a machine-readable catalog is to serve as a full

supplement to the card catalog, some means must be found to accommodate the many bibliographic records now unavailable in machine-readable form. This may involve beginning a series of separate card catalogs for special records, continuing to add to the old catalog, or even abandoning the idea of the full union catalog of materials in a research library system. In any case, these complex decisions will involve considerable bibliographic planning which should be based on user studies. Very few libraries are likely to have such a transition thoroughly planned and ready for implementation by 1981.

Secondly, users may ignore a COM catalog supplement including only a small portion of a library's holdings. At the University of Toronto, users frequently ignored the monthly supplements to the basic COM catalog.[5] A COM supplement to the card catalog or an add-on card catalog would probably meet the same fate. A limited COM catalog supplement would require the expense of equipping stations and instructing the users, yet it may be used relatively little. A delay to convert more records and produce a useful COM catalog would definitely be beneficial.

Third, producing a COM catalog will be eased after the major extant bibliographic data bases have converted to AACR 2 and automatic authority control systems are more highly developed. Even with the distribution of LC authority tapes, few libraries will be capable of producing COM catalogs which are completely compatible with AACR 2 in 1981. Maintenance of compatibility in machine-readable catalogs will continue to require a great deal of costly human effort. The retrospective conversion of local records into machine-readable, AACR 2-compatible form will be facilitated greatly by working from source data bases with authority control.

Finally, disassociating the change to COM from the implementation of AACR 2 may make both easier to explain to lay people. Some library administrators may find it convenient to treat AACR 2 implementation as a compelling force to make the library close its catalogs. The adoption of the new code may be described as a crisis which leaves no alternative in order to gain special funding. If a defensible appraisal of the effects of AACR 2 reveals this to be the case, there is nothing wrong with this approach, but as a ploy, it is shortsighted and potentially damaging.

Explaining the rationale for code revision to university administrators and faculty members poses a problem. Nonlibrarians don't understand why it is necessary, much less why it must be so expensive. If code revision is a crisis of such costly proportions, surely librarians have brought it on themselves. Code revision, after all, is a rather arcane technical matter. Specific examples of heading changes, particularly in relation to their cost, appear rather foolish to nonlibrarians. Their immediate response is why not just ignore the code, and LC, too, for that matter? After all, isn't the institution proud of its independence?

* * *

The discussion of AACR 2 in the library press has been marked by much speculative and passionate rhetoric. This article, too, borders on that tradition, if only to gain equal attention and because it is written before all supporting background studies have been completed. Some of the rhetoric has been entertaining, but it should not cloud the perspectives of librarians who must make sensible decisions and work realistically with their users and funding bodies.

The AACR 2 debate is reminiscent of the ALA conference of 1887, as reported in the New York World on September 7, 1877. "The party of the young librarians was eager for the adoption of Continental methods for decapitalization in the French style, and uniformity of labels, indexes, and calendars, to which the conservative majority gives guarded encouragement." The World tells us that the "frank Dewey" and "earnest, enthusiastic, young Tyler" enlarged on the advantages of omitting all capitals, while the "emphatic Spofford" and "Poole, of Chicago" protested against the "Neorepublicanism of letters and the beheading of capitals." The World reporter was so impressed by this scene he was moved to remark, "One was fain to look upon it as a chief earthly interest."[6]

Code revision and desuperimposition, like decapitalization and similar issues in the history of librarianship, should not be expected to impress nonlibrarians. The true reasons that COM and online catalogs must eventually replace the card catalog is their increased capacity for service and their long-term cost-effectiveness. These issues can interest users and administrators and should be promoted to achieve acceptance and fiscal support. Above all, the new systems must deliver what is promised, and the transition should neither disrupt service nor befuddle the users. In many libraries these goals can best be achieved by implementing the new code into a single card catalog while proceeding to plan for COM and online catalogs on a sound bibliographic, systems, and budgetary basis.

The transition from card catalog technology to progressively refined versions of the computer-based catalog will proceed deliberately over the next decade. LC's "day one" deadline may be appropriate to mark the beginning of the era of a new catalog code, but it need not mark the end of all card catalogs and the beginning of computerized catalogs. This transition should be a gradual, overlapping development in which an outmoded catalog will be supplanted by improved forms. The credibility of librarianship, and perhaps the future of the profession, will depend partially on our meeting this challenge in a professional and user-oriented manner, with a minimum of panic and rancor.

References

1. Richard M. Dougherty, "Closing the Card Catalog: A Survey of the Status of Planning in ARL Libraries," in Freezing Card Catalogs (Washington, D.C.: Association of Research Libraries, 1978), p. 2.

2. "AACR 2 Impact," document accompanying memo to directors of ARL libraries by John Lorenz, Association of Research Libraries, Aug. 4, 1978, p. 1.
3. Ibid.
4. Mary K. D. Pietris, "CCS Subject Analysis Committee," Library of Congress Information Bulletin, Vol. 37, No. 33, p. 501, Aug. 18, 1978.
5. Robert Blackburn, "Two Years with a Closed Catalog," in Freezing Card Catalogs, p. 61.
6. "The Librarians' Convention," New York World, Sept. 7, 1877, p. 5, col. 1. (The authors wish to thank Edward G. Holley, dean of the School of Library Science, UNC/CH, for calling our attention to this bit of ALA history.)

10. Closing the Card Catalog or Two Years Before the Blast*

by Mary B. Henry

Eye-catching headlines announcing the Library of Congress' plans to freeze its card catalogs and adopt new cataloging rules have been appearing more and more frequently in library literature. The conversion from manual to automated catalogs has become a topic of major interest at conferences, and most large libraries have formed task forces to plan the future of their bibliographic files in light of LC's decision. All this activity indicates a growing momentum away from the card catalog to automated alternatives, a trend which may presage an eventual revolution in bibliographic control.

Concurrent with the increasing interest in automated catalogs, there has developed a rising tide of concern that planning for the changeover has not been thorough enough and that library budgets and users will suffer because of insufficient preparation. For this reason, a group of distinguished library leaders recently met and persuaded LC to postpone the adoption of the second edition of Anglo-American Cataloging Rules and the closing of its catalogs from the originally planned date of January 2, 1980 until January 1, 1981. It is hoped that this delay will provide enough time for librarians to study the issues, decide the fate of their catalogs, and plan necessary changes in an orderly and deliberate manner. This paper examines some of the issues which currently confront library planners.

What's Closing?

The term "catalog closing" can be misleading. It has the connotation of locking up the card cabinets and making catalog records inaccessible to users. Actually, a closed card catalog is one that reflects a library's holdings only up to a certain date. Cards for new acquisitions are not filed into the closed catalog; instead, records for new materials appear in another catalog which can be in an automated form or even another card file. In the closed catalog, maintenance is still carried out for corrections and deletions of cards. Users are free to examine the closed catalog, although they should be made aware that it does not represent the library's full holdings. Freezing is a term often used synonymously with closing.

*Reprinted by permission of the author and publisher from New Jersey Libraries, 11 (October 1978), p. 11-14.

Sometimes the word freezing is used for a closed catalog with no maintenance of existing entries.

The catalog of the library's newer materials can appear in a number of formats, including cards, book, microform, and on-line. A new card catalog allows for quick entry of new titles, but it is expensive and tedious to maintain. Computer-produced book catalogs have the advantage of ease of use and maintenance but the disadvantage of expensive printing and cumulation. Computer output microform or COM catalogs can be prepared much more cheaply and cumulated more quickly than a book format. However, a microimage catalog is not as appealing to users. The on-line catalog offers one of the chief benefits of the card catalog--very rapid cumulation or updating. It is potentially much more flexible than cards in terms of providing more access points. The developmental costs of an on-line catalog are high, and as yet no on-line system provides the full service of the card catalog.

Some libraries partially eliminate the need for a closed catalog by photographing it and producing a book or microform version. In effect, a library can then "clone" its catalog, creating as many copies as needed. The drawback is that existing technology does not allow for the changing or correcting of records in a photographically produced microimage catalog. Unless a library has the means for displaying corrections and deletions to the closed catalog in the new catalog, it is necessary to continue to maintain the old catalog and photograph it periodically.

Then there are libraries which convert existing catalog records to machine-readable form or have it done by commercial vendors. Experts recommend this course of action for collections under 250,000 titles because a great percentage of the cataloging will already be in machine-readable form, for example, on MARC tapes or the OCLC data base. Retrospective conversion of the closed catalog to machine-readable form permits easy correction of records and makes it possible to integrate the old catalog with a new automated one. A library that has undertaken retrospective conversion can dare to throw out the cards.

Why Close?

The reasons why libraries are so interested in closing their card catalogs and changing to automated alternatives are numerous: 1) the cost of maintaining card catalogs is increasing as they grow in size and age; many wonder whether the amount expended is justified considering that with the growth in catalog complexity comes declining effectiveness; 2) it is difficult, costly, and tedious to carry out changes in card catalogs, for example, in filing rules, access points, and location designations; 3) an automated catalog can contain the complete holdings of a library system, and the full union catalog can be consulted at all branches; 4) as the catalog expands, it takes up valuable space; 5) as catalogs age, the cards deteriorate and eventually will become unusable; and 6) LC's decision to close its catalogs and adopt AACR 2 in 1981 is forcing libraries to decide whether or not to retain their card catalogs.

Of all these reasons, the Library of Congress' announced plans are of pressing concern because of LC's pervasive influence on the cataloging policies of individual libraries. Most libraries, from the smallest to the largest, utilize Library of Congress cataloging data to a great extent to avoid the expense of original cataloging. Many purchase card sets generated by jobbers from MARC tapes which consist of LC cataloging copy in machine-readable form. CIP catalog records prepared by LC and printed in new books are widely used, as are the National Union Catalog and the printed card sets sold by LC. A large portion of the OCLC data base is made up of MARC records and LC copy input by participants.

Thus, LC's internal decision to adopt cataloging rules will have an impact on all libraries. The second edition of AACR is expected to appear in November, 1978. Early predictions are that AACR 2 will require extensive changes in the form in which entries are established, which will cause conflicts with existing headings. For example, the works of an author using pseudonyms will appear under the name associated with individual works. So new entries for the author of Huckleberry Finn will be under Mark Twain, where old entries used Samuel Clemens. Another example is the more direct entry of corporate names; what was formerly entered under California. University. would appear under University of California.

The full extent of the changes required by AACR 2 are not yet known. Preliminary rough estimates by LC indicated that 37% of their current headings would be in conflict with AACR 2 headings; more recent studies at LC peg the discrepancy at 11% after some minor rule bending. The LC position is that the number of old headings needing revision to allow for integration with new entries is too great. Thus, they intend to close the catalog in 1981 and start a new catalog with new cataloging rules, hopefully in automated form but possibly in card form. At that time, many revisions will be made in subject headings (e.g. European War, 1914-1918 will finally be updated), and the 19th edition of Dewey will be adopted.

Whether other libraries will have to follow LC's lead to accommodate the changes brought about by AACR 2 is not yet clear. There is more than one method for dealing with entry conflicts, for example the following: 1) cards under the old entry can simply be interfiled with the new entries, a method which is sure to confuse users and filers; 2) cards under the old entry could be corrected to the new form by typing or writing, which is tedious and expensive; 3) new headings could be changed to the old form, which is called "superimposition," another costly operation; and 4) cross references can be provided between the old and new entries, a complicated procedure but probably more workable than the other choices.

Trying to choose an approach for coping with AACR 2 will be difficult for individual libraries because so far there has been little leadership from the Library of Congress and the American Library Association. Cost studies to determine the most efficient approach for a library will probably show that all methods cost more than present operations.

Implementation Concerns

If a library selects the option to close its card catalogs and begin a new automated file, there are still a myriad of questions to be addressed. For example, should closing be according to date of imprint or date of cataloging; will there be links (see also's) between variant forms of the same entry in the two catalogs; how will serials be handled; will the automated catalog be divided or dictionary; how many copies of the automated catalog will be needed; how often should it cumulate? An effective way of dealing with these detailed issues will be staff participation in carrying out studies, gathering information, and setting priorities.

Staffing considerations are important because of the need to reorganize once it is not necessary to keep the card file up-to-date. Since staff members might feel their job status threatened, care should be taken to keep them informed and involved in the planning process. The enthusiastic reception of an automated catalog on the part of staff members will help ensure more ready acceptance from users who interact with library personnel.

Since public and user support will be essential to a smooth transition, creative efforts will be needed in public relations and orientation. Convincing evidence for the need to convert to an automated catalog should be developed, especially for those holding the purse-strings.

In Conclusion

It is clear that there are no facile solutions for coping with catalog changes. So far, most planning has been done by libraries and systems in isolation from one another. What really is needed is for LC or ALA to issue guidelines and recommendations to assist libraries in deciding how to deal with AACR 2 and the proposed subject heading revision. At the same time, it is the responsibility of librarians to voice their opinions on the issues to those making decisions. The recent conclave of library leaders in which LC was convinced to postpone the adoption of AACR 2 demonstrated that the best way to be heard is through strength in numbers.

New Jersey librarians also have a forum for airing their concerns about LC's decisions: the Technical Services Section of NJLA. This author proposes that an all-day workshop devoted to catalog closing and AACR 2 be planned by the Technical Services Section for the coming year.

11. Close the Card Catalog?*

by Jeffrey T. Schwedes

It is sometime after January 2, 1981. The Library of Congress has adopted the new AACR 2 cataloging rules, closed its card catalog, and started a new catalog for materials processed after January 1.

You find yourself in a college library that you haven't visited in some time. You go to the area of the public catalog and peer around, searching for some sign that the library is freezing its catalog and beginning a new one.

You look for clusters of microform readers that weren't there before, or a lineup of new CRT terminals, or a new card file conspicuously set apart. You keep your eyes open for posted instructions directing patrons who seek recent materials away from the old catalog.

What will you find? The chances are better than average, if a recent ACRL survey is representative, that you will find nothing but the old card catalog.

When the Library of Congress adopts AACR 2 in 1981, the libraries that rely on Library of Congress cataloging will have to adjust to the changes in the form of entry called for by the new rules. The libraries polled by ACRL, however, will not necessarily follow the Library of Congress' decision to accommodate the new headings by opening a new catalog.

ACRL asked the libraries that are participating in the ACRL 100 Libraries project to answer a questionnaire on AACR 2 and the future of the catalog. Twenty-nine university libraries, forty-four college libraries, and thirty-three community college libraries returned questionnaires.

Of the 106 libraries that responded to the survey, 92 said they planned to adopt AACR 2. Of the remaining 14 libraries, 12 are community college libraries that have not yet decided what they will do about AACR 2.

---

*Reprinted by permission of the author and American Library Association from (College and Research Libraries News), 41 (February 1980), p. 25-27; copyright © 1980 by the American Library Association.

Among the ninety-two libraries that intend to adopt AACR 2, fourteen plan to close or freeze their card catalogs, and two are leaning toward closing. The largest number, forty, do not plan to close their catalogs in the near future, and two say they will probably not close. Twenty-three have not yet decided what they will do. Ten do not have card catalogs. And one library has already frozen its card catalog.

When the forty-two libraries that anticipate maintaining their existing card catalogs were asked to give the reasons for their decision, thirteen said they believed it would be more costly to start a new COM or on-line catalog; thirteen mentioned ease of use and service to patrons as important reasons for keeping an undivided card catalog (several libraries expressed concern that a divided catalog might create confusion and frustration among patrons); thirteen said they preferred to maintain a single card catalog until they can go to a single on-line catalog (one librarian commented that his institution was "close enough to a machine readable data base [retrospective conversion/OCLC] to not warrant an interim procedure"); twelve answered that the small size of their catalogs would make it relatively easy to adapt to AACR 2; six indicated that they didn't want to cope with multiple catalogs; and four said they did not have the technical capability yet to go to a COM or on-line catalog.

The survey asked the libraries that intend to keep their card catalogs open how they plan to deal with the changes in entry that the adoption of AACR 2 may require; in other words, how will they integrate the new headings called for by AACR 2 into their card catalogs? Four of the forty-two libraries that plan to maintain their catalogs said they would change existing headings (one of the four indicated it would also interfile entries where possible). Three said they would use see also cross-references to connect the new forms of headings to the old forms. Seventeen answered that they would both change existing headings and use cross-references (four of the seventeen said they would also interfile where possible). Twelve responded that they would use a combination of cross-references and superimposition. One library will both change existing headings and superimpose. Two libraries plan to change existing headings, superimpose, and use cross-references. One intends to change existing entries if relatively few are involved and move them to the correct location if many are involved. One said it would use computer-assisted editing to make the existing catalog work. And one institution is undecided on the issue.

Fourteen of the libraries polled plan to close their catalogs and open new catalogs. Two libraries are leaning in this direction. When asked why they intend to start new catalogs, eight of the sixteen cited the overall advantages of an automated catalog over a card catalog (particularly the advantage of distributed access). Seven of the respondents mentioned convenience to users and better service as a factor in their decision to close. Five pointed to the high cost of maintaining the catalog (especially labor costs) as a reason for closing. Interestingly enough, only three respondents mentioned the difficulty of adapting the catalog to AACR 2 as a reason for closing.

When asked what kind of new catalog they intend to open after closing the existing catalog, eight of sixteen said they would go to a COM catalog, six said they wanted an on-line catalog, and two indicated they would start a second card catalog. (Three of the libraries that want COM catalogs and one of the libraries that plan a second card catalog made clear that they look upon a second catalog as only a temporary bridge to a permanent on-line catalog.)

One should keep in mind that many, if not most, of the libraries surveyed are still in the early stages of thinking about what they will do about AACR 2 and their card catalogs. Thirteen libraries have not decided yet whether they will adopt AACR 2. Twenty-three libraries that plan to adopt AACR 2 have not decided whether they will close their card catalogs. Thirty-six libraries that have card catalogs and depend on Library of Congress cataloging have not yet begun any formal planning for what they will do when the Library of Congress adopts AACR 2. Only sixteen institutions have tried to determine the proportion of new headings prescribed by AACR 2 that would be incompatible with those already in their catalogs. And only fifteen have tried to estimate the cost of maintaining the current catalog as compared with the cost of opening a new one. (Of the eleven completed estimates, six showed that opening a new catalog would cost less, and five showed that maintaining an undivided card catalog would cost less.)

Because many of the libraries responding to the survey are still making up their minds, the results of the questionnaire must be regarded as tentative. Nevertheless, it does seem clear that the advent of AACR 2 will not necessarily compel libraries to close their catalogs. The fourteen libraries polled that intend to close their catalogs gave a variety of reasons for their decision. The adoption of AACR 2 by the Library of Congress was only one. The forty libraries that have decided to keep open their card catalogs believe that they can accommodate AACR 2 headings to their existing files, and they are inclined to postpone going to a new catalog until the issues of cost, service, technical feasibility, etc., are resolved to their satisfaction.

12. Catalog "Closings" and Serials*

by Jean S. Decker

An old friend is regrettably flawed. The rule changes, the local policy variations, the temporary little deviations, and the accumulation of human errors and omissions are there in plain sight. The reputation of the card catalog may be irretrievably besmirched. A mildly humorous line from a speech by John C. Rather is a clue to how the wind is blowing. "Somebody, speaking no doubt from bitter experience, said a card catalog is a place where bibliographic records get lost alphabetically."[1] With no attempt at humor, a report from the Processing Department of the Library of Congress states that an estimated 5 percent of the catalog cards are misfiled.[2] In spite of the flaws there is a great fondness in some quarters for a good and faithful servant.

In reviewing studies made mainly by large research libraries, one concludes that "closing" the large catalogs would have been an inevitable necessity even if automation, COM, desuperimposition, and AACR 2 had not appeared on the scene. AACR 1, obsolete subject headings, complex filing rules, size that precludes change, growing correction and revision backlogs, augmented costs, relentless demand for space, diminished staffs, and physical deterioration would have been enough to bring up the suggestion that we "close" the catalog. Perhaps a subconscious desire to be rid of the unmanageable mammoth prompted the choice of the word "closing." The author joins Art Plotnik, editor of American Libraries, in questioning the accuracy of the word to describe the action that some libraries are taking. "When a catalog is closed, it is not necessarily boarded up and left for archeologists."[3] Those libraries that can afford to convert the contents of the entire card catalog to machine-readable form or those that photograph the cards and freeze the records in books or on film, can in truth close their catalogs. The rest may "discontinue," "semiretire," "partially convert," "deactivate," or "give up on" our old catalogs. (The bomb-suggestive "deactivate" goes well with "information explosion" and "catalog card fallout," but as a serials cataloger, the author is partial to "discontinue.")

---

*Reprinted by permission of the author and publisher from The Journal of Academic Librarianship, 5 (November 1979), p. 261-65; © 1979 by the Journal of Academic Librarianship. All rights reserved.

Two Problems

Writing on card catalog "closings" combine, confuse, and possibly mislabel two distinct problems:

> Problem 1: To find a more flexible, more convenient, more easily maintainable, more accessible, and cheaper way to store bibliographic records. Technology gives a library an opportunity to choose to display records in books, on reels of microfilm, on microfiches, and/or on cathode-ray tubes. Whatever the decision, conversion to machine-readable records is the bottom line.

> Problem 2: To find a method by which a library can integrate or relate old records and new records created to be consonant with desuperimposition (i.e., changing names established under ALA rules to the forms required by AACR), AACR 2, current subject headings, and new romanization tables. The issue is record content rather than record storage and display.

The interrelatedness of the two problems is undeniable. The magnitude of Problem 2 makes a solution to Problem 1 all the more pressing. Whereas changing the content of records manually might be unthinkable, changing the content of machine-readable records could, by comparison, be quite easily effected. However, the focus here will be on Problem 2, particularly as it affects serials processing and control, and ultimately the seekers and users of information.

Serials and Standardization

The role of serials as the "Peck's Bad Boy" of information control is not about to change. Defying uniformity and standardization, serials display some perverse characteristics. Continuity is made uncertain by irregularities. Predictability is upset by unpredictable vicissitudes. Traditional behavior is abandoned in favor of separation and divorce. Indefinite publication abruptly turns definite. The ceased spring to life. By contrast, a monograph is static, stable, and unchanging. A serial, in theory, goes on forever. It can be erratic, unstable, and ever-changing. It resists "closing" or "freezing."

Given the nature of serials, automators are finding them something of a trial. Serials do not easily lend themselves to standardization. But why worry about "standardization"? Standardization is what control is all about whether one has a manual system, an automated system, or some combination of the two. The call for standardization has been sounded on numerous occasions. Margaret Mann, in 1929, stressed "the importance of system, accuracy and order"[4] in cataloging. Michael Gorman, in 1978, speaks of the "pressures for standardization exerted by the realities of international cooperation and modern bibliographic economics."[5] To maximize cooperation and the exchange of information the standards have been shaped to encourage international usage. At one time, a standard was designed to control only the collection in a local library. If one chooses to use products from the Library of Congress, the National Library of Medicine, the National Library of Canada, other national libraries, and all the libraries that are contributing members of cooperative processing systems, one has to try to live within the prescribed rules. However, creative catalogers, don't despair. Some flexibility remains. There are options and there are record levels. Gorman emphasizes this point in a recent article. "This rule [on supplements] is characteristic of a number of rules in AACR 2 in that it offers more than one method for dealing with a problem, recognizing that different contexts call for different solutions and that the task of a code of rules is not to create a Procrustean bed into which individual items are forced willy-nilly but to create flexible standards that allow for individual local interpretation while doing away with the necessity for petty local variation."[6] Agreement on what is "petty" will in all likelihood never be reached. But back to the specifics of serials control and catalog "closings."

The variations in serials themselves are matched by variations in processing procedures and the record-keeping habits of serials staffs. The "never-ending" feature of serials spawns a multiplicity of records: check-in, binding, payment, claiming, orders, vendor/publisher correspondence, holdings, and whatever additional records a library has deemed essential by experience or tradition. A study conducted at Berkeley "isolated two factors as essential to effective serial treatment: A. The importance of identical form of entry in several different files ... [and] B. The unacceptability of split files in the serial entering records."[7] These two factors loom large when one weighs the options for dealing with variant forms of entry.

More than a few libraries do not classify their periodicals. That being the case, their bound periodicals are probably alphabetically arranged. Any change in the form of entry requires answers to several questions. Shall we treat this new form of entry like a successive entry? Shall we alter the spine lettering to conform to the new form? Shall we ignore AACR?

One more file of records should be mentioned because it particularly affects interlibrary loan networks and their users: the union list of serials (ULS). In many academic and research libraries the ULS was the first file to be automated. For that reason, it will be the easiest file to manipulate. However, the ULS form of entry has to be identical to the form of entry in all other files and on the spines of unclassified bound periodicals.

Weighing Options

All considered, one cannot lightly lump serials with monographs in determining a course of action. Planners of catalog "closings" quite

uniformly recognize the complexity of problems in dealing with
serials. In a report from the University of California at Berkeley,
this conclusion was reached: "It is evident that serials because of
their ongoing nature, will present special problems no matter which
option for dealing with desuperimposition is selected."[8] The combination of multiplicity of records or files, and the importance of identical form of entry in every file, requires the weighing of more factors than those related solely to the bibliographic record in the catalog, even though it may be a separate serials catalog.

Even a cursory look at the studies which have been made of
options for handling entry conflicts will convince the reader that
hard decisions are ahead. The number of variables to consider,
the absence of reliable methods for measuring most variables, and
the tricky task of assigning a value or weight to each variable will
test administrators at all levels. Those groups who are wrestling
with the options and making difficult choices appear to ask similar
questions. Will the catalog retain its traditional functions? Will
the quality of service be decreased or enhanced? How will technical
processing be affected?

Functions of the Catalog

At least one traditional catalog function will be altered or eliminated.
In most libraries the collocating function, i.e., gathering into one
sequence the records describing an author's works, will no longer be
strictly maintained. Some of the reasons are clear. First, the new
rules for choice of entry will change many corporate main entries to
title main entries. Second, desuperimposition will give the corporate
form of entry a new look. Third, AACR 2 allows the cataloger to
choose more than one form of name or pseudonym for an author.

Although scattered records may force users into two- or
three-step searches, that inconvenience can be offset by the convenience of more accessible book, COM, or online catalogs in many locations. In selecting an option for making incompatible records intelligible and usable, decision-makers will most certainly retain two
basic catalog functions: to provide records of what a library owns
and to show where each title can be located.

Quality of Service

Is there any way to measure how an option will affect service? Not
very accurately or scientifically. Sally Hart McCallum was asking
how much users are bothered by inconsistent forms of entry. After
saying that there is no reliable data, she did cite a questionable
claim that has been made: "Each user is looking for only one specific heading. Thus ... the fact that some institutions are entered
under place, by the old rules, and others under name, by the new,
is not actually troublesome."[9] That thought, if it is true, will be
balm for the consciences of those who worry about users' time, lost

access, and unbearable frustration. Most commentators on, and students of, the catalog crisis are far from unconcerned about the impact on service. Paul Fasana of the New York Public Library is one of those concerned librarians:

> As a director of technical services in a large service-oriented research library, I am reminded every day by the users I serve that technical services is not an end in itself. It is not a <u>closed system</u> where I, or anyone else, is free to experiment with new ideas and concepts that change the way things are done currently, because such changes can affect files, catalogs, and collections which represent a large past investment in the organization and preservation of library materials. Technical services is first and foremost a means to an end--and that end is service. Therefore, <u>before</u> changes in practice, policy, and/or standards are considered, and <u>certainly</u> before they are implemented, we should know with some measure of precision what impact they will have on existing catalogs and records, so that we can predict <u>in advance</u> what effect they will have on service.[10]

Does he know how to measure the impact with precision?

Joan Marshall's concern is more specific: "... library users, despite their great differences, are expected to negotiate their own way through whatever catalog is presented to them. The catalog in each user's world, therefore, should meet individual information needs readily and with as much ease as is possible."[11] Is there an affordable option which will allow the user to find his/her way unaided to the information sought?

The impact of catalog "closings" on serials users will be no greater, and possibly less, than on other users. For instance, the disruption of the collocating function of the catalog may have less effect upon serials users than upon those using monographic records for a couple of reasons: (1) serials catalogers tend to avoid personal author entries because a human is finite and a serial is not, and (2) the subject headings in the catalog are less used since serials, notably periodicals, are frequently accessed through classified indexes. The library patron who seeks a serial has already had to sharpen his/her detective skills. Since the advent of the "successive entry" rule, the serial user, especially the periodical user, has had to interpret "continued by," "supersedes," "formed by the union of," etc. notes in order to conclude a search successfully. One more step will not discourage this hardy sort. Users of serials have added expectations which have nothing to do with the arrangement of bibliographic records. The final question is not, "does the library have this title?" but "does the library have this issue/edition and is the needed article therein intact?" An accurate holdings record is paramount no matter where or how it is stored. Serials users in all likelihood suffer more frustration from inadequate indexing and inaccurate holdings records than from catalog deficiencies.

Effect Upon Technical Processing

The effect upon technical processing is a variable, or group of variables, that can be measured. This very fact increases the danger that "the tail may wag the dog." In a time when accountability is king, the measurable factors may receive more than their fair share of weight. An option is apt to be selected or rejected on the basis of its measurable cost to the institution and not on the basis of the hard-to-measure effect on service and users.

One of the basic assumptions in the Berkeley study addresses processing costs. "While more economical and efficient technical processing should be a long term goal, added costs should be expected during a short term transition period. This will be true regardless of which option is chosen."[12] The cost of serials entry changes will be high.

When C-day (C for closing or conversion) comes in January, 1981, most serials departments will have to be ready to cope with conflicts in check-in, holdings or adds, payment, and bindery records, ULS, name authority files, and series authority files, in addition to public catalog records. For those who have not worked closely with serials records some examples which appeared in the Alternative Catalog Newsletter of June 1978, will illustrate the kind of complexities caused by desuperimposition and the new cataloging code.

> Further problems arise from the need to maintain current checking records and payment records in the Serials Department so that they can be readily located from the entry used in the catalog.
> Some of the problems can best be illustrated by examples. Suppose we have a number of standing orders for business services from Standard and Poor and they are entered under Standard and Poor (according to the old code). When a shipment arrives, the person recording them in the continuations file has the entire group in one spot in the visible file and soon learns that they are grouped there. But if a new title is added to our standing order and the new code calls for entry under title (if the new code is followed) this one title will be "out of pocket" in the visible file and the result will be lost time and motion in locating it. Of course a cross reference can and should be made in the central serials record, but space precludes cross references in the visible files. The checker will have to go to another file to learn the correct entry.... The entire process of checking in current periodicals and serials and paying for them will be considerably slowed down.
> The type of problem mentioned in the preceding paragraph is further complicated if the group of titles is in the periodical collection.... There is a strong possibility that the new code would call for the entry under title or under

a changed form of the corporate body's name. A related example is a title which is issued in parts A, B, and C, and part D appears or is newly acquired. The first three parts may be under one entry and the fourth under another. Recataloging and massive shifting of the volumes would be required to keep the relevant sections together under the new rules....

Serials classed together and analyzed constitute a different problem. The entry for the entire series and the analytics for the older books in the series would appear in the catalog according to the old code. But when the analytics for the new books in the series are made, the choice and form of entry would follow AACR 2. Unless massive recataloging were done, the cards for the series as a whole would follow the old code.[13]

It is primarily in the area of technical processing that serials characteristics complicate planning. Administrators are caught between a rock and a hard place: the rock being economic reality and the hard place being the need for continuity and the same form of entry on all records for each live serial.

Options

Those studying options have concentrated almost exclusively on what to do about catalog records for monographs. The suitability of different options to accommodate serials catalog records has received scant attention.

In the following review of options, "old entry" is used to refer to the established choice and/or form of entry presently in use and "new entry" to refer to the new choice and/or form of entry which conforms to AACR 2.

The first major choice is between revision and division. In Options 1, 2, and 3, below, a library would opt for one catalog and revised records. In Options 4 and 5 a library would opt for two catalogs and divided records. The pros and cons of revision versus division are many, involved, and available elsewhere in library literature.

OPTION ONE

One catalog consisting entirely of old entries.

Action: Revise LC or any cooperative copy the library may want to use so that the entries conform to its present old entries.

Effect on serials: Serials will be no special problem and serials users will be happy until entries in indexes, union lists of serials, interlibrary loan systems, bibliographic data bases, and other searching tools, produced outside the local library, begin to conflict with the library's old entries.

Decker   81

OPTION TWO

One catalog consisting of old and new entries interfiled.

<u>Action</u>: As conflicts appear, file unaltered old entries with new entries behind guide cards or correct old entries and file with new entries.
Cross reference from old entries to new.
Rework the present syndetic structure so that users can go directly to new entries.
Create and maintain an accurate authority file.

<u>Effect on serials</u>: Unaltered records filed as though they were new entries will confuse users and filers. Old entries pulled for corrections will be difficult to refile. Correcting only those parts of a record that affect filing has been suggested as a way to lessen confusion. Serials records which fall within a large corporate file require more than a change of location. Moving all the "Chicago University" entries to the "University of Chicago" location will not make those entries compatible with AACR 2. To quote again from Michael Gorman's article:

> The second rule (21.2B) prescribes corporate main entry for the following kinds of publications issued by, or caused to be issued by a corporate body:
> 1. administrative publications dealing with the body itself and its resources, e.g., catalogues, rules, membership lists;
> 2. certain legal publications, e.g., laws, treaties;
> 3. publications that contain the corporate thought of the body as a whole, e.g., reports of committees, commissions;
> 4. reports of conferences, expeditions, exhibitions, etc.; and
> 5. certain motion pictures and sound recordings that are the result of the work of a performing group.[14]

Under these new rules fewer serials will be cataloged with corporate main entries. Many serials records created because of the successive entry rule will have linking notes which will mislead users. From the serials standpoint this option is viable for coping with desuperimposition but not as a method for coping with AACR 2.

OPTION THREE

One catalog consisting of records made consonant with AACR 2.

<u>Action</u>: Recatalog all old entries to conform to AACR 2.

<u>Effect on serials</u>: The best of all worlds. Consistent serials records, to which accurate holdings records could be attached, would maximize service.

OPTION FOUR

Two catalogs consisting of old entries in the one, interconnected with new entries in the other.

Action: After a certain date, create new records which will conform to AACR 2.
Connect old and new entries in both directions.
Create and maintain an accurate authority file.

Effect on serials: The dividing date may be imprint date, cataloging date, date of receipt, or whatever date conditions dictate. Imprint date is a definite advantage for monograph users but less of an advantage for serials users. If the publication date is known and the new entry is known, a user may complete a search in one step. More often than not a serials user has no idea when a serial started, nor can he or she know when the library first acquired the serial. A 40-year-old serial may be acquired for the first time in 1981. Using the date cataloged or received as a dividing date would be an advantage to the processing department since one set of rules could be used. Whereas a split by imprint date means retrospective acquisitions would be cataloged by one set of cataloging rules and new imprints by another. Since live serials will be split between two catalogs, holdings records will also be split--not a boon to service.

OPTION FIVE

Two catalogs consisting of "frozen" old entries in the one and new entries in the other.

Action: After a certain date, create new records which will conform to all new rules.
Maintain the old catalog minimally or not at all.
Make changes in the old catalog records available to the public through a supplemental catalog of some sort.
Do not relate the old and new entries.
Create a new authority file.

Effect on serials: Problems for users will be similar to those with Option 4. Two- and three-step searches will be the usual, not the unusual. Dead serials are quite amenable to "freezing"; live serials are not. In view of the need for frequent maintenance, live serials records should be recataloged to fit into the new catalog.

Conclusion

The number of unanswered questions makes conclusions foolhardy. For example, where are the answers to the questions raised in the Berkeley study? How much of serials cataloging is useful? Are subject headings and added entries essential? Should serials be in the catalog? Can users identify serials? Do they know when to use the serials catalog?[15]

With a modicum of confidence, a few statements can be made about catalog "closings" and serials:
1. A dead serial can rest in a "closed" catalog in relative peace, if holdings records are kept in another location.
2. A live serial should be in a live catalog.
3. Split serials records will be particularly damaging to quality of service.
4. Authority files will be supremely important.
5. Considering current information, the best course of action appears to be a separate serials catalog with all records therein made compatible with AACR 2.

References

1. The Future of Card Catalogs (Washington, D. C.: Association of Research Libraries, 1975), p. 10.
2. The Library of Congress Card Catalog; an Analysis of Problems and Possible Solutions (Washington, D. C.: Library of Congress, Processing Dept., April 1972).
3. Arthur Plotnik, "Opening Minds to Closing Catalogs, or When Can We Throw Out the Cards?" American Libraries, 8 (December 1977), p. 594.
4. Laurel A. Grotzinger, "Women Who 'Spoke for Themselves,'" College and Research Libraries, 39 (May 1978), p. 181.
5. Michael Gorman, "The Anglo-American Cataloging Rules, Second Edition," Library Resources & Technical Services, 22 (Summer 1978), p. 210.
6. Ibid., p. 216.
7. To Close or Not to Close: Desuperimposition and the Future of the Catalogs. Report of the Subcommittee on the Future of the Catalog, Committee on Bibliographical Control, Phase I. (Berkeley: General Library, University of California, 1975), p. 18.
8. Ibid.
9. Sally Hart McCallum, "Some Implications of Desuperimposition," Library Quarterly, 47 (April, 1977), p. 113.
10. Paul Fasana, "Serials Data Control: Current Problems and Prospects," Journal of Library Automation, 9 (March 1971), p. 32.
11. Mary Kay Daniels Ganning, "The Catalog: Its Nature and Prospects," Journal of Library Automation, 9 (March 1976), p. 49.
12. To Close or Not to Close, op. cit., p. 5.
13. Mina Daniels, "Future of the Card Catalog Committee: Preliminary Report," Alternative Catalog Newsletter, 2 (June 1978), p. 38-39.
14. Gorman, op. cit., p. 219.
15. To Close or Not to Close, op. cit., p. 33.

13. Closing the Card Catalog*

by Ann Ekstrom

Few librarians today can imagine life without a card catalog. The card catalog as an index to collections within a library can be kept up to date with relative ease, and individual items can be analyzed and represented in the card catalog by as many entries as deemed necessary.

A card catalog increases in size by an average of six to ten cards per title added, each of which must be filed manually. With the rapidly accelerating cost of building space and staff salaries, housing and maintenance of card catalogs is becoming prohibitively expensive. Also as catalogs increase in size, entries--particularly subject entries--become more explicit and therefore more complex for the average patron to use.

Until the recent development of on-line computerized catalogs, there has been no viable alternative or substitute for a card catalog. Micro-form catalogs are in use, but usually as an extension of the card catalog rather than as a substitute for it.

With the availability of on-line catalogs, many libraries are seriously considering the advisability of closing card catalogs and using on-line access, perhaps with microform backup, to identify and locate the bibliographic materials in their collections.

OCLC is dedicated to providing full system support for those participating libraries that plan to close their card catalog within the next few years. To this end OCLC is considering the following: 1) subject access to bibliographic data, 2) on-line access to local data such as call numbers and departmental locations, 3) modified record displays for patron use, 4) less sophisticated, therefore less expensive, terminals, 5) the number of terminals required to replace a card catalog in a library of given size, and 6) where terminals should be located for optimum use.

Obviously an on-line catalog cannot function satisfactorily without subject access. OCLC has a prototype subject access system in operation at the present time. It works very well with a small catalog and a very limited number of users. However the computer

---
*Reprinted by permission of the author and publisher from Kentucky Library Association Bulletin, 41 (Spring 1977), p. 16-18.

time required to access all of the records that respond to a general subject, such as "Chemistry," is significant and if several such searches were in progress simultaneously, cataloging-related activities would be pre-empted. To avert such a catastrophe, OCLC must devise some means of implementing subject search that will not interfere with use of subsystems supporting various technical services.

Subject access, as conceived by OCLC, is not limited to the traditional subject approach used by most libraries, but rather provides for the combining of topical words, names, publishers, publication dates, etc. Hence a user, without intimate knowledge of subject headings structures, can search by terms that relate to a topic of interest and can delimit the search by a variety of other parameters. Using a card catalog to locate materials by subject, the user may have to examine hundreds of cards to find items within a specific time frame, or by a given individual should that person be a joint author. Complex searches such as these can be accomplished with comparative ease and speed in an automated system.

In a networking environment, on-line access to local data by each participant is another prerequisite to closing the card catalog in favor of an on-line catalog. OCLC has implemented a "local data" record for serials check-in and plans to design a modified version for monographs. A local data record might be equated to a shelf list card in that it contains a variety of information unique to an individual work in a single library. Each local record is machine-linked by control number to a bibliographic record in the on-line catalog.

To facilitate the use of the OCLC on-line union catalog as a catalog of an individual library's collections, the Center is planning the development of an integrated display, combining local call numbers and holdings information with the shared bibliographic data. As planned, this module will function as follows: from the authorization number of the user at a terminal, the computer identifies the institution from which a search originates; when a search is narrowed to a single bibliographic record, the computer will look for the institution code corresponding to the operator's authorization; if that code is present, the computer will select the call number and location from the linked local data record and display that data with the bibliographic record.

For patron use of the system, OCLC plans to further modify the screen display by omitting the fixed field, tags, indicators and subfield codes; in other words make the display more closely resemble a printed catalog card.

Perhaps the major concern librarians have expressed, regarding the closing of the card catalog, relates to training patrons to use an on-line catalog. Libraries that have placed terminals in public service areas for patron use report that a minimum of institution--in most cases a two or three page printed instruction placed at the terminal--is sufficient, and that patrons are more inclined to help themselves by using a terminal than the card catalog. Of course search skills, as any other skills, improve with practice and those who are interested may request additional guidance. Since patrons evidence little difficulty using the system as it is presently designed to support input cataloging, it seems reasonable to expect that there will be few problems with a subsystem designed primarily with the patron in mind.

The questions "How many terminals will a library need to replace its card catalog?" and "Where should public service terminals be located?" cannot yet be answered since libraries have no experience upon which to judge. The number of terminals required to replace a given card catalog will be affected in part by the location of the terminals. Decentralization of terminals for public use of on-line catalog will enhance its usefulness but might also increase costs.

The cost factor will certainly change over the next few years as new developments make it possible to utilize less sophisticated, and therefore less expensive, terminals for on-line searching.

It is inevitable that card catalogs be replaced by automated catalogs; it is only a question of how long it will take to accomplish the transition. Librarians should not bury their heads to avoid the inevitable but should use their heads to devise ways of exploiting the potential of on-line automated catalogs.

14. Closing the Card Catalog*

by Bill Caddell

The question of closing the card catalog is very far from the minds of librarians of small public libraries. We are more concerned about buying books and paying the increasing costs required to keep the doors open. As Gail Kennedy stated the University of Kentucky is only now beginning to look into the possibility of closing their card catalog. At a recent meeting of over 80 librarians and trustees from small and medium public libraries in Indiana, only one librarian responded to my request for comments on the closing of the card catalog. This librarian has been a leader in shared-cataloging and book-processing in Indiana.

Small and medium sized public libraries will continue to maintain their present card catalogs for many years to come. My reasons for making this statement are as follows:

    1. Large public and academic libraries have gone to book, micro-form or on-line catalogs so that they can save money by providing access to the catalogs at their many branch locations. Small public libraries cannot justify the catalogs for this reason.

    2. Small libraries do not have the financial resources needed to develop book, micro-form, or on-line catalogs and to maintain them on their own.

    3. In many small towns and rural areas the population has been stable or decreasing while that of urban and sub-urban areas has been increasing rapidly. Without an increasing population and an expanding tax base the financial picture becomes tight in the light of increasing inflation.

    4. The Library Board, community and staff acceptance of book, micro-form or on-line catalogs tends to be very slow. Small town library boards tend to be conservative. The "varied educational and experiential levels of users" in small public libraries works against new developments. The users in university and most large public libraries are more sophisticated. The staff in our library prefers to be in control of the selection, cataloging and processing of books. The more you rely on outside agencies the more

---

*Reprinted by permission of the author and publisher from Kentucky Library Association Bulletin, 41 (Spring 1977), p. 15-16.

problems you have in getting the current best sellers to the public while they are still popular.

  5. In Indiana we have recently formed the Indiana Cooperative Library Service Authority, a statewide network that is tied by phonelines to the Ohio College Library Center (OCLC). Through INCOLSA small libraries will be able to benefit from shared-cataloging by purchasing books cataloged and processed from the INCOLSA Book Processing Center. Unfortunately only a fraction of Indiana's small libraries have joined INCOLSA or purchase books through the Processing Center.

  6. Finally, I feel that the only way small libraries will be able to consider closing their card catalogs is through the assistance of library networks such as INCOLSA. The key to this situation is the Ohio College Library Center. When, and if, OCLC is able to provide subject access and local data on the book collection for each library then it would be possible for OCLC or the INCOLSA network to print book catalogs or produce micro-form catalogs for member libraries. With subject access and local data access for each library in the system you would have an On-line Catalog.

  An article in the January 1, 1976, Library Journal by Richard DeGennaro predicts that we will gradually move to computer assisted processing through a network and that book or micro-form catalogs will replace the card catalog. Although Mr. DeGennaro's prediction may one day come true, small public libraries in Indiana and elsewhere will not be able to participate until the financial picture brightens or our networks develop the system and provide it at a reasonable cost.

15. Living Amid Closed Catalogs*

by Sanford Berman

I didn't choose the title. "Living amid Closed Catalogs." And frankly, I don't like its implications. For the truth is that whether the University of California Library at Berkeley closes its catalog or not means nothing at all to the one- and two-room public libraries in Otter Tail County, Minnesota. And what the Library of Congress (LC) does to its catalog is equally irrelevant. Why? Simply because their catalogs never have been meaningful to the public and school libraries that service the majority of Americans. To argue that the form and substance of Otter Tail's card catalogs should depend on decisions made by the supernovas in Chicago, New York, or Washington and to maintain that Otter Tail's catalogs should be miniature versions of Berkeley's or Harvard's or LC's is to further promote a dependent attitude or syndrome that has generally resulted in awkward, ludicrous, inappropriate catalogs; frustrated users; and the progressive ruin of cataloging as an essential and creative art.

So let me first retitle this presentation from "Living amid Closed Catalogs" to "Who Gives a Damn about Closed Catalogs?" And then I want to state this basic axiom: <u>Each</u> library is responsible for what goes into its own catalog, just as it's presumably responsible for what goes into its own collection. Even the most rabid standardization freaks wouldn't claim that <u>Library Journal</u> or <u>Kirkus</u> or <u>Booklist</u> or Josten's should pick a library's materials for it or that Otter Tail ought to surrender its responsibility for collection development to these outside groups or publications. They're merely aids or tools. Similarly, should any library totally abdicate its cataloging function to the Catalog Code Revision Committee (CCRC), Library of Congress (LC) or OCLC? It's each library's duty to ensure that its own catalog works: that it provides full, fair, and intelligible access to the collection, to that library's resources; that it makes things easy to find through understandable entries, rather than placing barriers between users and materials.

This leads to another premise: Closing one catalog and starting another to accommodate rule changes, in other words,

---

*Reprinted by permission of the author and the publisher. Originally published in <u>Closing the Catalog: Proceedings of the 1978 and 1979 Library and Information Technology Association Institutes</u> (Oryx Press, Phoenix AZ, 1980).

creating a two-catalog system, is unthinkable precisely because it interposes a tremendous barrier between user and materials. Both information theory and common sense dictate single files, since ordinary people will not unless under great duress bother to look for the same or related items in two different catalog locations. Indeed, many won't realize there are two locations despite signs, handouts, and media blitzes. In short, "closing the catalog" is a misnomer. A more accurate phrase would be "murdering the catalog," or at least a large piece of it, for the convenience of librarians and no one else.

Now realists among us may rightly protest that however unfortunate or regrettable the dependence upon outside copy, upon standardized codes and centralized cataloging, that dependence is nonetheless real and must compel even the smallest nonarchival libraries to take the new code into account, for it will impact upon them. I agree. Clearly, few libraries can afford to do 100 percent original cataloging. For economic reasons alone, most necessarily get their cards or copy from vendors or other intermediaries. And these intermediate sources will surely be affected by the new rules, because they are themselves dependent upon Machine-Readable Cataloging (MARC) records. So, yes, school and public libraries should definitely take the new code into account, but its actual impact may be less pronounced than many think, for the following reasons:

First, public and school libraries largely stock English-language, American-published trade materials. On the whole, they get few government documents and not much that's produced by research centers and universities. Their holdings in "Law" and "Liturgy," for instance, are likely to be slight. Thus, the very nature of their collections will limit both the frequency and volume of conflict generated by Anglo-American Cataloging Rules, second edition (AACR2), which introduces major changes in the form of entry for legal and liturgical works, as well as for corporate bodies like universities, research centers, and government agencies. Many of those truly weighty changes just won't apply.

Second, the new, more generous approach to pseudonyms represents an ostensibly sharp departure from previous practice, from the dictum of "one author, one name." Now "Seuss" and "LeSieg" will be no less valid than the good doctor's real though seldom-used name, "Geisel." But will this change prove shattering to school and public libraries? No. First, this is simply title-page cataloging, which should unquestionably make popular works by familiar authors more retrievable both on the shelves and through the catalog. Second, LC has been favoring the most common name for some years, which, in practical terms, meant the salutary substitution of "Seuss" for "Geisel"; and third, a lot of libraries already perform title-page cataloging, so for them the new rule will merely sanction established practice and actually render much outside copy more usable. For example, MARC cataloging in 1981, will enter a novel by "Jean Plaidy" under "Plaidy" instead of "Hibbert," thus requiring no local alterations to make the existing and supplied name forms harmonize. And for those libraries not now into title-page cataloging, there are painless means for linking old and new name forms in the catalog and on the shelves.

Third, other conflicts, most notably between old and new geographical names, for example, "Paris" and "Chicago" of Anglo-American Cataloging Rules, first edition (AACR1) and "Paris (France)" and "Chicago (Ill.)" of AACR2, and between simpler and fuller versions of personal names, for example, the new "Lawrence, D. H." and old "Lawrence, David Herbert," don't need to become permanent conflicts at all. For instance, the new glosses for geographical names can be ignored and the original, pre-AACR2 forms retained; or the glosses "(France)" and "(Ill.)" be retrospectively added to existing "Paris" and "Chicago" cards, or the new and old can merely be interfiled, allowing natural attrition to eventually eliminate the earlier, unglossed forms. With personal names, a similar practice can be followed. At Hennepin County Library, there's absolutely no advantage in switching from the present, fuller "Lawrence, David Herbert" to the upcoming title-page form, "Lawrence, D. H.," because there's no conflict or confusion between these two forms and any other "Lawrences" currently in our catalog.

The "Paris," "Chicago," and "Lawrence" examples lead nicely to another topic, the opportunity afforded by implementation of AACR2 for reexamining current cataloging practice, determining what's useful and what isn't, deciding what reforms can be reasonably expected or induced outside, at LC, vendor, or network level, and then making a commitment, within the bounds of local resources, to assume genuine responsibility for the local catalog. Among other things, that means maintaining the catalog with cross-references and linking notes, something that no Good Fairy will ever do, and also exercising a little judgment and independence. For example, if a library produces its own cards or can tell a vendor how it wants them to look and that library finds International Standard Bibliographic Description (ISBD) formatting and abbreviations useless, if not irritating, it could drop the ISBD elements. (At least three county library systems in the Twin Cities area have done exactly that.) Likewise, since LC admits that its own institutional inertia makes extensive subject-cataloging reforms unlikely for a long time, such changes as the replacement of NEAR EAST by MIDDLE EAST, of GLACIAL EPOCH by ICE AGE, or of HAND-TO-HAND FIGHTING, ORIENTAL by MARTIAL ARTS, if they would obviously contribute to faster and better subject retrieval, could be introduced at the local level. And useful headings like JOB HUNTING, APPROPRIATE TECHNOLOGY, HOLISTIC or ALTERNATIVE MEDICINE, SELF-HELP PSYCHOLOGY, PSYCHIC ARCHAEOLOGY, and HOSPICES, which LC seems intellectually and spiritually incapable of creating, could be instituted and applied in-house. Further, if a local library concludes that AACR2's transcription of full names in parentheses following the shorter, title-page form, like "Lawrence, D. H. (David Herbert)," is either unnecessary or confusing or both, it could eliminate the glossed data on incoming cards or other copy and opt not to follow that practice in original cataloging.

What do these opportunities signify or portend from a management or policy standpoint? First, there must be a fixed, perhaps budgeted, responsibility for catalog input and maintenance, no matter how small the library. Second, to the extent local resources and methods of card production or acquisition allow, every library should:

    1. Initiate staff discussion on how well the catalog functions, how it can be made more useful, and which AACR2 rules and format elements should be approved, modified, or discarded, depending on whether they enhance or retard catalog access and intelligibility. Staff task forces or study groups, incidentally, should include paraprofessionals, clerks, and pages, not just professionals and supervisors.

    2. Establish authority control by creating an authority file or letting the catalog itself function as such a file. There's tangible help available. It's called Little Brief Authority: A Manual for Establishing a Name Authority File. Edie Baecker and Dorrie Senghas wrote it. DeDoss Associates sell it for only $3.50. Their address: 332 Railroad Avenue, Norwood, MA 02062.

    3. Either change established, existing entries to accord with acceptable and desirable AACR2 forms or link the variant forms with notes, still maintaining a single, organic, A-Z file. Here are a few idea sources that may prove helpful in handling changes both in subject headings and name forms:

        a. Marvin Scilken's "Changing Subject Headings" on page 26 of the first Unabashed Librarian.
        b. "Subject Heading Changes and the Catalogs," on pages 22-5 of Cataloging Service Bulletin, no. 119 (Fall 1976).
        c. Hennepin County Library's bimonthly Cataloging Bulletin and quarterly Authority File on fiche. The file includes all the linking notes between variant author names added to the catalog in the three years since we began title-page cataloging, together with data that differentiates between similarly named persons. Bulletin no. 36 (September/October 1978), addressed particular ramifications of AACR2. Issue no. 38 (January 1979) proposed AACR2 options and addenda for public and school libraries, in effect outlining a model cataloging code for nonarchival libraries. And no. 39 (March 1979) featured a major article by Arlene Dowell on how to accommodate rule changes in manual card systems. Moreover, the whole matter of how to maintain catalog integrity, quality, and usefulness on an ongoing basis in all sizes and types of libraries is nowhere better covered than in Dowell's 1976 volume, Cataloging with Copy, a Libraries Unlimited title.
        d. Implement AACR2 features that truly expand access, like the new pseudonym rule and A/V guidelines, even before 1981. If it's a good thing for patrons in January 1981 to directly find Jean Plaidy's historical romances in the

catalog and on the shelves under "Plaidy" instead of "Hibbert," why isn't it also a good thing now? Why continue for another two years to play a game of hide-and-seek that keeps users from what they want and makes the library seem like a perverse and antiquated ass?

The foregoing, admittedly decentralist, suggestions stem from a twin conviction that most of our centralized codes, schemes, and services do not serve public and school libraries very well and that there's no immediate likelihood that LC or any other vending agency will offer suitable alternative cataloging to nonarchival libraries.

In summary, there appear to be three possible scenarios for 1981, all within the framework of unclosed card catalogs:

1. Accept AACR2 on a critical, selective basis, resolving conflicts by either changing earlier entries or making links;
2. Accept AACR2 totally, irrespective of whether individual elements facilitate or impede catalog use, resolving conflicts as in the first scenario; or
3. Accept AACR2 totally and uncritically, allowing new and old forms to intermix without entry changes or links.

Since the third scenario requires the least imagination and effort, I predict it will be the most widespread. And the net effect will be an even greater erosion of catalog trustworthiness and utility. That isn't a particularly awful prospect to many of our born-again professional leaders who now peddle the gospel of salvation-by-hardware, apparently not realizing that the typical library hasn't even got enough money to adequately pay staff or buy books, much less install $3,000 tubes, and that even the value of what flashes on a CRT screen depends ultimately on the skill and wisdom of whoever decided what data to input and how to display it.

Bibliography

AACR 2 and Its Impact on Libraries: Papers Presented at the Academic Library Association of Ohio Annual Meeting and Conference on October 12, 1979, Worthington, Ohio. Compiled by Neal L. Edgar, edited by Pauline R. Bean and Sharon G. Fullerton. Columbus, Ohio, The Ohio State University Libraries Publications Committee, 1980.

Abbott, George L. Card Catalogs: Alternative Futures; A Selected Bibliography on Closing Card Catalogs and Alternative Catalog Formats With Separate Sections on AACR 2 and PRECIS. Syracuse: Information Yield, 1979.

Aroeste, Jean, and others. UCLA Working Group on Public Catalogs. Final Report. California University. Los Angeles, Library, January 1976. (ERIC number, ED 121 322).

Association of Research Libraries. The Future of Card Catalogs. Minutes of The Eighty-Fifth Meeting, January 18, 1975, Chicago, Illinois. Washington, D.C.: Association of Research Libraries, 1975.

Association of Research Libraries. SPEC Kit 46--Planning for the Future of the Card Catalog. Washington, D.C.: Association of Research Libraries, 1978.

Ayres, F. H. "The Code, The Catalog, and The Computer," Library Journal, 105 (April 1, 1980), 775-780.

Bennis, Warren G., ed., et al. The Planning of Change. 3rd ed. New York: Holt, Rinehart and Winston, 1976.

Berman, Sanford. "Living Amid Closed Catalogs," Originally published in Closing the Catalog: Proceedings of the 1978 and 1979 Library and Information Technology Association Institues, Phoenix, AZ.: Oryx Press, 1980.

"Bibliographic Control: Future Eyed," Library Journal, 102 (January 1, 1977), 22-23.

Bookstein, Abraham. "Congestion at Card and Book Catalogs: A Queuing-Theory Approach," Library Quarterly, 42 (July 1972), 316-328.

Bright, Franklyn F. "New Catalog for UW--Madison," Wisconsin Library Bulletin, 75 (May-June 1979), 129-130, 132.

_____. "A New Code! A New Catalog?" Wisconsin Library Bulletin, 74 (November-December 1978), 278-279.

Caddell, Bill. "Closing the Card Catalog," Kentucky Library Association Bulletin, 41 (Spring 1977), 15-16.

Carlson, Elliot. "The Library of Congress Ordains a New Catalogue, and Others Prepare to React," Humanities Report, 1 (February 1979), 10-14.

"The Catalog: Its Nature and Prospects," Journal of Library Automation, 9 (March 1976), 48-66.

Bibliography

Chan, Lois Mai. "The Closing of the Card Catalog: Introductory Remarks," Kentucky Library Association Bulletin, 41 (Spring 1977), 3-5.

"Closing the Catalog: Special Report," Library Journal Hotline, 6 (November 14, 1977), 2-7.

Colorado State University Libraries. Ad Hoc Committee on the Future of the Card Catalog. Report. Fort Collins, CO: 1978.

Cornell University Libraries. Task Force on the Future of the Cornell University Libraries Card Catalogs. Arlington, Va.: Eric Document Reproduction Service, 1978.

Crow, Rochell. "Where Will Your Card Catalog Be in 1980?" Alabama Librarian, 28 (September 1977), 12-14.

Decker, Jean S. "Catalog 'Closings' and Serials," Journal of Academic Librarianship, 5 (November 1979), 261-265.

Dougherty, Richard M. "Leaping into the Void," Journal of Academic Librarianship, 6 (July 1980), 131.

Dowell, Arlene Taylor. "Staying Open in 1981," Hennepin County Library Cataloging Bulletin, 39 (March/April 1979), 11-15.

──────. "What If We Had a Crisis, But Nobody Noticed? The Impact of AACR 2," The Georgia Librarian, 17 (May 1980), 5-8 (interim report).

Dusenbury, Carolyn. "Alas, Poor Card Catalog," Utah Libraries, 22 (Spring 1979), 30-38.

Ekstrom, Ann. "Closing the Card Catalog," Kentucky Library Association Bulletin, 41 (Spring 1977), 16-18.

Elrod, J. M. "Is the Card Catalogue's Unquestioned Sway in North America Ending?" Journal of Academic Librarianship, 2 (March 1976), 4-8.

Emmett, Robert C. "Automation and Its Impact on a Transportation Library," Special Libraries, 70 (November 1979), 479-486.

Fink, D. G. "Impact of Technology on Library Science," Special Libraries, 68 (February 1977), 76-80.

Fitzgerald, Michael. "LITA in New Orleans Eyes 'Closing the Catalog,'" Library Journal, 104 (March 1, 1979), 534-536.

Freedman, Maurice J. "The Automation of Cataloging--1976," Library Trends, 25 (January 1977), 703-721.

──────. "The Catalog: Its Nature and Prospects," Library Journal, 101 (February 15, 1976), 594-595.

──────. "Opening a Library Catalog," Library Journal, 104 (November 1, 1979), 2277-2280.

Freedman, Maurice J. and Malinconico, S. Michael, eds. The Nature and Future of the Catalog, Phoenix, Ariz.: Oryx Press, 1979.

Fussler, Herman H., and Kocher, Karl. "Contemporary Issues in Bibliographic Control," Library Quarterly, 47 (July 1977), 237-252.

The Future of Card Catalogs. Report of a Program Sponsored by the Association of Research Libraries. Washington, D.C.: Association of Research Libraries, 1975.

Ganning, Mary Kay Daniels. "The Catalog: Its Nature and Prospects," Journal of Library Automation, 9 (March 1976), 48-66.

Gay, Ruth. "The Machine in the Library," The American Scholar, 49 (Winter 1979-80), 66-77.

Gorman, M. "Osborn Revisited; or, The Catalog in Crisis; or, Four Catalogers, Only One of Whom Shall Save Us," American Libraries, 6 (November 1975), 599-601.

Grose, M. W., and Line, M. B. "On the Construction and Care of White Elephants: Some Fundamental Questions Concerning the Catalogue," Library Association Record, 70 (January 1968), 2-5.

Hazen, D. C. "Assumption of Automation; or, The Card Catalog Is Dead! Long Live the Card Catalog!" Cornell University Libraries Bulletin, No. 207 (January 1978), 1-5.

Henry, Mary B. "Closing the Card Catalog; or, Two Years Before the Blast," New Jersey Libraries, 11 (October 1978), 11-14.

Hewitt, J. A. and Gleim, D. E. "Adopting AACR 2: The Case For Not Closing the Catalog," American Libraries, 10 (March 1979), 118-121.

Information Systems Consultants, Inc. The Future of the Catalog: Background Paper for the Development of Cost Models for Alternatives to the Card Catalog, Boston: Information Systems Consultants, 1979.

Kennedy, Gail. "Problems With the Card Catalogs: Present and Prospective," Kentucky Library Association Bulletin, 41 (Spring 1977), 10-14.

Kline, Peggy S. and Taylor, Marion R. "Adapting an Existing Card Catalog to AACR 2: A Feasibility Study," Library Resources & Technical Services (Summer 1980), 209-213.

Lancaster, F. W. Toward Paperless Information Systems. N.Y.: Academic Press, 1978.

Leonard, W. Patrick. "The Card Catalog Mentality or We Have Always Done It This Way," Journal of Academic Librarianship, 6 (March 1980), 38, 64.

McElderry, S. "Alternatives to the Conventional Card Catalog From the User Point of View," IFLA Journal, 2 (1976), 232-236.

McMillen, Carolyn J. "Closing the Catalog," MSU Libraries Staff Information Bulletin, 211 (March 1977), 1-4.

Malinconico, S. Michael and Fasana, Paul J. The Future of the Catalog. White Plains, N.Y.: Knowledge Industry Publications, 1979.

Malinconico, S. Michael. "The Library Catalog in a Computerized Environment," Wilson Library Bulletin, 51 (September 1976), 53-64.

Mycue, D. "Librarians, Users, and the Electronic Library," Illinois Libraries, 59 (April 1977), 265-269.

Norie, Elisabeth. "False Economy: or, Sabotage at the Catalog!" Library Resources & Technical Services, 24 (Winter 1980), 69-70.

Plotnik, Art. "Opening Minds to Closing Catalogs, or When Can We Throw Out the Cards?" American Libraries, 8 (December 1977), 594-595.

Rather, John C. "The Future of Catalog Control in the Library of

Congress," The Journal of Academic Librarianship, 1 (May 1975), 4-7.
Reid, M. T. "LITA Offers Guidance on Catalog Closing," American Libraries, 10 (January 1979), 6.
Ricard, R. J. "ISAD/RTSD Institute on the Catalog: New York City, April 22-23, 1977," Library of Congress Information Bulletin, 36 (June 17, 1977), 430-432.
Schwedes, Jeffrey T. "Close the Card Catalog?" College and Research Libraries News, 41 (February 1980), 25-27.
A Study of Conversion of the University of California at Berkeley Library Catalog to Machine Readable Form, With Options and Cost Estimates. Berkeley: University of California General Library, 1975.
Thompson, James. "The 'New' Catalogs and the Unfinished Evolution," American Libraries, 10 (June 1979), 357-360.
——————. "Ten Ways to Profit From a Long Engagement," American Libraries, 9 (October 1978), 538-542.
Tolman, Lucille A. The Library Catalog and Its Future: A Bibliography. East Lansing, MI: Michigan State University, December 1977.
University of California. Library. Committee on Bibliographic Control. Future of the Catalogs: Phase 2 Reports. Berkeley, CA: University of California General Library, 1975.
University of California. Library. Committee on Bibliographic Control. Future of the General Catalogs: Phase IV Reports. Berkeley, CA: University of California General Library, 1978.
University of California. Library. Committee on Bibliographic Control. Future of the General Library Catalogs of the University of California at Berkeley: Report, Phase 3 on the Future of the Catalogs. Berkeley, CA: University of California General Library, 1976.
University of California. Library. Subcommittee on the Future of the Catalogs. To Close or Not to Close: Desuperimposition and the Future of the Catalogs. Berkeley, CA: University of California General Library, 1975.
Weiss, Carole. "Card Catalogue to On-Line Catalogue--The Transitional Process," Alternative Catalog Newsletter, No. 11 (February 1979), 31-43.
Wigington, Ronald L. and Costakos, Charles N. "Technological Foundations for Bibliographic Control Systems," Library Quarterly, 47 (July 1977), 285-307.
Yale University. Library. Committee on the Future of the Card Catalog. Preliminary Report. New Haven, CT: Yale University Library, 1978.

PART II. ALTERNATIVES TO THE CARD CATALOG

Before making a decision to freeze or to close the library's existing card catalog, some alternative forms of bibliographic access must be considered.

With the increasing number of options for libraries that choose to automate, the decision on what system best suits their needs becomes more difficult to determine. Much in-depth research should be conducted before the final decision is made. Such factors as patron use, size of collection, cost, library staff use, to name but a few, should be considered. More information on library automation is beginning to emerge in the literature and this can be very helpful in this research.

In addition to searching the literature, primary data can be used for evaluation. Visits to libraries already using automated systems can be quite helpful. Learning more about the advantages and "pitfalls" from someone who has "been there" can often be a meaningful complement to the secondary data.

Once a library has decided to use some form of automation, the next decision is to select the form to use. As noted earlier, there are several alternatives that should be considered. Any one of them can be adequate depending upon the size and make-up of the library. These alternatives include the book catalog, which was the first type used as an alternative to the card catalog; the Computer-Output-Microfilm (COM) catalog; and the more recent on-line catalog.

A library's holdings can be either fully automated or partially automated. With partial automation, the present card catalog can continue to be maintained. However, all holdings obtained after going to some form of machine-assisted bibliographic access would be entered into the automated data base, which could then be used to produce any one of the alternatives to the card catalog mentioned above.

In order to completely change to any one of the above mentioned forms of bibliographic access, all the library's retrospective holdings must be converted to machine readable form. Once this conversion has been completed, it can then be used for a book catalog, a COM catalog or an on-line catalog. A brief description of each of these three forms of bibliographic access follows.

<u>Book catalog</u>. Although the book catalog has been used in libraries for centuries, the one discussed here is the machine-

generated book catalog. Perhaps one of the strongest arguments for its use is the flexibility it offers for libraries with a number of branches. For example, filing a set of cards in each branch for the same book can be eliminated with the book catalog. There are some problems with the book catalog, however, such as the material not always being up-to-date, the cost of paper, the number of book catalogs needed, etc. Although it is easy and not too expensive to change access points in a book catalog, these corrections will not be available to the patron until the next supplement or basic edition is produced. In contrast, these corrections can be made immediately (staff time permitting) in a card catalog.

On the plus side, book catalogs can be more widely distributed. This makes the material within the library easily accessible to more users.

Computer-Output-Microform (COM) Catalogs. The COM catalog is somewhat similar to the book catalog in that it must be generated periodically and kept up to date with supplements. However, the COM catalog is in microform. As with the book catalog, the COM catalog is not always current. By being on microform, it is more compact than the book or card catalog, but requires the use of a reading machine. Many people feel that they cannot use a COM catalog, claiming that using the reader causes headaches, dizziness, and nausea. Nevertheless, it has been used successfully in many libraries and is very versatile in that a number of copies can be made and used in locations outside the library. As mentioned earlier, COM is based on a machine-readable record.

On-line Catalog. The on-line catalog came into being in the late 1960's. This type of system involves "... a computer terminal, a distant computer, and a communication system that brings the power of the remote computer to one's fingertips, to a typewriter keyboard in one's customary work environment."[1] One of the first on-line systems was OCLC. Others followed and there are a number of similar systems throughout the U. S. such as BALLOTS, RLIN, NELINET, B/NA, to name a few. These systems not only can facilitate shared cataloging or keep circulation records, but also offer interlibrary loan subsystems and one of the newer features, the on-line acquisition/accessioning subsystem.

A thorough study should be made to determine which of these alternatives to the card catalog best meets the needs of the library. The articles included in this section give an overview of various possibilities.

Dickinson, in "Of Catalogs, Computers and Communication," discusses the technological changes in bibliographic control. The emphasis here is to "communicate" with the patron through the cata-

---

1. Allen Kent, "The On-line Revolution in Libraries, 1969," American Libraries (June 1979), p. 339.

Alternatives to the Card Catalog 101

loging, whether in a card catalog or some alternative form of bibliographic control. One library, for example, has successfully used a book catalog in which changes in subject headings, authors, added entries, and the addition of cross references can easily be made.

In "Automated Network Catalog Products and Services," Freedman examines four categories of automated network catalog products and services. These include the on-line cathode-ray-tube (CRT) display, the line-printer produced card, the photocomposed book catalog and computer-based microforms. A description of each of these systems is given and the advantages and disadvantages are discussed. Reference is made in this article to the ways that various institutions throughout the country have made use of these systems.

McElderry, in "Alternatives to the Conventional Card Catalog From the User Point of View," looks at the strengths and weaknesses of the alternative forms of the card catalog and their implications for the user of research libraries. A brief description of each of these alternatives (book catalog, catalog in microform, Computer-Output-Microfilm (COM) and the on-line catalog) is given. Several reasons for changing from the traditional card catalog to some alternative form of bibliographic control are given, including the fact that this decision may be more product-oriented than consumer- or user-oriented.

In "Alternative Physical Forms of Catalogues in Large Research Libraries," Vervliet surveys the paths to an automated catalog production system. The cost of such a system is discussed along with some advantages of on-line systems and batch (off-line) systems. Although there are difficulties in automating, there are many arguments for automating the library catalog and some of these are listed at the end of this article.

In "Card Catalog to COM," North reports the results of an in-house study of the value of the card catalog in a growing and changing university. A step-by-step description is given of the process of converting to a microfiche catalog, and the closing of the subject and author/title card catalogs. The results of this action are summarized: the freeing of technical service staff to spend more time on public services, the increase in use of the library, and the access to a more up-to-date catalog. In addition, several problems associated with this change are mentioned.

Meyer and Juergens, in their article "Computer Output Microfiche Catalogs: Some Practical Considerations," compare the card catalog with the COM catalog. The results of a survey of library users' attitudes toward a microfiche catalog are reported. In addition, the article discusses the advantages and disadvantages that users found with the COM catalog.

In "Public Response to an Academic Library Microcatalog," Dwyer presents an analysis of a survey of user response to a microcatalog at a major university library. Items studied included adequate instructions on how to use the system, queues at viewers, physical facilities available at the viewers, comprehensiveness of the system itself, physical difficulties or ease in using a microfilm system, location of the viewers, etc. An evaluation of the microfilm catalog and its supplements is presented as well as some reasons for its nonuse. A final section is devoted to a comparison of the ease and speed of the card vs. the fiche catalog.

Horner, in his article "The Use and Economics of Computer-Generated Microfiche Catalogs," presents the advantages found in using a microfiche catalog at the D. H. Hill Library of North Carolina State University. The author uses the NCSU Serials Catalog as a model for this discussion, and compares its cost with that of a book catalog.

In "On-line Computer Terminal versus COM Systems," Malabarba and McCullough describe the technical aspects of the on-line computer terminal and COM for general use. The article also discusses how to determine which system to use and suggests how to go about setting up the use of such a system. A brief discussion is given on what the on-line system and the COM system can do for the organization and how their use can be integrated most advantageously. The advantages and disadvantages of these systems are pointed out as well as a look at the cost.

16. Of Catalogs, Computers, and Communication*

by Liz Dickinson

At the 1975 ALA conference Robert Wedgeworth made in his Executive Director's Report a 1984-like forecast for the library profession. A glimpse into the future of one segment of the profession, technical services, might reveal this analogous picture: Most of the libraries in the country have joined networking systems interconnected by CRT terminals. The cataloging information necessary for virtually all titles purchased by libraries of every type is available instantaneously through the on-line system. All of the information is standardized to conform to Library of Congress practice. There are few card catalogs any more. Most bibliographic information is provided in book, microform, or "electronic" catalogs.

As a result of the technological changes in bibliographic control and processing, the technical services staff of most small- and medium-sized libraries consists of a few clerical workers and a library assistant, who heads the Technical Services Department.[1] Only the largest libraries and processing centers employ real live M. L. S.-degreed catalogers, who are fully indoctrinated into the mysteries of cataloging at an LC training center. Since few libraries employ professional staff in technical services, library schools no longer teach the art of cataloging.[2] Consequently few reference librarians are given formal instruction in the use of the catalog. They are left to discover its benefits and pitfalls on their own. Vocation-technical centers around the country provide the training for those who become processing department technical assistants.

A rosy future?

Sounds, with a few exceptions, like an administrator's dream. And in many respects this scenario for the future would be a boon for libraries and their users. Materials can be processed and put on the shelves faster. The cost savings from a reduced technical services staff means that more money can be spent on collection development. Standardized bibliographic control through a networking system gives greater potential for interlibrary loan. The future seems rosy from a cost-and-time savings viewpoint.

*Reprinted by permission of the author and publisher from the February 1976 issue of the Wilson Library Bulletin, p. 463-70. Copyright © 1976 by the H. W. Wilson Company.

But how much self-satisfied confidence should we really place in that future? Let's examine the question with a few more scenes:

1. Imagine a young mother who approaches a children's librarian and requests an easy-level book for her daughter that will illustrate that girls don't always have to fit into a "feminine" mold. She explains that her daughter is being pressured at school to conform to a female sex role. Some good nonsexist children's books, the mother reasons, might help to reinforce her child's individuality. The librarian, who happens to be fairly experienced as a children's specialist, goes directly to the shelves and pulls out Elizabeth Levy's Nice Little Girls. (She doesn't consult the library's shiny new book catalog because she realizes that it provides no headings for easy-level books of this type.) If the mother had approached a librarian less familiar with the children's collection, it's quite likely that her request would have gone unanswered.

2. Another vignette: A retired man asks at his local library for some material on how to start a senior center. Although he's able to find some entries under AGED--SOCIETIES AND CLUBS, he goes away slightly miffed that in the eyes of librarians his with-it, not-about-to-die group is designated a "little old ladies' sewing club."

3. A third picture: A high school student comes into the library to research a project on Earth Resources Technology Satellites. Although the library has at least one title on the subject-- Lloyd Darden's The Earth in the Looking Glass--the student goes away with nothing. Neither she nor the librarian who helps with the search realizes that the material on ERTS is to be found under the general heading GEOGRAPHY or the obscure and technical rubric REMOTE SENSING SYSTEMS.

4. A student at a large university searches the new on-line catalog of her campus library for information on career counseling for minority women. Searches under COUNSELING, VOCATIONAL GUIDANCE and WOMEN--EMPLOYMENT--UNITED STATES in turn fill the screen with hundreds of entries. The student concludes that she does not have time to sift through all the entries for her specific topic. A librarian suggests that by waiting a few days she can get a printout of all the materials under the broad headings, but states that there's also a fee for the service. As the dissatisfied customer leaves, she mutters that she's going to pick a new topic--one that won't require her to waste her time at the library.

5. Another student, researching social values, approaches the same on-line catalog with his topic. He quickly leaves, however, after discovering that the catalog's conception of value does not match his: VALUE in the catalog refers strictly to economic value.

Failed searches and cluttered cataloging

Many other examples of catalog failure can be cited, not only because of subject heading inadequacies, but also as a result of missing cross-references, arcane punctuation à la ISBD, and puzzling abbreviations or filing arrangements. Puristic cataloging, which mandates "complete" bibliographic data, further obfuscates the catalog, at least for nonresearch users. Current LC cataloging clutters catalog entries with place of publication, book size, "Includes index" notes, and other information rarely consulted and almost never needed by garden-variety patrons.[3] Further, the catalog user is put off when he or she attempts, for example, to find Dr. Seuss books that are mysteriously cataloged under Theodor Seuss Geisel. Title-page, simplified cataloging versus puristic, formalistic cataloging emerges as a major issue when the catalog is examined as a communication tool.

The scenarios depicted above, of course, do not have to be placed in the future. Similar events happen constantly in libraries of all types and sizes across the country. The only difference between the current situation and that of the future is the medium used to impart cataloging information--the card catalog of today as opposed to the book, microform, or "electronic" catalogs of tomorrow. The point is, cataloging data that doesn't communicate with the public now will not, merely through a change of medium, communicate any better in the future.

Do subject headings really communicate?

More on trends and predictions later. First, to illustrate further the role of the catalog in the communication process, it's perhaps most fruitful to concentrate on subject headings. Although many other areas affect the information-giving function of the catalog, subject analysis probably offers the greatest opportunity for catalog interaction with the public, as well as the most frequent chance for squelching communication.

Many catalog-use studies have been conducted over the last 40 years. Even the most optimistic of these recognizes that the catalog frequently fails to communicate adequately with the patron. Such failure may be related to the fact that the LC list was not originally intended for general use. Curiously a 1916 report of the Librarian of Congress states, "There was ... no expectation that the scheme would be adapted by other libraries; much less was there any profession that it would be suited to their needs. ... Under the circumstances, the number of libraries that are already adopting it in whole or in part is somewhat surprising."[4]

A study of quantitative research on subject catalog effectiveness over a number of years in various types and sizes of libraries indicates that only a third of all subject searches meet with success. Hans Wellisch estimates "possibly fewer than 30 percent of all subject searches are successful" in public and university library catalogs.[5] The low success rate stems partly from a high rate of giving up. Users largely expect perfection from the catalog. When they don't find what they want quickly, they go away in frustration.

A quick lesson in patron disappointment

Catalog subject insufficiencies fall into several categories. First, subject headings do not adequately describe concepts, particularly those within disciplines that are exhibiting rapidly changing terminology. A few years ago this author conducted interviews with some University of Minnesota undergrads on their use of the catalog. Students who tried to use it for such topics as "the volunteer army," "sensitivity training," or "racial aggression among preschoolers" were stymied--and not altogether because the material wasn't in the cataloged collection. Two of the earlier examples--those on counseling and social values--were adapted from interviews conducted by John M. Christ and detailed in his 1972 publication Concepts and Subject Headings.[6] Christ, who compares the Library of Congress Subject Headings list (LCSH) with index terms from the 1968 edition of the International Ecyclopedia of the Social Sciences and other standard social science works, concludes that "a wide conceptual gulf exists between social science and library science."[7]

LC and subject specificity

Additionally LCSH lacks specificity. Although specificity is one of the basic tenets of subject analysis set forth by David Haykin in his Subject Headings: A Practical Guide (1951), the LC list has failed in numerous instances to implement the principle. Recently Joan Marshall, chief cataloger at Brooklyn College/CUNY Library, dissected the problem of specificity in a status report on her examination of LC subject authority records concerning women. Her investigations at LC--undertaken in the course of preparing a thesaurus of women-related descriptors--revealed the following:

> A basic fault with the subject headings relating to women's materials is the absence of specificity, or where almost specific headings do exist, the application of both the almost-specific headings and a general heading to materials rather than the establishment of a new and specific heading. Under WOMEN--EMPLOYMENT, for instance, are listed, in addition to other works, works on opportunities for employment, the health and safety hazards of employment, the wages of employment (although there is a heading WAGES--WOMEN), discrimination in employment, the problems of mothers, married and/or single women and employment, employment statistics, women in professional, business, trade, and home employment (although there is a heading HOME LABOR), the history of women's employment, and employment law.[8]

Marshall cites abundant examples (randomly selected and easily duplicated) of the absence of specificity. All of the following titles, for instance, are entered solely under WOMEN--EMPLOYMENT--UNITED STATES: Career Women of America, 1776-1840; The Female Labor Force in the U.S.: Demographic and Economic Factors Governing Its Growth and Changing Composition; Women View Their Working World, Based on a Study in Mental Health; and Counseling Girls and Women: A Guide for Jewish and Other Minority Women. The publication dates range from 1950 to 1973, indicating no change in the specificity of LC subject-access in this area since Haykin's principles appeared. Marshall concludes that through LC cataloging

> specificity is achieved only by matching the tracings. This "matching" approach may work (and is defensible) as long as a mass of material has not accumulated at ... [any] of the entry points. However, in the Library of Congress catalogs (and therefore in their book catalogs ... used throughout the country) and in smaller library's catalogs an indistinguishable mass of entries has accumulated at the WOMEN--EMPLOYMENT point.

The lack of specificity documented by Marshall's work on women's headings might be appropriately tagged under-cataloging on LC's part. It's a common problem with much of its cataloging copy.

How long, O Lord?

In another instance of under-cataloging, LC frequently fails to assign new terms in a reasonable length of time. Classic examples from the social sciences include "racism" and "sexism." Both are well established in the language, appearing in standard dictionaries, and both enjoy ample "literary warrant" for inclusion in LCSH. Yet, LC fails to employ either of these terms as a heading or as a cross-reference.

LC is particularly reluctant to change antiquated and awkward headings to "newer," more contemporary forms. We waited until 1972 for the change from ELECTRONIC CALCULATING MACHINES to COMPUTERS and until 1974 for the switch from AEROPLANES to AIRPLANES. ROCK MUSIC took ten years for LC recognition, while GOSPEL MUSIC became a full-fledged heading only last year. Still undone are the obvious changes from RIME to RHYME, GIPSIES to GYPSIES, CRUELTY TO CHILDREN to CHILD ABUSE, MOTORTRUCKS to TRUCKS, and EUROPEAN WAR, 1914-1918 to WORLD WAR, 1914-1918.

This author made an attempt to test LC's willingness to accept new terms by comparing the LCSH 7th ed. and supplements with The Barnhart Dictionary of New English Since 1963 (Barnhart/Harper Row, 1973). I chose dictionary terms capable of serving as headings or cross-references. Out of a random sample of 96

Barnhart Dictionary terms, 49 merited literary warrant based upon a search under likely headings in LC: Books Subjects and a check of titles in the Hennepin County collection that had also been cataloged by LC. I suspect that since my tools for determining literary warrant were limited, the 49 figure is probably too small.

Despite this possible bias giving LC, in effect, the benefit of the doubt, only 16 of the terms from the Barnhart Dictionary appeared as headings or cross-references in the LCSC list or supplements. In other words, the dictionary terms appeared as headings or cross-references just 33 percent (± 7 percent) of the time, a figure not unlike that which Christ reported in his study. Certainly the findings show that LC makes some changes. A 33-percent result is considerably better than zero. However, LC clearly does not exhibit enough sensitivity to new terms.

Moreover, terms relating to people often appear in the catalog in incorrect, derogatory, or inconsistent subject form. As mentioned earlier, seniors among our clientele might feel put off by the label AGED. Also, it was not until the July 1975 meeting of the ALA/RTSD Subject Analysis Committee that the Black Caucus received some assurance from the Library of Congress that the term NEGRO, which for many years has been considered highly offensive to a majority of Black Americans, will soon be changed in LCSH, depending on the context, to the preferable forms AFRO-AMERICANS or BLACKS. Other examples of LC's many shortcomings in the area of headings relating to peoples have been documented elsewhere. [10]

Do catalogers need assertiveness training?

Catalogers have never been very assertive in convincing the profession or the public that they play an important part in the information-transfer process. Now, possibly more than ever before, it is essential that all of us--catalogers and our out-front colleagues--work toward the establishment of bibliographic tools that communicate effectively.

The trends are unmistakably toward greater standardization, with LC cataloging data, insufficient or otherwise, at the core of bibliographic networking systems. It is likely that fewer catalogers will work at the local level to alter cataloging information to fit local situations, to make cross-references, to simplify bibliographic formats, to add notes or guides to local catalogs, or to help users and other librarians interpret cataloging information. The growth of OCLC and other networking systems is an indication of the direction in which cataloging will go in the future.

A further glimpse into the future is afforded through the report of the National Commission on Libraries and Information Science, which hopes to channel federal funding into networking systems. NCLIS recommends that funds be made available to libraries willing to cooperate in the exchange of standardized bibliographic information, using LC as a base for bibliographic control. The present flaws of LC cataloging may end up magnified and multiplied in the networking process.

The predictions given here should not entirely be taken as a message of doom--of technological obsolescence for catalogers or of limited local input into the catalog as a communication tool. It doesn't have to happen that way. The experience of Hennepin County Library is one example of what might be viewed as a success story in the melding of computerized cataloging with user-oriented catalog terms and format.

A book catalog that's flexible and dynamic

Hennepin County Library has developed--with the help of computer programs originated at the Institute of Library Research, UC/Berkeley, and programs from the New York Public Library--a book catalog system that serves as a dynamic link between the public and the collection. The key to the catalog's flexibility is an automated authority control system developed at NYPL that allows us to change subject headings, authors, and added entries and to input cross-references and public notes with far greater ease than is possible with the traditional card catalog or, it might be added, with most other computerized systems.

A brief digression is in order here to elaborate on the importance of authority control for automated cataloging systems. A flexible, changeable authority system like that first created by NYPL and adapted by Hennepin County Library assures consistent and complete author, subject, and cross-reference data that can be changed with relative ease to improve user access to cataloging information.

The same flexibility is not currently available through OCLC or LC's MARC data base. Neither base, at this point, has any automated authority control, although both will be developing at least name authority control systems within the next few years. Partly as a result of the lack of such control, OCLC might more accurately be termed a card production rather than cataloging system. In order to insure authority integrity and a better communicating catalog, catalogers within OCLC-affiliated systems must perform what might be termed "postcataloging," that is, amending cards after they have arrived from OCLC to fit local requirements, adding cross-references, guides, or more tracings, all before the cards are filed. Administrators frequently fail to recognize the difference between card production and cataloging concepts and are inclined to conclude that professionals are not needed--much to the detriment of catalog communication--once an OCLC terminal is installed.

The authority control systems developed by LC and OCLC in

the next few years are not necessarily going to feature the flexibility and ease of change for authority terms that are available through such systems as those of NYPL or HCL.[11] Furthermore LC is not planning at this point to undertake a thorough revision of its subject heading list to go along with its research and development into authority control systems, even though it would appear to be the ideal time to do so.[12]

Cataloging from "Dressing" to "Tantrums"

To return briefly to HCL experience, Hennepin County catalogers work closely with public service librarians to insure that the catalog will contain information that's useful and understandable for the system's clientele. For example, members of the cataloging staff consulted with children's librarians to determine areas where subject headings are very much needed for children's literature. Subject cataloging at LC is quite limited for children's materials, despite the Annotated Cards program. At HCL we added subject headings to children's materials that deal with such themes as skills (the HCL catalog includes headings for DRESSING and EASY AND DIFFICULT THINGS), family and interpersonal relations (e.g., COUSINS, AUNTS AND UNCLES, NEW BABY IN FAMILY), growing problems (such as BEDTIME and FIRST DAY IN SCHOOL), emotions and character traits (including TEMPER-TANTRUMS, BOREDOM, and HELPFULNESS), and so forth.

While LC assigned no subject tracings to Elizabeth Levy's Nice Little Girls, HCL supplied these access-points: 1. SEX ROLE--FICTION. 2. GIRLS--RIGHTS--FICTION. 3. CHILDREN'S LITERATURE, NONSEXIST. 4. FEMINISM AND EDUCATION--FICTION. 5. SEXISM IN EDUCATION--FICTION.

Hennepin County, however, is not the only library to decide that present LC cataloging of children's materials is insufficient. The Yonkers (N.Y.) PL Children's Services Division has produced A Guide to Subjects & Concepts in Picture Book Format (Oceana Publications, 1974) as a supplement to catalog access. The terms that Yonkers uses, based on actual requests from parents, teachers, and library school students, are similar to many HCL heads for children's material.

It is unfortunate that libraries must expend large quantities of time to improve LC cataloging. Standardization of cataloging information could be a boon to libraries if some of the changes developed at the grass-roots level to enhance access were incorporated into centralized cataloging services so that everyone might benefit from helpful changes. Lamentably, the likelihood is that cataloging information provided by the Library of Congress will continue to function inadequately in the communication process unless we at the local level do something about it.

AN ACTION GUIDE FOR CATALOGERS

For those of you who want to make a more positive contribution to the catalog as a public service tool, here's a list of actions toward that end. The list can also serve as a cataloger's survival checklist in an age of standardized cooperative cataloging systems:

1. Although time constraints and the inflexibility of card catalogs limit the number of changes that catalogers can initiate, certainly with the aid of your public service staff you can identify and set to rights certain aspects of the catalog that impede communication with the public. New headings, not yet established by LC, for instance, may be identified and introduced with relative ease. Additional LC headings might be given to materials that LC has undercataloged. Extra cross-references and notes may also improve public access. As you handle new materials, sensitize yourself to LC headings that communicate in antiquated or offensive fashion to your users. Those unable to deviate from LC practice can at least be aware of LC's deficiencies.

2. Although you may not have the resources to change inadequate or offensive cataloging data, you can lobby LC and other organizations involved in bibliographic control for more responsible cataloging. Flood LC with your comments. Request action in areas that dissatisfy you. Regarding subject headings, contact Edward J. Blume, chief of LC's Subject Cataloging Division. Blume's Descriptive Cataloging counterpart is Elizabeth Tate, while the head of the Dewey Office at LC is Benjamin Custer.[13] Share your ideas, questions, and experiences with others. Send a copy of your correspondence with LC or any remarks on user-oriented cataloging to the HCL Cataloging Bulletin,[14] Unabashed Librarian,[15] or SRRT Newsletter.[16] Note on your correspondence with LC that you've sent copies to the library press. It may produce quicker responses.

3. LC has shown a willingness to cooperate with groups lobbying for specific changes. Within the past year the Black Caucus and ALA/SRRT Task Force on Women have made presentations before the RTSD Subject Analysis Committee on LC's substandard treatment of materials about blacks and women. The committee endorsed positions of both groups, at least in principle, and LC has already acted on these recommendations. By no means is LC going to make all the changes suggested by the Black Caucus and Task Force on Women. The experience of these two groups, however, shows some promise for two-way communication between LC and organizations that make specific recommendations for changing the rules.[17]

4. You may want to start your own group. Consider forming a Social Responsibilities Round Table Task Force on Technical Services at the local or national level to examine and help correct catalog-access problems and to monitor LC, OCLC, and other networking efforts.

5. There is great need for more research on the catalog as a communication tool. We must develop more sophisticated methodologies to measure user needs. And we need to create imaginative but practical means of effecting changes. Research is always in order to serve as a weather vane on LC--to assess its willingness to make innovations that will expand public access to catalog information.

6. As you begin to develop cooperative cataloging systems, participate actively and argue assertively for those things essential to make cataloging information work in your local situation. Without such participation in decision-making cooperative cataloging stands a good chance of providing poorer service.

7. Most importantly, cataloging librarians must convince their own administrators of their professional worth. Unless we demonstrate that ours is a key, irreplaceable role in providing dynamic, user-oriented cataloging information, we may as well find ourselves some other line of work. And indeed we may have to.

References

1. Jolly, John. "Utilization of Paraprofessional Employees: a Panel Presentation." COLT Newsletter, 8:7, June 1975.
2. A decline in the requirements for cataloging in library schools is already evident, according to J. Balnaves: "The last decade has seen a reduction of course requirements in cataloging and classification in library schools generally, as much because of the existing cataloging environment as because of possible future environments. When ready-made cataloging data are available for up to 90 percent of English language materials and up to 70 percent of foreign language materials acquired by research libraries, there is a decline in original cataloging activity in individual libraries and a corresponding decline in emphasis on cataloging in educational programs." See his "Education for Cataloging." Library Literature 5--the Best of 1974. Metuchen, N.J., Scarecrow Press, 1975, p. 273.
3. For ideas on simplified, more intelligible formats, including the "Scilken Super Card," see Unabashed Librarian, 15:3, 8-13, Spring 1975.
4. Wellisch, Hans. "Subject Retrieval in the Seventies." Subject Retrieval in the Seventies. Westport, Conn., Greenwood Publ. Co., 1972, p. 12.
5. Ibid., p. 5.
6. Christ, John M. Concepts and Subject Headings. Metuchen, N.J., Scarecrow Press, 1972, p. ix-xii.
7. Ibid., p. 151. Christ notes that the LCSH 7th ed. does not list as primary headings, cross-references, or even as headings in similar form 23.5 percent of the index terms selected from the International Encyclopedia of the Social Sciences. More specific or interdisciplinary index entries chosen from

standard texts yield considerably fewer LCSH matches. For example, a check of the index of several interdisciplinary texts shows only a 19.5 percent match with LCSH, while 47.5 percent are not listed at all, and the rest appear in LCSH in either similar form or as cross-references. Further work is needed in the area of subject access to social science materials to substantiate Christ's research, since his methodology leaves something to be desired. He does not, for example, take into account literary warrant in the LC collection for the subject terms he compares. Christ's study, however, at least points in the direction of LC's failure to list headings directly in the form which researchers and students in the social sciences are apt to look for, particularly in more specific and interdisciplinary areas.

8. Marshall, Joan. "Sexist Subject Headings: An Update." HCL Cataloging Bulletin, No. 17, p. 38-42, Oct. 1, 1975.
9. Ibid.
10. See Berman, Sanford. Prejudices and Antipathies. Metuchen, N. J., Scarecrow Press, 1971; any of the 17 issues to date of the HCL Cataloging Bulletin; Dickinson, Elizabeth. "A Word Game." Emergency Librarian, 1:2-7, February 1974; Dickinson, Elizabeth. "Statement to the RTSD/CCS Subject Analysis Committee on sex-biased Library of Congress subject headings." July 10, 1974, available from the author; Kanwischer, Dorothy. "Subject Headings Trauma." Wilson Library Bulletin, 49:651-654, May 1975; Marshall, Joan. "LC Labeling: An Indictment." Revolting Librarian. San Francisco, Booklegger Press, 1972, p. 45-49; Wolf, Steve "Catalogers in Revolt Against LC's Racist, Sexist Headings." Interracial Books for Children Bulletin, 6: No. 3 & 4, p. 3, 16, 1975.
11. For further information on authority file control and the development of NYPL's control system, see: Malinconico, Michael S., and James A. Rizzolo. "The New York Public Library Automated Book Catalog Subsystem." Journal of Library Automation, 6:3-26, March 1973; and Malinconico, Michael S. "The Use of Automation to Maintain a Catalog and to Guarantee Its Integrity," a paper given at the ISAD/RASD/RTSD CCS Institute, "The Catalog--Its Nature and Prospects," Oct. 9-10, 1975 (proceedings forthcoming).
12. LC's future plans are outlined in Rather, John C. "The Future of Catalog Control in the Library of Congress," LCPA Newsletter, 6:6-7, May 1975; "High-level view: The Library of Congress as the National Bibliographic Center," American Libraries, 6:459 September 1975; and Welsh, William J. "The Continuing Role of the Library of Congress in the Future of the Catalog," ISAD/RASD/RTSD CCS Institute, Oct. 9-10, 1975.
13. All three are in the Processing Department, Library of Congress, Washington, D.C. 20540.
14. Sanford Berman, editor, Cataloging Section, Hennepin County Library, 7001 York Ave. S., Edina, MN 55435.
15. Marvin H. Scilken, editor and publisher, G.P.O. Box 2631, NY 10001.

16. Linda Katz, editor, c/o Wolfsohn Memorial Library, 180 Town Center Rd., King of Prussia, PA 19406.
17. Those interested in helping to index or critique the thesaurus being prepared by Joan Marshall in collaboration with the ALA/SRRT Task Force on Women--underwritten by a grant from the Council on Library Resources--should contact either Joan Marshall (Brooklyn College Library, Brooklyn, NY 11210) or Liz Dickinson (Technical Services Division, Hennepin County Library, 7001 York Ave. S., Edina, MN 55435).

17. Automated Network Catalog Products and Services*

by Maurice J. Freedman

This paper will concern itself with the kinds of catalog products and services a library can receive or share by participation in a computer-based network or through cooperation in the development of automated systems. Unless otherwise mentioned, all systems discussed are American and MARC monograph-based. The approach taken will be to deal with the products and services by categories of form. The assumption is that the networking which concerns us is computer-based, so the actual products and services described will all be directly or indirectly generated from machine-readable data.

The four categories or formats which will be examined are (1) the on-line cathode-ray-tube (CRT) display, (2) the line-printer produced card, (3) the photocomposed book catalog or catalog card, and (4) microforms produced on cpmputer-output-microfilm (COM) or digital-based graphics display microfilm. These categories each have differing technological attributes, costs, and advantages and disadvantages. Although monographic catalog products and services are the concern of this paper, these formats can be used for serials, any other category of library material, or for that matter a list of automotive parts.

The CRT Display or On-Line Access to the Computer

CRT terminals have been primarily used for input and maintenance of cataloging data. The Ohio College Library Center, the premier automated library network, consists of individual terminals located in institutions all over Ohio as well as most other areas of the country, all connected to a computer in Columbus, Ohio. The OCLC system allows participating libraries to first search via the CRT terminal the entire OCLC data base of over two million catalog entries.[1] Within seconds, the entry desired can be displayed on the screen, and the user can accept it or add, delete, or change it to render it consistent with the library's local cataloging requirements. Two other functional activities are performed. If the library can find no entry already in the data base for the title searched, it calls for a work-sheet display on the screen and locally enters the cata-

---

*Reprinted by permission of the author and the American Library Association from Journal of Library Automation, June 1976, p. 145-155, copyright © 1976 by the American Library Association.

loging as a new record into the data base. Finally, the union catalog function is available, and is particularly valuable to the original network participants, the academic libraries of Ohio, as well as other networks whose libraries are members of OCLC. Each time an entry is used or a new one added, a notation is affixed to the OCLC record indicating that the user library holds the item represented by that record. It is then possible using a simple search key to find out which libraries have a given piece of material. This information is of tremendous value both for collection development and inter-library loan. Expensive and unnecessary duplication of collections can be reduced and cooperative acquisition is facilitated through the use of an on-line union data base. These are especially important cost considerations which superficial analyses focusing on card costs and line charges tend to overlook.

In addition to OCLC, Stanford University's BALLOTS (Bibliographic Automation of Large Library Operations Using a Time-Sharing System) project allows on-line access to the MARC data base for the purpose of creating catalog cards for the Stanford University Libraries.[2] It has some similarities to OCLC, but it also has a particularly unique and distinguishing feature. It has a powerful search system: BALLOTS provides searches of its data base by virtually any combination of terms within the catalog record. It allows on-line subject querying of the entire machine-readable catalog file. On a daily basis, reference questions utilizing this capability are telephoned in from many libraries and individuals; these queries are manipulated through the search software in an on-line mode and appropriate citations are given. In addition, Stanford uses BALLOTS for ordering purposes. BALLOTS is developing the capability to include participation and use by other libraries and library networks.[3]

Although no large library currently uses a CRT terminal as a public on-line catalog, it is the Ohio State University (OSU) libraries' plan to do so in the not-too-distant future. The estimated date for this implementation is July 1976. At that time, the card catalog will be closed and no additional cards will be filed into it. Banks of CRTs will complement the card catalog, and the OSU users will have on-line access to the library's holdings.

A chief disadvantage of an on-line catalog is cost. One of the most important functions of a network is to spread the cost of maintaining a huge data base among a large number of libraries. It is most interesting that computer costs, particularly the cost of being on-line, have been going down, and there are indications that they will continue to decrease as methods and tools of storage and access become simpler.

There are also serious technical problems involved in the use of telephone lines and electronic transmissions. In addition, "Ma Bell" seems much less cooperative than she might be, as will be attested to by most anyone who has tried to schedule speedy installation of appropriate line facilities.

A disadvantage which pertains to the present on-line systems, but is not intrinsic to the on-line process, is the absence of automatic authority control. At present, the only way to change or control authority terms on the OCLC data base is to individually maintain (or change) each occurrence of the term, and to keep a manual authority file against which new authority terms can be checked and established.

The advantages of an on-line system are most attractive. Any library which has had to use a batch process for creating a catalog file will immediately appreciate its value. The batch process usually involves several trips back and forth to the computer. For example, a record is keyed and converted into machine-readable form; a printout or listing is then produced which is used for comparison with the source document. If a correction is necessary, the correction must be keyed and the whole process is then repeated. In addition, with the exception of the University of California's "FIX" program, usually the whole subfield or field must be rekeyed to make the correction.[4] This cycle continues until the proofreader sends an explicit approval to the machine or a sufficient time has elapsed for the computer to assume that the record has become cleansed of both typographical errors and tagging or coding errors. The on-line system allows immediate correction of any error, be it a single character or a whole record, thus obviating the tremendous loss of time and editorial expense involved in repetitive proofreading.

However, the on-line display is not as useful as a displayed page for the browser who does not have a specific title in mind or a precise knowledge of the author's last name. At most, a few entries can be viewed at once, while a printed catalog page allows one to browse large numbers of titles at a glance. The kinds of reduction and clarity true of the printed page are currently superior to the display of the CRT terminal. Yet, one should bear in mind that the computer printed catalog is out of date before the user sees it, as opposed to the immediacy and currency of the here-and-now on-line data base. The Ohio State University experience will be of great interest because it will involve the full use by the public of an on-line catalog in a large general research library collection.

Before going on to the next section, reference should be made to Information Dynamics Corporation's (IDC) BIBNET system. There are three separate components of BIBNET; two will be described in this section, and the third will be discussed below. In 1974, BIBNET, a commercial network service, consisted of a minicomputer terminal on-line via a dial-up telephone to the IDC computer. The primary use of the service was the on-line querying of a central bibliographic file for the dual purpose of creating and collecting cataloging records and holdings data, and printing card sets off-line. A recent enhancement of BIBNET was the loading of the entire MARC file and the additional non-MARC indexes created by IDC into a national data base service time-share network operated by the System Development Corporation. This recent development allows for the widest range of reference and subject queries, as well as the more "traditional" catalog use and addition of holdings for ILL purposes associated with the 1974 version of BIBNET. The New Mexico State Library, as of January 1975, was using the new BIBNET data base service for location searching and interlibrary loan.

Line-Printer Produced Catalog Card and/or Printout

These are the most common network products and the use of the service by which these cards or listings are produced is the most widespread of the four categories of products. The line-printer is the device on the computer from which printouts are produced. Large book vendors such as Blackwell North America, Bro-Dart, and Josten's all provide line-printed catalog cards to their customers, as do such institutions as OCLC and the University of Massachusetts. [5] These applications might all be viewed as network examples insofar as the central computer cost is defrayed by the libraries participating in the card service, and the cost of maintaining the data base is shared by the many purchasers of the service.

In addition, the MARC-O project in Oklahoma has been providing a printout service wherein Oklahoma libraries (and more recently other libraries) could request listings of MARC records. The printout service is valuable for the cataloging data and also for the SDI data provided to those wishing to know what is in MARC in a given area of the LC or Dewey classification.

Overall, the chief advantage of line-printed output is that it is inexpensive (or economical) to produce. One can purchase a set of cards from Josten's Catalog Card Corporation for less than thirty cents. All the commercial vendors mentioned provide card sets or kits at rates which cannot be refused unless one is already receiving free Title II depository cards (with their attendant obligations) from LC, or has a book catalog. Of course the vendors do not allow any significant options with respect to modifying those cataloging data. (Blackwell North America seems to offer the most flexibility.) It is difficult to compare the OCLC produced card set with that of the commercial vendors because OCLC's card set is an intrinsic part of a union catalog and national network and is not just a stand-alone card service. On the other hand, the total cost to a library for an OCLC card set is far greater than a commercial set because it includes such costs as line charges, maintenance costs, and terminal costs in addition to the price of the cards. One of the real cost savings OCLC provides libraries is that it delivers all of the cards to an individual library in ready-to-file main entry or title arrangement. It should also be noted that OCLC offers tremendous flexibility to its members in relation to the format of the card. OCLC was the first network to allow its users to alter any element of data in the catalog record. None of the commercial firms routinely offer this degree of flexibility.

A chief disadvantage of all of the extant card services, except

Blackwell North America's, is the absence of an internal authority control; none of them provide name or subject cross-references with their card sets, thus leaving a large part of the cataloging job undone or still to be done by those libraries still concerned with bibliographic control.

Perhaps the greatest disadvantage of network card services is independent of the network or the computer. As the size of the library increases, the cost of maintaining its card catalog grows. In OCLC's case, the libraries must pay both for the maintenance of the machine-readable data base and the maintenance of their own card catalog. Despite this, Dartmouth University, for example, estimates "(a) ... net annual savings of $25,000 to $30,000."[6] OSU may be the first to close its catalog and go on-line, but the overwhelming costs of maintaining large card catalogs will force other libraries to do the same.[7]

In balance we must note that although line-printed cards as commercial or institutional network products are economical, the data base from whence they came and the card catalogs into which they are going are costly to maintain.

The Computer-Produced Photocomposed Book Catalog

Next in line as a major product of networks is the computer-produced and photocomposed hard-copy book catalog. There have basically been three major book catalog products: (1) all of the commercially supplied catalogs which almost wholly have been sold to public and school libraries, as well as the in-house catalogs produced at places as disparate as Harvard (the Widener Library Shelflist), the University of California at Santa Cruz, and the State of Washington Library Network, etc.; (2) the phenomenon of the University of California Union Catalog Supplement for its many campuses; and (3) the development of The New York Public Library bibliographical control and book catalog system. The book catalogs produced in each of these situations represent significantly different approaches to bibliographical access and control.

The commercial book catalog producers have been in the game a long time. The reason public libraries have converted to book catalogs in large numbers is that generally they have many branches in addition to a central library or headquarters, and it is cheaper and easier to have a single book catalog in which an entry appears once rather than multiplied in the several branch card catalogs. It is clear that any system of library branches, be it public or academic, would find most valuable a single compilation of all the materials in the entire system. This in effect is the Sears-Roebuck concept: the smallest branch library provides direct bibliographic access through the book catalog to the total resources of the system insofar as the central data base contains everyone's holdings, and all of the members, large or small, have access to the materials. Depending on local arrangements, they will also share through interlibrary loan the materials described in that data base.

The University of California Union Catalog Supplement (UCUCS) represents the single largest library conversion project.[8] Keeping the cost down and accepting a relatively high error rate were two components of the project. In addition, the first effort at automatic field recognition (AFR) was made with UCUCS. All input was keyed directly from the catalog card rather than from some form of worksheet which included explicit tags and codes, the traditional method. The scope of the project was tremendous: 1.2 million cards were handled, or approximately 750,000 unique titles.

The New York Public Library attempted to create an automated bibliographical control system; in effect, this was an effort to have a computer system which would allow for the control functions associated traditionally with the official catalog. The net result is of great significance. For example, NYPL demonstrated and proved that sophisticated library filing rules can be observed by the computer in the creation of a catalog. (There apparently are those, and they are seemingly having their way, who advocate a wholesale departure from traditional filing rules to rules similar to those which IBM's machines observe.)[9] Of even greater importance is NYPL's solution to the age-old problem of authority control. Two of the salient features of the NYPL authority control system are: (1) any new term entering the file which does not match an existing term or cross-reference is automatically sent back to the cataloger for approval, thus eliminating the traditional search for establishing or verifying authority terms--all one deals with are the terms which do not match. The computer automatically takes care of the vast majority which matched existing terms or cross-references, while in a manual system a human being would have had to search each one individually; and (2) by the use of a single transaction, one can take all instances of a single term and transfer them to another term.[10] This technique solves the problem of manually having to change the term in every record in which it appears. It should be noted that Blackwell North America has developed a subject authority control system.

Several library agencies are served by each of the three kinds of catalog producers. (The New York Public Library consists of an eighty-three-branch system in addition to its several research libraries. In all probability there are many networks or consortia with fewer members.) The union catalog is the real foundation for networking, whether the catalog is used for cooperative acquisitions, shared cataloging, information retrieval, interlibrary loan, or other purposes. The book catalog in terms of economics is the most practical to produce and use. No terminals or special viewers are required, little special staff training is required, no telephone lines are needed, and most importantly no huge data base need be kept on-line at great expense. (The diminishing costs of on-line data storage are beginning to weaken this latter point.) On the other hand, the book catalog is obsolete the moment the cutoff for a given edition is established, and the printing and binding time can be extensive, as

well as having become increasingly more expensive.* Because of
the cumulation process and the intrinsic obsolescence of the data,
the reader is always forced to look in several places to complete
a definitive search; and bad entries, entries representing withdrawn
materials, and typographical errors must sometimes remain for as
long as an entire year (or even longer) because of the reaccumulation process.

In addition, all of the book catalog systems discussed use
the batch input process, which is much more time consuming and
troublesome than on-line input and/or maintenance. Keeping track
of the printouts and source documents is difficult under the best
circumstances, and all too frequently the best circumstances do not
prevail.†

Photocomposition or electronic composition has revolutionized
book catalog printing. It is important to note that this process
wherein the digital information is converted to graphic arts or
letterpress quality images, via the computer and the cathode ray
tube, allows much greater flexibility than the line printer. The research libraries particularly can go beyond the Roman language alphabets and the single font to which the ALA print chain, despite
all of its flexibility, perforce limits them.†† The Library of Congress (LC) and Xerox Bibliographics have used the photocomposition
process to produce catalog cards.

In the near future, particularly as long as on-line storage
and transmission costs are still significant, it seems that the book
catalog will be a valuable complement to the on-line data base.

Special note should be taken, before closing this section, of
the experience of Hennepin County Library (Minnesota) and Denver
Public Library. The "how to automate without doing it yourself"
theme pertains to the efforts of both of these libraries to transfer
The New York Public Library's system to their respective compu-

---

*The New York Public Library has been fortunate because its printer, Multiprint, Inc., New York City, has been able to keep costs
relatively constant and may even lower them because of the introduction of special printing equipment and processes which were not previously used in catalog production.
†The Hennepin County Library for its shelflist conversion project
was particularly vexed in trying to keep up with the flow of printouts
and corrections for 100,000 entries. Special stack space had been
set aside and a whole system of batch control had to be developed.
††The Research Libraries of The New York Public Library have recently published a book catalog containing vernacular Hebrew
characters. All of these characters were computer generated and
created on the Videocomp, a state-of-the-art photocomposition device.
This illustrates the difference between the line-printer with its
single alphabet limitation, and the photocomposition device which in
principle can handle a multiplicity of alphabets and type fonts.

ters. The research and development were done by NYPL and the software was freely given to these respective libraries. Libraries might well note that each network need not do an unique and massive research and development effort. Software sharing and transfer should have a special role in networking. The Hennepin County Library converted its 80,000-title shelflist to the MARC format by use of the University of California's MARC format recognition and MARC maintenance programs. It then had these records processed through NYPL's authority control and book catalog production programs to produce Hennepin's book catalog. Although Hennepin has successfully completed the software transfer, the Denver Public Library discontinued the project.

Software sharing and transfer is not only possible, but it is a practical approach to automated networking on a modest basis; the book catalog, because of its ease of dissemination (one can print many copies and distribute them enywhere), offers great opportunities for cooperation in acquisitions and collection development, cataloging, and interlibrary loan.

Note should also be taken of the University of Chicago's total data management system currently in the research and development stage. Its basic design criteria should be mentioned: the system will be both upward and downward transferable on IBM equipment; it is predicated on being usable by any kind of library, and, in principle, any number of libraries.

Computer-Based Microforms

During the 1970s, microforms have come into their own in library service. With the advent of computer-output-microfilm (COM), microfilm is playing a new and most vital role in library service and library automation. COM is available as an invaluable tool for networks.

Although COM either in microfiche or microfilm reel format was available well before 1970, it has become more heavily used in libraries, first in the area of acquisitions (e.g., the in-process file approach at Yale and Michigan Universities, and the on-order history files at Hennepin County and Los Angeles Public libraries) and ever more in the area of cataloging. The aforementioned Information Dynamics Corporation's Micrographic Catalog Retrieval Systems (MCRS) uses COM-generated indices and COM-generated card images for Cataloging-In-Publication data all on microfiche.

Information Design Incorporated's (IDI) CARDSET system is a wholly MARC-based system which uses indices to MARC, CIP, and full LC cataloging records which are displayed in full cardsets, ready for photocopying. Unlike other systems which photographed the LC card, an expensive and time-consuming process, the whole process is controlled by the computer. Actually IDI's reel microfilm is produced by a more sophisticated photocomposition device rather than the typical device used by the various COM service bureaus whose machines have limited character sets and lower-quality displays. Many libraries around the country are using COM catalogs for their patrons. Tulsa City-County Public Library (Oklahoma), El Centro Junior College (Dallas, Texas), Federal City College (Washington, D.C.), Tulsa Junior College (Oklahoma), the Georgia Institute of Technology, the University of Texas at Permian Basin are all examples of libraries using COM catalogs either in total or in part.

COM is important because it is the quickest and most economical means of disseminating multiple copies of reports, be they acquisitions, cataloging, or any other. It is not unusual for a COM service bureau to turn around an extensive report with multiple copies in appreciably less than one eight-hour shift. For example, a typical COM device (they are usually called cameras) will take the computer-generated reel of magnetic tape with its digital information and "set type" at the rate of 300-500 pages of printout per minute. One service bureau charges $1.80 per 207-page (or frame) four-by-six-inch microfiche master and $.09 per duplicate fiche. Reel microfilm, although more expensive per frame, is also quite economical.

One of the most simple yet valuable applications of COM is the Louisiana Numerical Register.[11] The Register is in effect a union catalog of library holdings symbols affixed to the LC card number for a given title. It avoids a number of bibliographical problems by simply relying on the LC card number. Of course, if one does not know the LC card number, the Register is useless.

A last advantage is that the film itself is virtually indestructible, and can be cheaply and quickly replaced.

The disadvantages of COM center around the microfilm medium itself. The display image tends to discourage use by individuals for extensive periods of time. It would be wonderful if the microfilm industry could in some way improve the traditional quality of display. The typical COM reduction is 42X, and experimentation is underway at reductions of 80X and greater. Three particular COM readers are library oriented.

IDI has developed the ROM III reader which is especially valuable for library use. A single reel of COM microfilm locks inside the reader, and all of the adjustment and controls are on the outside of the reader, thus enabling the library patron to access the data contained on the film without having to handle the film, as required with traditional readers. Because of the low cost of producing COM microfilm from a machine-readable data base, the availability of a relatively low-cost high-speed reader, and the ease of preparing fully cumulative and frequent updates on a single reel, we may see some major changes in public and technical service orientation. Science Press is now marketing microfilm book catalogs with the ROM III reader.

Autographics Corporation has recently announced the Library Catalog Reader (LCR) 500, a reader similar to the ROM III. It is noteworthy that Science Press and Autographics, two major commercial book catalog houses, have both committed themselves to microform catalogs. As printing and paper costs continue to increase, the shift to microform products from paper will also increase. These two suppliers are a further manifestation of a trend already established.

Northwest Microfilm, Minneapolis, Minnesota, has a microfiche reader which incorporates the best features of several microfiche readers presently on the market. Because of the many microfiche standards ranging in reduction from 16X to 48X, it is comforting to know that there is finally available a low-cost microfiche reader which permits the simple interchangeability of lenses. This solves the problem of needing several readers, one for each significantly different reduction.

Networks, the various micropublishers and those national distributors of data which have not availed themselves of COM's potential can all use COM in a variety of ways, many of which are just beginning to be explored.

In the balance, it would seem that the ROM III and the LCR 500 type of readers have more potential for use by the public at this time. Rather than having to deal with quantities of microfiche, the user can just push a button to scan an entire file on a single COM reel locked inside the machine. However, the ability of these machines to stand up to the daily wear and tear of public use must still be demonstrated. In the balance, though, it is a bright spot in what has become an increasingly dismal cost picture in the hard-copy book catalog world. Unfortunately, the initial capitalization of microform equipment is a problem. It is especially difficult because the equipment is not much beyond the prototype stage.

Conclusion

To close, a bright picture is before us. Shortcomings notwithstanding, there is a full range of products which networks can use to deliver needed services. From on-line CRTs to Catalog Cards to book catalogs to COM catalogs, there are enough tools available for networks to utilize in meeting the catalog and cataloging needs of participating libraries. The larger issue is: what is needed by libraries to get them to recognize that through networking, interlibrary cooperation and the sharing of resources, they will be able to serve their various publics better and cure themselves of some of the age-old problems that they in principle cannot solve by themselves? The economic picture of today underscores the urgency of this question.

References

1. OCLC Newsletter, no. 98 (April 30, 1976). As of this date 2,138,750 catalog records were in the OCLC data base.
2. SPIRES/BALLOTS Project Staff, System Scope for Library Automation and Generalized Information Storage and Retrieval at Stanford University (Stanford, Calif. 1970). 157 p. Also, "Stanford's BALLOTS Look to Network Operation," Advanced Technology/Libraries, 2 (Feb. 1973), p. 3-4.
3. BALLOTS Newsletter (Oct. 1975).
4. Maurice J. Freedman, "Cataloging Systems: 1973 Applications Status," in Library Automation: The State of Art II (Chicago: American Library Assn., 1975), p. 65.
5. International Business Machine Corp., Data Processing Div., Massachusetts Central Library Processing Service (White Plains, N.Y.: IBM, 1973), 14 p.
6. OCLC Newsletter, no. 57 (Jan 24, 1973).
7. Association of Research Libraries, The Future of Card Catalogs (Washington, D.C.: ARL, 1975).
8. University of California, Berkeley. Institute of Library Research. "Largest Computer Produced Book Catalog Completed by University of California." 4 p. press release dated 20 Sept. 1974.
9. John C. Rather, "Filing Arrangement in the Library of Congress Catalogs," Library Resources & Technical Services, 16 (Spring 1972), p. 240-61.
10. S. Michael Malinconico and James A. Rizzolo, "The New York Public Library Automated Book Catalog Subsystem," Journal of Library Automation, 6 (March 1973), p. 3-36.
11. William McGrath and Donald Simon, "Regional Numerical Union Catalog on Computer Output Microfiche," Journal of Library Automation, 5 (Dec. 1972), p. 217-29.

18. Alternatives to the Conventional Card Catalog from the User Point of View*

by Stanley McElderry

This is one of several papers being presented at this conference on new forms of bibliographic catalogs in research libraries. Our concern here is with the implications of these new catalog forms for the user. In exploring this question, attention will be given to the alternative forms which have been adopted, the advantages and disadvantages of each form, and the implication of these changes to the users of research libraries.

Alternative forms of the library catalog are perhaps best understood in the context of the factors which led to their adoption.¹ The card catalog has been the standard method for displaying bibliographic information in libraries of the United States for most of this century. It was derived from a sheaf or book format as a convenient form for updating and revising entries. The card size has long been standardized to facilitate the exchange of records from one library to another or to build a joint or union catalog of the holdings of more than one library. In the United States the card catalog is still the most common form for keeping bibliographic records.

Renewed interest in the book catalog emerged as research libraries became more dependent upon each other for access to resources or for authoritative cataloging information. The motivation to decrease costs as well as to increase the scope of information available to scholars and to avoid duplicate effort has dominated the search for alternative catalog forms. Outstanding examples of the book catalog are the catalogs of the British Library, the Bibliothèque Nationale, the Library of Congress, and the U. S. National Union Catalog in current and retrospective versions. The book format is frequently used for standard lists such as Books for College Libraries (American Library Association), national bibliographies, and indexing and abstracting services for serial literature. In more recent years catalogs of major collections in various research libraries have been prepared commercially by G. K. Hall by photographing card catalogs.

The book format is a convenient way of making cataloging and

---

*Reprinted by permission of the author and publisher from IFLA Journal, 2 (1976), p. 232-36.

holdings information available to a wide range of libraries. Catalogs in this format serve to guide collection development, to provide authoritative cataloging information, and to facilitate interlibrary lending. The existence of standard lists of resources has probably had a beneficial effect on commercial publishing as a guide to resources of scholarly significance. An additional advantage from the point of view of the user is the relative ease of searching. Entries may be scanned faster in book format and perhaps less orientation is required to use a book catalog effectively.

A disadvantage of the book catalog for the user has been the difficulty of keeping the information current. The effort to transform the catalog from card to book format is so great that the information may be several months behind by the time it is issued. The book catalog can be updated by supplements but these become cumbersome to use as the number of amendments increases. Unless the catalog is for a single library or collection it frequently does not include detailed holdings information or local classification numbers. Hence a separate catalog to assist the user in locating material in an individual library is required.

A major problem of the book catalog has been production costs. Typesetting of all entries used in earlier forms of book catalogs quickly became prohibitive since the market was generally not large enough to recover publication costs. Photography provided a faster and cheaper alternative for a time and made limited editions economically feasible, but even this technology is rapidly increasing in cost. Creation of a machine readable data base for generation of book catalogs and catalogs in other forms is the most current technology and can be most cost effective where the information is captured only once and can be reused repeatedly by many libraries in a variety of products. The MARC Distribution Service of the Library of Congress is an example of data collection and dissemination that supports this approach. Another alternative form of a bibliographic catalog is the catalog in microform. As the previous discussion suggests, this form has gained currency primarily because of cost advantages. It is not only cheaper to produce a catalog photographically, but the catalog can be produced more quickly and frequently. The micro-image catalog is frequently the format elected when the book catalog becomes large and costly to update. The book catalog has generally been adopted in large public libraries where many copies of the catalog are required and the objective is to make the resources of the system readily available at all service points. The micro-image format is being used more frequently to update such catalogs. Most bibliographic catalogs in common use by the public are in fiche format. A microfilm version may be used as the security copy for archival purposes or for infrequently used materials. It is generally less convenient than fiche for general use.

The disadvantages of the micro-image catalog are the difficulty of making additions and corrections to the catalog and the limitations of the medium itself. The apparent ease of production is a disadvantage in that until relatively recent times few standards existed. Consequently quality control was lacking, reduction ratios were not standardized, and equipment for reading and reproduction was relatively costly and of poor quality. Users could adapt quickly to the reading equipment but often complained of eye strain with prolonged use. As a result the medium tended to be used more as a substitute for print for lesser used materials. The limited reports on user reaction of micro-image catalogs suggests a similar pattern-the greater the dependence on the catalog the greater the resistance to the medium. But there is some evidence to suggest that familiarity with the medium reduces resistance. [2]

Computer Output Microfilm (COM) is a relatively new method of producing a micro-image catalog from machine readable information stored in a computer. Its characteristics are similar to microfiche and will receive increasing attention as more bibliographic information is available in machine readable form.

Another major alternative to the card catalog is the on-line catalog. This form of catalog exists more in concept than reality, but there are several institutions developing this approach.[3] The general characteristics of the on-line catalog are: 1) bibliographic information is stored in a computer in machine readable form, 2) the data are accessed on-line by terminal but are also available in various batch-produced forms such as a printed list, COM, or cards, 3) information is accessible by a variety of "keys," primarily author, title, author-title, subject, call number, LC card number, record number, International Standard Book Number (ISBN), etc., 4) access keys may be approached algorithmically and in various combinations (i.e., Boolean logic), and 5) the search is conducted inter-actively (i.e., in real-time) so that the user can respond to the data displayed in refining the search. On-line bibliographic systems in the United States usually contain Library of Congress MARC data and data input locally in MARC compatible format.

The primary advantages of the on-line catalog are its improved search capability, its accessibility over wide geographic distances, and its ease of update. There are more access keys available and these keys may be used in a variety of combinations to narrow the search. The catalog can be updated almost immediately and a variety of status information can be added to the bibliographic file. Records can be updated, merged, and arranged in a variety of sequences. Access is virtually instantaneous with average response times in the range of 5-10 seconds or less. The record can be modified and updated by a terminal operator or automatically by comparing one file with another. Information can be copied electronically from one data base to another and a variety of sub-data bases generated and displayed on a terminal or by a variety of off-line products such as cards, print-outs or COM.

The major disadvantage of the on-line catalog is its cost. To exploit the advantages of this format a medium to large computer is required and the data base, generally large, must be shared by a number of libraries. The file structure must accommodate local library holdings information and call numbers if the catalog is to substitute for the card catalog. The on-line catalog generally requires an intermediator (librarian), who is familiar with the terminal, the file structure, and the data bases, to conduct efficient searches. Training and experience would be required for the average user to access on-line catalogs successfully. It is anticipated that a variety of formats from the conventional card catalog to the on-line approach will be employed, with the medium adapted to a particular function of the conventional catalog (i.e., bibliographic identification, finding local call numbers, finding alternative locations, etc.). Analysis of the literature on the alternative forms of the card catalog reveals that most writers proceed with only an implicit understanding of what a catalog is. The examples cited represent various forms of bibliographic display. Consequently almost any tool which contains bibliographic information is admissable under this definition of a catalog. If on the other hand, one accepts the more formal definition of a catalog such as the following: "The Paris Principles identify two functions of a catalog--location and collocation. These functions are realized in a file of bibliographic information through authority control over heading forms and entry control over heading use as entry such that all works by a particular author or about a given subject and all editions of a particular work may be brought together,"[4] it is evident that many of the examples cited earlier do not qualify.

The preceding analysis is a valid description of various bibliographic formats which could be used to construct a library catalog as specified in the Paris Principles. This distinction may prove useful as further analysis identifies the medium which is most appropriate to serve specific functions under stated conditions such as locating or collocating information. As the generation of cataloging information becomes more centralized, a hierarchy of functions becomes possible. The conventional card catalog as a general purpose tool may be replaced by a variety of tools in varied formats generated nationally as well as locally.

The foregoing analysis indicates that the primary motivation for changes in the format of the catalog has been product oriented more than it has been consumer or user oriented.[5] Research Libraries have experienced rapid growth in resources over the past several decades and the user population has also increased rapidly. It has become apparent that no single library could provide for the range of needs of its local clientele. At the same time labor costs have increased more rapidly than income. The necessity to increase access to a broader range of resources than were available locally and to reduce unit costs of processing materials provided strong motivating factors to explore new approaches to producing catalogs. These factors and the availability of new technological devices, particularly photography and computers, provided fertile ground for exploring new forms for the bibliographic catalog.

At the same time we have witnessed the trend toward greater

centralization and coordination of collection development and the preparation of bibliographic information as near the sources as possible. In the United States these efforts have evolved from the Farmington Plan, a systematic plan for the collection and cataloging of foreign publications on a cooperative basis, to the National Program for Acquisition and Cataloging (NPAC) centered at the Library of Congress. Further initiations at the national level have resulted in the Cataloging in Publication program (CIP) and efforts to capture bibliographic information on an international level as a by-product of preparing national bibliographies. Meetings have also been held with representatives from the commercial and private sectors to promote greater standardization and reduce duplication of effort.

Little attention has been given directly to a systematic appraisal of user requirements in adoption of new forms of the catalog. [6] Efforts have been concentrated on increasing the scope of catalogs and reducing duplicate effort in generation of records. Consequently we know little about users' behavior in the use of catalogs or the influence of new forms on information gathering habits. We may anticipate continued preoccupation with the scope and costs of catalog generation in the immediate future. Increased centralization and the adoption of new standards in bibliographic records will eventually follow from these efforts.

The computer will increasingly serve as a base for operation of bibliographic records. It is the most flexible tool we have for inputing information from a wide variety of sources and manipulating data to produce a wide range of products to serve multiple uses. Initially, and to a large extent currently, the computer application has been limited to generation of conventional bibliographic products. As the flexibility of the medium is better understood we may anticipate a wider range of products. The appropriate strategy for providing access, whether on-line or off-line, will evolve with greater experience and improved communication capabilities.

Much of the study of user behavior in the use of bibliographic products has been confined to smaller, special purpose data bases and has been conducted by persons associated with information science. We may expect to see continued attention to analysis of user needs and information gathering habits. Empirical studies in this area may lead to refinements in vocabulary for subject analysis, definition of more effective search strategies, extension of descriptive information, and other elements. Refined cost studies will likewise identify more cost effective approaches to construction of bibliographic tools.

Even though more attention may be given to generation of bibliographic information than improving searching techniques in the immediate future, the computer based bibliographic record provides a flexible medium for improving the quality of catalogs and for serving the user more effectively as our information about improved techniques increases.

In summary a variety of alternative formats to the conventional card catalog have emerged in research libraries in the past several decades. From the point of view of the user these formats have increased the range of access to scholarly resources but have not necessarily improved the efficiency of the catalog for the retrieval of information. The computer produced catalog provides a more flexible medium for developing more efficient and cost effective bibliographic access in the future.

References

1. For a review of current literature on this subject see Kenneth John Bierman. "Automated Alternatives to Card Catalogs: The Current State of Planning and Implementation." Journal of Library Automation 8, (December 1975), p. 277-298, and Annual Review of Information Science and Technology, Washington, D.C., American Society for Information Science, 1966-.
2. New York Public Library. Research Libraries. The Use of Microfilm in Relation to the Retrospective and Prospective Catalogs of the Research Libraries of the New York Public Library: A Report to the Council on Library Resources, New York. (New York Public Library, Research Libraries, 1972. 39 p. [ED 067 107]) Cited in Kenneth J. Bierman, "Library Automation." Annual Review of Information Science and Technology. Vol. 9. Washington, D.C.: American Society for Information Science, © 1974, pp. 123-172.
3. Some of the major systems in the United States are described in Herman H. Fussler. Research Libraries and Technology: a report to the Sloan Foundation. Chicago and London: The University of Chicago Press, © 1973.
4. Requirements Report: The Quadraplaner Structure for the Bibliographic Item File. Chicago: Library Data Management Project, The University of Chicago Library. May 3, 1976. p. 3.
5. A careful assessment of current problems and needs in bibliographic tools of research libraries is contained in Fussler, op. cit.
6. An example of research on user studies of research libraries is contained in Swanson, Don R. "Requirements Study for Future Catalogs." The Library Quarterly, 42 (July 1972), p. 302-315.

19. Alternative Physical Forms of Catalogues in Large Research Libraries*

by H. D. L. Vervliet

The title of this paper implicitly departs from the usual framework of the idealized automated library based on a totally integrated system, in which all the following functions are merged: 1) acquisitions; 2) periodical control; 3) cataloguing; 4) circulation control; 5) reference retrieval through externally or locally produced bibliographic databases. Very few, if any, large libraries have succeeded in automating these five functions in one step. Most libraries, while recognizing the (theoretically) ultimate necessity of a totally-integrated system, proceed by implementing the system step by step, in as modular a fashion as possible in the circumstances.

It is, therefore, necessary to establish which of these functions should be automated first. The choice essentially depends on the facilities and software available to the given library, and on the importance of each function in a given situation. A public library with several hundred thousand circulation transactions per year may reasonably prefer to automate its circulation function in the first instance, whereas a large research library or a large public library system with many branches, having to cope with a large intake of new titles, may prefer to start with the automation of the cataloguing function. The term "cataloguing function" is used here as referring to the totality of the public catalogue, including the traditional access points of author, title, subject, shelfmark, references, and authority control. In this term partial catalogues, e.g. of periodicals only, are not included.

This paper endeavours to sketch the various possibilities, costs, and problems associated with the various forms of output from automated catalogue production systems, as seen from the point of view of a librarian. For a more documented survey, the reader is referred to the recent state of the art of American library automation by Bierman.[1] It is not the intention in this paper to discuss such issues as input, processing techniques and formats, these being technical and beyond the scope of the paper. A good general introduction has been produced by Wainwright.[2]

Two main classes of automated systems can be distinguished,

---

*Reprinted by permission of the author and publisher from International Cataloguing, 6 (Jan./March 1977), p. 6-8.

namely: 1) on-line systems; 2) batch (or off-line) systems. In an on-line system the user is confined to a typewriter terminal operating usually at speeds in the region of three to thirty characters per second or to a VDU (visual display unit) operating at speeds of between thirty and two hundred and forty characters per second.

Most on-line systems tend to be used by library staff only; the catalogue creation (input and editing) is done on-line, but the catalogue proper is produced in batch mode. This is the case at OCLC (Ohio College Library Center) and in fact in most other networks where the catalogue entry is created on-line, but the catalogue itself is produced later, in the case of OCLC in the form of cards to be filed manually into the main catalogue.

Terminals, mostly VDUs, for public use are exceptional at present. The National Library of Medicine in Bethesda experimented, early in 1974, with CRT (cathode ray tube) terminals to its on-line catalogue file (CATLINE, 150,000 titles) but the experiment was discontinued. The National Agricultural Library recently studied the feasibility of closing its card catalogue by January 1976 in favour of on-line access to the CAIN (Cataloguing and Indexing) data base. The study concluded that it was not feasible to take this step before 1980 (1, p. 289). Ohio State University, however, is reported to be starting in summer 1976 with free user access to its electronic catalogue through nine VDU terminals. [3]

The reasons for this hesitant approach are evident: a public and exclusive on-line catalogue is quite expensive. There are substantial costs to be borne for the constant connection and access to a large main-frame computer. No exact figures are available for these costs, which can vary considerably depending on the number of hours connected, on the size of the catalogue, and on the on-line system used. In a large research library, open for say eighty hours per week and with half a million catalogue entries, it is estimated the cost would be around $200,000 to $300,000 per year. These would be minimal operating costs, no software or maintenance expenses being included. However, library networking and time-sharing is likely to diminish these costs in the future. Cost-effective library networking is essentially a matter of scale; the costs of on-line computer processing being what they are today, it is doubtful whether a network with less than twenty or thirty participants (of medium or large research library size) is economically feasible.

In addition to connection costs, there are also investment costs. A suitable VDU costs between $1,500 and $3,000 in Europe. In order to avoid queueing at the terminal, [4] a library may need, it is estimated, one VDU per two hundred students (in a university library) or one VDU per twenty regularly-occupied seats. In a medium-sized university, with say 10,000 students, this would amount to the acquisition of fifty VDU's or a capital investment of between $80,000 and $150,000. This is much more than Ohio State University intends to invest, but these figures bear on a totally electronic catalogue, with no further availability of other catalogue forms such as card and book catalogues, etc. Most libraries refrain from such an investment and prefer to wait for a substantial decrease in price and to consider intermediate or mixed systems.

Batch systems currently tend to be six to ten times cheaper than on-line systems, [5] but have certain side-effects, less acceptable to the library. They are operated by means of one or more discrete computer operations. Input, updating, editing is done perhaps every day, every week, every month, and so on. Output in batch mode is mainly in one or more of the following forms:

1) line printer output,
   --either on cards,
   --or on paper sheets (possibly multiple part stationery),
   --or on master plates for offset printing;
2) magnetic tape driven photosetting;
3) COM (computer output microform).

In the United States, printing catalogue cards by computer is usually the first step in automated cataloguing. It allows the use of externally-produced tapes, mostly MARC, or of a network such as OCLC or Libcon; it is relatively simple because:

1) it allows manual corrections and additions to the cards;
2) it can co-exist with a partially manual production of cards, for example of non-MARC items;
3) it can co-exist with the older stock of catalogue cards and thus avoids closure of the old catalogue and a painful division of the catalogue;
4) it avoids major filing problems, inherent in most other solutions, but requires the filing to be completed manually.

From the point of view of management, however, card production by computer is a weak solution which fails to use the computer's inherent capacity for sorting, merging and filing huge quantities of records both rapidly and, inasmuch as the software is effective, faultlessly. Moreover, card catalogues are "user-unfriendly" in that the economics inherent in this option severely inhibit the possibility of further reproduction of the catalogue.

In continental Europe the tendency has been to use line-printer output. The line-printer easily produces up to three readable copies; if more copies are needed xerographic copying or photo-lithographic offset can be used. For small catalogues, say less than 10,000 entries, line-printer output is the cheapest unless it is intended to reproduce the catalogue in more than ten or twenty copies. If more copies are needed, COM-microforms (-fiches or -films) are cheaper. Even the rather expensive phototypesetting may be more cost-effective, if more than 500 copies are needed.

The production of library catalogues by line-printer has some awkward side-effects, namely:

1) the closing of the old card catalogue;
2) the problem of the possible reconversion of the old card catalogue;
3) the problem of the periodicity of the update;
4) filing problems of the new catalogue.

These negative side-effects also occur in other batch formats and reference will be made again to these at the end of this paper. A supplementary adverse effect of the book catalogue, whether generated from line-printer output, or from computer-driven photo typesetting, is the lag between cutoff date for data entry and the final production of the book catalogue, which tends to increase as the catalogue grows in size.

Besides line-printer output, there is much interest, especially in the United Kingdom, in COM-produced catalogues. These are usually produced either as COM-fiches (105 x 149 mm reduction: 24 x, 42 x or 48 x) or as films (spools or cassette, 16 mm: reduction 24 x). COM is probably the cheapest form of catalogue production, [6, 7] cheaper than line-printer output, even for one copy, except if the catalogue is quite small, say less than 10,000 entries.

The investment in the acquisition of readers and the problem of educating the library user in the new medium should be taken into account. Neither, however, pose serious problems.[8] Good microfiche readers generally cost no more than $200 to $300, the equivalent of the price of ten card cabinet drawers. It should also be remembered that the number of readers is not related to the number of entries, but to the number of users. In academic libraries the ratio of one reader for two hundred students may be appropriate. For a university of ten thousand students, fifty readers may be needed, requiring an investment in the region of $10,000 to $15,000.[9]

Ultrafiche (105 x 149 mm: reduction 150 or more) or similar highly-reduced microforms tend to be uneconomical except where a large catalogue of around one million entries is to be published in large quantities, perhaps more than one thousand copies.

Computer-assisted typesetting is generally the most readable output format. It is regularly used for producing bibliographies, indexes, and book catalogues. It is always more expensive than microforms but on the whole is less expensive than line-printer output if more than five hundred copies are required. This is because typography allows a much smaller typesize for an equivalent legibility and a greater economy in paper and printing time.[10]

To return to the negative side-effects of batch-produced catalogues mentioned above, there is no solution to the problem of closing the old catalogue, unless a library is prepared to convert it into machine-readable form or to continue to produce cards and file these manually. Most libraries will take the painful step of having two catalogues during the next decade; the National Agricultural Library and the New York Public Library have closed their existing manually-produced catalogues.[11] The Library of Congress intends to do this in 1980.[12]

Updating, and showing the updating to catalogue users on a continuous basis, is only possible in an on-line catalogue system or in a well-kept card catalogue. In both cases the latest information is always available to the user: in the other forms it is not. If the catalogue is reproduced at the end of every week, the information of the first five days will only be shown at the end of the sixth day. In fact, the nuisance is small in daily or weekly merged catalogues. But the merging of a catalogue of around 100,000 items is an expensive procedure, particularly if full bibliographic standards of filing are to be maintained. Each merging may take up to twenty hours on a fast and large computer, e.g. an IBM 370/145, and at commercial rates it may cost anything up to $10,000 depending on the number of catalogues (author, title, subject, etc.) to be produced. Most batch-processed catalogues, therefore, are only cumulated once or twice a year or produced in the so-called "two-snowball mode": the main catalogue is cumulated perhaps once a year and the accessions of the current year in perhaps monthly cumulations. Only very small or very wealthy libraries will be able to escape this dilemma.

Another problem is caused by filing procedures. Trivial differences in headings, caused by hyphenation or by a small addition, will be adjusted spontaneously in a manual context by the filing personnel. In on-line cataloguing the constant availability of an authority file may prevent most variants. In batch-mode, it will be necessary afterwards to chase misfilings generated by slightly different entries; it is necessary that appropriate techniques be implemented to ensure the homogeneity of the catalogue.

A last consideration bears upon the standard of cataloguing itself. Every character of a bibliographic description will give rise to costs when regenerated or updated; in an on-line system it will constantly generate costs, whether used or not. A standard catalogue, whether made by hand or generated by computer, can contain up to eight hundred characters. After the initial cost of generating the text, it will not matter whether the card contains two hundred, four hundred or eight hundred characters. This is wholly different in an automated context. It can be said that a catalogue with an average length of entries of six hundred characters will cost substantially more than a catalogue with an average entry of three hundred characters. In batch systems these costs will recur at every periodical updating and in on-line systems the cost will constantly be doubled.

From the point of view of economics, therefore, it is of the utmost importance to restrict as much as possible the extent of each bibliographic description. In this context it is unfortunate to speak of minimal or medium cataloguing as opposed to full cataloguing (whatever this may be). Each library or each group of libraries will have to define very stringently the average extent of its bibliographical descriptions. It will have to define the boundaries of what may be called "essential catalography." Researches into the use of the different fields in bibliographic entries seem to show that certain elements are not wholly necessary in every context. Simply copying the fullness of MARC or even of ISBD may eventually generate unnecessary and unaccountable processing costs.

In spite of studies by Lipetz, and others, [13] "lack of knowledge about how library catalogs are used (or might be used) seemed to be a major reason for making the automated catalog as nearly like the card catalog as possible on the assumption that the 'new' catalog will then at least be as satisfactory as the 'old' catalog, which is assumed to be at least adequate".[1] In many cases an automated catalogue looks like an old lady dressed in young clothes!

There are difficulties in automating but there are also major advantages, as follows:

1 the convenience of remote catalogue access or the reproducibility of the catalogue, which may lead ultimately to a catalogue on the desk of every user;
2 the ease of creating union catalogues and shared cataloguing, which makes the automated catalogue a powerful instrument towards effective resource sharing and greater accessibility of regional or national holdings;
3 versatility and the hospitality to change, by which one description can be used in a different layout in different files: alphabetical catalogue, title catalogue, classified catalogue, subject catalogue, shelflist, accession list, etc. ;
4 the perfectibility, or ease with which corrections can be made at any stage within a properly designed system;
5 the speed with which accession can be processed.

It is suggested, therefore, that automation is not necessarily "Russian roulette,"[14] and that within the next ten years all major research libraries will have automated their catalogues, albeit with output in mixed physical forms.

References

1. K. J. Bierman. "Automated alternatives to card catalogs: the current state of planning and implementation." Journal of Library Automation, vol. 8, 1975, p. 277-298.
2. J. Wainwright. Computer Provision in British Libraries. London: Aslib, 1975. (Aslib occasional publications; 16).
3. H. Atkinson, director of the Ohio State University Libraries, quoted in: Mary K. Daniels Ganning. "The Catalog: Its Nature and Prospects." Journal of Library Automation, vol. 9, 1976, p. 62.
4. A. Bookstein. "Congestion at Card and Book Catalogs--A Queueing Theory Approach." Library Quarterly, vol. 42, 1972, p. 316-328; A. W. Knox & B. A. Miller. "Predicting the

Number of Public Computer Terminals Needed for an On-Line Catalog: A Queuing Theory Approach." Library Research, 2, 1980-81, p. 95-100.
5. A set of catalogue cards, generated from an existing MARC data base, may cost about $2.00 in an on-line context, but only $0.30 in batch mode--cf. M. J. Freedman. "Automated Network Catalog Products and Services." Journal of Library Automation, vol. 9, 1976, p. 148.
6. Even existing or planned on-line systems now hold back and turn to COM systems--cf. A. Hackli. "Census Data: From Magnetic Tape to Microfiche." Illinois Libraries, vol. 54, 1974, p. 279-282; R. M. Landau. "New economic factors in the system integration of computer terminal on-line retrieval systems and large microform data banks." Journal of Micrographics, vol. 5, 1972, p. 125-129; J. R. Spencer. An Appraisal of Computer Output Microfilm for Library Catalogues. Hatfield, 1974; B. J. S. Williams. Microforms in Information Handling. Hatfield, 1975, (microfiche).
7. C. J. Tucker. "A Comparison of the Production Costs of Different Physical Forms of Catalogue Output." Program, vol. 8, 1974, p. 59-74; Ph. Hull & Porter. "Use of COM and OCR in Guelph Cataloging Systems." Computerised Cataloging Systems, 1:1, 1974, p. 95-103; P. Bryant and A. Needham. Costing Different Forms of Library Catalogue. Bath University Library, 1975; S. M. Malinconico. "The Display Medium and the Price of the Message." Library Journal, vol. 101, 1976, p. 2144-2149.
8. A. Needham. User Reactions to Various Forms and Orders of Catalogue. Bath University Library, 1974; A. Needham. Performance of Four Physical Forms of Catalogue: User Times and Success Rates for Catalogues on COM Fiche, Cassetted COM Roll-Film, Printout and Card. Bath University Library, 1975; H. Spencer and L. Reynolds. Factors Affecting the Acceptability of Microforms as a Reading Medium. London: Readability of Print Research Unit, 1976.
9. This is much more than the "rule of thumb" of one reader per 40,000 circulations, mentioned at the ALA Centennial Conference (Library Journal, Sept. 1, 1976, p. 1707). The figures here are deduced from the use of a COM-catalogue in the real situation of an academic library. They are the equivalent of one reader per 4,000 circulations.
10. J. L. Dolby, V. J. Forsyth, H. L. Resnikoff. Computerised Library Catalogs: Their Growth, Cost, and Utility. Cambridge, Mass., 1969.
11. Lois Mai Chan. "Year's Work in Cataloging and Classification: 1975." Library Resources and Technical Services, vol. 20, 1975, p. 214.
12. M. K. Daniels Ganning, p. 59, reference (3) above.
13. B. Lipetz. User Requirements in Identifying Desired Works in a Large Library. Washington, 1970; A. Maltby and A. Duxbury. "Description and Annotations in Catalogues: Reader Requirements." New Library World, vol. 73, 1972, p. 260-262, 273; A. Maltby. U.K. Catalogue Use Survey. London,

1973; G. Ford. "Research in User Behaviour in University Libraries." Journal of Documentation, vol. 29, 1973, p. 85-106; P. Simmons. "Studies in the Use of the Card Catalogue in a Public Library." Canadian Library Journal, vol. 31, 1974, p. 323-324; 330-337; A. Scott. "Catalogue Use: the Staff User's Viewpoint." Catalogue & Index, no. 38, 1975, p. 8-9; C. Sheridan & P. Butcher. "A Comparison Between Short and Full Entry Catalogues at the City University Library." Catalogue & Index, no. 53, 1979, 3-5.

14. The term is Elsworth Mason's, the most vocal critic of unwise library automation. Cf. Proceedings of the 1972 Clinic on Library Applications of Data Processing. Urbana, 1972, p. 138-156.

20. Card Catalog to COM*

by John North

Since its creation in 1947, Ryerson Polytechnical Institute has grown from a small trades school for returning servicemen to a multidiscipline university situated in the downtown core of one of the largest metropolitan areas in North America. At the start of the 1974/75 academic year, in attempting to provide services for 9000 full-time day students and up to 15,000 extension students, the library of Ryerson was at a crossroads. Having been relocated from cramped, inadequate quarters to a new ten-story building the library then had adequate short-term book budgets, new degree programs to support, spacious well-furnished facilities, a new director, and no possibility of increased staffing. In the old quarters, the staff had been adequate to service 8,291 square feet of floor space; however in the new building of 84,414 square feet, they seemed to virtually disappear.

Stress Brings Questions

A shift in library policy which broke up the collection of periodicals, government documents, and reference books to form subject-based departments greatly increased the number of service points and dispersed the staff even further around the building. At this time the prospect of the lean years of funding for post-secondary education in Ontario had loomed out the "probable future" into the "palpable present." The writing had come off the wall and was appearing in the budget.

With no prospect of increased funds for new staff positions, and user demands for better services in the new facilities, we were forced to examine our operation for unnecessary practices, to see whether we could modify or discontinue unnecessary operations and to use the staff in more meaningful ways. This questioning process, together with the inevitable residual problems of the recent move and the onslaught of a new influx of students caused extreme pressure in all areas of the library. It has been said that only in moments of severe stress do entrenched beliefs and faiths get questioned and abandoned. It was stress of this magnitude which caused us to question the usefulness of our largest and most time-consuming sacred

---

*Reprinted by permission of the author and publisher from Library Journal, October 15, 1977, p. 2132-34. Published by R. R. Bowker Co. (a Xerox company). Copyright ©1977 by Xerox Corporation.

cow--the card catalog. One catalog source in a ten-story building provided too many ups and downs for readers and staff alike.

Card Catalog Problems

There were many problems with the card catalog: it was isolated from most of the staff and the collections; its apparent complexity baffled or frightened many students and faculty (and, one suspects, some library staff); there was always a huge filing backlog which could never be eroded despite desperation raids on staff from other areas. Misfilings and duplicate sequences were rampant, cross-references had been virtually abandoned, and enormous amounts of scarce staff time were being expended on the perpetuation of inadequacy. Its one benefit was that most of the library staff felt comfortable with it.

Fortunately our automated circulation system (which contained some wrong data due to compilation from order files, rather than catalog records) enabled us to produce fragmentary author and title listings for the entire library. The placement of these lists on all floors of the building ameliorated the book location problem to some extent, provided that students knew which books they were seeking. An expensive and erratic KWIC title index was available, but this seemed to aggravate rather than solve the perplexities of a subject search outside the card catalog.

The Data Source

Before it was elevated (?) to university status, Ryerson had been a founding participant in a cooperative acquisition/cataloging venture called College Bibliocentre (CB), which was established in 1967 to serve the bibliographic needs of the new Ontario community college system. Since its inception the CB had recorded full cataloging and holdings data for all material it acquired for member institutions, and in 1975 the data was stored at the Library Automation Systems of the University of Toronto (UTLAS). Although Ryerson predated the CB, it had, in the interests of a potential union catalog and to set up an automated circulation system, entered its complete prior holdings into the CB data base and maintained the currency of such records.

Since machine-readable records for all library stock were available, it seemed theoretically possible that we could recall all records flagged with the Ryerson location code, arrange them in any order (subject, author, title, etc.), and produce listings which would serve as catalogs. Having made this apparently simple, logical deduction, we decided to test it. Since some listings of author and title were available as by-products of the circulation system, we decided in November 1974 to experiment with the production of a subject catalog. At this time paper costs were escalating to even more unreasonable levels, and the decision was made to use microform. After considering purchase and maintenance costs, ease of operation, and other factors, it was decided that microfiche would be preferable to roll-film.

A New Sequence

Because of past experiences with the vagaries of computer listings, we tried to predict the pitfalls to be faced in an alphabetical listing of LC subject headings. The eighth edition of the subject headings promised some changes to the "traditional" sequencing, although the placement of "parenthetically qualified" entries still left them in places unlikely to be found by anyone except a librarian. We therefore decided to discard tradition and file all subject entries word by word and ignore all punctuation. It was reasoned that this would be simpler for all users (including the librarians), since it was basically the same as one of the most commonly understood, detailed reference books, the telephone directory. This system of arrangement with interfiled subdivisions, names, hyphenated phrases, and the ubiquitous "parenthetically qualified" was seriously questioned by the librarians. However, after serious discussions in which all peeves and prejudices were exposed, it was decided to press on with this format since, as one staff member put it, "it is a logical progression and may be worked out, and in any case it's no less comprehensible to the average reader than the old system (or possibly systems)."

Editing the Entries

Having decided how to arrange the entries, the problem of what to include in them was undertaken. Because we were used to seeing masses of closely-typed data on 5" x 3" cards, and because full cataloging data was available for retrieval, we instinctively concluded that all the traditional data was absolutely essential. After discussion of how much of this information was ever read (let alone understood) by most catalog users, we decided to list only those items from the catalog entry which were essential to the user. We came to the conclusion that the most common information required from a subject catalog was "What does the library have in this subject?" and "How recent is it?" Having been unable to part with the main entry and title, we decided that the subject catalog could be kept to the following elements: subject heading, main entry, title, date, call number. At this point it was discovered that many of the records entered into the data base were in unedited form. To correct the data as errors were discovered, we included the accession number for each item since it facilitated faster and easier corrections to the data base.

Accession numbers for all items were assigned by the CB during processing, and were therefore the same for all participant colleges. Since the CB could obtain access to the cataloging record by accession number, corrections to our data updated records for all other colleges. Some time was spent on designing the format in which the fiche would appear, and we finally decided that maximum clarity could be achieved by using 42X, two columns per frame, subject headings in capitals, main entry alphabetization under each subject heading, with headings repeated only if a new column on frame was used, and an index frame which listed only the first entry for each frame of each fiche. Having accomplished this much, we made the official request to extract the data in May 1975, and waited and waited!

"Pioneering" Problems

Due to the largely experimental nature of the project, various technical things went wrong with extract programs, sequencing errors, data dumps, and fiche production. The heavy technical (and largely incomprehensible) explanations of these did cause some questioning of the benefits and desirability of pioneering anything. We learned that "firm deadline" was often a meaningless phrase to UTLAS, and that not only did they speak with forked tongues, they seemed to have one fork firmly in each cheek as they spoke. Finally, in September 1975, the first fiche sets arrived and, with some trepidation, were examined in the blue glows of the untouched fiche readers. At this point we finally understood the perils and problems of "unedited data." When the data base was created, CB keypunchers had transcribed exactly what was on the cards (plus and minus errors of transcription). Thus we found that we now had separate sequences under United States history, labelled:
    U. S. --Hist.
    U. S. --History
    United States--Hist.
    United States--History
Leaving aside the sporting possibilities posed by such entries as:
    French balls and songs
    Education, Compulsive
    Canada--Hisotry
we decided that a lot of work would have to be done before the subject catalog could be inflicted on the Ryerson population as a substitute for the card catalog. By fall 1975 the collections of the library totalled about 160,000 items, and the total subject entries (equivalent to 275 drawers of cards) were contained on 36 fiche, each with 208 frames, and an average of 25 entries per frame. As we were about to start a new academic year, nothing could be done to edit the fiche or replace the card catalog until the following summer. We decided to test the reaction of readers by placing uncorrected fiche sets and viewers in all areas of the library on the principle that however bad the fiche were, they were still better than nothing. Since, due to prohibitive costs and the way the base had been originally compiled, it had not been possible to incorporate cross-references into the fiche, each viewing station was equipped with a new (eighth) edition of the LC Subject Headings, and a copy of the Index to the Library of Congress Classification (Canadian Library Assn., 1974) in the hope that these would suffice to supply cross-references. Surprisingly,

this worked quite well, and the Index not only enabled readers to more easily understand the classification system, but also allowed more general queries to bypass the catalogs completely.

Editing the Fiche

By the spring of 1976, there was consensus that despite its gross errors, the fiche catalog was worthwhile. To facilitate internal location of material, and to enable us to relocate items from one collection to another, we decided to include location data to each fiche entry. In the interests of accuracy and consistency, it was decided that if the fiche were to be edited this would have to be done by the librarians who were ostensibly in the best position to recognize and correct errors. In an unparalleled effort of self-sacrifice, and with only minor coercion, each of the nine librarians agreed to personally edit and correct four fiche. A brief error reporting form had been designed so that the CB would correct the data base records, and the ordeal began in May 1976.

It was agreed that each librarian would finish their allotted fiche by June 30, 1976, so that corrections could be made, a new fiche produced for the 1976/77 academic year, and the subject card catalog removed entirely. Each librarian met the deadline, the CB staff coped with the flood of corrections, and despite the usual delay from the computer service, we started off the academic year with no subject card catalog. Apart from the general unease of the library staff and the gap left in the Information Centre furniture, the transition was relatively smooth. Two written complaints concerning the need for full bibliographic data appeared in the suggestion box, and some verbal comments were made by readers. The student response was generally enthusiastic, they were able to see a display of books at one time, and seemed to find the abridged data much easier to understand. One of our concerns had been how we would cope with constantly showing readers how to use the new catalog, but we were pleasantly surprised to find that a fair percentage already knew, and that those who did delighted in showing off their expertise to others. We do, however, have a few chronic cases who will never be able to understand the machines, and who have to be shown each time.

When the editing process was finished in 1976, we began to consider the feasibility of replacing the author/title card catalog with microfiche. Over a period of several months we considered the problems of format and content of separate main entry and title fiche, and decided that we would test them in the 1976/77 academic year with a view to removing the last card catalog before the 1977/78 academic year, if the system worked.

In considering author/title listings on fiche, we decided to try dividing the catalog into two sequences to test the assumption that students considered names and titles as two separate things. We decided to construct two sequences, one of authors and one of titles.

The "author" sequence was designed to include all personal or corporate name entries whether they appeared as main, added, or series entries. The title sequence included all title entries whether main, added, series, or uniform, and all main, added and series entries for conferences and meetings. The removal of main entries for conferences and meetings into the title sequence was designed to assist students and met with general approval. The destruction of the main entry concept has, however, been questioned by some librarians.

The liberties which appear to have been taken with traditional catalog practices have, in our library at least, been well-received. One of the advantages of the computer-based catalog is that the various elements may be assembled in a variety of sequences to meet particular needs. We have decided that, at least for the present, all our computer output microform (COM) will continue to carry abridged information i.e. main entry, title, date, location, and call number only. A small percentage of catalog searches need more information than this and will continue to be sought from other sources. To assist this, the shelf-list, so far still retained in card form, will be relocated close to the main reference desk.

The Results

Our experiment on the staged withdrawal of the card catalog has now been completed, and by the time you read this all public card catalogs will have been removed from the library. We now face the question of whether or not to replace the shelf-list with a COM using complete bibliographic data.

What have we gained from this transfer? A lot of staff time is now spent on public services rather than card filing; a catalog which is in a correct and comprehensible sequence; public catalogs which are 50 percent less out-of-date than before; multiple access points to our collections; a 20 percent increase of library attendance and circulation; and the satisfaction of having accomplished something which many others are still only contemplating.

Many of the anticipated disadvantages did not materialize. The education of catalog users was generally much easier than was expected. The "resistance to change" syndrome hardly appeared at all. The expense of microfiche readers was less than forecast, and should be offset by the sale of our card catalog units. Abridged entries have not caused users as many problems as we thought, although time spent in showing readers how to use bibliographic tools may have increased.

The one disadvantage which still causes concern is that we no longer have internal control of our catalog. We are at the mercy of the computer people, who can change schedules or increase prices and upset our budgets. Transferring our data to our own computer may be the answer to this potential problem. It is recognized that we were in a fortunate position to change from a card catalog to a COM because our data was pre-assembled and available due to our membership in a cooperative acquisition scheme. However if our "abridged" COM catalog continues to meet the needs and expectations of Ryerson students, it should be within the reach of, and possible for, many other types of libraries. The hardest part was the questioning of the norms of library operation. Once we learned to do this, the rest was relatively easy.

21. Computer Output Microfiche Catalogs:
Some Practical Considerations*

by Richard W. Meyer and Bonnie Juergens

Introduction

As more and more libraries seek alternatives to the card catalog, Computer Output Microfiche (COM) is becoming more important as an alternative form for the catalogs of library collections.[1] This is really a return to the book catalog concept, which has become cost effective and viable through the power of the computer. While the use of the computer certainly makes on-line catalogs possible, it also implies the potential for restructuring the format, record arrangement and record length of the catalog in printed forms. Before looking at the practical considerations involved with the structural characteristics of a COM catalog, the reader is reminded here that the two major issues are cost and practicality of COM versus card catalog.

It should be kept in mind that while comparing the card catalog versus the COM catalog, the kinds of costs offset are manpower, including filing and authority work, versus machine costs and data base maintenance costs. The former costs are nearly always hidden in-house, while the latter two may be included in the billing from the service agency utilized. Detailed cost information on COM will be reported later by the AMIGOS Bibliographic Council under a grant from the Texas State Library for a project to generate a union catalog.

The practicality of COM versus the card catalog centers around the advantages of one over the other. These advantages may include timeliness. The card catalog is a real-time system, but card production and filing delays often make it approach a batch system like COM. Advantages in favor of COM are its ease of duplication, wider distribution, and ease of maintenance. What may prove a disadvantage of COM is the necessity for reallocating personnel expertise from cataloging into computer data base management.[2] The reader is left to resolve these considerations as befits the particular situation.

This paper is concerned with and reports on a number of

---

*Reprinted with permission from the Journal of Micrographics, (Nov. Dec. 1977), Vol. 11, No. 2. 1977. National Micrographics Association. ALL RIGHTS RESERVED.

practical considerations centered around the structural characteristics of the University of Texas at Dallas (UT Dallas) COM catalog. It is hoped that some of the significant but less decisive issues are herein isolated for the reader.

Background

Early in 1971, UT Dallas and two other newly formed UT campus libraries, during their search for an alternative to the card catalog, were approached by Blackwell North America, Inc. (B/NA; formerly Richard Abel and Company). The three libraries accepted the proposal of B/NA to develop programs and provide data base management for COM catalogs for each library. The first catalogs were produced in 1973 from the data bases managed by B/NA.

The data bases of the three libraries are composed of LC-MARC records and contributed records in the MARC II format. The computer programs, which include complete subject authority control and which are very complex, manipulate these records to produce the COM catalogs. Since the flexibility is available to produce a variety of record formats, UT Dallas decided to analyze acceptance levels of several different layouts. A user survey was designed. B/NA set up the programs and produced two different author catalogs, four title catalogs, two subject catalogs and one shelf-list for UT Dallas' first master catalog based on about 20,000 titles. The entry elements and some samples are indicated in Tables I and II and Figures 1 through 4.

Analysis and Survey

The statistical analysis of the various catalogs is documented in Tables I through III. The analysis attempts to explicate catalog size variations resulting from various record lengths and page formats. The layout of the microfiche itself is based upon standard software of a COM vendor local to B/NA.

The survey was conducted by constructing and distributing a questionnaire. Of some 500 questionnaires distributed, 94 were completed and returned. Most of these were from library science graduate students from several institutions participating as an educational experiment. Slightly more than 1.5% of local student and faculty users participated. Such low local response may indicate that the questionnaire was poorly constructed even though it was designed with the help of two librarians, an industrial psychologist and a communications specialist. A realistic explanation for minimal participation might also reside in the library's failure to publicize the project more widely and public service staff members' failure to solicit more user response. The library was new and understaffed.

The questionnaire was divided into eight sections. Sections

one and two requested personal information about the user and the user's familiarity with microfiche readers. Sections three and four solicited user preference for record length and entry alternatives. Section five dealt with the layout of the microfiche. Sections six and seven requested the user's reaction to the concept of microfiche catalogs versus the card catalog and a potential book catalog. Section eight, which was open ended, asked for additional comments.

Results

An analysis of the data shown in Table I demonstrates the following: the greater the length of the record, the larger the catalog. As shown in Table I, the addition of place of publication, publisher, collation, notes and tracings to records containing author, title, date and call number more than doubles the size of the catalog. There is a 100% increase in one case and 140% increase in another case. The reason for the difference in these percentages is because the column format provides greater utility for brief records than it does for full records.

Table I. Increase in number of frames based on difference in extent of entry.

Catalog	Number of columns per frame	Entry elements	Number of frames required	Increase
A-1	3	A, T, D, C#	1307	*72.7%
A-2	2	A, T, Imp, Coll, Trac, C#	2257	
T-1	2	A, T, Imp, Coll, Notes, Trac, C#	1535	100.4%
T-4	2	A, T, D, C#	766	
T-2	3	A, T, Imp, Coll, Notes, Trac, C#	1503	140.1%
T-3	3	A, T, D, C#	626	

*Comparison somewhat invalidated because column format differs.

The effect generated by varying the number of columns can be seen by reviewing Table II. Going from a three column per frame format to a two column per frame format with brief records causes a 22.4 percent increase whereas the same progression utilizing full entries produces a 2.1 percent increase. Moderately full entries yield an increase rate which falls between the 22.4 percent and 2.1 percent, as might be expected. The data seems to support the logic that longer records will more effectively utilize space. This happens because the blank area following the call number, for instance,

Table II. Increase in number of frames based on difference in column format.

Catalog	Number of columns	Entry elements	Number of frames	Increase
T-3	3	A, T, D, C#	626	22.4%
T-4	2	A, T, D, C#	766	
T-1a	2	A, T, Imp, Coll, Trac, C#	1298	6.4%
T-2a	3	A, T, Imp, Coll, Trac, C#	1220	
T-1	2	A, T, Imp, Coll, Notes, Trac, C#	1535	2.1%
T-2	3	A, T, Imp, Coll, Notes, Trac, C#	1503	

represents a smaller percentage of the total page area with the more complete entry. Logical extrapolation from here indicates that either a one or four column format would waste space. Therefore, if space utilization is important, the three column format seems best.

The information shown in Table III demonstrates the ratio of entries to bibliographic records. There is an average of 5.3 entries per record, which supports the generally accepted norm.

In discussing responses to the questionnaires, all of the percentages indicated are based on the answering of specific questions, not on percentages of total number of questionnaires returned. Percentages were calculated both ways, but in no case were the results significantly affected by the different calculations.

As reported above, the majority (72 percent) of respondents were graduate students, largely on campuses other than UT Dallas. Nearly 90 percent indicated they used the library more than once a week. Responses suggest that those people who care about what kind of catalog a library has are the ones who use it frequently. A little less than half indicated that the instruction given in the use of the microfiche reader was inadequate; half indicated it was adequate and a few thought that it was good. Many expressed concern over machine failure and lack of access to the catalog due to an insufficient number of machines. Most of this concern was from respondents not on the UT Dallas campus who used machines provided by their respective schools. When UT Dallas conducted the study, 800 students and 75 faculty members constituted the user base, and just four readers were provided for public access to the catalog. No queuing problems were evident. There were three back-up readers in other parts of the library which were occasionally used.

Table III. Overall comparison.

Catalog	Number of microfiche	Number of frames	Number of entries*	Average number of entries per frame	Number of entries per record
A-1	6.28	1307	32635	24.96	1.58
A-2	10.85	2257	32635	14.46	1.58
T-1	7.38	1535	21644	14.10	1.05
T-2	7.23	1503	21644	14.10	1.05
T-3	3.01	626	21644	34.61	1.05
T-4	3.68	766	21644	28.26	1.05
T-1a	6.24	1298	21644	16.67	1.05
T-2a	5.86	1220	21644	17.74	1.05
S-1	10.64	2214	34973(42816)	15.80(19.34)	1.69
S-2	6.88	1431	34973(42816)	24.75(29.92)	1.69
Shelflist	9.50	1976	20664	10.46	1.00

*Figures in parentheses shows counts including cross-references.

Reader malfunction presents an insignificant problem if low-maintenance readers which minimize machine failures are chosen.[3] Experience indicates that adequate service can be provided if a ratio of one catalog and microfiche reader per 250 users is observed and routine maintenance is provided by a media technician.

The majority of users (62 to 72 percent) prefer full bibliographic records rather than brief records when a choice is available. Eighty-six percent indicated that brief entries will not always meet needs. However, many indicated that the brief entries were quicker and easier to scan than the full ones. It appears that a brief entry would be satisfactory, provided that a full bibliographic entry is available somewhere in the catalog for each title. UT Dallas uses a brief entry under author and a full entry under title.

Eighty-six percent of the responses indicated that subject tracings shown with entries can be helpful. A frequent comment was that subject tracings here provide alternative places to search. Interestingly, there were a number of comments, even from graduate library school students, suggesting that as long as there are cross-references, the subject tracings are not needed for alternatives. That would seem to indicate some misunderstanding of LC subject heading structure.

Answers to questions comparing the page format using two columns of entries with that using three columns indicates that a slim majority (65 percent) prefer two columns. Since the three-column format may make a 22 percent better use of space, some judgment is required in determining which will be used. When asked if a single column format would be desirable, 75 percent indicated this would not be necessary. Indeed, without a specially designed reader this approach would waste some space. With a very full record such as the shelf-list, space utilization is good enough for single column microfiche to warrant the ease of scanning afforded by this approach, but any indenting or paragraph structure would use up extra space.

Presently used headings and indexing on the microfiche were judged adequate by 72 to 86 percent of respondents. There is nothing special about these headings; they were generated directly from the standard software of a typical COM vendor.[4] Indexes exist at the bottom of each column of frames of the microfiche with eye-readable headings at the top. Experience with other microfiche files indicates that a single index in one corner of the microfiche is easier to use. What appears most apparent here is that no special programming is required; many COM vendors already have standard software which works very well.

When asked to compare their feelings about microfiche catalogs to card catalogs and book catalogs, a slim majority (52 percent) prefer the card catalog over microfiche. When asked about the possibility of having many microfiche catalogs around campus versus one card catalog in the library, the majority swung the other way. Many expressed concern over the loss of microfiche and the inability of frequent updating. This indicates that there are misunderstandings about the concept of microfiche catalogs. It should be kept in mind that microfiche are easily and cheaply duplicated, thus minimizing the concern over loss and providing the capability of placing many catalogs around campus. In addition, it should be noted that five or more microfiche readers can be purchased for the price of one 72-drawer card cabinet. Updating of microfiche is no less difficult. The catalog at UT Dallas has been updating as often as biweekly with a cumulative supplement. The turnaround time here matches card production and filing time of comparable libraries. [5]

Some of those surveyed indicated they would like a book catalog because of its obvious advantages over microfiche. Less than 50 percent of the respondents indicated they would borrow readers and microfiche if they were available to take home. Publication of a book catalog for 50,000 titles with very brief author entries only would result in a 200 page document costing about $5,000 for the first 1,000 copies. That same $5,000 could buy 45 copies of the catalog with readers for loan. Thorough market analysis is required before a full commitment to either approach would be warranted.

Conclusions

If a microfiche catalog is chosen as the alternative to the card catalog, the format should be based on standard products available from COM vendors. If possible, a two or three column frame layout optimizes scanning and space utilization, with three columns the best. A brief entry under either author or title with a full entry under the other and subject entries which include subject tracings, make for a good balance of providing adequate information while utilizing space effectively. Standard indexing techniques of many COM vendors are adequate. Users need to be educated to the advantages of microfiche over card catalogs.

As a further consideration, it should be remembered that microfiche catalogs may be interim between card catalogs and on-line computer catalogs. The building of a computer data base required to provide COM catalogs implies the future possibility of an on-line catalog. Once on-line catalog access has been achieved, the microfiche catalog does not automatically become obsolete but its role can change to that of an adjunct access tool capable of being located remote to the library or of being carried home by the user.

References

1. "More libraries switch to COM cataloging," Library Journal, 101:2213-14 (November 1, 1976).
2. Landau, Herbert B., "Can the librarian become a computer data base manager?" Special Libraries, 62/3:117-24 (March 1971).
3. "Microform readers for libraries: a survey," Library Technol-

ogy Reports, Appendix E (November 1975); Ballou, Hubbard W., Guide to Micrographic Equipment (Silver Spring, Maryland: National Microfilm Association, 1975); U.S. National Archives and Records Service. Records management handbook. Managing information retrieval. Microform retrieval equipment guide, (Washington, D.C.: Government Printing Office, 1974).

4. U.S. National Archives and Records Service. Records management handbook. Managing information retrieval. Computer output microfilm, (Washington, D.C.: Government Printing Office, 1975); Spigai, Frances G., The invisible medium: the state-of-the-art of microfilm and a guide to the literature (Washington, D.C.: ERIC Clearinghouse on Library and Information Sciences, March 1973) ED 075 029.

5. For some interesting reading on computer filing see: Books in Print (New York: Bowker, 1975), v. 1, preface; U.S. Library of Congress, Films and other materials for projection, 1974 (Washington, D.C., 1975), p. vii-viii.

22. Public Response to an Academic Library Microcatalog*

by James R. Dwyer

In May 1975 the University of Oregon took the first step toward closing its card catalog by filming the existing catalog which, at that time, contained approximately 750,000 records on 3.2 million cards. Since that date all bibliographic records have been entered into the Blackwell North America data base. BNA sends card sets to the U of O along with computer output microfiche (COM) supplements to the filmed catalog. Over 100,000 new records have been entered into the system in the last four years along with over 10,000 recats and reclassifications.

In September 1976 microcatalogs were established at seven locations in the main and branch libraries. Since then the card catalog was removed from the Architecture and Allied Arts (A & AA) branch (in August 1977) and the subject card catalog in the main library was closed (in November 1977).

Purpose of the Study

A change in the mode of access to the collection might be expected to have a major impact on the public. Since microcatalogs are a relatively new tool, and since the U of O "basic" catalog is a form of "frozen" catalog, à la LC, it seemed particularly important to measure public response. A reader survey accompanied by an analysis of previous related research was chosen as the most effective means to this end.

The literature search revealed that the vast majority of articles about microcatalogs focused on applications and economics rather than on patron response. When readers were mentioned at all it was typically as part of an impressionistic statement such as "Both faculty and student users of the library have commented favorably on the catalog...."[1]

McElderry reports that "the primary motivation for changes in the format of the catalog has been product-oriented more than it has been consumer- or user-oriented.... Little attention has been

---

*Reprinted by permission of the author and publisher from The Journal of Academic Librarianship, 5 (July 1979), p. 132-141; © by The Journal of Academic Librarianship. All rights reserved.

given directly to a systematic appraisal of user requirements."[2] Scott[3] and Bierman[4] note a lack of research on the subject, while Maltby and Duxbury observe that "too often, like the proverbial good little boy, our readers are seen and not heard."[5]

Money, or the lack of it, may be the main reason for the lack of research. Gatenby reports that at Australia's Milperra College of Advanced Education "No formal studies were carried out to determine the acceptability of the new catalog ... as there seemed no economic alternative to it."[6] The potential effects of such one-dimensional planning could be particularly damaging when it takes place on the national/international level: "The headlong rush to close the catalog--stampeded in part and unintentionally by LC's decision to close its own catalog because of internal problems--must be tempered by a concern for the library users who will be ravaged by the multiple lookups forced on them by cost- but not service-oriented administrators."[7]

Some studies, such as Salmon's,[8] analyze public response to microforms but concentrate on research materials in this format rather than on catalogs. As the trend toward alternatives to the card catalog intensifies,[9] more research specifically concerned with microcatalogs should be conducted since "There still remains a serious question ... whether or not users will accept microforms."[10] By identifying existing problems we can design better catalog delivery systems and expect less public resistance to them.

To date the author has located only four sophisticated microcatalog user studies. Reports on the LENDS system at Georgia Tech analyze a remote access system and are of the greatest value to libraries fortunate enough to be considering such an expansion of their services.[11] The Bath University Comparative Catalog Survey (BUCCS) may be the most comprehensive one of its type. It has been mentioned only briefly in library literature,[12] but complete sets of ten reports can be acquired through the Bath University Library. A major COM catalog system at the University of Toronto has been the object of scrutiny by DeBruin and Weiss.[13] The fourth study was conducted by Cox and Juergens of the AMIGOS Bibliographic Council at five Texas libraries.[14] They compare reader reaction to film and fiche catalogs and evaluate the effectiveness of microcatalogs in performing various types of bibliographic searches.

The University of Oregon microcatalog study differs from previous research in that statistical methods are used to test hypotheses about reader behavior. It compares responses to card and microcatalogs and attempts to determine not only how people reacted, but why they reacted as they did.

Hypotheses

Based on previous research, observation of catalog users, and direct experience with the microcatalog, the following hypotheses were formulated:

1. Frequency of use and acceptance of the microcatalog would vary over time, by total microfiche use, by academic status, and by distance from the card catalog. Acceptance of the new system would vary directly with distance and total use and inversely by status.
2. The number of first-time users would drop as the study progressed.
3. Problems with the legibility of the basic (filmed) catalog would emerge over time resulting in an increasingly critical reception and inhibited use of the microcatalog.
4. Nonuse of the supplements would be a major problem and a split file (basic and supplements) would not be fully utilized. It was expected, however, that awareness, use, and acceptance of the supplements would improve over time.
5. The microcatalog would be considered to be as easy and quick to search as the card catalog.

Other hypotheses were also tested. These are presented in the context of the major hypotheses in later sections of this report.

Research Methodology

Three weeks before the end of the academic quarter in Autumn 1976 (Period I), Spring 1977 (Period II), and Autumn 1977 (Period III) questionnaires were placed at seven microcatalog stations. Four were in the main library (Education-Psychology, Social Sciences, Humanities, Oregon Collection) and three in branches (Architecture and Allied Arts, Science, Law). Due to a low rate of response in the Law Library, that branch was dropped from the survey beginning with Period II and the new station at the Catalog Information Desk was substituted.

Complete questionnaires were collected at the end of each quarter. A total of 790 usable questionnaires was collected: 235 from Period I, 215 from Period II, and 340 from Period III. Responses were transferred to keypunch cards and a Statistical Package for the Social Sciences Crosstabulation program was used to analyze the results.

The major methodological problem from Period I was that many of the questionnaires were incomplete. Because this was a particularly serious problem on questionnaires submitted by "Staff" or "Other," these two groups were excluded for the first phase of the survey. Rather than discard the remainder of the incomplete questionnaires, "corrected totals excluding nonrespondents" were included in the tables when appropriate. After Period I the questionnaire was redesigned and nonresponse was substantially reduced.

Another problem was that the time to select a truly random sample and administer the questionnaires in a more scientific manner was not available. With questionnaires openly placed at every viewing station results are subject to skewing through self-selection. Because those whose reaction is particularly positive or negative are more likely to respond than those who are indifferent, we might expect a flattening of the curve to take place. Under ideal testing circumstances we might expect a slightly greater number of median range reactions.

Delivery of the System

Previous reports[15] have demonstrated that environmental factors have a substantial effect on the acceptance of microforms. Lack of adequate eye-legible indexing, queues at viewers, overcrowding, and a lack of writing space all inhibit microform use. Because not all readers are accustomed to using microforms, it is essential to keep the viewing process as simple as possible and to provide adequate instruction.

At the University of Oregon brief instructions are posted on placards and more detailed manuals are also left at each viewing station. Seventy-five percent of the respondents found these instructions clear and easy to follow, although another 30 percent required assistance by a librarian. Fortunately, 98 percent of those requiring assistance found it readily available.

This is not to imply that disruptions are not to be expected during the transition from card to film. At the New South Wales Institute of Technology librarians discovered that "an intensified reader assistance program was required."[16] After the card catalog was replaced by microfiche in the Architecture and Allied Arts branch a substantial increase in catalog-related questions was encountered as well.

Greene[17] and DeBruin[18] report a positive response to having viewers located around the library and the campus. Many respondents to the U of O survey commented favorably upon this aspect of the microcatalog and over 96 percent considered the viewers to be conveniently located. By stressing the advantages of having the catalog available in multiple locations librarians might expect to lessen initial resistance, especially from faculty.

Even if the full potential of campus- or network-wide distribution of the catalog is not realized, it is still crucial to provide an adequate number of viewing stations within the library. Since we still have a dual system (card and fiche) at the University of Oregon and readers can go to the card catalog if viewing stations are crowded, it is impossible in this survey to try to determine the correct number of viewers for a library of a given size. According to 88 percent of those surveyed, no waiting was required to use the microcatalog. Of those who did not have immediate access, one-third waited less than three minutes, one-third waited three to seven minutes, and still another one-third had to wait seven minutes or

longer. These figures may be the result of skewing by self-
selection, since many of those who had to wait may have gone to
the card catalog instead without filling in a questionnaire.

Because complex or comprehensive searches may take a
great deal of time, reader comfort must be taken into account. We
discovered that at stations where viewers were placed on abdomen-
level tables, readers requested stools or suggested that the viewers
be placed on standard height tables with chairs. Requests for more
writing space were frequent.

Nearly 20 percent of the respondents reported physical difficulties in using the microfiche, including eyestrain, headaches,
nausea, and pains in the neck, back, etc. Some of these ailments
might be traced to the sometimes fuzzy reproduction of the basic
catalog (rated "poor" by nearly one-third of the sample), but it
would be unrealistic to blame poor filming exclusively or to hope
that this sort of problem will go away over time or to expect that
people will become desensitized. According to Lewis, "There appears to be no reason to expect a change in attitude ... unless
there is a much greater emphasis on overcoming problems involving
user comfort, convenience, personal preference and research
habits."[19]

Librarians instituting microcatalogs can reduce the "nuisance
factor" by providing standardized equipment (including standardized
placement of fiche in the viewers), comfortable viewing stations with
adequate seating and writing space, and sufficient eye-legible indexing of the fiche. Prior training of librarians and staff should result
in enhanced service and heightened acceptance and use by staff and
clients alike. Self-instruction modules and inclusion of microcatalog
training in orientation programs and classes should also be considered.

Level of Use by Location and Status

In order to measure level of use, three experience categories were
established. Those who indicated more than ten searches were placed
in the "Often" category ("frequent users"), those with two to ten
searches were termed "Occasional" users, and beginners were considered to have used the system "Rarely."

It was hypothesized that the number of frequent users would
increase as the percentage of neophytes dropped. This would appear
to be the case; between December 1976 and December 1977 the percentage of frequent users nearly doubled (from 35 percent to 63 percent) as other categories declined.

It was also assumed that frequency of use would vary directly
with distance from the main card catalog. Within the main library
this was borne out with the exception of the relatively little-used
catalog in the Oregon Collection. Note in Table 1 how the percentage
of frequent users rises continuously from the Catalog Information

Table 1
Use by Distance from Card Catalog

Location	Often (%)	Occasional (%)	Rare (%)	Number of Responses	Percent of Total
Catalog Information	37	35	27	106	13
Education-Psychology	44	43	12	73	9
Social Sciences	61	33	5	117	15
Humanities	65	32	2	193	24
Oregon Collection	53	37	10	49	6
Architecture & Allied Arts	67	30	3	122	15
Science	35	48	17	130	17
The Mean	53	36	10		

Locations listed in order of distance from card catalog, location increasing from left to right.

Service (CIS) through Humanities for each period. Note also that the largest total number of readers, nearly one-fourth of the total sample, is concentrated in Humanities. (Humanities is located further from the card catalog than any other major service point in the main library.) Dozens of favorable comments about the microfiche catalog as a time- and step-saving device came from this division.

One might therefore expect that microcatalog use would be highest in the branch libraries since they are so much farther away from the main card catalog. While this was true for the Architecture and Allied Arts Library, it was not the case at the Science Library. This is probably because Science has a separate card catalog for its own collection (not yet separately available in fiche) and because use of indexed periodicals is particularly high at this branch. It was suspected that the introduction of a "new toy" would be most popular among science students, but this did not turn out to be true. Indeed, many science students and faculty remarked that this was an "inappropriate application of technology."

The A & AA Library demonstrates an interesting use pattern; it is near the average for the first two periods, but sharply higher during the final test. This can be traced directly to the removal of the card catalog in that branch in August of 1977; no one reported being a first-time user during Period III.

An analysis of status by location provides some insights into these use patterns. CIS has a less experienced clientele both in class standing and total microfiche use. The heaviest concentration of graduate students was in Humanities, the main library location with the highest number of frequent uses. Because variations by location closely resemble variations by status we can explain divisional and branch response largely in terms of the perceptions and needs of differing clientele.

It had been predicted that the highest degree of use would be by graduate students and the lowest by faculty. Measured in terms of either total numbers of readers or frequency-of-use percentages, this did not turn out to be entirely true. Of all respondents 43 percent were undergraduates, 43 percent were graduate students, and 7 percent were faculty. Although the number of graduate students in the sample may seem disproportionally high compared to enrollment and the number of undergraduates disproportionally low, these figures may be a reflection of actual library use rather than enrollment.

In Period I, frequency-of-use percentages among the three groups (undergrad, grad, faculty) are remarkably even. Everyone was just beginning to use the new system. Over time, however, both graduate students and faculty show a much higher frequency of use than undergraduates. Four partial explanations occur: (1) undergraduates are more likely to be casual or occasional library patrons, (2) graduate students and faculty are more likely to work in a single subject division of the library and take advantage of the viewers in that area, (3) graduate students and faculty carry a greater burden of responsibility for catalog efficacy than do undergraduates, and (4) graduate students and faculty are more accustomed to completing questionnaires than undergraduates. The third factor may result in some degree of nonrandom self-selection of participants, but the random variety of responses from all sections of the sample implies that there was no crucial skewing of the data.

Evaluation of the Basic Catalog

As was mentioned earlier, the U of O microcatalog consists of two major sections, a microfilmed basic catalog and two COM supplements. A concern arose that the supplements were more consistently legible and that readers might find the basic catalog less than acceptable as they became more experienced in its use. (It should be noted that the microfilming of the basic catalog was professionally done but that even the best constructed and maintained card catalog is likely to contain some misfilings, some breakdowns in the syndetic structure, and some inaccurate information. This is particularly true of large research library catalogs which were developed under a variety of cataloging codes. Even the best microfilming job can't eliminate the legibility problem completely.)

A crosstabulation of "Quality of the basic catalog by use" confirms our concern regarding negative reception of the basic catalog. Over the course of one year the percentage of those considering the basic catalog highly legible dropped from 35 percent to 15 percent while the percentage of those who consider the basic catalog unacceptable rose from 14 percent to 36 percent. Given that there was no noticeable physical deterioration of the film this would reveal an increasingly negative reaction as familiarity increased.

This observation is further verified by the fact that first-time users were considerably less critical than their more experienced peers, indicating that some dissatisfaction was already reached after only two to ten searches. The number of written complaints regarding illegibility, misfilings, and inaccuracies was disconcerting. Pasternack's observation that "the most frequent negative comments were that the fiche were some times difficult to read"[20] definitely applies here.

The greatest amount of criticism regarding the legibility of the basic catalog came from the Architecture and Allied Arts Library. Only 12 percent of the respondents there considered it to be a good reproduction compared to 20 percent of the total sample. This is especially significant when one considers that this is the only branch relying exclusively on microfiche and is also the location with the greatest concentration of frequent users.

It was also hypothesized that acceptance of the basic catalog would vary in inverse proportion to academic standing. This was the case, with the percentage of acceptance highest among freshmen (35 percent) before dropping steadily by class through seniors (21 percent), graduates (16 percent), faculty (14 percent), and staff (9 percent). Conversely, over half the faculty and staff considered the basic catalog to be "poor" compared to only 15 percent of the freshmen. Comments of different client groups varied as well; a faculty member suggested computerizing the entire system while a frustrated sophomore had a different plan: "The basic catalog stinks. Buy a copy of The Exorcist."

The basic catalog has not been the victim of neglect, only 13 respondents (1.6 percent of the total sample) having reported that they had never used it. Five of them were from the Catalog Information Service and they were presumably using the COM supplements to the closed subject catalog.

Evaluation of the Supplements

Readers who had used the supplements were far less critical of them than they had been of the basic catalog. Unfortunately, the positive response to the supplements was marred by a low level of use. It was predicted that awareness, use, and acceptance of the supplements would increase over time and with total microcatalog use. In Table 2 we find only partial confirmation of this hypothesis. Although the popularity of the basic catalog dropped off sharply after Period I, this was not the case with the supplements which were rated "good" by 39 percent in Period I and 34 percent in Period III. Nearly twice as many respondents rated the supplements "good" (36 percent versus

Table 2
Quality of Supplements by Use

Quality of Supplements	Period	Often (%)	Occasional (%)	Rarely (%)	Mean (%)	Corrected (%)
Good	I	37	27	35	31	39
	II	47	13	28	35	36
	III	37	23	26	32	34
	Combined	40	22	30	32	36
Fair	I	16	12	17	14	17
	II	18	19	0	17	18
	III	24	24	7	22	24
	Combined	21	18	9	18	20
Poor	I	3	5	7	4	5
	II	0	9	0	3	3
	III	12	10	13	11	12
	Combined	6	7	8	7	8
Not Used	I	25	34	35	31	39
	II	31	57	56	41	43
	III	23	40	29	28	30
	Combined	25	42	37	32	36

20 percent for the basic catalog) and only one-fourth as many considered it "poor" (8 percent to 30 percent for the basic catalog.)

Frequent users were more likely to give the supplements high marks than occasional or first-time users (61 percent "good" or "fair" versus 39 percent "good" or "fair"). The increase in the "poor" category during Period III was a result of dissatisfaction with the microcatalog at the Architecture and Allied Arts branch; nearly half of the negative responses in Period III came from that location.

Because they were most critical of the basic catalog, one might expect faculty to be highly critical of the supplements as well. Except for Period I, this was not the case. During Periods II and III faculty and staff gave the supplements higher marks than any other group did, a reversal of the results obtained in the evaluation of the basic catalog. The moral here might be that you can only teach an old dog new tricks by offering the reward of improved services.

As mentioned earlier, the level of nonuse of the supplements was stunning. This was expected to be a problem during the initial test period, but it was hoped that awareness would rise and nonuse drop over time. Once again, the faculty was the only group to show a substantial improvement in attitude and use, with nonuse dropping from 45 percent in Period I to only 9 percent in Period III. Even among frequent microcatalog users nearly one-fourth were still unaware of the supplements or had not used them by the final round. More than one-third of the total sample were using only the retrospective part of the system.

There is further evidence which indicates that people will not take advantage of supplements even when they are aware that such things exist. At the University of Toronto, although 63 percent of the undergraduates were aware of supplements, only 8 percent of these students used them frequently and nearly 40 percent never used them at all.[21]

Considering that the U of O supplements contain records for all materials acquired and/or cataloged since May 1975 as well as all recataloged and reclassified records, an overall figure of 36 percent nonuse is unacceptable. Furthermore, the survey could not measure the problems encountered when readers assumed that the basic catalog contained an accurate record of current holdings and left the library unsatisfied because (1) there appeared to be no post-1974 materials on a given subject or by a popular author, (2) the item sought had been recataloged or reclassified and was "lost" under the old call number, or (3) they were confused by divergent forms of names or subject headings in the card and basic fiche catalogs. Have we discovered the most effective tool for keeping readers away from library holdings? Is an inscrutable multiple file system even more intimidating than an inscrutable reference librarian?

An Analysis of Nonuse Based on Research in Information Seeking

As librarians, we often assume that the public speaks our language, or that its needs are what we perceive them to be from our position of greater authority, or that everyone possesses the same thoroughness and search sophistication that we do. Consider this statement: "One limitation of the fiche catalog that has not been overcome is that we have no means of changing the basic catalog file.... The recommended practice of always consulting the supplements circumvents this difficulty."[22] And unfortunately, "the fact that too high a number of users (other than staff) were unaware of the existence of the supplements is disturbing."[23] Those troublesome readers, they just don't behave! We set up supplements and they ignore them. Why?

Two theories we should keep in mind when developing bibliographic access systems such as catalogs are the "principle of least effort in information gathering"[24] and the "principle of information processing parsimony."[25] These theories have been tested and verified in a variety of settings and apply here as well.

"Least effort in information gathering" postulates that people will put as little time and effort as possible into finding out what they perceive that they need to know. In a library "More than 50% ... will look up only one entry and then stop--regardless of whether or not they have found what they are looking for."[26]

Those of us who work at public service desks know that a certain amount of guidance and encouragement may be required to be sure that our clients check a variety of possible entries or sources. Since we can't (and shouldn't have to) monitor all searches, it is imperative that we keep the catalog simple, with as few steps as possible. Ideally we might like to think of supplements as additional access points, but in practice multiple files are rarely consulted and the existence of a complex system may discourage readers.

Respondents were vocal in their opinions on a multiple file system. "Too many places to look which is frustrating and time consuming." "Put it all in one sequence." "The triple system [basic plus two supplements] is irrational, time-consuming, and confusing." "Prevents me from checking an interesting subject." "Some technologies complicate life rather than simplify it ... the new or transfer student is put off from doing research." "I had trouble determining the order. Is it different in basic and supps?" These remarks came from all levels, including one from a library school faculty member.

The other theory to keep in mind, the "principle of information processing parsimony," takes us one step further. It maintains that people not only minimize their search efforts, but neither need nor want all the information which is available on a given subject. This is a natural reaction to information overload and is similar to the phenomenon of people "spacing out" while watching television. People cannot be expected to look in supplements if they can get a few citations from a basic file. If they discover those books are missing (recataloged, checked out, withdrawn, etc.) they have a choice of leaving the library or starting their searches from scratch. In either case, split files are a source of misinformation and wasted time.

One respondent noted, "I do not trust its [basic catalog's] contents thoroughly" yet that same person had never used the supplements. Was this the sort of problem Bierman had in mind when he predicted that "exclusively microimage catalogs for large collections will not be acceptable because of user interface and acceptance problems...."?[27]

Judging from what we know about how people approach information, we should not be surprised that more than one-third of those surveyed did not use or did not know of the existence of the supplements. With this in mind, isn't it a form of professional irresponsibility to construct "frozen" catalogs which do not accurately reflect library holdings? Conceptually, a frozen catalog is a contradiction in terms; in practice it is a source of misinformation and confusion.

Bates proposes that we reconsider assumptions about our clients and reformulate our service patterns accordingly: "[The traditional] model is the industrious searcher who does for him or herself, and if not willing to is considered 'lazy' and not deserving of our attention. I'm not suggesting that we turn library service inside

out and do everyone's searching for them. But I do suggest that it
is our responsibility as information professionals to know and understand people's search behavior and to design services to optimize
the likelihood for people getting the information they need given their
patterns of behavior."28

Considering the problem of nonuse of multiple files, Vervliet's
observations are particularly apropos: "There is no solution to the
problem of closing the old catalogue unless a library is prepared to
convert it into machine readable form or to continue to produce
cards and file them manually."29 Participants in the University of
Oregon survey proposed both options: "The expense of computerizing
the whole thing is probably prohibitive, but the resulting ease of use
would justify it." "I don't want to look through the frigging supplements again. Get the card catalogue back so we can look up everything at once."

Given the substantial problems users have with multiple files,
librarians should consider microcatalogs to be a viable option for
their libraries if and only if they might reasonably expect to enter
all bibliographic records into a single data base.30 As time passes,
frozen catalogs, be they fiche or card format, are increasingly less
representative of library holdings and are increasingly a source of
confusion and frustration. Although card catalogs have many faults
and are expensive to maintain, they are nonetheless online in the
sense that they are immediately accessible and that they are more
comprehensible to the public than a multiple file microcatalog. A
live white elephant is preferable to a series of dead armadillos.

The idea of appending COM supplements to a frozen card or
filmed catalog is a prime example of library misapplication and
underutilization of promising technologies. Such a practice seems
particularly shortsighted when one considers the advantages of a fully
automated system in COM or online form. With all bibliographic information in a single data base, one can produce an up-to-date, accurate and totally manipulatable record of library holdings. When a
major entry or subject-heading change is made (such as Negroes to
Afro-Americans), all records with that heading can be changed to
the new form by relatively simple program manipulation. Freedman
calls this the "global fix" capability: "The net result of this automated catalog control is to maximize the probability that the authority terms for a given network will be correct, consistent with respect
to each other, and not redundant."31

In a dual system one must not only change the program but
must also either manually revise the card catalog or be faced with
increasing numbers of inconsistencies. Hence the major disadvantage
of card catalogs (maintenance costs) remains part of a new dual system. With a frozen filmed catalog one has no choice other than an
increasing level of inconsistency and inaccuracy.

Ease and Speed Factors

In the final section of the questionnaire respondents were asked to compare the card and fiche catalogs regarding ease and speed of use. This approach was chosen because it was feared that asking, "Do you prefer the card or fiche catalog?" would be tantamount to operating a superficial popularity contest. We were attempting to determine not only which form was preferred, but why.

It was initially assumed that there would be a near perfect correlation between ease and speed factors. A cross-tabulation of ease by speed reveals a strong but imperfect correlation, with 62 percent of those who found the microcatalog easier to use than its traditional counterpart finding it also faster to use, and 87 percent of those who found it harder to use wasting time as well. The largest single group, 292 respondents or 37 percent of the sample, reported that the microcatalog was both harder and slower to use than the card catalog. Conversely, the second largest group, 150 people or 19 percent of the sample, rated the microcatalog superior on both counts.

A librarian at the CIS desk has observed that most clients seem totally unaware of the supplements. Readers may think they have completed a search after looking in only one of the three sequences and may thus believe that the search had been faster than a card catalog search regardless of whether or not they had successfully located desired information.

The literature is replete with other undocumented testimonials to universal reader acceptance of fiche catalogs. Considering these statements and the results of surveys at the University of Toronto,[32] Brighton Polytechnic,[33] and AMIGOS,[34] one might expect high user acceptance of microcatalogs.

The University of Oregon Microfiche Use Study did not elicit such a positive response. Only 23 percent reported that the microcatalog was easier to use, 29 percent considered it comparable to the card catalog, and 47 percent found it harder to use. The most optimistic interpretation of these results would be that just over half consider the fiche catalog to be at least as acceptable as the card catalog.

Considering that long-established work patterns can be the most difficult to change, it is not surprising that acceptance of the microcatalog varied inversely by status. Faculty were consistently the most critical, followed by graduate students, down through the freshmen who were least critical and, judging from their comments, most enthusiastic. In similar situations one might reasonably expect that faculty will be the most difficult group to wean from the card catalog.

In Period III there was a sudden increase in "Harder" responses from seniors. Once again, this phenomena can be attributed

Table 3
Ease by Status

Status	Easier (%)	Same (%)	Harder (%)
Freshmen	41	26	30
Sophomores	35	36	27
Juniors	32	28	40
Seniors	23	22	52
Graduates	18	28	53
Faculty	12	35	52
Staff	36	36	27
Other	19	46	32
Mean	23	29	47

Table 4
Quality of Supplements by Ease

Ease (%)	Good	Fair	Poor	Not Used
Easy	44	18	0	28
Same	38	16	3	32
Hard	24	20	12	35
Mean	32	18	7	33
Corrected	36	20	8	36

to the removal of the card catalog from the A & AA branch where many of the students are seniors or fifth-year students, who are considered to be seniors. Acceptance of the microcatalog did not vary significantly by location otherwise.

According to McElderry, "there is some evidence to suggest that familiarity with the medium reduces resistance."[35] Greene, however, in his Georgia Tech study, reports that "a strong relationship between microform attitude and frequency of microform use was not found."[36] U of O discovered a relationship between acceptance and use, a negative one. Between Periods I and III those who gave the microcatalog an "Easier" rating dropped from 29 percent to 21 percent while the percentage of users who found the microfiche more difficult to use than the card catalog rose from 42 percent to 53 percent. Although one might expect greater ease of use with experience (number of uses), this did not turn out to be the case.

One explanation of this pattern might be that the more often one uses the basic catalog, the more likely one is to encounter inaccurate or illegible records. A strong correlation exists between the public's evaluation of the legibility of the basic catalog and its rating as to ease of microcatalog use. The largest group of respondents to this question, 168 or 21 percent of the sample, considered the legibility of the basic catalog to be poor and the fiche catalog harder to use than cards.

Nonuse of the COM supplements also contributed to dissatisfaction (see Table 4). Note that while nonuse of the supplements is unacceptably high among all groups, it is lowest among those who rated the microcatalog easy to use. Conversely, 85 percent of those who found fault with the supplements also claimed that the microfiche was harder to use than the card catalog. By increasing awareness of the supplements one might expect an improvement in the acceptance of microcatalogs. Unfortunately, as reported earlier, awareness of the supplements is not increasing nearly fast enough to substantially offset dissatisfaction.

Likewise, one might hope that an improved refilming of the basic catalog would lower resistance to it. Refilming, however, would be a mere palliative because (1) the new basic catalog would soon be out of date, (2) readers would still be likely to limit their searches to a single file, (3) older, lower quality cards will not produce high quality reproductions. It would seem that the only way to significantly improve public acceptance of the microcatalog would be to produce a significantly improved catalog, i.e., a single portable catalog containing current records of all library holdings.

Search time is a crucial factor when considering the value of a particular catalog format. Considering the number of work hours spent on catalog searches by library staff (order, cataloging, verification, etc.), and considering that readers can be discouraged by long or fruitless searches, it may well be the most important factor of all, given equal reliability of data in either file.

Are we to expect improved search speed from microcatalogs? The literature presents conflicting evidence on this point. At the Royal Melbourne Institute of Technology "microform catalogues ... took longer to search than full print catalogues."[37] Likewise, at the University of Toronto a card search was shown to be slightly faster than one using fiche or film.[38] Conversely, the Bath University Comparative Catalog Study found fiche and rollfilm searches to be substantially faster than card searches.[39] Of course it is possible that Bath University maintains a single file without encumbering supplements.

In the University of Oregon study respondents gave no clear indication as to whether or not the microcatalog is more efficient for searching purposes than the card catalog. One should realize that what is being tested is not objectively measured search time, but the experiential perception of search speed. The perception of whether the catalog is easy or hard or fast or slow to use can have a major impact on total microcatalog acceptance. The largest group, 43 percent of the sample, reported that the fiche was slower, 23 percent thought both took the same amount of time, and 31 percent considered the microfiche faster. The optimistic interpretation is that more than half the people discovered that the microcatalog is as fast or faster to use than cards. The pessimistic view is that nearly two-thirds think it is the same or even worse than an already ungainly access tool.

Analysis of the speed factor is complicated by the fact that viewing stations are scattered throughout the libraries. This is a real step-saver for readers, and one might expect a more positive response to the speed question. Some people commented that the elimination of trips to the catalog was appreciated, but that once at the catalog or viewer, it actually took longer to search the fiche than the cards.

As with ease, it had been hoped that search speed performance would improve over time and by total number of uses, an overoptimistic prediction. Response was actually more critical during the final period than during the initial one. There was no strong correlation between speed and frequency of use, even though frequent and occasional users responded more negatively than neophytes in Period III (52 percent "slower" among veterans versus 29 percent for beginners). These results are similar to those in an ease-by-use test, and this parallel drop in acceptance can be most likely traced to the split-file system and the legibility and filing problems of the basic catalog.

Search speed evaluation, like ease, varied inversely by status. Faculty were consistently more critical of the microcatalog on this account than were graduate students who, in turn, were more negative than the undergraduates.

There was little variation in evaluation of speed by location. Results obtained from the Catalog Information Service are consistently more positive than the mean, but this is to be expected considering the high percentage of undergraduates and the frequency of search assistance by a librarian at that location. Once again, readers at the Architecture and Allied Arts Library were most negative, particularly during Period III when only 7 percent of those respondents reported that fiche was faster to use than cards, while an overwhelming 73 percent claimed that the fiche was slower. The librarians at that branch report that some faculty members and students refuse to use triple file fiche catalog, preferring to make the often drizzly walk to the main library. Staff from the A & AA Library prefer to use the main card catalog for verification searches, but it must be understood that the main title catalog, unlike the fiche, includes temporary records for items on order or in process.

Conclusion

Alternative forms of catalogs have become increasingly popular within the past few years. Unfortunately they have been established primarily because of cost considerations, with little regard to reader habits and preferences.

This paper has pointed out some of the disadvantages of a partially frozen, multiple file system. Given the principle of least effort and the principle of information processing parsimony, it is unrealistic to expect readers to employ such complex devices to full advantage. Indeed, many may be confused and discouraged from using a library thus equipped. By avoiding frozen catalogs and placing greater emphasis on retrospective conversion of bibliographic data, individual libraries and networks can eventually overcome these problems and offer genuinely improved access systems to the public.

* * *

The author wishes to thank those who have assisted in the preparation of this report, particularly Barbara O'Neill and Claire Meyer of the University of Oregon and Marcia Bates of the University of Washington School of Librarianship.

References

1. William C. Horner, "The Use of Economics of Computer-Generated Microfiche Catalogs," North Carolina Libraries 33 (Winter 1975):31-33.
2. Stanley McElderry, "Alternatives to the Conventional Card Catalog from the User Point of View," IFLA Journal 2 (1976): 234-35.
3. Aldyth D. Scott, "Catalogue Use: Staff Talking," New Library World 76 (May 1975):93-94.
4. John K. Bierman, "Automated Alternatives to Card Catalogs," Journal of Library Automation 8 (December 1975):277-94.
5. A. Maltby and A. Duxbury, "Description and Annotation in Catalogues: Reader Requirements," New Library World 73 (April 1972):260.
6. Jan Gatenby, "The MARC Based Microfiche Catalog at the Milperra College of Advanced Education," LASIE 7 (May-June 1977):23.
7. Maurice J. Freedman, "The Automation of Cataloging--1976," Library Trends 25 (January 1977):703-21.
8. Stephen R. Salmon, "User Resistance to Microforms in the Research Library," Microform Review 3 (July 1974):194-99.
9. "More Libraries Switch to COM Cataloging," Library Journal 101 (November 1, 1976):2213-14.
10. Philip J. Schwarz, "COM: Decisions and Applications in a Small University Library," ERIC Document ED-135-391:6 (November 1976).
11. Robert J. Greene, "Microform Library Catalogs and the LENDS Microfiche Catalog," Microform Review 4 (January 1975): 30-34 and idem., "Microform Attitude and Frequency of Microform Use," Journal of Micrographics 8 (January 1975): 131-34.
12. Philip Bryant and Angela Needham, "You Need Long Nails," Catalogue & Index 33 (Spring 1974):10-12 and Philip Bryant,

"The Bath University Comparative Catalogue Study," Catalogue & Index 41 (Summer 1976):6-8.
13. Valentina DeBruin, "Sometimes Dirty Things are Seen on the Screen," Journal of Academic Librarianship 3 (November 1977): 256-66 and Carole Weiss, "Card Catalogue to On-Line Catalogue: the Transitional Process." Unpublished report, University of Toronto Library, 1977.
14. Carolyn M. Cox and Bonnie Juergens, Microform Catalogs: A Viable Alternative for Texas Libraries (Dallas: AMIGOS, 1977).
15. C. W. Christ, "Microfiche: A Study of User Attitudes and Reading Habits." JASIS 25 (January-February 1972):30-35 and Donald Holmes, "Determination of the Environmental Conditions Required in a Library for the Effective Utilization of Microforms." ERIC Document ED-046-403 (1970) and Ralph R. Lewis, "User's Reaction to Microfiche," College & Research Libraries 31 (July 1970):260-68 and Arthur Tannenbaum and Eva Sidhom, "User Environment and Attitudes in an Academic Microform Center." Library Journal 101 (Oct. 15, 1976):2139-43.
16. D. G. Peake, et al., "Use of Microforms at the New South Wales Institute of Technology," LASIE 6 (May-June 1976):33.
17. Greene, "Microform Library Catalogs."
18. DeBruin, "Dirty Things on the Screen."
19. Lewis, "User's Reaction to Microfiche," p. 264.
20. Howard Pasternack, "Microform Catalog Retrieval Systems," Library Technology Reports 12 (July 1976):401.
21. Weiss, "Card Catalogue to On-Line Catalogue," appendix.
22. Edward G. Roberts and John P. Kennedy, "The Georgia Tech Library's Microfiche Catalog," Journal of Micrographics 6 (July 1973):251.
23. DeBruin, "Dirty Things on the Screen," p. 261.
24. Victor Rosenberg, "Factors Affecting the Preferences of Industrial Personnel for Information Gathering Methods," Information Storage and Retrieval 3 (1967):119-27.
25. George H. Haines, "Process Models of Consumer Decision Making," in Buyer/Consumer Information Processing. (Chapel Hill: University of North Carolina Press, 1974).
26. Paul E. Baldwin, "The B.C. Union Catalogue Project." An unpublished paper presented at the "After the Card Catalogue" workshop held at the British Columbia Institute of Technology, March 3, 1978.
27. Bierman, "Automated Alternatives to Card Catalogues," p. 293.
28. Marcia Bates, "User Studies: What Are They Good For?" an unpublished paper. (Seattle: University of Washington School of Librarianship, 1976), p. 8.
29. H. D. L. Vervliet, "Alternative Forms of Catalogues in Large Research Libraries," International Cataloging 6 (January-March 1977):7.
30. Although this is being done in many public libraries, many academic librarians balk when faced with a project of such magnitude. If the central research library at NYPL can accomplish such a feat, though, so can they. For a suggestion re-

garding how retrospective conversion can be accomplished more easily at a lower cost see James R. Dwyer, "Single File Full Speed Ahead," Hennepin County Library Cataloging Bulletin 34 (May-June 1978):21-23.
31. Freedman, "The Automation of Cataloging--1976," p. 713.
32. Fifty-four percent found the microcatalog easy to use compared to only 7 percent who found it hard to use. DeBruin, "Dirty Things on the Screen," p. 262.
33. "63 percent were satisfied; 31 percent preferred this form." Aldyth D. Scott, "Catalogue Use Survey," New Library World 75 (February 1974):31.
34. 34 percent very easy; 58 percent easy; 8 percent difficult or impossible. Cox and Juergens, "Microform Catalogs: A Viable Alternative," p. 22a.
35. McElderry, "Alternatives to the Conventional Card Catalog," p. 234.
36. Greene, "Microform Attitude," p. 131.
37. Elizabeth Stecher, "RMIT COM Catalogue Study Results," Australian Library Journal 24 (October-November 1975):386.
38. DeBruin, "Dirty Things on the Screen," p. 266.
39. Bryant and Needham, "You Need Long Nails," p. 11.

Questionnaire on Microfiche Catalog Use
(Period I)

Beginning this term the catalog of the University Library is available in microfiche format. In order to make this system as usable and useful as possible, we would like to know your reaction to it. We would appreciate it if you would take a moment to fill in this questionnaire. Thank you.

Status:
___ Freshman ___ Sophomore
___ Junior ___ Senior ___ Graduate
___ Faculty ___ Staff ___ Other

Have you ever used microfiche before:
___ Yes
___ No

How often have you used the microfiche catalog?
___ Often (more than ten times)
___ Occasionally (two to ten times)
___ Rarely (once)

Were written instructions clear and easy to follow?
___ Yes
___ No

Was assistance in using the fiche necessary?
___ Yes   If yes, was assistance readily available:
___ No   ___ Yes ___ No

Was the reader conveniently located:
___ Yes
___ No

Was the reader readily available for use:
___ Yes   If no, how long did you
___ No   have to wait? ___ minutes

There are two separate files, the basic catalog and the supplements to it. What is your evaluation of the quality (legibility)
Of the basic catalog: Of the supplements:
___ Good   ___ Good
___ Acceptable   ___ Fair
___ Poor   ___ Poor
___ Did not use   ___ Did not use

Do you find that the microfiche catalog is:
___ Easier to use than the   ___ Quicker to use than
    card catalog?   the card catalog?
___ About the same?   ___ About the same?
___ Harder to use than the   ___ Slower to use than the
    card catalog?   card catalog?

We welcome your comments, suggestions, etc. (use back of page, if needed):

Questionnaire on Microfiche Catalog Use
(Periods II and III)

Beginning this year the card catalog is also available in microfiche format. In order to make this system as useful to you as possible, we would like to know your reactions to it and would appreciate it if you could take a moment to answer these questions. Thank you.

Status:
___ Freshman ___ Sophomore
___ Junior ___ Senior ___ Graduate
___ Faculty ___ Staff ___ Other

How often have you used the microfiche catalog?
___ More than ten times
___ Two to ten times
___ Once (first time)

Were written instructions clear and easy to follow?
___ Yes
___ No

Was assistance necessary?
___ Yes   If yes, was help available?
___ No   ___ Yes ___ No

Was the microfiche reader (machine) readily available for use?
___ Yes   If no, how long did you
___ No   have to wait? ___ minutes

There are two separate sections, the BASIC CATALOG and the SUPPLEMENTS. How would you rate the legibility of the BASIC CATALOG?
___ Good
___ Fair (Acceptable)
___ Poor (Unacceptable)
___ Did not use

Rate the legibility of the SUPPLEMENTS:
___ Good
___ Fair (Acceptable)
___ Poor (Unacceptable)
___ Did not use

Do you find that the microfiche catalog is
___ Easier to use than the card catalog
___ About the same
___ Harder to use than the card catalog

Do you find that the microfiche is
___ Faster to use than the card catalog
___ About the same
___ Slower to use than the card catalog

We welcome your comments and suggestions (use back of page if needed):

23. The Use and Economics of Computer-Generated Microfiche Catalogs*

by William C. Horner

The D. H. Hill Library of North Carolina State University is currently producing three computer-generated catalogs on microfiche. They are: The Cooperating Raleigh Colleges History Union Catalog, consisting of about 16,000 titles in the Library of Congress "E" and "F" classifications held in the libraries of the six colleges and universities in Raleigh, N.C.; the NCSU Working Collections Catalog, consisting of about 11,000 volumes located in departmental working collections on the North Carolina State University campus; and the NCSU Serials Catalog. Experience with these catalogs has convinced us that they have a number of advantages over printed book catalogs. They are significantly cheaper to produce and particularly to update, and more convenient to use. They are quite acceptable to library users. Their single disadvantage, the fact that they require a microfiche reader, is far outweighed by these advantages. This article will describe the NCSU Serials Catalog and, using it as a model, the production processes, use, and economics of microfiche catalogs and the responses of library staff and library users will be discussed.

The NCSU Serials Catalog consists of approximately 30,000 main entries and cross references and is contained on five 4" x 6" microfiche produced at a reduction ratio of 42X. Each fiche contains 224 computer page images of sixty-four 132 character lines. Each page image is formated into two columns of entries and cross references and is, in fact, precisely the format that would have been used for a printed catalog. Each title record contains the complete main entry, location, call number, library's holdings, and the language of publication.

The 224 page images on each fiche are arranged into rows and columns. The top row contains the first 20 characters of the first entry on that fiche, the date that the fiche was created, and the sequence number of that fiche in the set--all readable without magnification. The last page image on each fiche contains an index to that fiche. The titling and indexing features enable the user to find the entry he is seeking substantially faster than he could in a printed catalog, although to use the indexing effectively the fiche must be read on a reader especially equipped for computer-generated microfiche.

---

*Reprinted by permission of the author from North Carolina Libraries, 33 (Winter 1975), p. 31-33.

The master file of serial records is contained on magnetic tape and is updated monthly. The cost of producing and updating the master tape file is the same whether the final output is a printed book catalog or microfiche. The new monthly master file is processed to produce a computer tape formated for processing into microfiche on a COM (Computer Output Microfilm) device. This tape is sent by courier to a service bureau in Winston-Salem for processing and the microfiche are returned by courier the following day. One-hundred duplicate sets (i.e., 500 microfiche) are produced on the library's microfiche duplicator for distribution to both on- and off-campus locations. There are 17 readers located in the D. H. Hill Library and the three school libraries on the NCSU campus. Fourteen academic departments of the University have purchased readers and receive catalogs. The other 70-odd sets of the catalog are sent to other libraries in the Southeast--university, public, and special.

The serials project at NCSU was begun before the commercial development of COM techniques and the original plan envisioned the production of a printed serials catalog in book form. Fortunately, the service bureau that produces the fiche began solicitating business just at the time the catalog was ready to be printed.

The production of 300 copies of a paperbound book catalog would have cost approximately $3500. Such a catalog would, of course, have been out of date before it was distributed and it would have been necessary to produce supplements to keep it current. The printing costs for 11 monthly supplements would have at least equalled the original printing costs so that the total annual cost for a respectably up-to-date printed catalog would have been approximately $7000. Furthermore, the campus computing center would charge about $35.00 for each camera-ready catalog printout. It is not necessary to produce computer printouts for production of the microfiche since the fiche are produced directly from computer tape.

In comparison, the cost of producing one original microfiche is $3.80 so that the total cost of an original catalog set is $19.00. The cost of duplicating a microfiche is 8 cents (4 cents for material, 4 cents for labor) so that the total cost for duplicating one catalog set is 40 cents. The total monthly cost for producing the sets needed for use in the library is $25.80, or about $310 per year--and there are no supplements to contend with.

There are, however, one-time equipment costs to be considered which include a reader for each location of the catalog and a microfiche duplicator for the production of multiple copies of the catalog. There are a variety of COM microfiche readers available ranging in price from about $100 to $250. These vary in both quality of construction and versatility. At the low end of the price range the readers are cheaply constructed and in practical application their use is restricted to a single fiche format. The more expensive models provide better construction and optics and greater versatility in handling a variety of microfiche formats. After investigating several models the D. H. Hill Library chose the Realist "Vantage II" microfiche reader. This machine is relatively well constructed and provides the capabilities required to use the indexing feature of the microfiche system. Moreover, it offers seven different lenses that can be interchanged instantly by the machine operator so that it can be used for all fiche formats except ultramicrofiche. Most importantly, it provides for variable magnification with the same lens--a feature unique to these machines at the time they were ordered. This last feature enables the library to read government documents produced at 24X and COM catalog fiche produced at 42X on the same reader equipped with a single lens. It is true that the 24X fiche image is somewhat larger than the original and the 42X fiche image is somewhat smaller than the original computer page, but this is a trivial defect. The list price of the "Vantage II" is $180, but, by ordering in quantity, the D. H. Hill Library obtained their readers at a cost of $155 each. The microfiche duplicator cost about $1100, and a binder with inserts costing $3 is also provided with each catalog. Therefore, the total initial equipment and material cost required to issue the microfiche serials catalog and to provide readers at all useful locations in the library approximated $3800, but these were one-time costs. Furthermore, the microfiche duplicator has made it possible to make copies of any of the microfiche in the library's collection and to preserve the integrity of this collection by eliminating the need to circulate the original fiche. Duplicates are provided at nominal charge to users who wish to take the documents from the library.

In summary, the library is able to produce newly updated and complete monthly editions of its microfiche serials catalog with one-time equipment costs of $3800 and annual costs of about $310 as opposed to a book catalog with supplements at an annual cost of over $7000.

When the decision was made to produce the catalog on microfiche, there was considerable concern about how library users and staff would receive this format. Such concern was needless. Both faculty and student users of the library have commented favorably on the catalog and the only complaints expressed related to minor adjustments needed by the readers--not to the catalog format. The library has received many unsolicited complimentary letters from the off-campus subscribers, some of whom requested information to enable them to implement such a system themselves. The reaction of the library staff has been most illuminating of all. After some initial doubt their acceptance is now complete. In fact, the most doubtful member of the staff complained rather bitterly when she was asked recently to work temporarily with a printout instead of the microfiche.

It is the conclusion of the D. H. Hill Library that computer-generated microfiche catalogs are substantially cheaper to produce, more convenient to use, and at least as acceptable to users as are printed book catalogs for applications involving fairly large catalogs and lists. Nevertheless, for some applications we regard microfiche catalogs as a transitional step between card catalogs and real-time computer catalogs accessed by remote terminal. We are presently converting our shelf-list from 1969 onward to machine-readable form using MARC II format and hope to have that portion of the general catalog available for library users at CRT terminals in the library by the end of next year. For the longer term we envision a state-wide or, better yet, a regional system encompassing shared cataloging with data entered into a central computer and made accessible to users at remote terminals in the member libraries. Yet, for some time to come, we believe that microfiche will satisfy the need for inexpensive and timely catalog maintenance.

24. On-Line Computer Terminal Versus COM Systems*

by Frank J. Malabarba and William D. McCullough

The use of on-line systems and COM has increased dramatically over the past 5 years. Every indication points toward continued growth at an increasing rate. Both media, individually or collectively used, can solve many of the problems associated with computerized information systems.

Unfortunately, many organizations overlook the potential cost reduction and system enhancements that are possible by merging on-line and COM technologies. All too often on-line systems are developed without considering the roles micrographics could play in meeting the systems' requirements. Frequently, the resulting systems incur unnecessary cost in software development and added computer hardware.

A number of factors contribute to this problem, primarily, systems designers' ignorance regarding ways in which COM may be used effectively with on-line computer systems. Their ignorance of COM's benefits stems directly from the parcity of user education sponsored by the COM industry, especially in comparison to the computer industry's successful educational efforts related to on-line technology.

This article discusses COM and on-line systems in the following areas: (1) systems design and programming, (2) data retrieval and output speed, (3) distribution, (4) comparative costs, (5) real time/current status and (6) history/audit trails. We will objectively discuss the factors involved and the possible alternatives for combining the two media for maximum effectiveness.

System Design and Programming

Most computer professionals realize that designing an on-line information retrieval system is a lengthy and expensive undertaking, which requires a maximum effort from even the most sophisticated systems and programming staffs. This fact is particularly true if the CRT (cathode-ray tube) is the principal or only medium used to deliver required information from the total on-line information data

---
*Reprinted with permission from the Proceedings of the 26th Annual Conference, Part IV. 1978. National Micrographics Association. ALL RIGHTS RESERVED.

base. Let's consider the more important aspects of on-line system design and programming. These aspects include:

1. Loading (data identification and preparation and file design/allocation and loading).
2. Maintenance (programs for updating, retrieving from, integrity of and purging the data base).
3. Backup (media conversion, distribution and fail soft).

At this point it would be relatively easy to construct a case against a true on-line system, particularly if we examined the steps involved in each of these actions. Rather than rejecting on-line systems, however, we want to point out how much easier system design may become when micrographics, specifically COM, is combined with the on-line system.

For example, the loading task can be reduced to dealing with key fields; the computerized index, to the COM data bases. The maintenance task can be similarly simplified to updating index pointers in the reduced size data base. Programming for data retrieval from only a few fields, where not all of the information is in the total data base, is proportionally reduced. Backup can be virtually built in, since COM-generated indexes could substitute in the event of system failure.

Perhaps the most difficult task when considering COM in conjunction with an on-line system is to define the system requirements and how extensively COM might be used. If the data base already exists, then the COM formatting software for creating the indexes described above are normally available from COM manufacturers and service bureaus.

The programming involved generally concerns incorporating this software with the host programs that maintain the data base. Usually, this is neither a difficult nor lengthy task.

Retrieval and Output Speed

In discussing retrieval and output speed in relation to on-line systems, we must note the glamorous aspects of the data-processing field that were created during the 1960s. Although it is still very much alive today, the 1970s have been dominated by first the mini and now the microcomputer.

People who are familiar with CRTs and on-line information retrieval systems know that it is difficult to beat their output speed. But what did the user have to input to obtain that output? How easy was it to learn the particular retrieval language of the system, and can the user find the answers he/she is really looking for--only if the data is there and is addressable. At the cost of becoming all encompassing, some systems become too cumbersome, which jeopardizes their processing time advantage.

How can an on-line system become more effective, while maintaining those features most wanted by its users? A careful (and unbiased) analysis of the information contained in any large, on-line data base should provide statistics on the key fields, activity percentages, summaries versus details and accuracy.

In analyzing the findings, several distinctions should soon become evident. First, a disproportionate share of the file receives the majority of the activity. Second, a small number of the data fields receive the majority of the action.

Considering the steps that were probably enacted during the design phase of an on-line system to separate "the wheat from the chaff," data will still remain that is not worth the time and expense of storing, updating and retrieving it. At this point an integration of COM-generated microfiche and the on-line system can best be introduced. Overall speed of key information retrieval through the CRT can be increased at no expense in data availability. The data-entry, or keying, part of the retrieval can be simplified and combined with smaller files, with less data to search and less to output to the CRT, resulting in a net increase in throughput. All of the noncritical and detail information can be moved off-line to microfiche and, if needed, referenced on the CRT by fiche number and grid coordinates. Certain functions, however, do rightfully belong to on-line systems; what we are attempting to emphasize is a method to enhance those functions and provide an even better total information retrieval system.

A variety of alternatives for using COM and on-line systems in conjunction to meet the requirements of a given information system exist. The key factors in determining which alternative to use are to clearly define the requirements of the system and to determine what the organization is willing to pay for the system.

The first alternative is to maintain only the most current or critical information from a data base on-line and store the entire data base in a COM file. Defining current or critical data is a management decision and depends on the requirements of the particular system.

An index to all items in the data base would be maintained on-line for rapid access to detail information in the COM file. The advantages to this alternative are:

    1. The COM file would provide backup to the on-line system in the event of computer failure.
    2. The on-line update capability is maintained.
    3. The amount of mass storage required for the data base could be reduced substantially, thereby reducing costs.
    4. Using index sequential software for creating the COM file and index could provide an audit trail on all file activity.

A possible disadvantage to this alternative might be that file inquiry could require two steps.

The next alternative is to put the entire data base on COM and maintain only the index to the COM file on-line. Retaining the on-line update capability may be a requirement of the system.

The COM file and index could be updated on a daily basis if the user is using a COM service bureau that provides overnight turnaround or has an in-house COM system. The advantages of this alternative are the same as those outlined previously, with the added savings in mass storage space.

A third alternative concerns the initial planning for the system. After the system requirements have been defined and weighed against the cost of an on-line system, is it necessary for the data base to be on-line at all? If the system does not require an on-line update capability, could a current COM system meet the retrieval and display requirements of the proposed system? If it could, then the third alternative is a COM system with daily updates.

The primary advantage of a COM-only system would be a dramatic reduction in the time and cost required to implement the system. If the data base already exists, the COM software could be implemented in less than a month in most cases. The disadvantage to this alternative would be the absence of an on-line file update at the point of need.

Distribution

When we discuss distribution in relation to on-line systems, we might be referring to one of two methods: the actual transmitting of data to the requesting terminal(s) or a possible hardcopy followup sent by normal channels, e.g., mail, hand carrying or transmission. Remote batch work falls into the latter category even though it is the primary output simply because it typically means paper, even though dependent on transmission.

Let's examine these two methods from both a pro and con viewpoint. Data transmission has long since lost its novelty and has fast become an everyday part of most computer operations. Data transmission is such an integral part of so many businesses that they would be lost without it. Between airline and motel reservations, checking accounts and credit card electronic funds transfer, point of sale (POS) system and the FBI's NCIC network, data on each and every one of us is transferred around the country every day. Whether it is to verify a charge or to check on a stolen car, the speed with which these systems function usually pleases us, as customers, very much.

Now that we can in some way relate to a personal experience with an on-line system of some sort, I think we can safely say that they have earned their place in the sun. Well, being inanimate objects, computers and their terminals also get their share of a different spotlight, the one we all shine on the culprit when something goes wrong. How recently, not if, but when, have you been told, "The computer is down" or "the line went dead," or worse yet, "it doesn't like that number?"

How do you argue with a computer that is hundreds or thousands of miles away? You don't. But if you could see the files, or information that is being referenced, you could tolerate the waiting time. Watching a clerk weed through a large printout binder or file drawer is just as frustrating, but more understandable.

How about the paper output of on-line systems? Is it really cost effective to use a remote batch terminal (RBT) to print reports which must then follow the traditional route of reproduction and distribution or to supply hardcopies of the data in the on-line files for those "down" times? The answer to both questions is certainly not, especially if you were to compute the cost per character to deliver the data to the end user. It is this facet of on-line systems that makes systems analysts look for alternative methods of information dissemination.

If we really strive to do a better job of information management, we cannot afford to approach the job wearing blinders, like a race horse, but rather we should take the slow approach, looking around at all options before detailing any specific design feature.

Used in conjunction with an on-line system, COM can play a significant role in information distribution. Internally, it may not be necessary for all departments to be on-line to the computer via terminals. If the department in question is merely making inquiries against a file, then having that file on COM in the department may satisfy their requirements for information.

The same philosophy may apply for remote or branch locations. If the data base is not updated on-line from these locations, then perhaps the file on COM at these locations would suffice. Certainly the paper reports generated from on-line systems would be more cost effective if they were sent to remote locations on COM.

Cost

To address the true cost of an on-line information system, many individual components must be examined and costed out. In addition, the characteristics of these components add a degree of difficulty to the costing process. The following chart enables us to examine most of these factors and helps explain why we cannot simply present a one line picture of cost. (See p. 184.)

There are endless varieties of terminals, from teletypes to intelligent terminals, costing from $700 to over $10,000, or $30 to over $300 a month. Phone line costs can be over DDD at long-distance rates (direct dial), WATS lines at a flat rate for unlimited usage or dedicated leased lines at the typical rate of $0.015 per day per mile.

Component	Characteristic
Terminal (printer)	
Lines	
Communications	
Controller-processor	Dependence
CPU and peripherals	Variations
Modems	Sophistication
OS and DBMS overhead	
Backup	

Communications controller-processors run from $50 to $30,000 per month or from $2,000 to over $1 million purchase. Mainframe computer systems capable of on-line operation can cost on rental from $2,000 to $50,000 a month or from $50,000 to over $30 million to purchase. Modems, on the other hand, are relatively inexpensive, renting from $8 to $105 a month and costing from $135 to $9,000. Operating system and data-base management software is supplied free by "unbundled" vendors; but others, including independent software houses, charge up to $1,000 a month or up to $69,000 purchase.

Obviously, the cost of servicing even one terminal cannot be derived from figures like these because most components are used to perform a multitude of tasks, and the amount of time they are shared would require microsecond time accounting in order to allocate costs. Further, the component characteristics indicate that there are endless variations in configurations and degrees of sophistication. Most important, however, is the fact that each component in a typical system depends on the other. If the line is "hit" or a processor goes down, the entire system is affected. The backup components can be added, at extra cost, if priorities dictate, but this simply increases cost a little more.

Although on-line systems are expensive, there are many instances when an on-line system is the only solution and even others where almost any cost is justified. In the military world of command and control systems, for example, you cannot afford the time it would take to identify and allocate your resources on film or paper and then feed parameters to a tactical computer system. It all has to be in the system, instantly updatable and readily transmittable. Or consider the decision a corporate executive must make on a moment's notice requiring up-to-the-minute financial status on the entire corporation, when minutes can cost millions. Obviously, almost any reasonable cost would be justifiable.

Cost/COM Systems

If it is determined that COM can meet the requirements of an information system, then the costs, when compared to an on-line system, are very much less. It is difficult to make an accurate comparison between the two media without specific facts concerning file size, update frequency, number of terminals, etc. A few comparisons that may be meaningful are:

1. A COM viewer can be purchased for less than 1 month's lease of an IBM 3270 terminal.
   2. A COM recorder can be leased for about the same cost as one IBM 3330 disk drive.
   3. A 500,000 page data base could be produced on COM and kept current on a daily basis for less than $6,000 a month.

The major area to look for possible savings in system planning is to use COM in conjunction with on-line systems as a replacement for mass storage devices.

Real-Time/Current Status

Before discussing the topic of real-time/current status, it is important to define these terms. Real time is a term used to describe the characteristics of a computer system that can provide not only on-line access to information but allow immediate update and processing of any new information. This latter feature is the key to the uniqueness of real-time systems. An on-line teller system at a bank is a familiar example.

A teller terminal is connected directly to the bank's computer(s), and all transactions are immediately acknowledged and acted on. Deposits are posted; withdrawals are checked and posted; and mortgage and other time payments are credited while you wait, usually in a matter of seconds. Such a system allows bank officials to know at any time the complete financial picture of the bank, a capability that is mandatory when dealing with millions of dollars that, if not properly managed, can cost the bank thousands a day in either interest penalties or lost income from short-term investments, particularly if the bank also handles demand deposits that fluctuate daily.

When we discuss real time, there are certain functions of an information-processing system that can only be accomplished on-line to a computer. The above are only a couple of examples that demonstrate the power of the computer, the most dynamic example, however, might be airlines reservation systems.

Now that we have real time in perspective, let's examine the chart in Figure 1 showing the demand for information as it relates to the allowed time to provide that information.

Our reservation, banking and inventory systems all fall into the 2- to 5-second response range, and total transaction time may move them into the 1-minute range. Even if we proceed to the 8-hour point, it is still difficult to produce and distribute any appreciable volume of information within that time, certainly not on paper and in only certain cases via COM. But let's look at the 80 percent of information demands that are not needed within 8 hours, those overnight or longer. Now we can open the door to COM-produced information which can satisfy most demands.

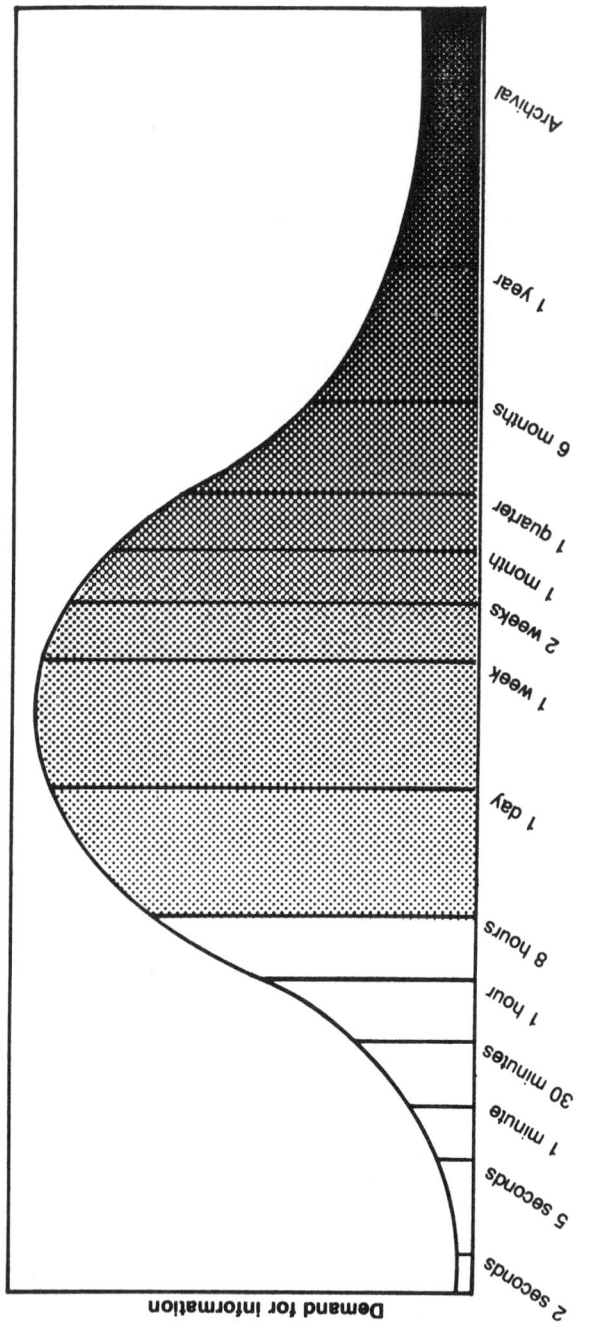

Figure 1 The demand for information in relation to time.

If we consider that the greater majority of inquiries into a data base are usually answered using a small portion of the total data available, we can conclude that there is room for improvement in the structure of the on-line data base. Also, considering that some small percentage of inquiries require information from the total data base, what is the best way to improve such systems?

If cost is a consideration, then possibly the best way to improve the system would be to purge all data over 24 hours old to a COM file. Using the COM software discussed earlier, the index to the COM file could remain on-line to provide for rapid access to the information in the file. This procedure would not degrade the system in any way.

History/Audit Trails

History/audit trails are, in the long run, the most significant factors. The potential to capitalize on the use of information that has been preserved is great, but it can be quickly diminished if it proves impossible to find, read, process or understand. We all know that this has traditionally been an area in which microfilm has fostered as the great preserver in record retention. What we may not realize, however, is that far better systems can be and have been designed and implemented that utilize not only the computer but micrographics, and not separately but together.

In addressing the history/audit trail issue with respect to on-line systems, we must emphasize the accessibility of information as the key feature. With this fact in mind, what happens to data that has outlived its useful on-line life but must begin a new life off-line? In almost every aspect of business today, in one form or another, are regulations that require far more detailed and prolonged record keeping than ever before. Whether one must satisfy the IRS, ICC, FBI or just the consumer, the fact remains that you never know when you are going to need that information. Since it is in our best interest to have data available, we must therefore return to the computer and make better provisions.

When on-line systems design reaches this particular stage, the questions usually faced are: Where do we put this old information and in what format? The first step is usually to purge the data onto magnetic tape and provide for accessing when the need arises. But let's not forget that audit trail is a much more ominous term than history file. Implicit in the term audit trail is the ability to trace cumulative transactions results all the way through a system.

In order to accomplish this procedure on-line, "pointers" are usually provided in the files that send the inquiries either forward or backward through a file to the most current or previous record data. This is necessary because, unlike tape file, disk files are not maintained and updated in the traditional father/son/grandson batch method. Therefore, all transactions are usually saved on tape in case files must be reconstructed from some point in time.

Eventually, the string of information that is tied together by pointers grows too long, becomes outdated and is a burden on the data-base system itself. It is time to purge.

At this point the data can either remain on magnetic tape, be printed out or be preserved on microfilm somehow. It is only lately that this latter format has been recognized as the most cost-effective responsive method. Joining the two technologies together at this point is another of the more versatile examples of the power of COM/micrographics.

If maintenance of an audit trail is a significant requirement of a particular information system, then COM should receive serious consideration. The COM software to accept computer data, files changes, create indexes and maintain an audit trail on all file activity is readily available from most major COM companies. It is neither difficult to install nor expensive.

* * *

In summary, we do not propose COM as a replacement to on-line systems. In most cases, it simply is not possible. However, if COM is integrated into the planning of information systems, it could result in overall system improvements and, in most cases, a significant reduction in the cost of the system. An increasing number of companies are now using on-line and COM technology with great success.

Bibliography

Abbott, George L. Card Catalogs: Alternative Futures; A Selected Bibliography on Closing Card Catalogs and Alternative Catalog Formats With Separate Sections on AACR 2 and PRECIS. Syracuse: Information Yield, 1979.

Altman, E. "Reactions to a COM Catalog," Journal of Academic Librarianship, 3 (November 1977), 267-268.

Altman, Ellen. "On My Mind ... Reactions to a COM Catalog," Journal of Academic Librarianship, 3 (November 1977), 267-268.

American Library Association. Book Catalogs Committee. Guidelines for Book Catalogs. Chicago: American Library Association, 1977.

American Library Association. Reference and Adult Services Division. Catalog Use Committee. Commercial COM Catalogs: How to Choose; When to Buy. Chicago: American Library Association, 1978.

Aveney, Brian and Ghikas, Mary Fischer. "600 Users Meet the COM Catalog," American Libraries, 10 (February 1979), 82-83.

Bath University Comparative Catalogue Study Final Report. Bath: University Library, 1975.

Bierman, K. J. "Automated Alternatives to the Card Catalog," Catholic Library World, 47 (Spring 1975), 74-77.

──────. "Automated Alternatives to Card Catalogs: The Current State of Planning and Implementation," Journal of Library Automation, 8 (December 1975), 277-298.

──────. Automated Alternatives to Card Catalogs for Large Libraries. Washington, D.C.: Council on Library Resources, 1975.

Blackburn, Robert H. Management Experience with COM Catalogs in a Large Academic Library. Toronto: 1977.

Bookstein, Abraham, and C. E. Rodriquez. "Bibliographic Access to Full Descriptive Cataloging with COM," Journal of Library Automation, 11 (March 1978), 41-46.

Bourne, C. P. "Initial Article Filing in Computer-Based Book Catalogs: Techniques, Problems, and Article Frequencies," Journal of Library Automation, 8 (September 1975), 221-247.

Butler, Bret, West, Martha W., and Aveney, Brian. Library and Patron Response to the COM Catalog; Use and Evaluation. Los Altos, CA: Information Access Corporation, 1978.

"COM, Automated Printing Processes and Future Applications," Journal of Library Automation, 10 (March 1977), 86-87.

COM and Its Applications. Silver Spring, MD: National Micrographics Association, 1976.

"COM Database at Columbus for Rent," Library Journal, 103 (November 15, 1978), 2290.
"COMCAT, The Revolutionary Computer Output Microfilm Catalog," Southeastern Librarian, 26 (Summer 1976), 110.
Carter, R. C. "Steps Toward an On-Line Union List," Journal of Library Automation, 11 (March 1978), 32-40.
Cheney, B. J. and others. "Computerisation of the Union Catalogues in CSIRO," LASIE, 8 (March/May 1978), 13-19.
Christoffersson, John G. "Automation at the University of Georgia Libraries," Journal of Library Automation, 21 (March 1979), 22-39.
Chwe, Steven Seokho. "A Study of Data Elements for the COM Catalog," Journal of Library Automation, 12 (March 1979), 94-97.
Cooper, M. D. "Input-Output Relationships in On-Line Bibliographic Searching," American Society for Information Science Journal, 27 (May 1977), 153-160.
Cox, Carolyn M. and Juergens, Bonnie. Microform Catalogs: A Viable Alternative for Texas Libraries. Dallas, TX: AMIGOS Bibliographic Council, 1977.
Cramer, S. A. "Computerised Catalogue in a University Library," Libri, 26 (March 1976), 38-54.
Dataflow Systems, Inc. An Introduction to COM (Computer-Output-Microfilm). Bethesda, MD: Dataflow Systems, Inc., 1975.
DeGennaro, Richard. "Library Automation: Changing Patterns and New Directions," Library Journal, 101 (January 1, 1976), 175-183.
Dewe, Ainslie. An Annotated Bibliography of Automation in Libraries, 1975-1978. London: ASLIB, 1980.
Diaz, Albert J. Microforms and Library Catalogs: A Reader. Westport, CT: Microform Review, 1977.
Dickinson, Liz. "Of Catalogs, Computers, and Communications," Wilson Library Bulletin, 50 (February 1976), 463-470.
Divilbiss, J. L., ed. The Economics of Library Automation. Papers presented at the 1976 Clinic on Library Applications of Data Processing, April 25-28, 1976. Urbana-Champaign, IL: University of Illinois, Graduate School of Library Science, 1977.
Dodd, Sue A. "Building an On-Line Bibliographic/MARC Resource Data Base for Machine-Readable Data Files," Journal of Library Automation, 12 (March 1979), 6-21.
D'Ooge, C. "Computer Catalog Center Greeted With Enthusiasm," Library of Congress Information Bulletin, 36 (September 23, 1977), 662-664.
Dougherty, Richard M. "Adoption of AACR-2 and Alternative Forms of Catalogs," Utah Libraries, 22 (Spring 1977), 25-27.
Doyle, J. M. and Bosler, G. F. "COM Catalog: It's Progress If You Plan For It," Michigan Librarian, 43 (Winter 1977), 7-8.
Dusenbury, Carolyn. "Alas, Poor Card Catalog," Utah Libraries, 22 (Spring 1979), 29-38.
Dwyer, James R. "Public Response to an Academic Library Microcatalog," Journal of Academic Librarianship, 5 (July 1979), 132-140.

Edelhoff, E. and Lehmann, K. D., eds. On-Line Library and Network Systems. Symposium Held at Dortmund University, March 22-24, 1976. Frankfurt Am Main: Klostermann, 1977.

Emmett, J. "Year in the Life: In March 1976 North Brisbane College of Advanced Education Provided Its First COM Fiche Catalogue for the Library's Users," Australian Library Journal, 26 (May 6, 1977), 108.

"Fairfax County Public Library: COMCAT (Computer Output Microfilm Catalog) Is Coming!" Virginia Librarian, 21 (December 1975), 15-16.

Ferguson, Douglas. "Marketing Online Services in the University," Online, 1 (July 1977), 15-23.

"First Card-to-Micro Catalog Claimed by Harford, Md.," Library Journal, 101 (May 15, 1976), 1164.

Folk, Clara A., Campbell, Bill W., and Bloomfield, Masse. "A Microfilm Card Catalog at Work," Special Libraries, 67 (July 1976), 316-318.

Force, Ronald W. and Force, Jo Ellen. "Access to Alternative Catalogs: A Simulation Model," College and Research Libraries, 40 (May 1979), 234-239.

Freedman, Maurice J. "Automated Network Catalog Products and Services," Journal of Library Automation, 9 (June 1976), 145-155.

Freund, Clare E. "Catalog on Microfiche at the Eastman Kodak Libraries," Special Libraries, 68 (1977), 375-382.

Friedman, Elaine S. "Library Applications of Computer Output Microfilm: An Annotated Bibliography," Special Libraries, 68 (December 1977), 447-454.

Gatenby, J. "North Brisbane College of Advanced Education, MARC Based Microfiche Catalogue," LASIE, 8 (September 1977), 55-56.

Greene, R. J. "Microform Library Catalogs and the LENDS (Library Extends Catalog Access and New Delivery Service) Microfiche Catalog," Microform Review, 4 (January 1975), 30-34.

Grosch, Audrey N. Current and Retrospective Sources of Machine Readable Cataloging Records: A Study of Their Potential Cost and Utility in Automated System Development at the University of Minnesota. Minneapolis, MN: University of Minnesota Libraries, March 1975. ED 107 280.

_____. "Fourth Generation Systems for Libraries: The Marriage of Data Base Management Systems and On-Line Minicomputer Hardware," Special Libraries, 68 (July/August 1977), 221-227.

_____. Minicomputers in Libraries, 1979-80. White Plains, N.Y.: Knowledge Industry Publications, 1979.

Hadlow, J. F. "Some Problems With COM Catalogues," MICRODOC, 16 (1977), 75-76.

Hall, Agnez. "Computer-Produced Book Catalogue for New Brunswick Public Library System," APLA Bulletin, 41 (1977), 33-35.

Harbord, H. "Computer Catalogue at the Dartmouth Regional Library," APLA Bulletin, 41 (1977), 31-32.

Harris, B. "Practical Consideration of the COM/CIM (Computer Input Microfilm) Marriage," Information Hotline, 9 (November 1977), 6-9.

Hill, J. and Brown, N. A. "COM Catalogues at the University of Guelph Library," Microform Review, 7 (July 1978), 213-216.

Hodgkinson, L. "Computerisation in the Lancashire Library," Program, 9 (October 1975), 184-197.

Horner, William C. "Use and Economics of Computer-Generated Microfiche Catalogs," North Carolina Libraries, 33 (Winter 1975), 31-33.

Horny, Karen L. "NOTIS-3 (Northwestern On-Line Total Integrated System): Technical Service Application," Library Resources and Technical Services, 22 (Fall 1978), 361-367.

Howell, John Bruce. "Computer Output Microfilm (COM): Alternative Technology for the Catalogs of North American Research Libraries," Alternative Catalog Newsletter, No. 18-20 (May 1980), 1-67.

Hyatt, Dennis. "COM Catalog vs Card Catalog: The Experience of the University of Oregon Law Library," Law Library Journal, 71 (November 1978), 668-672.

Kaye, Sheldon. "Ms. Clark Meets a Computer: Automation Possibilities for Smaller Libraries," Wisconsin Library Bulletin, 73 (May-June 1977), 109-110.

Kent, Allen. "The On-Line Revolution in Libraries, 1969- ," American Libraries, 10 (June 1979), 339-342.

Kimber, R. T. Automation in Libraries. 2nd ed. Oxford: Pergamon, 1975.

Kimzey, A. C. and Smith, R. "Automated Book Catalog for a Learning Resources Center Periodicals Collection," Serials Librarian, 2 (Summer 1978), 405-410.

Kloepper, D. "Nebraska Union Catalog on COM? Not Enough!" Nebraska Library Association Quarterly, 9 (Spring 1978), 17-18.

Kopischke, J. L. "Community & Technical Colleges Get COM Catalog," Nebraska Library Association Quarterly, 8 (Winter 1977), 4+.

Kountz, John C. "Library Support Through Automation: The California State University and Colleges Plan for Library Automation," Journal of Library Automation, 8 (June 1975), 98-114.

Krikelas, James. "Thinking About Automation? Consider These Factors in Making a Decision," Wisconsin Library Bulletin, 73 (May-June 1977), 98-100.

Kuhner, D. A. "Sprague Library Adopts Microfiche Catalog," Sci-Tech News, 29 (July 1975), 84.

Le Croisette, J. C. "Microfilm Catalogs in a British Public Library System," Microform Review, 4 (April 1975), 104-107.

Leide, J. Development of Automated Systems at Columbia University Libraries. Tempe, Ariz.: LARC Association, 1975.

"Libraries and Co-Ops Go With COM," Library Journal, 102 (April 15, 1977) 864.

"Libraries Expand Use of COM Catalogs," Advanced Technology/Libraries, 6 (February 1977), 1-3.

"Los Angeles & Cook Co. Switch to COM," Library Journal, 103 (January 1, 1978), 10.

Bibliography

"Los Angeles Public Library Moves to COM," Journal of Library Automation, 10 (December 1977), 377.

McElderry, Stanley. "Alternatives to the Conventional Card Catalog From the User Point of View," IFLA Journal, 2 (1976), 232-236.

Magarrell, Jack. "Ticking in the Card Files," Chronicle of Higher Education, 16 (April 3, 1978), 1.

Maguire, C. "Is On-Line In Line? Some Thoughts After a Visit to the United States," LASIE, 7 (January 1977), 2-8.

Malabarba, Frank and McCullough, William D. "On-Line Computer Terminal versus COM Systems," Proceedings of the 26th Annual Conference, National Micrographics Association, Part IV, 1978, p. 116-119.

Malinconico, S. Michael. "Bibliographic Terminals, Development Status--United States--1977," Libri, 28 (June 1978), 101-102.

Malinconico, S. Michael. "Computers and the Catalog Librarian's New View of Reality," Bookmark, 36 (Winter 1977), 30-35.

Markuson, B. E. "Ohio College Library Center System: A Study of Factors Affecting the Adaptation of Libraries to On-Line Networks," Library Technology Reports, 12 (January 1976 issue).

Markuson, Barbara Evans and Tolliver, Don L. Factors Affecting the Adaptation of Academic and Other Libraries to On-Line Networks, a Study of Ohio College Library Center (OCLC) Users Final Report. Washington, D.C.: U.S. Department of Health, Education and Welfare, Office of Education, Bureau of Libraries and Educational Technology, 1975.

Martin, Susan K. "An Odd Couple--AACR2 and Automation," American Libraries, 9 (December 1978), 689-691.

Meyer, R. W. and Knapp, J. F. "COM Catalog Based on OCLC Records," Journal of Library Automation, 8 (December 1975), 312-321.

Meyer, Richard W. and Juergens, Bonnie. "Computer Output Microfiche Catalogs: Some Practical Considerations," Journal of Micrographics, 11 (November/December 1977), 91-96.

"Michigan Public Libraries Converting to COM: Lower Costs a Major Factor," Advanced Technology/Libraries, 5 (January 1976), 1-2.

"Microfilmed Catalog Slated for Baltimore County," Library Journal, 100 (May 1, 1975), 802.

"More Libraries Switch to COM Cataloging," Library Journal, 101 (November 1, 1976), 2213-2214.

Murray, Carolyn K. "Teaching the COM Microcatalogue," RQ, 19 (Fall 1979), 52-58.

National Micrographics Association. COM and its Applications. Silver Spring, Md.: National Micrographics Association, 1977.

North, John. "Card Catalog to COM," Library Journal, 102 (October 15, 1977), 2132-2134.

"OCLC Public Access: Test Run Successful," Library Journal, 101 (October 15, 1976), 2126.

O'Brien, P. M. "COM Comes to the Chicago Public Library," Illinois Libraries, 60 (April 1978), 397-402.

"On-Line Catalog Conversion Commercially Available," Journal of

Library Automation, 11 (June 1978), 171-172.
Painter, Reed B. The State of the Card Catalog: Proposals and Alternatives for the Future. Logan, Utah: Merrill Library, Utah State University, 1976.
Remington, D. G. "Automating LC's Catalogs, " Kentucky Library Association Bulletin, 41 (Spring 1977), 5-9.
Revill, D. H. "Computer Output Microfiche Catalogues, " MICRODOC, 17 (1978), 14+.
Richmond, P. A. "Research Possibilities in the Machine-Readable Catalog: Use of the Catalog to Study Itself, " Journal of Academic Librarianship, 2 (November 1976), 224-229.
Rogers, J. A. "From Cards to COM in St. Louis County, " Unabashed Librarian, No. 25 (1977), 27-29.
Rogerson, M. "Choosing a COM Bureau, " Australian Library Journal, 27 (September 15, 1978), 253-254.
Ross, Joan. "Great Output Race: COM Joins the Winners' Circle, " Journal of Micrographics, 10 (September 1976), 11-15.
Saffady, William. Computer-Output Microfilm: Its Library Applications. Chicago: American Library Association, 1978.
_____. Computer-Output-Microfilm (COM) Hardware and Software: The State of the Art. Chicago: American Library Association, 1977.
Schwarz, Philip. "Computer Output Microfilm: Stout Uses a New Library Tool, " Wisconsin Library Bulletin, 72 (May 1976), 125-126+.
Simpson, George A. Microcomputers in Library Automation. McLean, VA: MITRE Corporation Metrek Division, 1978.
SOLINET Committee on COM. Computer Output Microfilm (COM): An Alternative to Card Catalogs for SOLINET Members. Atlanta, Georgia: Southeastern Library Network, February, 1977.
"Southampton University Library Changes Over From COM Film to COM Fiche Catalogues, " Program, 11 (July 1977), 115-116.
Spaulding, C. M. "Primer on COM (Computer Output Microfilm), An Alternative to Computer Printout, " American Libraries, 7 (July 1976), 468-469.
Spigai, Frances G. , Grams, Theodore W. , and Kawabata, Julie, eds. Information Roundup: Proceedings of the 4th ASIS Mid-Year Meeting, Portland, Oregon, May 15-17, 1975. Washington, D. C.: American Society for Information Science, 1975.
Teague, Sydney John. Microform Librarianship. London, Boston: Butterworths, 1979.
Tedd, L. A. Introduction to Computer-Based Library Systems. Heyden and Son, 1977.
Terry, B. "Microfilm, The Computer and The Librarian, " State Librarian, 24 (March 1976), 2-3.
Thomas, S. M. and Needle, L. P. "Application of COM (Computer Output on Microform) in the Library System, " Microform Review, 4 (April 1975), 95-96.
Thompson, J. "New Catalogs and the Unfinished Evolution, " American Libraries, 10 (June 1979), 357-360.
"University of Birmingham: Microfiche Trial, " VINE, No. 20 (February 1978), 14-17.

Vervliet, H. D. L. "Alternative Physical Forms of Catalogues in Large Research Libraries," International Cataloguing, 6 (January/March 1977), 6-8.

"Virginia: COMCAT (Computer Output Microfilm Catalog) Is Coming!" Southeastern Librarian, 26 (Spring 1976), 42-43.

Wassom, Earl E. and Jones, Richard A. "Bibliographic Access to Full Descriptive Cataloging with COM," Journal of Library Automation, 11 (March 1978), 47-53.

Weiss, Carole, "Card Catalogue to On-Line Catalogue--The Transitional Process," Alternative Catalog Newsletter, No. 11 (February 1979), 31-43.

Weissman, E. "Now Is the Time; or, How I Learned to Stop Worrying and Love an Automated Catalog," Cornell University Library Bulletin, No. 208 (April 1978), 2-7.

West, Martha W., comp. Bibliography of Library Automation. Chicago: American Library Association, 1975.

Williams, Martha E. and Shefner, Gordon J. "Data Element Statistics for the MARC II Data Base," Journal of Library Automation, 9 (June 1976), 89-100.

PART III. PREPARING FOR AN ALTERNATIVE FORM
OF BIBLIOGRAPHIC ACCESS

First, it should be kept in mind that libraries exist to store information and to organize it so that the patron receives the best possible service. Therefore, before making any decision on what type of alternative bibliographic access system the library will utilize, including continuing with the conventional card catalog, user needs should be given top priority. Although there have been some libraries that have done extensive research on closing the card catalog and the alternatives to it, there seems to be no simple solution to this question. And, although a few libraries have closed their card catalogs, it is still too early to tell if this action is the most advantageous to the library user.

It is naturally extremely important for library planners and administrators to examine thoroughly all the facets of changing from a card catalog to some other form of bibliographic access. This includes conversion to an on-line system or a computer generated system, the costs involved, the administrative problems that may arise, and the staff considerations.

Automation Concerns

The library administrator must be aware of the many problems he or she will encounter when automating a library. In addition to those mentioned above, the administrator must be aware of the effects of library automation on the library as a whole and also on the entire university or other parent organization. In order for library automation to be successful, one of the most important factors is institutional commitment. It is necessary for the library administrator to make all the facts known to the necessary institutional administrators. In addition, the library staff needs to be kept aware of the changes as well as the planning involved. The management decision-making process is extremely important in order to provide an efficient transition to an alternative form of bibliographic control.

If the decision is to change to a completely machine-assisted catalog, the existing holdings must be transferred from manual to machine-readable form. This is called conversion. Since cost is an important factor in the conversion decision, many questions must be answered before a library decides to convert its retrospective holdings. For example, why are we converting? Is it for the use of the technical services staff, ease of the user, acquisitions lists, alternative means of displaying bibliographic information, a means to

prepare a catalog for public distribution, interlibrary loan use, etc.
Once the goals have been determined, then the feasibility of conversion can be determined. Next, the decision must be made on how much information is necessary to put into machine readable form. There are several choices here: search key only, a brief record or the complete record. This will depend largely on for whom the library is converting. Whatever method is chosen, careful control of the process must be carried out. Since this process involves the use of staff as well as the use of hardware, it can be very expensive and it is up to each individual library to determine if the benefits of a machine-assisted catalog are worth the cost of providing such a catalog. In order to hold down conversion expenses to some extent, the process can be based on prior conversion of regional, national, or international files already in existence. The development of high quality resource data bases by the Library of Congress and others makes possible considerable cost savings to libraries who wish to build a collection data base.

The Conversion Process

Gorman lists three aspects involved in the conversion process. These are: (1) the selection of data to be converted, (2) the coding of that data to make it acceptable to the machine system, and (3) the transfer of the coded data from human-readable to machine-readable form.* However, the final determination on the conversion decision deals mainly with cost. This is fundamental in the decision-making process.

Perhaps one of the biggest costs involved in conversion is for personnel. This can involve the reorganization of staff within the library to accommodate the conversion activities as well as the hiring of new staff for these duties. However, in many cases, the existing personnel can be reassigned to new duties involved with the machine-assisted system. This does mean that their former duties must be handled by other staff. There can be potential major savings by trading professional positions for library assistant positions or perhaps even by reducing some clerical positions. There will be some training costs involved.

Another cost is for the equipment itself, including the cost of using records on such systems as OCLC or BALLOTS, for example. These costs would consist of the fee necessary to join the system plus use fees.

In addition, libraries converting to an alternative form of catalog will have a start-up cost such as buying or leasing equipment

---

*Michael Gorman, "The Economics of Catalog Conversion," in J. L. Divilbiss, The Economics of Library Automation, (Urbana-Champaign, IL, Graduate School of Library Science, University of Illinois, 1977), p. 124.

Preparing for an Alternative Form   199

in addition to the expense of conversion. This can be somewhat offset, however, by the savings made in card catalog upkeep. The administrator and the library planners need to do extensive research into the most advantageous way to handle this area of library reorganization in order to improve service to the public while still operating an efficient library.

Another alternative to the choice of form of bibliographic access, as mentioned earlier, is simply to freeze the current card catalog. For many libraries, due to the cost and staff necessary to convert, this will be the only alternative.

The articles included in this section are directed mainly toward the administrative aspects of the future of the card catalog. Also included are some views on catalog conversion.

The Readings

Krikelas, in "Thinking About Automation? Consider These Factors in Making a Decision," provides the reader with some reasons why a library should automate, giving special attention to small- and medium-sized public and academic libraries. He outlines the basic steps necessary in this operation and touches on ways of learning more about computers in libraries. The value of shared systems for the smaller library is discussed.

In "Card Catalog to On-Line Catalog--The Transitional Process," Weiss outlines the steps involved in the transition from a card catalog to a microcatalog at the University of Toronto Library. A brief description is given of a user study done at this library. The article also discusses how they use a microcatalog and how the library deals with a closed catalog. User preferences were considered as well as their complaints about the new form of catalog. Some of the problems involved with changing to a new form of bibliographic access are mentioned along with plans for the future to improve their system.

In his article "Automation--Planning to Implementation: The Problems En Route," Pizer discusses the problems which can arise in automating library procedures. The library administrator must be aware of such concerns as institutional commitment to the project, cooperation with institutional data processing departments, personnel, budget, etc., before automation is instituted. Although this article deals with the automation of a circulation system, perhaps some points can be gathered from the experience at the University of Illinois Medical Center that would be useful to a library administrator planning to automate other library operations.

Daily, in "Financial Considerations Involved in Closing the Catalog," gives the reader information on the financial considerations involved in closing the card catalog. The author reviews the cost implications of a new catalog and those involved in the most common alternatives to the card catalog: COM catalogs, book catalogs, and on-line catalogs. Examples of cost figures are discussed for several institutions and some suggestions are given for cutting costs of changing to another form of bibliographic access.

In another article on the managerial approach to the future of the card catalog, "Planning for the Catalogs: A Managerial Perspective," Rosenthal focuses on the decision-making process in changing from a card catalog to some alternative form of bibliographic access. The problems inherent in this transition are discussed along with some recommendations for arriving at these decisions. The plans used for changing the catalog structure at Berkeley are discussed, listing the twelve underlying assumptions on which the detailed plan was based. He also suggests some data that must be in hand before an administrator can make a decision on the future of the card catalog.

In "Automation and the Library Administrator," Montague traces the development of automated systems in libraries through three phases: developmental, operational, and integrative. The article first looks at the changing characteristics of the development of automation in libraries, and the management procedures involved with the changes. The management process of an automated system once it has been implemented is discussed. Also, seven areas of library automation are described. In the integrative phase, the effects of management policy--as well as the way management decisions can affect the success of the system--are considered.

Pflug, in "The Effects of Automation on Library Administration," stresses the importance of proper planning before automation and discusses the side effects that can occur after automating library procedures. This article deals generally with the automation of all library processes and how it will affect the staff, work processes, etc. Although this article does not deal specifically with the card catalog, it is important for the library administrator to take an overall look at how automation of one operation will affect the library as a whole.

Before any library can totally change to a machine-assisted system, it must convert its retrospective holdings to the new system. Several articles on this topic are included here. In the first one, "The Retrospective Conversion Project at the University of Utah Marriott Library," Kao describes the conversion techniques and strategies used at this large academic library. Included in the discussion are staff training procedures as well as statistics on the number of records converted and those found in OCLC.

Watson, in "Converting a Card Catalogue to Microfiche," gives the step-by-step process followed in converting the holdings in the Footscray Institute of Technology Library into a microfiche format, a first step to a COM catalog. Six stages for preparing the card catalog are listed, with time frames and cost figures for this particular library and some suggestions for future improvements.

The final article in this section appeared in a recent issue of the Library of Congress Information Bulletin. "Freezing the Library of Congress Catalogs" discusses the timetable and procedures the Library of Congress has prepared for freezing its card catalogs. The policy on descriptive cataloging of post-1980 records and updating existing MARC bibliographic records is discussed, along with other important topics such as subject headings, serials check-ins, linkages, etc.

25. Thinking About Automation?

Consider These Factors in Making a Decision*

by James Krikelas

With the passing of time, arguments in favor of using computers in libraries--what may be termed library automation for brevity--will continue to mount. The question of a decade ago, "Is automation really feasible?" has changed to the question "Isn't automation inevitable?" It is in the realm of possibility that by the 1990s the library without some type of computer may be as rare as libraries with computers were in the 1960s.

With an increasing number of apparently successful applications of library automation, some librarians will begin to feel greater pressure to automate now! It seems appropriate, therefore, to stop for a moment and ask the single, most important question: "Why automate?" The answer to this question is neither simple nor self-evident. It is the purpose of this brief essay to look at some of the reasons others have given and to look at some potential library operations that can be automated. Special attention will be given to the needs of small- and medium-sized public and academic libraries.

There are at least two very obvious reasons for automating library operations. First, the manual system becomes so overloaded that it is breaking down and needs to be replaced. The second reason frequently given is that the manual system's cost of operation is rising so rapidly that some change is imperative.

Atwood and Livingston, in an article appearing in the April 1969 issue of Special Libraries, identified three other reasons for employing computers: fashion, curiosity and challenge. For some librarians, the very idea that computers were something new was enough to motivate them to automate. For others, curiosity about the machine's potential and the library were the rationale for automation.

The authors called these three reasons "unmentionables" which could imply that they were "bad" or, at least, "wrong" reasons. It would be more profitable, however, to recognize that

―――――――――
*Reprinted by permission of the author and publisher from Wisconsin Library Bulletin, 73 (May/June 1977), p. 98-100.

there is nothing wrong with any of them although each becomes less justifiable as time passes. In fact, the library profession is indebted to these pioneers for having accepted the challenge to satisfy our collective curiosity and for helping us learn through their experiences.

It is obvious that as each librarian contemplates library automation, much can be learned from the experience of others and it is hoped that these lessons will continue to be shared. The decision to automate, however, must be made on objective grounds and should be based on the factors relevant to the local library situation (whether it is a single library or a library system).

Under what circumstances, then, is it most plausible to consider the use of a computer in the library? The most rational response, of course, is the one in which the computer appears as a viable alternative to other, usually manual, systems. And the major reasons for seeking such alternatives, as noted above, tend to be a breakdown in the current system due to work overload and staggering increases in the funds required to provide normal library services.

Seeking alternatives and planning for change can lead, under the most ideal circumstances, to traumatic moments. For those who can afford the luxury, advanced planning and evaluation is much less painful than the planning that must be done in a crisis situation. (In fact, librarians must recognize the importance of the planning function as part of their professional activities. The individuals who are "too busy" to plan because they are "busy doing" may want to pause for a moment--because they are likely candidates for change!)

The first step in the planning process is the most difficult; it requires an explicit statement of the library's objectives. The next step involves the evaluation of the various library programs and routines to ascertain how they serve to achieve these objectives. Quite frequently objectives and routines are stated in terms of the familiar--that which can be done--rather than in terms of the desirable.

If there is one major benefit derived from planning library automation it is that the process has permitted librarians to envision a wide range of programs and operations which were once thought to be impossible. Of course, many of these may still be economically prohibitive, but the listing of all objectives frequently stimulates ideas about possible alternative methods. To determine the feasibility of the use of the computer requires some knowledge about the nature of the machine. And it is lack of such knowledge among many librarians that becomes a barrier to planning.

Assuming a decision has been reached at least to consider the possibility of automating, where does one learn about the computer? Getting to know about computers is about the same as getting to know about anything else that is mysterious or unfamiliar (mechanical or otherwise). Some will find it plausible to learn through reading! The library often will own enough material on the subject to permit a simple, basic grasp of the computer's potentials and limitations. Others may find it desirable to take formal courses. Such classes may be found in the local high school (as evening courses), at the area technical and vocational schools or at a nearby college or university.

Additional assistance can be sought from various state institutions including the state library agency and the university's extension division. Equally important as a source of information are the numerous librarians who have already done some work with the computer. It is expected, however, that since for most librarians the computer is such a "technical monster" a combination of approaches will be desirable.

As one acquires some familiarity with the computer's capabilities the natural subsequent question becomes "Is it economically feasible?" It is unfortunate that no simple answer can be provided for this question; the answer depends on many local variations and conditions. But the factors to be considered can be broadly sketched. First, comparisons of cost must be made on the basis of concrete evidence: "What does your current system cost?" Then, one needs to be able to determine what the costs will be in the future, projecting estimated costs over the next five or ten years.

For many large libraries, automation was the only solution because it was determined that although there was a high initial cost for conversion, the projected cost for future years of using the manual system would exceed the projected yearly costs--for the same period of time--for the computerized system. Thus the slower rate of increase, rather than lower costs, was the determining factor in reaching the final decision.

Although larger libraries have concluded that it is economically feasible to convert many of their operations from manual to computerized systems on their own, it is a less likely prospect for small- and medium-sized libraries. The potential for automation for smaller units, therefore, rests upon the development of shared systems: systems developed by groups of libraries working cooperatively or systems purchased (or rented) from a vendor.

What library operations are candidates for such cooperative development? Virtually every type of library operation has been successfully implemented in individual libraries and many could serve as the basis for expanded, joint development. The practicability of large-scale multi-purpose networks has also been demonstrated. The Ohio College Library Center (OCLC) and Stanford University's Bibliographic Automation of Large Library Operations using a Timesharing System (BALLOTS) are the two prime examples of the latter. At the same time, there continues to be a paucity of data that could serve as the basis for making decisions about the appropriateness of automation for individual libraries.

The experience gained from current practice appears to justify two very tentative conclusions. First, operations that require the creation and maintenance of large files of bibliographic records in machine-readable form tend to be cost effective only for the largest libraries or library systems. Second, it appears that routines that utilize a combination of computer-assisted operations with certain manual processes are much more likely to be cost effective. If these conclusions are valid then the most likely candidate for automation for smaller library units would seem to be circulation. With adequate planning, this semi-automated system could serve as the basis for subsequent computerization of other library operations.

It is beyond the scope of this brief essay to detail any particular system that would be appropriate for any specific library. Indeed, the principal theme has been that the ultimate decision to automate can be made only at the local level. Systematic analysis of current operations and critical investigation of alternative methods will benefit the library regardless of the nature of the final decision: to automate or not to automate!

26. Card Catalogue to On-Line Catalogue--The Transitional Process*

by Carole Weiss

I. Preparation for Closing

Plans to use the computer to improve access to the diverse and decentralized libraries at the University of Toronto began at least 15 years ago. Our collections, totalling over 4,000,000 items, are housed in about 50 libraries which seem to be constantly shifting as University needs change. In 1965 we began conversion of catalogue records to machine form; by 1967 we adopted the first LC/MARC format for these records. Our new research library for humanities and social sciences was designed with facilities for computer terminals which would provide an eventual on-line catalogue.

Despite this long history and seemingly clear objective, it came as a profound shock to library staff when the decision was made in July 1975 to close the card catalogue in one year's time. The reasons for this decision are ones with which you are no doubt familiar from discussions in your own library. The card catalogue did not provide the capabilities offered by the computer:

- to update and change subject headings and location information
- to decentralize access to a union catalogue
- to produce one integrated file of various bibliographic records through machine translation programmes
- to apply Boolean logic in searching records.

By 1975 the cost of maintaining even one card catalogue--in a system such as ours--had resulted in huge backlogs particularly in updating of location information for collections which have been transferred or closed. The timing of the decision to close the card catalogue was partly determined by a substantial reduction in the library budget and our resulting inability to continue a manually filed card catalogue while developing a new computer based system.

Reader Services staff had not been involved in planning for automated catalogue systems and to us, the frequently postponed predictions of library automation staff had seemed unreal. However, when it became clear that the primary tool for access to the collec-

---
*Reprinted by permission of the author and publisher from Alternative Catalog Newsletter, No. 11 (February 1979), p. 31-43.

tion was about to be drastically changed, reader services staff finally woke up and decided it was time to have some influence over the outcome of that change.

I should note at this point, that a key factor in our library climate at that time was our recent involvement in the Association for Research Libraries' Management Review and Analysis Program. This self study had involved a large number of staff from all parts of the library and had greatly improved communication between areas. It had also provided us with the skills and knowledge needed to contribute useful input to the decision-making process.

Reader Services staff decided that what was needed was a position paper that would generate discussion and increase awareness of the library users' requirements. Reference staff immediately did a literature search. We found several studies which stimulated our thinking: the Bath University study suggested some possibilities on user preferences for catalogue formats, New York Public Library's experience provided background on the question of freezing versus closing of the card catalogue, and particularly useful was Richard Palmer's study, a survey of user requirements conducted at the University of Michigan. No model existed, however, which provided definitive answers to our problems in a large decentralized academic library. We therefore initiated two simple surveys.

In the first, we analyzed in-person and telephone requests at our Catalogue Information Desk to determine what information users expected to find in the catalogue and which access points they most frequently used. In person over 60% wanted a specific work, 29% asked by author and 33% by title. About 30% wanted material on a given topic. Nearly all telephone callers were looking for specific items, 42% requested by author, 53%, by title.

Users' perceptions of their own needs were somewhat different. In answer to a questionnaire distributed at our three main libraries, 77% of the users were looking for a specific item; 85% said they would look first under the author's name. Few thought they looked for material under title. Their most frequent complaints about the card catalogue were the two classification systems, old and new (LC); difficulties caused by filing rules; and inadequate subject headings. When asked about preferences for an alternative to card catalogues, 37% said they would prefer computer terminal access, 30% a book-form catalogue, 26% wanted to keep the card system, and only 6% wanted a microform catalogue. A large number of users expressed dissatisfaction with the possibility of a microform alternative, because of problems with handling and eyestrain. Their negative reactions seemed generally based on past experiences in trying to consult newspapers on microfilm.

With this much information a group called the "Reader Services Task Force on the Design of Services in a Machine-Readable Environment" drafted a list of guidelines which was intended to state general goals for the provision of services when the card catalogues were closed. It was noted that our card catalogue system, which attempted to give a fairly high standard of bibliographic information to all users, failed to provide the majority with the speed of access they desired, and also failed to provide many of the access points and descriptive information the more specialized users sought. To cope with increasing demand and diminishing resources it was considered essential that we create a system in which the majority of users could find what they wanted independently.

Reader Services proposed 1) a simplified on-line finding list giving location and availability information which would satisfy the 60-80% of users looking for known items; 2) an improved subject retrieval system making use of on-line search capabilities; 3) full bibliographic records made available, on a more limited basis, not necessarily on-line.

Near the end of this intensive planning period, some of our most valuable information was gathered through experimentation with a public on-line shelflist. The Call Number Query System was an interactive computer programme which provided call number access to the Library's database in a compressed format. The user could display a particular record, browse forwards or backwards through the shelflist, and if desired, print out bibliographies of selected records.

Computer terminals placed in five sites in the Library were closely monitored for type and frequency of use. In the two sites where terminals were placed in locations freely accessible to the public, use was extraordinarily high. The terminal in our main catalogue room had constant line-ups. After the first week we had to insert a message asking users to give those waiting in line a chance. We were surprised to find that users asked for very little instruction in the system, and were extremely inventive in finding what they wanted using the limited call number access. Although some assumed that this system was the rumored replacement for the card catalogue and expressed dismay at having no author or title access, most complaints stemmed from overly high expectations of "The Computer." Some users would type in very specific topics, for example: "I have to write about the influence of Dante on three nineteenth century writers" and hope that a nearly finished essay would be printed out. One unexpected but logical result was that most of these specific requests could be answered by our traditional reference services or by other computer databases offered through the Dialog or Orbit systems. Use of these commercial database services mushroomed during the three month period.

The conclusion of this experiment was that user reaction was in fact too positive. It became apparent that to add on-line access by author, title and subject, we would need much more terminal access than our system could then provide. The added speed and convenience of the system increased the demand for the service far beyond our original estimates, which had been based on use of the card catalogue.

Various planning groups worked intensively from January to June 1976 in an effort to overcome problems without compromising our objective: a replacement for the card catalogue that would improve services for the user and stay within budgetary limitations. In addition to the management team ultimately responsible for decisions, the key groups which accomplished this task were two implementation teams: one charged with working out all details related to data base integration and application; the other, with coordinating orientation and training. Both teams were made up mainly of non-administrative staff from all areas of the library. Their attention to detail, and their sense of responsibility in keeping other staff in touch with new developments and consequent alterations in plans were absolutely crucial in creating staff confidence in the new system. The orientation team distributed frequent newsletters. They also held general and small group sessions to train all staff in the new system and to allay fears about the impact of technology on library jobs. Reader Services staff conducted a comprehensive user instruction programme employing various media, the most successful of which were flip charts, brochures and seminar sessions.

II. What We Have Now

Our card catalogues were closed as scheduled on July 1, 1976. The main union card catalogue is not completely frozen. New serial holdings and non-Romanized entries are added. When corrections are made, cards are pulled and the corrected version appears only in the machine records. Since records for some material, mainly in affiliated libraries, are not yet in the database, we expect to retain the card catalogue for some time.

What replaces the card catalogue? The least preferable alternative, according to our prior user survey, a microform catalogue. Fortunately for everyone, the users love it.

The microcatalogue now includes about 1,300,000 records with nearly 6,000,000 access points. Old class and Library of Congress classification systems are interfiled. We have begun adding our government documents, and audiovisual material; which are classified in separate schemes. The whole catalogue is cumulated annually, with monthly cumulative supplements.

Our microcatalogue is arranged in four separate sequences, by shelf list order, by author, by title and by subject. The full bibliographic record, i.e. the usual information found on Library of Congress cards, appears only in the Shelf-list section. The other listings are brief form indexes giving author, title, edition statement, date of publication, call number, holdings, and location of the item. This division of indexes was perhaps our most hotly debated issue. The controversy among librarians appeared to be largely an emotional one, some maintaining that a dictionary filing arrangement would result in total mayhem and others asserting that a classified catalogue was the only logical choice. The breakdown seemed to be along lines of national origin and library school training rather than the result of concrete evidence. In the end the Chief Librarian cast the deciding vote and made the choice. The separation of author and title has proved a distinct improvement for users who did not know what to look under when confronted by our author/title card catalogue. No one seems confused by the change in the split.

Other significant improvements are the inclusion of all titles including general ones such as Handbook of psychology and all series, for example, Penquin books. These have proved extremely useful in reference work. Filing is strictly alphabetic as in a telephone directory: umlauts are ignored, Mac and Mc file separately, and punctuation is ignored in the subject arrangement. Most important, it is no longer necessary for a library user to learn what we mean by main entry to find the complete information about a work. The amount of frustration this saves is impossible to calculate. We have kept the main entry concept for the internal purposes of construction of the database. For those who want to know, the main entry is in capitals. The user, however, can find his book without learning cataloguing rules.

The microcatalogue is produced on both microfilm and microfiche. At present we have 67 permanently loaded motorized microfilm readers in high use locations and 75 fiche readers scattered throughout the library stacks and around campus.

What has happened to on-line access for the public? We have new plans which will come into operation this fall when we begin to implement a Circulation and Inquiry System operated on a minicomputer. Although I hesitate to predict at this point, it appears that the development of mini-computers will bring costs to a level at which extensive on-line public access is feasible. Meanwhile to everyone's surprise, our computer print-out bibliographies have been superseded by the relative ease and low cost of microfilm print-outs. The now antiquated Call Number Query System is used only in the production of overdue notices. Our cataloguing system operates online, but is not used directly by the public. Reference staff use it on a limited basis for verification and interlibrary loan purposes.

We also have some computer produced book-form catalogues for smaller collections such as the Government Publications collection. Even these locations find the amount of paper and the cost of updating serious disadvantages and now prefer the main microcatalogue.

III. How It Has Worked Out From a Reference Point of View

In general, library users are enthusiastic about the microcatalogue. Staff fears of having to face increasing numbers of hostile and dissatisfied users never materialized. From the first day students appeared to prefer looking for material on a screen to looking in drawers of cards. It amazed us to find people choosing to wait for a microfilm reader rather than use the card catalogue in the same room.

It is possible that after years of being accustomed to the television screens, younger users actually feel more comfortable with the similar microcatalogue screen than they do with paper catalogues. Most users needed little or no instruction, and in retrospect, I think that our comprehensive orientation programme satisfied our own staff needs more than the users'. Very few users ever understood the intricacies of our card catalogue and seemed virtually unaware of what we regarded as revolutionary changes in the catalogue structure.

Our evaluation of the first year's operation of the new system included collection of use statistics as well as another questionnaire. Again, in the main catalogue areas title access tended to be used slightly more than author. Use of the shelflist with full bibliographic information represented less than 10% of the total use. In answer to the questionnaire, users continued to say they mainly consulted the author section, however. With the exception of library staff more than half said they never consulted the full bibliographic record. Those who did, used it mainly for its classified subject approach rather than to find bibliographic details about a work. (Orientation staff are now planning better publicity to explain the potential uses of the shelflist approach.) A majority of undergraduate and graduate students found the microfiche catalogues easy to use. Most faculty, however, ranked it only fairly easy. The motorized microfilm catalogues were considered easy to use by all groups. Nearly 90% found the present division of catalogues into author, title, subject, and shelflist sections satisfactory.

The most frequent user complaint was that there were not enough machines. Some people, particularly those with poor eyesight found the microcatalogues hard on the eyes. Problems cited included glare, entries too crowded, print too small, dirty screens, poor lighting, and difficulty of keeping one's place when copying information.

Numbers of favorable comments such as "excellent innovation," "vast improvement," "very convenient tool" outweighted the unfavorable "I don't trust them," "I inherently dislike machines." One graduate student wrote "For years I pined away for a catalogue of some sort that would be on hand in the stacks near to where I do most of my work. The microcatalogues you have installed save me a great deal of time, and I'm grateful."

Library staff, although pleased with the user reactions, are more aware of problems with the system. Until all material is included in the database, there are more places to search. For staff, who know all the possibilities, this means more checking to be certain that we do not have an item. The removal of cards from our closed catalogue when records are corrected or copies added has created more difficulties than were foreseen. Our thinking in making this decision had been that anyone using the card catalogue would find only correct information. For example, users would not be sent to wrong locations because of failure to check the microcatalogue. However, when new editions or copies of works are added, the cards are withdrawn, resulting in surprising gaps in the card catalogue listings for the most widely read authors. I am not sure that there is any good answer to questions of how to close the card catalogue, but we probably would have been better off not to have withdrawn cards so extensively.

Until we have an automated authority system, probably two years away, we lack cross-references in the microcatalogue. While users undoubtedly miss finding some material, the problem is partially offset by the additional entries provided, particularly for corporate bodies and journal titles.

Obtaining good quality film reproduction of the length required for our film readers was an unexpected problem at first. On the other hand loss or theft of microfiche was not a problem at all as some people feared; nor has breakdown of the machines been a burden.

In the next cumulation of the complete catalogue we hope to correct most of the record errors found in the first edition and to improve legibility.

Probably the most difficult part of the transitional process is a general human impatience with imperfections, especially on the part of professional staff who feel a responsibility for providing good quality service. We have made great efforts to clear up minor problems and to agree on priorities for attacking major ones. But the librarian who is blocked in a search by an error or omission, normally reacts first with feelings of annoyance and frustration rather than calmly thinking, oh yes, this problem is priority number 17 and will be solved in 1979. Staff must clearly devote an unusual amount of energy to problem follow-up during the change process.

Another general problem is the difficulty of predicting all the ramifications of a change. This discovery of unexpected uses is at the same time, the most exciting and rewarding part of the effort. For example, use of our old classification material more than tripled when the microcatalogue was introduced. Reference staff in exploring the cataloguing databases discovered the economical use of different search keys such as ISBN for verifying recent publications. Based on experiences with search systems for databases available from commercial sources, reference staff have also been able to provide proposals for improved subject access to our own collection. Technical services staff, in their eagerness to add as much as possible to our database found new ways of handling records. This effort, while extremely beneficial from many points of view, unfortunately resulted in an unexpected growth of the catalogue supplement and consequent budgetary problems.

Further complications are introduced by constant change in

technology. The development of the mini-computer has greatly altered the focus of our planning within the last year. Present user preference for our microfilm catalogue seems largely based on our selection of a particular machine. If inexpensive portable fiche readers were made available, reader demand might change completely. I know that one smaller library which has converted to a microform catalogue, can afford to cumulate completely every month and change the arrangement as often, thus making the fiche catalogue quite a different tool from ours. The potential for flexibility is so great and so tempting that there is a danger of going off in too many directions. Especially in a large library, a tremendous effort must be made to keep communications going so that changes do not have unwanted effects.

From our experiences so far, I can only conclude that what we are involved in is much more complex than a transitional process from A to B, Card Catalogue to On-line catalogue. With so many variables, I do not think that anyone can predict quite where the process will lead. Perhaps our biggest mistake was in not introducing small experimental changes in our system to users sooner, so that we would not now be facing so many unknowns. The present technology offers exciting potential for librarians to improve access to information. Reference librarians, with daily experience in using a multitude of indexes requiring different search strategies, have a unique knowledge of the vast range of possibilities and the likely impact on users. We are in a strong position to influence the future systems of bibliographic access if we only take advantage of the present opportunity.

27. Automation--Planning to Implementation; the Problems En Route*

by Irwin H. Pizer

"The best laid schemes of mice and men gang aft a'gley." These words, penned by Robert Burns some 200 years ago, are especially appropriate for those who have experienced the difficulties of bringing an automated system into being. The course of automation, like true love, never did run smooth, and there are many pitfalls that must be avoided in the accomplishment of the goal.

Anna Russell gave the following bit of advice to those determined individuals who have turned IBM's motto of THINK into SCHEME. First, make a list of all the things you want out of life. Next make a list of all the people you know who have those things. Then you can set about getting them in an organized, systematic fashion--Sic semper automation.

Institutional Commitment

Probably the most important element leading to the successful completion of any automation effort is institutional commitment. Unless the parent organization which the library serves, and from which funds must be obtained, is fully in agreement regarding the advantages which will accrue from the projected system, then an almost insurmountable obstacle exists. The librarian must, therefore, be knowledgeable and must understand clearly what the planned automation project will and will not do; why the project is important to the library and its effective functioning; and how the project will help to meet the goals of the institution. Together with institutional approval must come an institutional commitment of funds, and perhaps more important, there must be an institutional priority for the project which is compatible with the needs of the library. For example, many systems have foundered late in the game because the needs of other departments ranked higher and were thus attended to first. Suppose that the automation project for the library is being performed by the data processing department of the institution. If the work of another department with a higher priority expands, then less time may be available for the library program, or if there is an emergency, and it comes to a choice of running the library program or producing the pay checks for all employees, it is clear which task will take precedence.

*Reprinted by permission of the author and publisher from Bulletin of the Medical Library Association, 64 (January 1976), p. 1-4.

In many institutions, the acquisition of a large computer can initially produce a situation where there is more capacity than there are tasks. This is a wasteful state with which no administrator will be pleased. As a result, the canny computer center manager or administrator will look for projects which can be developed to use this excess capacity. One should be wary if the library program is used for filler, for it can be readily foreseen that the time will come when other projects will push the library program off the computer. This phenomenon is not limited to small projects and small libraries.

Consider the history of the circulation automation program at the Denison Memorial Library, University of Colorado Medical Center. Here, an excellent system was developed, programmed, tested, and was ready to become operational when the library was informed that no computer time was available for running the system. The expenditure in both state and federal funds for the system was thus wasted, and a system which many people hoped would prove a prototype for other libraries cannot be used.

A hazard which is totally uncontrollable is that of change of administrative personnel and a consequent change of institutional direction. Because there is little that can be done about this situation, it is simply mentioned so that we do not forget that it can occur.

Problems With Institutional Data Processing Departments

Another serious problem is that of an institutional data processing department which is sure that it can do the job that is needed by the library, but the department encounters various problems in performing at a satisfactory level. The reasons for such problems are varied, but several examples will illustrate the point. No one programmer may be given the responsibility for all of the library program; it is farmed out in bits and pieces to many people, none of whom has the opportunity to become sufficiently expert to perform quickly or well. The data processing group, not completely understanding the requirements of the library system, may try to mold it to fit standard data processing methods and techniques used for handling business data. Data processing personnel may find that the requirements of the library system are considerably more sophisticated than they had first supposed and as a result the system is difficult to program. In this case the library may be told that the "machine" cannot do the things that the library needs to have done. A response of this kind should serve as an immediate warning that the library will end up with a system which is unsatisfactory from its point of view and will only be second-rate at best. Because of the likelihood that such a response may be received, the library should have either a knowledgeable staff member (in a big library there should be a systems librarian) who can deal with this problem or should have access to impartial outside people for advice who are knowledgeable about library automation.

A case in which some or all of these problems have occurred is at the University Library at the Urbana/Champaign campus of the University of Illinois. Here a planned circulation system for the undergraduate library has never become operational, and the automation of the acquisition department records has generated more problems perhaps than it has solved. Note that the problems with circulation systems recur and one can cite many examples of unsatisfactory automation attempts in this area, partly because the task appears to be simple and akin to store inventory, but is actually more complex.

Automation of Circulation at the University of Illinois at the Medical Center

A problem that is happily uncommon, terminated four years of work on a circulation system for the University of Illinois at the Medical Center. In 1970/71 specifications were written for a circulation system to meet the needs of the library. We hoped to use the work done in Colorado, and as a result, the same type of equipment was specified. (As a general rule of thumb, it is cheaper to tie into an existing system than to create a new system.) As the implementation phase progressed, it became clear that there would be differences between systems, but the differences could be handled by the terminals and hardware that were originally specified. Because of the cost of the system, it was necessary to place the purchase order for the hardware by bid; the vendor who placed the lowest bid was the same vendor used by Colorado. This was a small manufacturer of hardware with an excellent reputation, and it had been noted that this firm was flexible and willing to work closely with the library to customize the necessary terminals to meet the needs of the library. Because of the time involved in bidding, it was not until early 1973 that the actual order for the machines was placed, for delivery at the time of the opening of the new library building. Due to a change in manufacturer specifications, the system was slightly altered, requiring the whole package be rebid, but the same vendor again won the bid. Concurrently with these procedures, the library was producing the necessary machine-readable book cards, was preparing to produce machine-readable user identification cards, and had purchased terminals from another vendor for printing notices and date due slips, as part of the total system.

The library then received word that the small manufacturing firm with which we had been working for three years had been sold to a larger company. Although that news was not entirely welcome due to the reputation of the larger firm, assurance was given that there would be no affect on the library's order. Then came the first delivery date in the fall of 1973, and no equipment arrived. The library was informed that the manufacturing plant was being moved and that there would be a delay of a couple of months in delivery. With the next missed delivery date, the library was promised that a delivery date of October 1974 would be met. In October 1974, the delivery date came and went, and the library was told, with profuse apologies, that delivery would take place in December, absolutely. In December the library was informed that certain vital documentation, necessary for building the computer interface equipment, had been lost in moving, and that delivery would take place in the spring of 1976. It was now clear that the manufacturer's own internal priorities had been reordered and that library systems were no longer a primary product. At that point, and because the firm was now on the brink of bankruptcy, the library faced the difficult decision to scrap the entire project as it had been originally planned, and begin again. Other libraries caught in the same double play with this manufacturer are still hoping to receive equipment at a future date.

One reason that reconsideration of the library's system was not altogether unattractive in 1975, was that in the years since 1970, considerable technological advances had taken place in two areas, both of which may have significant impact on library automation. Relatively inexpensive minicomputers now seem to provide an attractive and practical solution to many of the problems which have been noted. In addition, light pens for reading bar-coded markings, like those we are seeing with increasing frequency on grocery product labels, have been developed. Although the initially specified system would have been satisfactory for the needs of the library, the new technology makes it possible to explore and integrate other library operations, both in-house and with other libraries in the geographic region.

Personnel

Personnel are the key factor in any library automation program, and because automation is usually a threatening experience for most people, the problems with acceptance of automation are vitally important. Automation does not usually eliminate jobs in libraries, but rather frees staff members to perform additional tasks and to provide additional services. It should be clearly put to administrators that hopes for automation to reduce the cost of running the library are largely illusory. What will be achieved is a slowing of the rate of growth of library expenditures for personnel, if the system works. Besides convincing the administration on this point, it is important to make it clear to library staff. It is also helpful to conduct training programs for the staff so that they lose their initial fear of "the machine" and learn to regard it as just another piece of office equipment, like the typewriter.

Budget

One should also take an honest look at the budget for a proposed system. An overzealous salesman will make many claims and promises as to the cost of the system, and it is wise to make sure that the estimates are realistic (barring the uncertainties of inflation) so that one is not caught in the position in which the allotted funds run out midway in the implementation of a project. The institution must also be prepared to make a long-term funding commitment for an automation project. Once a library automation program begins, it is painful and very expensive not to complete the task.

Conclusion

If one is entering the field of library automation anew, take the time to talk to people who have experienced putting together their own system, preferably in a similar environment. The pioneer days are over and it should not be difficult to find an analogous situation for comparison. Do not think that frank discussions of the problems of a library automation program will be found in the published literature. There is very little in print to indicate what can and did go wrong with plans for many libraries. No one likes to admit failure, especially in print. One may find a published description of automation plans for a library in the literature, and then find no further reports. This is often a good indication that something went wrong, and that the system is not working as planned, or not working at all. It may be just as important, if not more so, to talk to the staffs of those libraries as to the ones who succeeded.

The library staff with plans for automation should be prepared to modify those plans if it is found that all of the things wanted are more than can be afforded. We all start by imagining the best of all possible worlds, but it is often possible to live with less, and not have a system which is the worse for compromise. Just be sure that the compromises made are those which are based on the needs of the library, and not on what data processing people said could or could not be done by the machine.

The problems are great, but the rewards are even greater.

28. Financial Considerations Involved in Closing the Catalog*

by Kazuko M. Dailey

I have been asked to speak about financial considerations involved in closing card catalogs. It is an extremely complex question, there are no pat formulae to follow, and all I can do is merely to touch on the points I think are important. At the outset, let me make some assumptions: any alternative means of bibliographic data display selected will be accomplished through the use of computers and that the computerized data can be used directly to construct the new catalog. I must warn you also that I will quote many figures, but they should be treated only as examples. Quoting figures can be hazardous because people may use them without knowing precisely the elements which support the figures being quoted or use the figures out of context. Nonetheless I think it is helpful to use numbers first, to suggest the magnitude of the resources involved, and second, to provide some bases for comparison among available alternatives.

Authority control system and staff training are certainly substantial cost factors but for the purpose of today's discussion I will not discuss them in view of time constraints for this presentation. Let me indicate only that I believe the authority control mechanism should reside in the technical processing system so that the data derived from it are ready for use in a public access file. If the technical processing system does not have a heading validation mechanism, libraries will continue to have a considerable cost item in catalog maintenance. Simply put, what I am talking about today is the effect on the cost of purchasing catalog card stock and the cost of labor necessary for production of catalog cards, sorting and filing into catalogs and maintaining if we close the card catalog. In such an event the cost of these operations will be either eliminated completely or partially displaced.

The other side of the question is the amount of funding required to start-up and maintain an alternative method of bibliographic data display, and to what extent the new mode of catalog display will displace the current costs involved in maintaining our present card catalog.

First of all let me talk a little about the current costs of

---

*Reprinted by permission of the author and publisher from Alternative Catalog Newsletter, No. 6 (September 1978), 7-17.

maintaining card catalogs. I will use the University of California, Davis costs as illustration. These figures are extremely raw, and as a consequence, I do not know how closely they reflect the real costs.

* Filing of cards into the main card catalog	$ 54,900	per year
* Filing and refiling into the main shelflist	8,100	
** Card preparation	15,100	
* Card handling	14,500	
* Catalog maintenance, excluding authority work	27,600	
Catalog cards, including catalog cards produced by BALLOTS	10,000	
	$130,800	

   * the Main Library only
 ** includes references, authority cards, and non-standard cataloging. This category represents about 25% of all cards produced.

(If we take over $250,000 for Berkeley, as cited by Joseph Rosenthal, $130,800 for Davis seems reasonable.) All but $10,000 of the annual cost is in personnel cost.

    The next step is to identify which of the cost elements will be eliminated or reduced by closing the catalog and adopting a new mode of catalog data display. Any decision one makes will have its cost consequences. For instance, if a library decided to convert the entire catalog to machine-readable format, the one time cost of conversion can be very large, but on the other hand, a completely machine readable catalog may mean that most of the current costs of maintaining the card catalog will disappear. If the decision is to close the card catalog but the alternative catalog will contain only records produced from point X forward, this decision will entail a host of ancillary questions:

    1. Do we mean freezing the catalog as of point X?
    2. Shall we continue to up-date the manual catalog to reflect changes in names, subject headings, etc. ?
    3. Whenever any maintenance is required, shall we pull out entire sets of cards and submit the revised data to the new form of catalog?
    4. Shall we provide references from the manual catalog to the new and vice versa?
    5. If the catalogs are split into new and old, should we maintain an integrated shelflist in card format?

and so on. Each of the choices mentioned will have its own individual cost configuration, and the cost impact will vary a great deal among the available choices. Take for instance, a decision to keep the closed card catalog current with the prevailing practice would mean that maintenance work will be required every time that the LC issues a change in a subject heading or name, and catalog editing is an expensive cost item. Let me illustrate.

At Davis, we recently concluded a project of completely overhauling geographic headings in the card catalog to be in conformance with the recent change. The labor cost of this project was nearly $8,000. Anticipating the implementation of the AACR-2 and the adoption of machine filing rules, this particular choice indicates a high price tag. If such maintenance cost is more than the library can bear, then we must consider and decide to what extent we are willing to live with, and indeed more importantly, we are willing to subject our patrons to, inconsistencies and discrepancies between the old and new catalogs. Inevitably, the more effort we devote to keeping the two catalogs in close conformity, the higher the cost will be. On this issue particularly, librarians will find themselves asking a philosophical question about their own stance in regard to bibliographical control. Where does one stand between the two extreme positions; on the one extreme a position that believes that the integrity and consistency of the catalog is of an overriding importance, and the other which believes that the only important thing is to get the desired book in the user's hand. However sincere and difficult the soul-searching may be, the final arbiter of the question for the library is likely to be the dollars available. I must add, however, that operating within the constraints of a given budget, there is always room to make judicious decisions and injudicious ones.

Let us now turn to the costs involved in alternative methods of display. But before we discuss alternatives, I think it may be useful to review the scope and function of the new catalog that one contemplates, for decisions regarding the scope and functions will have the most serious cost implications.

1. The extent of the library's collections which will be represented in the new catalog. At a recent meeting on the closing of catalogs, John Knapp stated that if a library collection is smaller than 250,000 titles, it may be worthwhile converting the entire collection, but if it is larger than that, the one time cost of conversion becomes too great for most libraries to undertake. At the moment, the cheapest method of conversion is to use OCLC, but that may change. There are a number of commercial firms which offer this service, but the cost varies from firm to firm, and will depend also on the requirements of the library. One factor to keep in mind is that cost of conversion is directly proportionate to the amount of data to be converted. A recent study by Butler and Aveney indicates that the average cost of converting records with 200 characters is $1.06, while 400 character records will cost $1.95, and 600 character records, which is the average length of catalog records, will cost $3.28.
Since Tacoma Public Library's success story in converting its files to install an automated circulation system, there has been a dramatic rise of interest in B/NA's conversion technique. Whether conversion for circulation purposes satisfies

the requirements of a catalog is a question each library must consider.

2. Language. There is not a technical processing system that I am aware of which can accommodate non-Roman alphabet languages, with the exception of the New York Public Library's system which has Cyrillic and Hebrew characters. We may be quite willing to compromise and accept transliterated data only, but will our users be satisfied?

3. Types of materials. Do we want to include in the new data base, not only books, but also scores, maps, tapes, recordings and all other media. even though MARC formats may not be available? If the answer is no, we will have to maintain small catalogs and work units for card production, filing and maintenance. It is quite possible that even libraries which opt to close their catalogs will have to continue to maintain for many years card catalogs for special materials and languages.

4. Function. Is the new form of catalog to be a complete repository of bibliographic data? Or is it conceived primarily as a finding tool for users? If it is the latter, the level of fullness of catalog data can be reduced to only a few elements, but if it is to serve the library workers as well, the level must be raised significantly to include complete or nearly complete records. If the pattern of catalog use can be determined fairly precisely, more than one form of display might be cost effective. For instance, in an on-line catalog, the on-line storage is a significant cost factor, therefore, the record length will have a direct impact on cost. Toronto and other studies on catalog use indicate that 90% of catalog consultation is satisfied by a limited number of data elements. If this is the case, it would not be cost effective to store full MARC records on-line. Rather, it would be far more economical to store full records in cheaper formats, such as off-line storage, microform or even a manual shelflist to accommodate the 10% which requires display of full records.

5. Access points. If the access points you wish to provide in the new catalog are exactly the same as in the card catalog, linear display of catalog data would be satisfactory, thus microfiche or microfilm would provide the necessary access. Of course, KWIK and KWOK indexes can provide another dimension to access points. But when applied to a large number of entries that are likely to be present in a catalog, their effectiveness as a search tool becomes questionable, and certainly there will be added costs. On the other hand, if you wish to provide a flexible search mechanism to allow access through name or partial name, title, series and subject word or phrase, call number and other numeric identifiers such as LC card number, ISBN and so forth, then the data must be stored in a random access storage. Clearly, the more

access points you provide, the more storage capacity will be required for storing a larger number of data and for indexing, and the more sophisticated the search algorithm, the more expensive the software package will be.

It must be clear by now that the cost of an alternative form of catalog depends on what one requires it to do and how one intends to use it. Therefore, it is extremely important that we study these questions in depth and arrive at a clear understanding of the library's requirements by carefully defining the purpose and function of the alternative form of catalog that is being proposed.

At the risk of repeating old information, I will discuss briefly the relative costs of some of the more common alternatives being talked about, namely, microform catalog, book catalog and on-line catalog.

The University of Toronto and Los Angeles County Library System are two examples of large library systems which have successfully implemented microform catalogs. But there are several smaller and younger institutions, such as the University of Texas at Permian Basin, which started out by using only microform catalogs. According to all I have read, these catalogs have proved to be cost effective and satisfactory as a public access tool. At Toronto where the user population is about 40,000, and the size of the collection is 1.2 million, the catalog records are contained in 514 pieces of fiche or 5 reels of microfilm, 700 feet long. 59 ROM III film readers, at $800 each, and 43 fiche readers, at $250 each, were installed for a total cost of $58,000. The only information I was able to gather about UTLAS system's cost of creating a microform catalog system is based on the collection size of 10,000 items. The one time cost of creating the software package is $1,130, and the operating cost for the first year is $2,718. But this COM catalog does not include the authority file or references.

To give you another example of microform cost, at UC Davis, we formerly issued hard copy serial lists, but two years ago, we abandoned the paper issue in favor of COM. The current cost of creating a master COM list, which contains some 49,000 entries in 10 fiche, is $43.78. Each additional set of the fiche list costs $1.50. Thus our cost of producing 200 sets of the fiche list is $344, at the unit cost of $1.72. With the money saved by converting to COM, we were able to purchase a requisite number of fiche readers which are placed in strategic points throughout the library.

If we were to publish the same list in hard copy, the cost would be prohibitive. One proposal we received for a high quality product indicated that the list would require 2600 pages at the cost of 6¢ per page. The total cost of producing 200 copies will be $31,200, or $156 per copy. Fortunately, this was the most expensive quotation we received. Two other quotations received for usable but less pleasing products were $65 per copy and $57 per copy. The point of the story then is a library, when ready to produce a catalog or serial list, must shop around carefully for the cheapest price which satisfies its requirements.

Book catalogs are admittedly more expensive than microform catalogs, but those libraries which have used book catalogs feel that the book catalog is by far the more economical when compared to card catalogs. One such example is the book catalog system used at University of California, Santa Cruz. The library's collection is about 290,000 volumes with annual additions of 24,000 volumes. The entire catalog is in machine readable form. The book catalog is divided into an author/title section and a subject section, and each of the sections is cumulated in alternate years. The basic cost of producing the hard copy--magnetic tape through photocomposition-- is $1.44 per page unbound and $1.55 per page bound. The cost of last year's author/title cumulation, which was 29 volumes per set in 20 copies, was a little over $20,000. This year's subject cumulation cost was about $19,000. In addition, the currently cataloged titles are cumulated into quarterly cumulative supplements, and the annual cost of producing the supplements is roughly $10,000. Thus the present cost of Santa Cruz's book catalog is about $30,000 a year, but the cost will increase as new titles are added to the data base.

As I have already mentioned, the amount of data has a very direct relation to cost. Therefore, the selection of data elements must be examined critically and the decision for inclusion should be based on utility. Most book catalogs have full catalog data only under the main entry, and all other entries carry only the essential information. I was surprised to find some years ago that addition of even a small data element, such as the LC card number, can add significantly to the cost of a book catalog. Another way of cutting cost is by compaction of data; this again relates to the number of pages of the catalog.

Both in the case of COM and book catalog, many attractive type fonts are now available, but inevitably one must pay for fine appearance and legibility. Likewise, if the ALA character set of non-Roman alphabet is required, the cost will rise considerably.

On-line catalog is the most intriguing of alternatives, but it is still the most expensive, although computer experts tell us that the cost of hardware, particularly the storage cost, is steadily declining. Since I am not a computer expert, I can speak only in the most gross terms. Merely as an experiment, I tried to calculate the cost of an on-line catalog for a library of Davis' size--requiring manipulation of 1 million records, and to accommodate a user population of between 25,000 to 30,000. The result showed that it would cost $260,000 to acquire the basic hardware. This price would include a CPU of the size of PDP 11/70, 40 terminals, 2 tape drives, 1 printer, 4 disc drives (300 megabytes each), and 8 disc packs. But the $260,000 does not provide for the necessary software which must be written in-house or by a service bureau. As we all know, software is probably the most expensive aspect of computer use, therefore, $260,000 is only the beginning. As a consequence, it would seem advantageous to buy a system with vendor maintained software. The question is, "Is there such a system commercially available?"

As a matter of fact, there is a system with a potential capability of becoming an on-line catalog in the reasonably near future. That system is CLSI. The idea of using CLSI is quite attractive because it will combine the public access catalog and circulation functions in one system, thus reducing the cost of each of the components.

Assuming that a library already has a basic LIBS 100 system which can accommodate the size of its catalog (rather a large assumption), the addition of a required number of terminals is the only further expenditure to be anticipated. At CLSI's current price for CRT's, $8,000 a unit, the addition of 40 terminals alone will amount to $320,000, and the annual maintenance at the current rate will cost $19,200. But this package does include the software. (Parenthetically, I should mention that the system is not yet able to accommodate such a large number of terminals, but the company promises that capability in the near future. Another point of serious concern would be the effect that a heavy transaction load created by public catalog query will have on the system's response time.) Admittedly, CLSI equipment is very expensive, but if the proposed public access catalog system fulfills the library's requirements, it is an alternative definitely worthy of consideration. In the same vein, Toronto's UTLAS is a system which deserves a serious review.

Another obvious alternative is a direct link with one of the bibliographic utilities, but I doubt that either OCLC or BALLOTS can handle the traffic load such operations will place on the system. As a matter of fact, this question was raised by the University of California, and both utilities indicated that they could not accommodate the UC system. In addition, imagine the poor freshman who finally locates the book he wants on an OCLC terminal and finds 75 holding libraries listed on the screen!

The on-line catalog is probably the softest cost area because prices of computer and related equipment change from month to month, and because there are many methods of manipulating catalog records. In addition, the technological changes in the computer field are so rapid that a library cannot do without expert assistance in designing an efficient and economical on-line system. At least we know the initial capital outlay for the hardware will be enormous, but without knowing the cost of necessary software, it is difficult to predict whether an on-line catalog will be affordable or eventually prove cost effective. The Berkeley campus, which has done a detailed study, has concluded, however, that it would indeed realize cost savings in several years.

I have drawn a somewhat simplistic picture in which a library has just one catalog and one collection, and all users make one level of demands on the catalog. That, as you know, is far from the reality, but I will only add that the more complex a library system is, the more difficult it will be to assess what alternative form of catalog is desirable, and the more complexity one builds into the new catalog, the more the cost is likely to escalate.

In the process of working through the various options available, I find myself compelled to conclude that, at least in the Davis situation, we will go from the card catalog not simply to another form of catalog, but rather to a variety of displays--card catalog format for the retrospective collections and possibly for specialized collections, on-line catalog for current and prospective collections, supplemented by a COM catalog in one or more forms.

In coming to grips with financial questions involved, it seems exceedingly important to keep in mind that closing the catalog can be and should be an opportunity to improve service to our users. Any medium you choose to use will have its own particular physical, functional and economic constraints. In the era of steady state and tax-payers' revolt, we cannot purchase only Rolls and Cadillacs, and we must make absolutely certain that changes and enhancements we introduce to our library service are purchased at a cost/effective level. Whether a price paid is cost/effective depends on the real utility the library and its patrons get out of the bibliographic access system. The only way that we are going to be able to predict the utility is by knowing with considerable precision how our patrons and staff use the catalogs and what they want out of it. It is an extremely complex problem, but at the same time, it is an equally great challenge for those of us whose business is to provide both bibliographic control and bibliographic access to the library user.

29. Planning for the Catalogs: A Managerial Perspective*

by Joseph A. Rosenthal

Introduction

Unexpectedly, the federal government will soon be a major source of assistance in helping us face a future dotted with frozen card catalogs. I refer not to Title II-C or to the Library of Congress, but to a hitherto little-known agency within HEW that is contemplating a new series of pamphlets and other aids for nonprofit organizations. The initial group of items includes the following titles: <u>How to reduce your library fuel bills through the use of pulverized catalog cards</u>; <u>Remodeling card catalog cabinets into cathode-ray terminals, microfiche reader-printers, and planters</u>; and what will probably be a best-selling videocassette, <u>Retraining filers for library management positions</u>.

This paper looks at the bibliographic prospects for research libraries during the next few years and touches on some of the data that either are available or needed for planning and decision making. Using some work done at Berkeley as a point of departure, the paper also makes some recommendations with regard to both the means for arriving at decisions and, to some limited extent, the content of the questions that must be asked and of the decisions that must be made. An underlying assumption is that most North American research libraries are either participating in or about to join a machine-based bibliographic processing system.

Implications of AACR 2

Let's face it: chronologically divided catalogs constitute a fact of life staring us directly in the face. With the issuance of the second edition of the <u>Anglo-American Cataloguing Rules</u> and its subsequent implementation by the Library of Congress, the rest of us cannot afford to maintain cataloging practice according to AACR 1. There is, of course, the option of perpetuating a single card catalog while adopting AACR 2, but as John Rather and others have pointed out, this is simply a masking device for maintaining two sets of files within one physical entity.[1] That is, as time goes on, an in-

---

*Reprinted by permission of the author and the American Library Association from <u>Journal of Library Automation</u>, September 1978, p. 192-205, copyright©1978 by the American Library Association.

creasing number of name headings will be represented in the file under two different forms. The tasks relating to linkage of the different forms of headings are similar, though not identical, whether a library chooses to split the catalogs at the time of implementation of AACR 2 or decides to maintain a single catalog indefinitely.

Apart from the issuance of AACR 2 and its implementation by LC, card catalogs are increasingly coming to be recognized as a costly and relatively ineffective means--in light of present and future technology--of bibliographic display for large collections.

Considering the available forms of display, cards require large accompanying expenditures of manual effort as well as indefinitely expanding spatial requirements, and the expenditure curve for maintaining card catalogs rises as the size of the files increase. Book catalogs for large collections are relatively expensive to produce, and present difficult choices between large financial outlays necessary to provide frequent updating and recumulation or user frustration in using multiple alphabets or segments to perform comprehensive searches. On-line access--for certain types of queries--has a great deal to offer but is very expensive, limited at present for search capability, and generally will not be feasible for most libraries by January 2, 1981.

This brings us to computer-output-microform, a medium that is operationally viable, cheap, and highly acceptable for many users and types of use. Regardless of the development and implementation of on-line access, COM should be considered as an effective display mechanism answering a considerable portion of bibliographic queries for some time to come, and I believe it will be obligatory as a back-up to most on-line installations.

With COM as a practical display mechanism, two other factors, if available, would make the closing of any library card catalog a breeze. Unfortunately, few libraries will have either of these features on hand by 1981. They are: 1. An authority control system providing automated linkage back and forth between bibliographic records and the established forms together with their associated cross references of names and subject headings embedded in those bibliographic records; 2. a completely machine-readable file, i. e., a catalog that is already converted to machine-readable form.

I will spend some time on each of these concepts:

Authority Control System

The authority control system, first brilliantly executed in a computer milieu at The New York Public Library, holds the greatest promise of allowing us to overcome the problems posed by the second edition of AACR and, perhaps more importantly, to deal with future changes in cataloging policy and practice over the long haul. Devoutly as we might hope, it now seems very clear that the Library of Congress will not have a well-functioning on-line authority control system linked to its machine-readable bibliographic records by the beginning of 1981, and unless a miracle occurs in the next two years, the name headings in the MARC files at LC will in large measure not be compatible with forms called for by AACR 2, notwithstanding a valiant attempt at LC to build in the changed form of names manually between now and Day One.

Of equal consequence is the present inability of two of the major data processing utilities, OCLC and BALLOTS, to cope in machine-based or automatic fashion with the problems of linking changed forms of name headings and associated pre- and post-1980 bibliographic records. To my knowledge, neither system has announced a strategy for dealing with this set of problems as it affects the files at Columbus and Palo Alto, much less the use consequences that will become all too quickly apparent at libraries throughout the United States.

UTLAS, the University of Toronto Library Automation System, seems to be well on the way to developing an authority control system, and WLN, the Washington Library Network, is the first major processing utility to offer this capability on an on-line basis. Utilization of an effective authority control system should go far toward reducing the unpleasant bibliographic and financial effects we can anticipate with implementation of AACR 2.

Machine Readable File

As has become evident at the University of Toronto, an integrated file of machine-readable bibliographic records representing nearly the complete library collection has been for Toronto--and would be for other libraries--a significant factor in mitigating the difficulties otherwise faced by users in accessing two separate files. It is of some interest, then, to take a look at the individual and collective prospects for conversion to machine-readable form of retrospective bibliographic data. To begin with, John Knapp has put into a handy little algorithm some guidelines for individual libraries considering retrospective conversion.[2] For libraries holding fewer than 250,000 titles, the chances are that quite a high proportion of those titles will already be available in machine-readable form, and a conversion project utilizing access to an existing large machine-readable bibliographic file should probably prove to be cost beneficial within a matter of a few years. The choice is not so clear for libraries holding between one-quarter and one-half million titles, Knapp believes, and for libraries holding more than one-half million titles, the decision to convert retrospective files on an individual institutional basis is probably not economically justifiable at the present time.

Two important provisos should be attached to these guidelines. First, the economic feasibility of retrospective conversion is changing on an almost monthly basis because of the de facto growth of files, changes in methodologies for inputting and verifying bibliographic records, and changes in the machine/manual labor cost ratio. Second, the economic constraints and costs applicable to retrospective conversion undergo significant change when contemplated on a multi-institutional basis. The major libraries of the province of British Columbia are embarking on massive and comprehensive retrospective conversion. The disposition to act in concert coupled with a history of favorable relations between libraries and the provincial government has led to substantial backing for this program. Imaginative library leadership and a history of successful applications of machine techniques bode well for the enterprise, which is utilizing the UTLAS system and its bibliographic files as the basis for conversion.

The UTLAS file along with those of Blackwell/North America and OCLC are some of the major data stores that might be given consideration for retrospective conversion programs. Each of the files has its own quantitative and qualitative characteristics, and these along with the charges for utilizing any particular file should be very carefully evaluated before any library or group of libraries begins retrospective conversion. After the RECON studies and reports in the early 1970s, the Library of Congress decided that conversion of LC's main retrospective files would not be afforded a high priority. Breakthroughs in the technology of optical character recognition might drastically change the economic parameters of this situation, and ultimately the policy of LC. In any event, I suggest that the early 1980s, with a decade of development since the RECON work, might be an appropriate time for reexamination by LC of the possibility of converting its manual bibliographic files.

PLANNING AT BERKELEY

Returning to the more common situation of no automated authority control system and massive retrospective files in manual form, a planning approach for changing the catalog structure was adopted at Berkeley and a detailed planning document was developed. A close inspection of the questions and decision points contained in that document make it apparent that a great many problems disappear with the operational availability of the two features just mentioned above: authority control and retrospective conversion. The planning document sets forth basic working assumptions, a methodology, and an outline of specific questions to be answered by teams assigned to carry out the planning itself. While some of the details are specific to Berkeley's institutional environment, this outline of the contents of that planning paper should give some idea of the number and variety of decisions, mostly technical, that research libraries can generally expect to encounter.

Assumptions

Twelve underlying assumptions established the constraints within which the detailed plan would evolve. These assumptions were:

1. The General Library will freeze its present card catalogs at approximately the same time the Library of Congress closes its card catalogs, now scheduled to occur January 1, 1981.
2. All, or substantially all, of the General Library's cataloging data will be either received or input in machine-readable form by 1981.
3. The General Library will be participating in an on-line cataloging/technical processing system for the foreseeable future.
4. The bibliographic system for the General Library will be developed so as to be consistent and compatible with university-wide planning and implementation in this area of library operation.
5. National bibliographic standards will be followed, in order to facilitate the potential for cooperative and networking activities and to minimize costs. These standards include:
    a) Anglo-American Cataloguing Rules as interpreted by the Library of Congress, including Library of Congress established forms of entry for both print and nonprint materials.
    b) Library of Congress subject headings and classification.
    c) MARC formats as developed by the Library of Congress.
    d) Filing rules at such time as a national standard for arrangement of computer-based bibliographic records is developed.
    e) Romanization system.
6. Various formats will be used for display of data both centrally and locally. No one form--card, book, microform, on-line display, or listing--will be used exclusively. The choice of display format will depend on the use intended and the cost of the product in light of rapidly changing technology. Criteria will be developed to enable the General Library to choose among various modes of display and arrangement of bibliographic data.
7. For the immediate future, a primary display mode for bibliographic data will be microform. The specific microform format(s) will be related to and developed on the basis of experience with the present Catalog Supplement and Berkeley Serials Union List. In order to lessen the number of separate displays of bibliographic records, plans should be developed to integrate the display of records for on-order, in-process, and fully-processed library materials.
8. Records in the machine-based bibliographic file will be displayed under at least the same access points found in the present card catalog system: main entry, name and title added entries, and series and subject added entries. (It should be noted that not all of these access points are provided currently for all types of material.) The microform display will be based on the premise that full bibliographic data for any record will be found in only one place: this might be either in the register listing of a register/index display or under a basic access point, as in the microfiche display now used at the University of Toronto. Choices here will depend on evaluation of public service utility coupled with cost considerations.

9. For a number of reasons, including anticipated adoption by the Library of Congress and the General Library of the second edition of the Anglo-American Cataloguing Rules and an increased pace of revision of subject headings by the Library of Congress after 1980, many access points in the new bibliographic display will differ from corresponding headings in the existing card catalogs. The General Library's policy will be based on liberal provision of references in the new catalog system; however, alteration of headings and provision of additional references in the existing card catalogs will be on an exceptional basis only.
10. Planning for the modes of bibliographic display will be on the basis of anticipating a modest extension of on-line access to General Library bibliographic data during the period from the present through 1985. By 1980, on-line access should be available at the presently covered units in the acquisition and catalog departments, in the undergraduate library, in the general reference service, in the loan hall, and in at least one branch library location.
11. Materials received and processed after the beginning of 1981 will be integrated into the new bibliographic system, regardless of date of imprint. This principle is in accord with the decision of the Library of Congress on the same point, and is intended to lessen the difficulties and costs of processing library materials in the context of two major systems for bibliographic display.
12. The General Library will expand and improve its program of orientation and assistance to users of bibliographic data that represent the Berkeley collections.

Planning Methodology

For each phase of planning for the General Library's Bibliographic system, a number of staff members worked either individually or in small groups on particular aspects and problems related to freezing the present card catalog system and changing to new forms of display. For most assignments, a written report was prepared; these reports should serve as road maps for the implementation period covering the next several years.³ All those engaged in these assignments met approximately once each month as a group, along with the coordinating group for this phase of the planning--the university librarian, the associate and assistant university librarians, the head of the catalog department, and the head of the systems office.

As written reports covering the various assignments are finished, they will be circulated widely in the General Library for comment, discussion, and suggestions for revision. After an appropriate period for evaluating reaction and making requisite changes in the content of the reports, the actual work necessary to build and implement the new bibliographic system will begin.

Assignments

Once we had a good idea of the assumptions and the methodology, it remained for us to package areas of concern into specific assignments. What follows is a fairly detailed description of issues and especially the questions to be answered by teams working in each of the areas we finally agreed upon. Brief papers drawn up in each of these areas should serve as a point of departure for more intensive planning efforts. It was expected, of course, that there would be some overlap in the various areas, but monthly meetings of everyone involved in planning and the existence of the coordinating group helped to lessen the amount of duplicative effort.

TEAM 1: BRANCH CONSIDERATIONS A

Scope extends to catalogs and files other than author/title, subject, official, loan stack shelflist, depository, and CSR (Central Serial Record) catalogs.

What should the configuration for bibliographic display consist of in branch libraries and other specialized public service units of the General Library for the period from the present through 1985? When should card catalogs in these units cease to be maintained?

What provision should be made for continued access by call number (shelflist)? Should a catalog card continue to be provided for all branch shelflists? What requirements should be set in order to cease maintenance of branch shelflists in card form?

What opportunities should be provided, if any, for local deviation from basic General Library cataloging policies (i.e., conformity to and compatibility with Anglo-American Cataloguing Rules, Library of Congress practice, LC Subject Headings and classification)? What policies and practices should govern the possibility of branch library additions to a bibliographic record such as 1. additional added entries--including variant titles, additional name headings, variant or additional series, 2. additional subject entries, 3. other information in the form of notes? If any such additions are to be permitted by policy, what specific mechanisms should be developed for submission and review of such data?

To what extent should "temporary" or "special" locations be reflected in the bibliographic data base? That is, should the bibliographic data base include and display 1. reserve status, 2. reference status, 3. other special locations? If so, what procedures should be adopted for including these data?

What "authority" or cross-reference information should be provided for branch bibliographic display? (To be coordinated with work of links and authorities team.)

TEAM 2: BRANCH CONSIDERATIONS B

This team should work within the context of general recommendations regarding branch bibliographic display developed by branch considerations A team.

What specific policies should be followed for units that now deviate significantly from our basic cataloging policies? To what extent should differing practices regarding name and subject headings and classification policy be continued? For each of these units, how should data be submitted to the basic bibliographic file? For the above units and for the undergraduate library, in what form should bibliographic data regarding holdings of these units be distributed? Should there be any distribution of bibliographic data other than that contemplated for other units of the General Library? If so, what should be provided? (Any recommendations for additional bibliographic products should be accompanied by specifications as to format, content, access points, frequency, and cost estimates.)

TEAM 3: RECORD FORMATS AND DISPLAY SPECIFICATIONS

Develop in specific detail the configuration of bibliographic display for the General Library system through 1985.

Assume that the "new" catalog data will be displayed principally in microforms for public use but that a transition over the period from 1980-85 will occur, with on-line access to bibliographic data increasing substantially.

What specific configurations should be adopted for the microform display? Register/index? If so, what data elements should be provided in the various indexes? What pattern of indexes should be adopted?

Main and added entries and titles
Subjects
Call number

Main and added entries
Titles
Subjects
Call number

Name headings (personal and corporate)
Topical subjects
Call number
Series

OR, should the microform configuration be based on brief entries under all but one of the various indexes, with one index providing a full bibliographic record?

Provide a recommendation for a specific frequency pattern for the microform display configuration.

Assume the desirability of combining the microform display configuration for fully cataloged materials with records for on-order and in-process items (the categories of records now represented in the Catalog Supplement). Will this be possible? If so, formulate specific proposals for clear user identification of items in various stages of processing. Will the recommended pattern of issuance for this microform display configuration for public use necessitate an additional microform product or set of products for internal (technical service) access? Or should internal access be based on on-line access to records maintained in one or more processing utilities?

What provisions should be made for shelflist access a in the immediate future, i.e., during the period when retrospective bibliographic records are for the most part in manual form only, and b on a long-term basis, looking toward the time when most or all bibliographic records for general library collections are in machine-readable form?

Indicate, with regard to specific recommendations in this area, the degree to which specific aspects of the display formats can be changed with comparatively minor cost burdens and disruption of public and technical service functions, and which aspects (once adopted) should be regarded as relatively fixed in view of these considerations.

TEAM 4: SERIALS

Develop the configuration of bibliographic and holdings display for serials in the General Library system through 1985, with particular attention to the following points.

To what extent should information regarding serials be reflected in the bibliographic display for the General Library?
- Should serials be represented at all?
- If so, under what access points should they be represented? Main entry? Title? Added entries? Subjects?
- To the extent that serials are represented, should the representation follow the same pattern as for monographs if a register/index format is adopted?
- Should any holdings information be provided in such representation, and if so, under which access points? Beginning date? Complete holdings for inactive titles?

If a separate display is to be provided for serial information (whether or not some information regarding serials is to be included in the display(s) for monograph items), describe the nature of this display with regard to:
- access points
- completeness of bibliographic and holdings information under all categories of access points
- frequency
- microform and/or hardcopy

Describe the relationships these displays bear to files containing serial data now existing in the General Library:
- Berkeley serials union list
- author/title catalog
- official shelflist
- central serial record
  - entering files:
    - serials department
    - documents department
    - branch and other locations
- branch card catalogs.

In view of what is known regarding the choice of a bibliographic utility for the UC library system, recommend steps to be taken regarding the integration or linkage of the Berkeley serials system with the bibliographic utility (BALLOTS or OCLC).

Identify in chronological order, and with estimates of personnel needs and other requirements, the steps to be taken to accomplish the recommendations made above through 1985. Operations should be characterized as "essential" or "desirable," and goals (such as completion date or number of records to be processed on an annual basis) should be stated.

TEAM 5: AUTHORITY STRUCTURE AND LINKS

What general and specific policies should be adopted regarding references from variant forms of names and subject headings in and between the old and new systems of bibliographic display? In addressing this point, consider the adoption of AACR 2 by the Library of Congress and the UCB General Library in 1981 and an expected substantial increase in the number of headings to be changed beginning at that time.

Will the policies recommended be applicable to any form of display for the new catalog, i.e., card, microform, on-line?

What policies should be followed by catalogers regarding the establishment of names and subject headings for the new catalog? In what instances should the old catalog be searched for identical, variant, and conflicting headings? What practices can be adopted to minimize the human effort and cost, while assuring adequate bibliographic access to the collections?

For such links as are recommended between the old and new catalogs, what legends should be provided in the bibliographic display? Should the legends explicitly refer users to the other display? Should the legends reflect a time distinction (i.e., "For works cataloged before 1980...")?

What policies should be adopted when records in the old catalog system are modified? Consider modifications based on transfer, change of format (i.e., hardcopy to microform), additions to multiple-volume sets, closing of serial titles, and added copies in different locations.

TEAM 6: NON-ROMAN ALPHABET RECORDS

Present specific recommendations regarding the inclusion, exclusion, and romanization of bibliographic data representing items in non-roman alphabets acquired and added to the General Library collections in 1980 and after. With reference to particular existing card catalogs, indicate how these policies should affect the maintenance or closing of the card catalogs.

In view of anticipated technological and cost developments with regard to representation of various character sets in machine-readable form, set forth guidelines for the General Library's long-range policies in this area. What long-range goals should be adopted regarding separate or integrated files for bibliographic records representing roman-alphabet and non-roman alphabet materials?

TEAM 7: PUBLIC AND STAFF RELATIONS

List all groups likely to be affected by the changes in bibliographic display to an extent that warrants special attention directed toward informing these groups regarding likely changes, securing feedback and participation in planning, and preparing for effective use of the changed bibliographic system.

Develop a program, with accompanying chronology, of specific informational and "public relations" efforts that should be directed to these various groups.

Make recommendations regarding people and units to be assigned to this program; estimate costs.

Participate in all public and staff relations activities connected with the bibliographic system planning from January through April 1978.

TEAM 8: PHYSICAL FACILITIES AND EQUIPMENT

Develop equipment, space, building modification (e. g., wiring) needs for the future system of bibliographic display. Include a phase transition to on-line access for a major portion of public and staff access to bibliographic data. Restudy, refine, and verify previous projections of use under the future system; relate these findings to the needed number of access devices of various types.

What organizational assignments should be made for continuing review of equipment and physical facilities: microform readers, microform reader-printers, on-line terminals, file and display arrangements for microforms (e. g., fiche holders); use justification for additional equipment?

Recommend specific policies for purchase, lease, and maintenance contracts with regard to specific types of equipment.

Develop cost estimates through 1985 for equipment, maintenance of equipment, and building modification.

TEAM 9: LIAISON WITH UNIVERSITY-WIDE

Maintain liaison and work towards compatibility with university-wide planning for a UC union catalog system. Communicate budgetary, technological, and networking developments to university-wide staff members and to appropriate general library personnel.

TEAM 10: LIAISON WITH BIBLIOGRAPHIC UTILITY (BALLOTS or OCLC)

Serve as coordinator(s) between the bibliographic utility and persons and groups involved in planning future bibliographic operations and display in the General Library. Based on the evolving assumptions regarding record format and bibliographic display, develop cost parameters and specific methods for delivery of various bibliographic products--encompassing the bibliographic utility, any other non-UC agencies (such as microform service bureau), UC Data Processing Center, and specific library units and personnel.

TEAM 11: TECHNICAL/COST CONSULTANTS

Advise on feasibility and prepare cost estimates as requested by individuals or teams working on various assignments.

TEAM 12: CATALOG USE CONSULTANTS

Advise on issues relating to public use of catalogs as requested by individuals or teams working on various assignments. Review working papers for public use implications.

Using this team approach it seemed possible to assign personnel already working in the library to the tasks of filling in much of the necessary detailed data for decision making.

Areas for Managerial Decisions

I would now like to go over some of the more global data that I feel may be useful, individually and collectively, in making managerial decisions regarding future systems of bibliographic display and access. To begin with, present costs of personnel, equipment, space, and maintenance are essential, and projections of these cost categories, as applied to maintenance of the current system of processing without significant change, should be valuable in developing justifications for future action.

A listing, description, and quantitative analysis of all present catalogs and other files of bibliographic records with accompanying growth rates should be developed, if these data are not already available. If it seems likely that planning will include the possibility of on-line and/or microform displays of bibliographic data, an analysis of spatial requirements and capacities at appropriate public and technical service points and a determination of power and telecommunication needs and capacities will probably be necessary; and, as an adjunct, cost estimates should be made to bring present capabilities up to anticipated requirements under a changed system.

Though it may be difficult to obtain, it would be very useful to have some indication of peak load in terms of queries by staff and other users of the present bibliographic files; and if at all possible, some estimated breakdown by type of query and length of examination or perusal of the file. In other words, how many people are apt to be using the present bibliographic files at any one time? How are these users likely to be divided in terms of known item search versus subject search? Approximately how long do they spend at the catalogs for any single search?

The Library of Congress estimated in 1977 that approximately

49 percent of the records in the existing MARC file will need to have headings updated to bring them into line with AACR 2. We do not know how to apply this projection to the records of any particular library other than LC, and we have very little idea of the rate at which name headings established after 1979 will constitute changes to previously established forms. For example, how many name headings can the catalog department of a university research library with a collection of two million volumes and an annual cataloging rate of fifty thousand titles expect to encounter during 1981, which will need to be reconciled with different forms of names established prior to the implementation of AACR 2? Three thousand? Ten thousand? Twenty thousand? What will happen to the rate of changed headings during the first five years of implementation of AACR 2? Will there be a decreasing rate of change; and if so, what kind of declining curve will that decrease take?

We have few guidelines to tell us whether these changes are likely to have more, less, or about equal impact on monographs as opposed to serials. Such information might be valuable in terms of the allocation of staff and the organization for the processing of serial and monograph material in a library, relative to the serial holdings and intake in a particular collection. For example, Berkeley, which has long prided itself on the massive strength of its serial holdings, 65 percent of which are entered under corporate body, is particularly concerned with the AACR 2 rules changes as they affect serial publications.

For longer range planning, as well as the immediate prospect of closing card catalogs, data enabling us to project the amount and cost of on-line usage of bibliographic files would be enormously helpful. There would seem to be a large number of variables associated with the quantity of on-line queries: size of file; ease of access; nature of the instructional and research programs; training and assistance provided for users; declining costs of computer storage; and other factors. Manipulating estimates of all of these in order to provide a projection that would assist a given library in allocating funds for on-line terminals at its public service stations is probably about as difficult as fashioning a Leontief matrix for the gross national product. Nevertheless, even a much cruder handle on these costs might at least give us some rough basis for budgetary projections of what will certainly be an important aspect of library service.

In company with any other major change in library operations, the closing of library card catalogs places library administrators at the center of various categories of constituents, and thus poses delicate questions in political and public relations strategies. The cast of characters is familiar: user groups from the academic community --faculty, students, and staff. Certain other users should be considered as well: borrowers of library materials through interlibrary loan, particularly borrowers from institutions with which a given library has formal network connections. Previously established rapport, or the lack of it, with these various constituencies will contribute a good deal to the kind of reception given to plans and proposals affecting our present systems of bibliographic display.

The planning work underway at Berkeley also exemplifies an attempt to involve library staff members in the decision-making process. Despite what may seem to some administrators a troublesome inefficiency engendered by dispersed responsibility for decision making in this area, the widespread participation of staff--professional, nonprofessional, public service as well as technical service and systems-- can and should offer a series of payoffs. Staff involvement should enhance the intrinsic quality of the planning; in a complementary fashion, the process of planning should lead to increased awareness and knowledge among a large segment of the library staff. Moreover, it should strengthen the quality of library service during a period of dramatic bibliographic change because of greater staff commitment to the implementation of plans resulting from group effort.

Concluding Remarks

I've tried to outline some major concerns most of us face in contemplating the closing of library card catalogs. Some of these concerns are institutional-specific, but others are general and could well be addressed by the library community acting in concert. The investments we have made individually and as a group in our bibliographic files are sizeable--in almost any league except perhaps AT&T, General Motors, and the U.S. defense budget.

There may be a few library operations that will not be affected by the closing of existing card catalogs, but I would find it difficult to name more than half a dozen. Most technical service functions will feel the impact immediately and seriously, and even more significant will be the reverberations in public service and the costs of those operations.

It is disquieting to realize that while most of us are aware that the closing of card catalogs will be a major event--in terms of costs, quality of service, organization and deployment of library personnel, and reactions from users--we have a very imprecise idea of the nature or extent of the consequences. Lucia Rather of the Library of Congress remarked at LC's excellent presentation at ALA Midwinter 1978 that one of the recurrent fears within the group of staff members planning for LC's freezing of its catalogs was that a completely new and unanticipated result--one for which there would be no obvious solution--would occur in the period immediately after the official freeze and the beginning of a new era. This could certainly happen; all of us will probably experience a few rude shocks as we pass through the coming retooling of our bibliographical systems.

In retrospect, careful managerial attention to these issues should have begun with the decision in the early 1970s to proceed with work on a second edition of the <u>Anglo-American Cataloguing Rules</u>, or even earlier in the previous decade when Bill Welsh and others at LC began to examine the possibilities of changing the structure of LC's catalogs.

Despite what we might have done, I am inclined to regard the bibliographic horizon, on balance, as very promising. There is work cut out for all of us; with some diligence and imagination we need not lament--with sackcloth and ashes--the closing of card catalogs. Quite the opposite--the future holds for us the exciting promise of truly opened catalogs.

References

1. The Future of Card Catalogs (Washington, D.C.: Association of Research Libraries, 1975), p. 14-17.
2. "How to Close," presentation at "Closing the Catalog: Automated Alternatives to the Card Catalog," seminar sponsored by METRO (New York Metropolitan Reference and Research Library Agency), 4 Nov. 1977.
3. These reports are available as a group from Room 245, General Library, University of California, Berkeley, CA 94720. The cost of the reports is $7; checks should be made to Regents of the University of California.

30. Automation and the Library Administrator*

by Eleanor Montague

Introduction

"If you have the urge to automate, sit down and calmly wait for it to pass!" was a common piece of advice to library administrators in the mid-1960s. The news of large money expenditures, problems, and pitfalls spread even when system developers and administrators went to great lengths not to divulge such problems or mistakes. At the same time, computer specialists likening libraries to screw and nut inventory problems promised that our concerns were trivial; that library processing would occupy only seconds of computer processing time. Administrators were promised "instant computerization" of library functions as a remedy for problems of spiraling labor costs, increasingly complex procedures, growing manual files, and other ills.

While no library administrator involved with early automation efforts will claim it was easy, thanks to advances in technology, networking, and turnkey systems, examples of successful applications of computer technology to library processing and services abound. The computer has become a fast new tool, both in the backroom and in the front lines of patron service; it has brought greater flexibility, speed, and the potential for expanded cooperation and service. The computer has been a significant agent of change in libraries and we can be assured that future developments will bring even more dramatic changes and challenges.

Early soothsayers predicted an instant organizational, management, and service revolution to go along with the instant computerization--a new order of things. While there has been change, it has been evolutionary rather than revolutionary, and we have a long way to go. In looking at the impact of automation on administration, it is also important to remember that automation has not been the sole agent of change in libraries recently. Pressures for sound management practices and the need to manage for innovation as well as for the status quo have increased during the 1970s, including demands for greater accountability, pressures from the changing economic and social scene, inflation, staff demands for greater role in

---

*Reprinted by permission of the author and the American Library Association from Journal of Library Automation, December 1978, p. 313-323, copyright © 1978 by the American Library Association.

the management and decision-making process, networking capabilities and national developments, competing demands for limited resources, and a leveling or constriction of budgets.

The purpose of this paper is, first, to look at the changing characteristics of the development of automation in libraries over time; second, to examine the reaction of management to these developments; and third, to list the management challenges for the future. For the purposes of discussion, the development of automation in libraries is divided into three phases:
1. The Developmental Phase--The period through the early seventies, characterized by system experimentation, development, and entrepreneurship in a limited number of institutions around the country.
2. The Operational Phase--The period beginning in the seventies through the current time, characterized by system sharing and electronic networks, vendor supplied systems, competition, and broad library participation.
3. The Integrative Phase--The period emerging now and going into the future, characterized by the integration of systems across functional lines, the definition and implementation of national networking capabilities, greater cooperation, a more substantial impact on processing and service capabilities, greater information industry involvement, and continuing technological innovation.

The Developmental Phase

In planning for automation, library administrators counted on a number of effects: speedier and simplified processing procedures, greater sharing of bibliographic information, improved access to collections, and reduced staffing. In general, the practical goals for automation were (1) to do what was currently being done better, faster, or more effectively, and (2) to provide services and products that were infeasible or impossible with the manual system. In addition, many hoped that this would be a period of research into the applicability of computers to help libraries achieve their missions, unfettered by many of the constraints imposed by manual systems.

The period was characterized by generous foundation and government funding for several large system development projects in individual libraries throughout the country, numerous small automation projects in individual libraries, little interaction or coordination between development projects, and substantial schedule slippages.

The concept of total system design was alive in the literature, but, with only a few exceptions where systems were indeed designed with the totality in mind, applications were typically restricted to one or a few functions. The prime candidates were serial processing and lists, circulation, acquisitions, and book fund accounting (and occasionally cataloging), depending on pressures being felt in the institution, the interests of library management, the interests of funding sources, available expertise, and the computer facilities or services available.

Just as we lauded the potential situation in which a book would be cataloged just once in the country, the management hope for system development during the period was that a system developed once at one institution could be transferred to another institution. This management dream was thwarted on a number of counts. Hardware and software operating systems differed from place to place. Library application programs were integrated into computer systems in various ways. But more importantly, libraries did not agree on a standardized way of doing things. An output format found quite acceptable at one institution would be found woefully lacking by the staff at another institution; a data element deemed essential by institution X would be scoffed at by institution Y, and so on. At each library, the application of automation even to similar functions appeared different and incompatible.

There were two significant national developments during the period: the MARC Pilot Project and the initiation of the regular MARC subscription service. These developments established for the library community an exhaustively complete, standardized bibliographic record content and format definition for the communication of bibliographic information that could still be utilized by the individual institution to fit local processing requirements and priorities.

Several challenges faced management in planning for this new tool. First, the technology itself was evolving rapidly. A 1967 White House report on computers in higher education begins with the statement that "after growing wildly for several years, the field of computing now appears to be approaching its infancy."[1] Management inclined to pursue automation was faced with making decisions without the benefits of personal expertise or prior experience in the midst of rapid hardware and software changes and technological developments. Expert computer advice was available but suffered from both ignorance and underestimation of library requirements and the same rapid technological changes.

Second, there were few librarians trained in the new technology. Therefore, the application of computer technology required the integration of expertise from three different groups of people: librarians, programmers, and computer experts. Finding no immediate common ground of terminology, priorities, or concerns, the seeds of miscommunication, misdirection, and misunderstanding flourished. Salary scales, work habits, work hours, and views of the work to be done varied widely between library and computer personnel, with library managers expected to play referee and interpreter.

Organizationally, a common management decision was to create a systems office, populated by systems analysts and programmers given the responsibility of designing, testing, and implementing the computer application in the library. On the positive side during the developmental period, this brought the people charged with automation together in one place in the organization. On the negative side, the isolation occasionally fed the suspicion of the staff, caused miscommunication, and often led to a situation in which the systems staff ignored the real requirements and priorities of the library. The concentration of responsibility in a systems office frequently robbed the line manager of the opportunity to understand the automated application in the context of the total operation of the unit or department. In addition, the majority of the time, library management did not possess the expertise to properly direct or evaluate the system development effort. Unfortunately, the result was often an autonomous systems staff.

Third, change is ideally predicated on a long-range plan, a thorough knowledge of the present system in totality--including procedures, files, historical precedent, and resource allocations, and a method for evaluating the change. Regrettably, there were numerous management failures during this period: (1) failure to clearly articulate the goals and priorities of the organization; (2) failure to fully understand the current system that was to be modified by automation; (3) failure to analyze costs of the manual system prior to automation as a benchmark against which to compare the costs after automation; (4) failure to develop evaluation techniques to measure the efficiency or effectiveness of the automated systems; and (5) failure to establish an ongoing methodology for monitoring costs.

Fourth, resource allocation (always difficult at best) became a real challenge. Most early automation efforts resulted in no staff savings, requiring that automation development and operating costs come from other sources, including local institutions, the government, foundations, or reallocations from other areas in the budget. The challenge to the library administrator was not only to explain to funders and higher administrators the potential benefits of automation, but also to educate them as to how a library works. The real costs of computer processing in library applications were virtually unknown by library administrators making decisions to automate. Budget estimates repeatedly evaporated in a sea of red ink as libraries learned more and more about the job to be done and as computer experts learned that library requirements were different from industrial inventory applications. Additionally, influxes of grant money and "free" (contributed) computer time from local computer facilities distorted the real potential impact on the operating budget.

The myth was still very much alive that automation would save money. As this myth turned to smoke toward the end of the period, the management argument turned to increased services rather than cost savings. To some, the argument of dealing with spiraling costs for the future (slowing the rate of rise of costs), rather than cost saving in the present, became an attractive alternative way of justifying automation in libraries.

Fifth, management attempts to utilize information from other libraries engaged in automation efforts usually proved impossible because of different system designs and requirements, different data elements and data bases, different computer center charging algorithms, hidden charges, internal money transfers, differing products, and so on. The automated bibliographic wheel was reinvented at each library; meaningful comparisons were nearly impossible.

Sixth, more than ever before, the dedication of management to communication (up and down) was essential and never were the cases of abysmal failure more prevalent. Out of ignorance and fear of the unknown, typical resistance to change, and skepticism about the benefits of the computer and the interests of the systems analyst and designer in their real requirements, the staff waited to see what the result would be. Where communication was open and frequent, where the operational staff was consulted, and where training was constant and thorough, the chances for a successful implementation increased dramatically. Where these actions on the part of management did not take place and staff resistance built up, change was made more difficult, if not sabotaged altogether.

In summary, it was a period of trial and error, experimentation, and learning. By and large, the new technology touched few libraries and, in these, the change touched only small segments of the total library operation. Where it did touch, there was frequently not a revolutionary change. As a matter of fact, in many cases, the automated systems were merely superimposed on existing manual systems with little change or true integration.

The local focus on development allowed the system designers to tailor the system design to the local environment, without changing local idiosyncrasies or procedures, even when these were inefficient. On the other hand, a frequent cause for frustration in the library was the computer experts' dismissal of our requirements with the observation that "the computer can't do that." Often, library management never asked, "Why not?"

Also as a result of local development, capabilities were programmed around the country to take MARC records and massage them to fit local conventions. Decisions to deviate from the MARC content and format were the rule rather than the exception, causing problems with interinstitutional information or system sharing. The siren call of cheap, very fast computer manipulation of information caused libraries to believe that the perfectionism attempted in the manual system could be finally achieved, without additional cost. For example, failure to understand the real costs of automation led the library community to specify every conceivable piece of information in the MARC format without asking what the price tag would be; we are still paying the price of that completeness in our systems of today.

A backward look into the times reveals an agonizing lack of leadership and planning on the part of library management. Managers trying to cope with change and many unknowns abdicated, in my view, their responsibility to give a sense of direction to the internal organization or to exert control over the external agents of change. The technological tail wagged the library and bibliographic dog. The staff tail, wedded to historical procedures and practices, wagged the development dog. Managers struggling with the new technology failed to follow the basic steps of systems analysis and development or the rational decision-making process in which change is made in the context of goals and priorities and the long-term view. Facing the prospect of staff resistance to change, the temptation to program the manual system was unbearable for many managers. The failure to comprehend the potential impact of automation on traditional procedures and services and the resulting failure to take full advantage of the new tool is evident in our systems of today.

The Operational Phase

The benefits of automation hoped for in the 1960s were still needed in the 1970s. It was clear that the challenges of continually escalating labor costs in the manual environment could not be met merely by cutting staff; while efficiencies were undoubtedly possible in the majority of manual systems, gains in efficiency alone could not hope to meet the challenges faced by libraries. The social and economic pressures building during this time, the end of the era of unprecedented growth in libraries, the need to compete more aggressively for resources, and a society accustomed to technological advances, brought the necessity to automate into clearer focus for most library administrators.

It was during this phase that libraries witnessed the development of successful networks, the sharing of computer systems, proven on-line applications, turnkey library systems, vendor-supplied automated capabilities, minicomputer applications, the promise of microcomputer applications, and greater competition among systems. The earlier management prospect of having to replicate systems developed at one institution in another was largely replaced by the capability to share hardware, software, and data bases. With the availability of choices and advances in the technology, it was possible to differentiate those library applications best handled cooperatively with large data bases, such as cataloging, from those high-transaction-volume, specifically local applications, such as circulation, which could be handled in-house by stand-alone systems.

As a result, libraries of all types and sizes that were unable to invest the horrendous financial and human resources necessary to undertake system development efforts could now utilize this new tool. For library management, the risks were now less, there was more flexibility, there were choices, there was an ever-growing community of libraries utilizing similar or the same systems, the mystique surrounding computer systems was reduced, and the general acceptance of the capabilities of automation was increasing throughout the ranks of the profession. Accordingly, and in line with other pressures, the challenges involved in the management of automated systems shifted from development to implementation, integration, and greater staff involvement.

- Technical Knowledge. The developments in automated library applications have become such that the technical knowledge required for intelligent decision making is well within the capabilities of virtually every library manager. Rather than having to rely solely on outside experts, we have in libraries of all sizes and types a growing number of managers and staff able and willing to specify needs, evaluate alternatives, and make decisions. As a result, in many libraries there has been a shift of responsibility for system definition and implementation from a systems department or outside experts to those line managers ultimately responsible for the integration and operation of the new system. Larger libraries engaged in local system development still often utilize systems departments of experts, but the clear and welcome pattern of greater involvement for the line manager and staff seems to be an established one.

Except for a certain level of expertise and understanding required to evaluate computer capabilities specifically, the management planning and decision-making processes involving automation have proven to be identical to those necessary for other change factors requiring rational decisions--the accountability for managing the change so that it matches the needs, priorities, and goals of the organization is the same and clearly resides ultimately with the library administrator.

- Decision-making Process. The successful introduction of any change involves the development of a consistent, logical process and framework for short- and long-term planning and decision making. The essential first step in this process is the preparation of a clear statement of goals, objectives, and priorities for the organization as a whole, including specific goals and expectations for the area to be impacted by the change. This plan should be formulated only after (1) wide consultation in the internal environment; (2) wide consultation in, and education of, the external environment; (3) a thorough analysis of the current environment, including bottlenecks, constraints, limitations, and inadequacies; (4) a clear understanding of current resource allocation decisions and current costs; and (5) a carefully prepared statement of the anticipated impact of automation on the organization.

Based on the analysis, it is possible for library administration to identify appropriate steps and choices. Assuming the decision is to apply new technology, the next step is to prepare a comprehensive statement of requirements, expectations, and priorities for the automated application, conducted with an air of imagination and creativity so as to fully utilize the automated capabilities, with an air of questioning tradition-bound procedures, and with a goal to supply capabilities for the library and its users impossible in the manual system.

The third step in the management process is the evaluation of all available systems against the stated criteria. Once the choice is made, the organization must construct a detailed implementation plan, a timetable for implementation, and a statement of formal organizational structure in which to make fullest use of the factors of change. Meaningful staff input to the process is essential, as are truly effective training programs and a two-way communication environment. Finally, this whole management decision-making process must take the whole organization into account, not just the segment of the organization involved in the change.

Unfortunately, examples of management failures to follow this logical process persisted in the 1970s. One of the most important steps--to define an ongoing, efficient mechanism for feedback, evaluation, and improvement--is one of the most neglected. So often, the tendency is to think that the system of today will remain unchanged over time, yet we know that technology and our utilization of it will certainly evolve and change. For this evolution to be effectively guided, it is essential to monitor the system, provide a feedback channel, evaluate the system's performance against changing requirements, and factor improvements into the ongoing system.

● Buy or Make. The decision to make or to buy an automated system is still a very real one for libraries. The management process to build, or have built, a system is similar to buying into a network or a turnkey system, but additional specifications must be prepared for system and vendor performance, hardware, system and user test procedures, error correction, system maintenance, implementation, evaluation and future improvements, and penalties for vendor nonperformance.

● Competitive Bidding. Many library managers face the requirement for competitive bidding in the choice of systems. Where it is desirable or mandatory, the preparation of a request for proposal (RFP) or request for quotation (RFQ) is an important management responsibility. Since these requests constitute specifications for what is needed, their preparation requires extreme care in order to ensure that all requirements are fully and unambiguously stated, according to the statement of the organization's plan, goals, and analysis of needs. In both substance and process, management has to evaluate the bids so as to comply with legal requirements. The evaluation process consists of a number of steps, starting with the determination of each bidder's qualifications, the extent of the bidder's compliance with the request, an analysis of costs, and the applicability of the suggested system design or configuration to the existing organization and staff. While a numerical scoring process to evaluate a bidder's promises to meet requirements is a useful tool, decisions of this magnitude cannot be decided purely on the basis of numerical scores or lowest cost. Management must factor judgment and nonquantifiable considerations of significant issues into the decision-making process. For those libraries wishing to use a numerical scoring system as one component of the evaluation process, there are numerous computer programs and consulting firms available to aid the decision maker.

● Management Techniques. The opportunity for library management to make rational decisions based on a logical process has always been present, but during this period there has been a proliferation of articles and conferences on how to apply decision-making and evaluation techniques from other disciplines in managing change in the library, including operations research, cost-benefit analysis, management by objectives, theory X and theory Y personnel management, socioeconomic factors of motivation, and many others. In addition, a number of self-analysis techniques have appeared within the last several years, designed to provide a systematic internal review of a library's organizational and management structure and functions. MRAP (Management Review and Analysis Program) is an example for the large institution; less exhaustive versions and variations exist for the smaller library.[2]

The challenge for management is to apply the technique that best fits the situation; to choose a technique that fits the resources available; and to choose the simplest technique, or a collage of techniques, that will get the job done. Forgetting the chaotic consequences of the failure to use any recognized management techniques for planning, we have many examples of the other extreme, namely "overkill." The national network could probably be funded if we had a dollar for every elaborate study, every committee report, or every pound of statistical data compiled as an aid to a management decision that went unused or provided no real assistance in the process. Almost as much care is required in the choice and process of analysis and evaluation as in the decision itself. Occasionally, a half a day of intelligent, directed analysis is a perfect substitute for five or six days' work, if the manager knows what he or she wants and needs and takes the time to define it. Library managers must make some fundamental decisions about the allocation of their time. It is not sufficient to manage for the status quo or the short-term future. Yet, we all know that these concerns can fully occupy every waking hour. What is required is a decision to allocate time for the long-range planning that is essential in order to influence the process of change and not merely react to it.

● Communication and Staff Involvement. The introduction of change, to be effective, requires a management dedication to (1) involve the staff in the definition of requirements and the implementation of the system and (2) provide training so that they fully understand the system, its role in the mission of the library, and their role in making it run. Experience and common sense indicate that a properly trained and motivated staff can provide imaginative and dynamic ideas for change and the utilization of new resources that rival those of most outside experts. Staff members today are looking for job satisfaction and a share in the objectives of the organization, based on mutual trust and confidence with library management. It is management's responsibility to provide opportunities in which this kind of staff participation and involvement can grow and flourish.

● Impact of Automation. The utilization and impact of automation has varied significantly among libraries. Some have increased staff, some have decreased staff, some have stayed the same; some have realized the goal of processing more material with the same staffing level, some have not. The difference is dependent on a number of factors, including conditions before automation; staffing levels before automation; the attitudes, interests, and philosophy of library management; and the extent to which the staff has been prepared or encouraged to deal positively with the change.

A major technological reason behind these differences has been the flexibility of the automated systems. Almost without exception, automated systems and networks have allowed each participating library utmost flexibility in the use of the system, allowing a library to perpetuate local idiosyncrasies and procedures if it wishes. Given this degree of flexibility, it has been utterly possible to use the automated system as inefficiently and ineffectively and with as little knowledge of what is going on as with the manual system.

In summary, in contrast to the earlier period of development involving a small number of libraries, during the seventies there has been a widespread application of computer systems in libraries of all types and sizes, thanks to advances in on-line technology, communications, and networking. As a result, the emphasis for management has shifted from entrepreneurship and systems development, design and experimentation, to system specification and choice, implementation, functional integration, measurement and evaluation, and greater interlibrary cooperation and sharing.

The new technology has created a challenge for management that has taxed planning and decision-making skills; however, the technology has not produced a revolution either in the way libraries go about their business or, to much of an extent, in the ways in which patrons are served. We have not simplified the procedures for or interaction with the bibliographic apparatus; instead, the automated systems are as complex as our previous manual systems. In general, staff savings have not been realized as a result of automation, nor have libraries really tested the hypothesis that the same staff could process more materials due to automation, since the era of unprecedented growth came to an end as the operational phase began. The rule rather than the exception is still to view automated capabilities as one-to-one replacements for manual systems--as an opportunity not only to perpetuate local variations but frequently to consider more of them, given the speed and apparent ease afforded by the computer. By specific multiple, exhaustive MARC formats and applying them to retrospective as well as current records, we have failed to examine cost as a function of benefit for the retrieval of library materials. Years ago when systems were first designed, we failed to ask whether the abundance of data we specified was required and whether we could afford it. Rather than using the computer tool to create new ways of doing things, we applied it to our historical practices with little creativity. It is still too early to tell what price we have paid for those decisions.

As we find more functions in the library that can be efficiently and effectively automated, including some front-line services to patrons, our challenge is to integrate these parts creatively into one compatible whole which is greater than the sum of the parts. As a group, however, I maintain that we have rested too comfortably on past accomplishments; we have had insufficient influence on network managers or designers concerning the priorities or schedules of future developments; and we have been so happy to see the successful application of on-line networking to the cataloging function, for example, that we have failed to plan sufficiently for (1) other applications, such as acquisitions or book fund accounting, (2) bibliographic control of collections other than monographs and serials, (3) the ripple effects coming from our current systems, (4) future technological developments, (5) the integration of applications, or (6) the potential impact of these developments on the role of the library in a changing society.

The Integrative Phase--Challenges for the Future

It is reasonable to assume that technological advancements and pressures for sound management and accountability from the changing economic and social scene will continue, and may well affect more aspects of our business or raise more questions of our relevancy in society than developments to date. In all probability, the changing situation will put the traditional library into greater competition for resources and with other segments of the economy for the control and delivery of information. For the future, library administrators will have to deal with the ripple effects arising as a result of current systems, networks, and national planning, and plan for the future with full recognition of past accomplishments and failures. The limited growth expectations for book, materials, and building project budgets, plus developments in national network planning, will result in greater reliance on information about holdings of other libraries as recorded in the bibliographic data bases available on-line throughout the country. The opportunity for more systematic acquisitions decisions based on knowledge of other collections, and the multilateral agreements for cooperation and resource sharing that will follow, will have an impact on internal procedures and priorities. A major impact involves the collection development function, where decisions must be made about in-house holdings versus materials of potentially lesser use than can be gotten through a cooperative arrangement. In turn, this instant access capability will affect (1) patron service goals, (2) views on ever-expanding collections and collection-development policies, (3) views on centralized, shared storage facilities for lesser-used materials, and (4) space needs and plans for new library buildings.

These effects will result in an impact on our interlibrary loan functions, which will have to accommodate the increased traffic of both borrowing and lending transactions. The load-leveling effect of multiple locations shown in bibliographic data bases may offset the burden currently borne by a few large collections, but the extent of that impact is not yet known. In all probability, current interlibrary loan staffing patterns will not be sufficient to handle the increased volume likely to build as on-line systems are used in collection development and acquisitions decisions. This will necessitate a shift of resources to the interlibrary loan function, since speed and accuracy will be required to make the system of resource sharing work.

Another major ripple effect is the strain on large collections heavily used by other libraries, where the priorities of handling local needs must be juggled with the needs of other libraries wishing to borrow books. When these problems are solved, libraries will still be faced with improving both the communication of interlibrary loan requests and the physical transportation of the materials. Unless we can deliver the material in a timely fashion, the speed of access to location information in on-line systems is for naught.

An inevitable outcome of the efforts to date is the replacement of the three-by-five-inch card catalog in the local library with an on-line catalog, either centrally maintained on shared equipment or maintained locally on a stand-alone system. Unless we are fooled into accepting merely a machine equivalent of our unwieldy, increasingly difficult current card files, the on-line catalog with its multiple access points and capabilities for Boolean search operators will revolutionize the use of the catalog as a bibliographic tool, our reference service, and our interaction with the patron. As we try to learn from the past, it is distressing to note that the on-line catalog (frequently viewed as a one-to-one replacement of the manual file but utilizing a different medium) is more often heralded as a way to reduce filing costs in the manual card files than as a refreshing, dynamic new tool for access to the collections, with the potential of being integrated with other capabilities to form a total library system.

Challenging questions of resource allocation remain. Capital and operating costs of automation must be offset by staff savings, budget increase, reallocations from other areas in the budget, a charge for services, or a combination of these. For example, if libraries are to support the costs of patron access to on-line catalogs once the card catalog is closed, there must be a shift in resource allocation from manual filing and maintenance to the costs of building, maintaining, and operating the on-line catalog. If the shift does not result in savings, libraries will have to face reallocations from other parts of the budget, charge fees, or argue for a budget increase. The fee-for-service controversy already sparked by the issue of charging for computer literature searching may well be just the beginning as we face the on-line catalog, full text retrieval capabilities on demand through a computer system, and additional capabilities that may come about in the future.

With enhancements in on-line systems and the emergence of vendor-supplied systems, we can look forward to significant changes in our way of acquiring material. Some libraries are already electronically ordering material from vendors and there is no reason to believe that this capability will escape general library use. Advances

in direct communication with the vendor, plus the on-line catalog
with authority control and electronic interlibrary loan switching and
accounting and an interface with circulation systems, will have a
substantial impact on library operations. As these developments unfold,
it is essential that library management plan for a true integration
of automated capabilities across functions, ask hard questions
about the long-term cost-benefit tradeoff of decisions, question historical
sacred cows, establish effective communication links with
staff, and take a more aggressive role in shaping capabilities,
schedules, and priorities in future network and national planning
developments.

In summary, we have assumed that libraries are a societal
good beyond question and have immersed ourselves in detailed questions
of bibliographic access and control without regard to possible
shifting trends and priorities in society. In an era of tax revolution
(as witnessed in California by the passage of the Jarvis proposition),
libraries cannot assume automatic public support. Library administration
must assume an outspoken and dynamic leadership role in
the definition and development of future capabilities utilizing the computer
and must do so with imagination, questioning, and real attention
to priorities. Management must provide direction in selling funders
and taxpayers on the role of libraries in the society and the importance
of the new technology in this task. And most importantly, we
must understand the real requirements of the user--one of our most
critical reasons for existence.

References

1. President's Science Advisory Committee, Computers in Higher
Education (Washington, D.C.: The White House, 1967), p. 1.
2. Michael Buckland, ed. "The Management Review and Analysis
Program: A Symposium," Journal of Academic Librarianship
1, no. 6 (Jan. 1976).

31. The Effects of Automation on Library Administration*

by Günter Pflug

Thoughts on Side Effects and Their Causes

The decision to computerize a library or some of its departments is a decision of basic importance and is therefore always the concern of the library administration. Usually the specific consent or approval of superior administrative levels or authorities is also required. They would evaluate the reasoning which has led to this decision, consider the respective advantages and disadvantages of the conventional and automated systems, and, if indicated, would make available the means necessary for a systems change of the library. The introduction of a computer in a library consequently involves a process which is based on thorough evaluation. The result of this process is characterized by the realization of a goal which is intended to bring about a more favorable economic relationship between the financial outlays and the productivity of the library.

In spite of all efforts to incorporate in the process of clarification which precedes the decision all expected consequences of the introduction of EDP (electronic data processing), experience has shown that in many instances side effects which develop could not be fully anticipated in preceding planning.

Experiments with simulated models have been carried out in accordance with numerous recommendations in the expectation that in this way side effects would be discovered including those which could not be isolated by rational analysis. These experiments, preceding a library's changeover to EDP, did not bring the desired results. The development of simulation techniques and corresponding models, which show a satisfactory agreement with reality, has proven highly complex. The work involved in this development is much more risky than a concrete experiment in an actual situation. Therefore it was considered preferable in nearly all cases to have the change of a library to automated procedures preceded by a trial phase under actual conditions rather than by the utilization of a simulated model.

By being applied, this method of change to EDP installations

---
*Reprinted by permission of the author and publisher from IFLA Journal, 1 (1975), p. 267-75.

introduces a considerable risk factor, since only the trial phase discloses the extent to which in the course of the changeover side effects appear which in kind and intensity could not be anticipated by theoretical speculations; or, which at any rate were not anticipated, even if it was possible to foresee them.

Finally it should not be overlooked that neither the librarians nor the computer experts possessed the integrating, comprehensive expert knowledge necessary for carrying through electronic data processing. With such knowledge, the deliberations and experiments of the early years would have facilitated a satisfactory logical analysis of the consequences of electronic data processing. The courage to experiment, even though possible side effects could not be satisfactorily recognized, cannot be underestimated as a strong force to move the library towards the epoch of automation. It is therefore not surprising that today everywhere the question is raised regarding the side effects which library automation exercises on the structure of the work processes of the library.

It is easier to ask this question in a general way than to answer it. When these side effects were first made the subject of theoretical considerations, the side effects did not as a rule become phenomena. This is the case essentially because they are not derived from abstract, basic conditions of EDP utilization but are rather caused by certain accidental, usually locally determined special situations. Therefore, it is not only difficult to generalize but also to determine the logical and analytical direction of the side effects. An ex-post facto typification, which is required if a unique experience is to become the basis for decision making for subsequent experiments, is also rather difficult. These side effects are, as it were, meandering disturbances which represent the accumulation of multiple factors for which a rational basis can be found only under certain conditions, especially since psychological, social and conventional attitudes may also be factors which leave their impact. If it is nevertheless here attempted to characterize several types of side effects which have occurred when libraries have been automated, it must always be kept in mind that as a matter of principle, in all cases the side effects can be eliminated by a change in the conditions of work. It is thus theoretically possible to retain the library structure unchanged in the transition from conventional to automated work processes. In this way, undesirable side effects can be eliminated. As a rule, however, this would cause a considerable restriction of the effectiveness of automation. One should also resist the temptation to attach a prejorative coloring to the concept of "side effect". The experiences gained in the area of pharmacology are not necessarily identical with those in the field of librarianship. However, there is a wholesome urge to eliminate the side effects as will be shown by the following examples.

The side effects, which usually occur when work processes are automated by the utilization of EDP, may be assigned roughly to four categories:

1. Personnel problems
2. Problems caused by the departmental arrangement of libraries
3. Problems of work processes
4. Problems of libraries shaped by library autonomy and by outside forces, respectively.

These spheres are naturally connected with each other and, moreover, occur with different intensity depending on the choice of the EDP system. They are considerably influenced by the choice of either on-line or off-line routines, by the degree of accessibility of processing installations, and by the extent of automation within the libraries.

1. Personnel Problems

A conventionally organized library is characterized by a largely homogeneous personnel structure. It is true that the necessary work can be divided into a certain number of levels of complexity which make different demands on the workers of each level as to training and performance. Within a class, however, the work requirements for the individual tasks are largely identical. In conventionally organized libraries it may be assumed that a worker of a certain rank is also capable of performing the tasks of his colleagues who are in the same rank. A librarian who is assigned to circulation work must be capable, as a matter of principle, to perform corresponding tasks in accession or in cataloging. Such interchangeability of assignments is specifically required by the German salary regulations. It is a prerequisite for the assignment of staff members to certain salary levels. In conventionally organized libraries this potential of interchangeable assignments suffers only few exceptions in its application. Exceptions apply, for instance, to professionally trained bindery employees assigned to library-maintained bindery departments or to photographic technicians assigned to library-maintained photographic departments, as well as to some other specialists in the lower salary levels (for instance, operators of motor vehicles, janitors, and cleaning personnel).

The invasion of libraries by EDP destroys this homogeneity of the staff and thus confronts the library administration with new organizational problems. Suddenly the library finds itself in the situation where it has to employ highly paid specialists who can be used only in their area of specialization and who, therefore, can easily become foreign bodies in the library. (A similar situation also occurs if a library has an audio-visual center which is not only responsible for the procurement and incorporation of pertinent materials, but to a certain extent, also for the production of such materials.)

This kind of personnel development confronts the library administration with three special problems. On one hand the range of unhampered decision making on the part of the library administration is being considerably narrowed. In case of sudden loss of a staff member, as for instance through sickness, it is no longer so easily possible to transfer staff members of a certain level and to assign them other tasks either on a temporary or an extended basis. As a rule, personnel assigned to electronic data processing can be used only in that area. The more highly qualified staff members are, the less there is the opportunity to use them outside of the EDP area. This restriction of the library administration is considerably intensified if compared with the previously existing limitations (for instance, those regarding bindery workers and operators of motor vehicles). This may be explained by the fact that staff in the EDP area belong mainly to the higher salary groups who in the library's hierarchical order occupy position levels with which, up to now, the library's administrator could deal without any restrictions.

The second problem which results from a change in the personnel structure is caused by the differences in the salary structure for the several groups of staff members. Countries such as the Federal Republic of Germany have salary categories fixed by law or established by contract for persons in the government service. Under these circumstances the library administration has little or no leeway in determining individual salaries, and striking discrepancies between the compensation of library staff members and those in EDP may easily develop. The general demand for staff members with comprehensive knowledge and experience in this sector is generally high, at any rate higher than for library trained staff. When establishing salary rates for the EDP area, the state is therefore compelled to grant higher salaries than in other areas in order to find a sufficient number of experts who accept employment in government service rather than in trade and industry. (A special investigation seems indicated to evaluate this problem in countries which have a different economic structure.) However pleasant it may be on one hand that the administrator of the library has the possibility of employing EDP experts at higher salaries than comparable staff members working as conventional librarians, it should not be overlooked that this will automatically produce tension within the organization. Inasmuch as the preferred salary treatment of EDP personnel is not limited to highly qualified programmers but extends over all levels, even down to temporary replacements, the resulting area of friction is extensive.

The third problem is closely connected with these organizational and psychological problems. Since EDP personnel cannot be used for other tasks and since these persons are in higher compensation levels, EDP staff members often acquire an esoteric attitude which furthers the formation of groups or cliques within the library. The problems caused by this situation are of course not unique to libraries. Similar developments occur in industry. From general statistics regarding the mobility of staff members, it can easily be seen that electronic data processing personnel has developed its own forms of group loyalty. They feel strongly tied to each other through their common problems, a bond which extends beyond the confines of the commercial or other establishments with which they are connected. They have indeed a diminished sense of identification with their own organization.

To direct this development and to keep it within those limits which are indispensable for a tolerable work climate is one of the new responsibilities of the library administration. These are tasks which must often be handled without sufficient practical experience. The decisions are quite easily influenced by the desire to hold on to a staff member with EDP experience who had been found only through great effort. The resulting difficulties cannot be fully envisioned. Most libraries have sought alternatives suitable to eliminate part of the difficulties produced by the problems which were previously discussed. In this process two methods have been used as a rule and repeatedly tested. On one hand, libraries have made an effort not to integrate EDP personnel into the libraries but to utilize other forms of service. Here again, two channels are open, at any rate as far as programming is concerned. (For the servicing of the installations the problem does not usually occur, inasmuch as the number of libraries which have their own electronic data processing centers is very small. For EDP work most libraries utilize the computer centers of the agencies or institutions to whom they are subordinated.) The programming function may be transferred to the computer center which is already in charge of electronic data processing for the library. The incorporation of programming into this computer center does not create significant personnel policy problems, since here the homogeneity of the staff is left undisturbed. The library may, on the other hand, enter into a contract with a software firm which would undertake the programming work. There is no difference between these two ways as far as problems of management are concerned. In both cases the significant problem lies in the increasingly difficult coordination of work in comparison to the situation which prevails when the programmers are library staff members. In both instances, however, the success of automation depends decisively on the productivity and cooperativeness of an organization over which the library administration can exercise only limited influence. The problems resulting from this situation will be discussed later.

The other, more widely adopted procedure is to forego the employment of experienced EDP personnel and to systematically train library staff to handle EDP problems. Most of the libraries, which in recent years have dealt with such automation processes, have gone this way--at least for parts of the programs which were to be developed--and they have in addition arranged for the training of librarians as systems analysts and as programmers. It is evident that this method is preferable. In the problems we have discussed here, this method solves certainly some of the difficulties which are caused by the slight opportunity to incorporate EDP personnel into the organization of a library. The aspect of the difficulties which results from the salary structure cannot be eliminated in these situations, inasmuch as librarians who perform the work of systems analysts or programmers have naturally a claim to the higher compensation. Consequently the area of friction within a library persists.

2. Problems of Departmentation of the Library

The problems treated above are naturally, to a not insignificant degree, problems of departmentation. A new department for systems analysis and programming must be added to the library. By its structure this department represents, as it were, a foreign body within the conventional library organization. The problems to be discussed here are, however, of opposing nature: The isolation of the new departments as well as the breaking down of hitherto strictly fixed departmental boundaries within a library are certainly not unintended and unexpected side effects, but intentionally sought results of automation. These results are viewed with the perspective of a general exploitation of data once they are captured and put into machine-readable form. This goal which is usually designated with the term "integrated system" will not be described nor discussed at this juncture. There are probably no planners of EDP utilization in librarianship who do not work towards an integrated system. However, we shall discuss here two side effects: one, organizational, and the other, psychological. In a conventional library the departments are largely autonomous. The establishment and modification of work processes usually affect merely the department in which such changes are to be carried out. If a department does not change the boundaries for its work processes, a change in the work sequences does not have any influence on the other departments. For this reason, in a library in which a sensible delegation of authority has taken place, the library director may grant to the department heads a large measure of decision making power, even in organizational matters, as long as the decisions do not have any influence on the inflow or outflow of the material which is to be handled, but affect only the internal work processes of the department.

The introduction of EDP installations in libraries has not changed their structure to any appreciable degree inasmuch as only certain departments were taken over by the electronic data processing unit. In these cases the relationships with the other departments have usually remained unchanged. Nearly all library automation projects, which have been put into effect until now, have left the library's organizational pattern untouched. So far the extent of automation has been delimited by the conventional departmental boundaries. In only a few cases have integrated systems, in the narrow meaning of this term, been conceived; still more rarely have steps been undertaken, to translate these concepts into reality; and where such initiatives have been undertaken, the realization has been achieved in several steps whose sequence has been determined by the conventional departmental organization.

Within the framework of the present discussion, it is not essential to ask whether the conventional organization of a library is so strongly determined by the subject division that such division must also form the basis for the organization of an automated library. In whatever way a library may be organized, it must be aligned around a data bank which influences the work processes of the individual department. This is very different from the role of

catalogs in a conventional library. This tying of all departments to
a data bank results in a considerably stronger interrelatedness between the departments with the effect that, in the interest of reducing
friction, the sphere of action of the department heads must be more
limited than in conventional libraries. In an integrated automated
system, organizational decisions, which up to now could be handled
on the departmental level, will become the responsibility of the top
administrative level of the library. Simultaneously this also brings
about a change in the structure of the decision making process since
the library administration must take into account, to a higher degree
than has been necessary up to now, the effect of such changes on
the several departments or work processes even if the changes are
concerned with only a single work process. Ad hoc decisions are
fraught with a considerably higher risk in the planning stage. For
this reason, each decision process requires thorough preparation.
Also for this reason, steps must be undertaken which prevent procedures concerned with the organizational structure of a library from
becoming so complex as to lead to immobility. It is particularly
important that a sufficiently flexible decision making machinery exists
for necessary organizational changes, since adoption of EDP has a
powerful impact on the efficiency of the library.

3. Problems of the Work Process

The tying of a library to an electronic data processing installation
imposes on the library certain working conditions which result from
the structure and method of work of such an installation. The problems which are hereby encountered are not at all technological in
origin but may be ascribed to economic conditions. For this reason
they may be easily eliminated on a theoretical plane, though in actuality they usually resist solution for economic reasons.

All systems of automation which were put in operation in the
early years of library automation--from about the early 60's to the
early 70's--were off-line systems which necessitated batch processing.
This form of an electronic data processing setup leads necessarily to
a periodicity of the work processes. This interferes deeply with the
work structure of conventionally organized libraries.

A conventional library usually has a continuing flow of work.
Even material coming into the library in a disconnected fashion (e.g.,
large shipments of books from book dealers or binderies) or by disconnected decision processes (e.g., periodically occurring purchase
meetings) is handled by means of continuing work processes. It is
true that in the work processes disconnected units are always being
created, for instance by temporary storage of materials on book
trucks. The work rhythm, however, is not thereby influenced. It is
determined exclusively by the work attitude of the staff members.

When an EDP installation is utilized, this continuous work
flow is transformed into periodic segments. Since the EDP installation is available only at specific periods for the handling of library

programs, work in the several automated departments is tied to a rhythm which is determined by the EDP unit. It is true that subsequent manual treatment will still occur in a continuing fashion. However, even here a structure involving periodic handling has been superimposed. It compels the staff members to complete before the next period a certain workload prescribed by the computer in order that the whole system may remain in step.

The sociological background of this development can be generally delimited in nearly all areas of activity at a time when the utilization of large pieces of equipment is increasing. Pieces of machinery which exceed a certain size lose their identity as tools of man, which can be characterized by the fact that man uses them when he needs them. They acquire their separate identity and, on their part, expect to be served by man.

The tension which exists between the servicing of an EDP installation and the installation's servicing itself represents a problem which has effects even on the daily operations of the automated library. This tension is distinctly articulated by librarians in their demands for more flexibility in the utilization of the EDP setup. As a rule, they propose the replacing of the batch system by forms which are capable of dialog. Such a form would, of course, free librarians from having to take into account the work structure of the EDP installation. The fact that such demands are made in a vague, general way without examination of individual cases shows that the demands are based not only on rational considerations but also on psychological forces from which they hope to be freed by their demands.

Such arguments, formed by a strange mixture of emotional and rational causes and directed against work processes which are largely determined by EDP, are, of course, not peculiar to librarians. Similar kinds of arguments can also be found in other areas of higher learning or of public affairs.

Many librarians overlook that the alternative between on-line and off-line utilization of EDP, a favorite topic of discussion, is based on incorrect assumptions. In this case, antagonism is constructed instead of a rational evaluation of the potentials of both the batch process and the need for interactive routines. It is not within the scope of the present discussion to take a stand on this controversy which will have a decisive influence on the further utilization of EDP. However, the need to apply the batch process is without doubt in the sphere of side effects which must be treated here.

It is necessary to examine much more closely than has been the case up to now to what extent the requirement of using the batch process must be accepted and where this requirement may be set aside by a change in the application of the EDP system. However, even now it can be stated with certainty that this requirement, which is derived from the internal structure of the computer, cannot be fully eliminated even in quite perfect on-line systems. Experience with such systems has shown that periodicity of work processes will soon be replaced by a considerable increase in the waiting period for handling the dialog. The time frame, which batch process users can easily tolerate, has an immediate effect on the manual processes if an interactive mode is involved. It is evident that in the matter of work processes, the application of EDP will to a certain degree entail side effects.

4. Problems Shaped by Library Autonomy and by Outisde Forces, Respectively

The problem area which was discussed above already revealed a distinct influence on the library's work processes by an institution which is usually outside of the immediate sphere of influence of the library administration, namely the computer center which handles library tasks. In only rare instances is the EDP installation directly incorporated in the library. For this reason it is usually necessary to determine, together with agencies which are outside of the library, the needs of the library for computer work both as to quantity and as to termination dates. Inasmuch as the need for computer time has significantly increased in all phases of public affairs and inasmuch as this need as a rule exceeds the available computer capacity, a situation has been created which considerably restricts the sphere of action of the libraries in their use of the computer.

Theoretically the library may avoid being governed by outside forces simply by acquiring its own EDP unit. In actuality, however, this method has its limitations because of the considerable cost of such a unit. This is certainly always the case if the unit must have such large dimensions that it can handle an integrated library system which uses the interactive method. There are certainly more advantageous cost comparisons between smaller, partial systems, as for instance library-owned mini-computers for the automation of circulation, and the tying of the library to a large computer housed in a computer center. For fully integrated on-line systems, however, the library-owned computer does not, as a rule, offer an economically advantageous alternative to the system which ties the library to a computer center.

By a different structuring of the computer center, libraries have tried to eliminate or at least to weaken, this nearly unavoidable pressure caused by the setting of library policy by outside forces. At the least, libraries have tried to soften the impact resulting from this situation. For several years attempts have been made in several countries to effect a combination of the computer requirements of the libraries of a region through utilization of a library-dedicated regional computer center. This idea has already been put into effect in several localities. In these instances local or regional peculiarities have influenced the varied goals and organizational patterns.

For the problems under discussion here, it seems to be of some significance to establish the extent to which libraries combine and affiliate with a library-dedicated computer center either on a voluntary basis or by law. However, this distinction is of no practical importance since the requirement to cooperate exists once the decision to automate has been made. As experience has shown, such a decision to change can be reversed only by considerable expenditure of new labor. The advantages library-dedicated computer installations have over general computer centers, for instance in institutions of higher learning or in communities, lie both in the greater familiarity of dedicated centers with specific library problems and in the setting of priorities which are more favorable to libraries. While library tasks are matters of first priority in a library-dedicated computer center, such tasks are in continuing competition with the needs of other agencies in general computer centers.

Of course, the changeover to a library-dedicated center reduces the problem of heteronomy considerably: however, this problem is not being eliminated. Whatever outside agency may handle the computer requirements, any such arrangement means a restriction of the library's autonomy. Those work processes which are dependent on EDP are no longer within the sole jurisdiction of the library administration as to their timing, character, and scope. The work processes are dependent on discussions with authorities outside of the library.

Such a limitation of the autonomy of a library should not necessarily be viewed as a deficiency. It is not surprising that the library administration, which is used to independent decision making, at first views this restriction as an imposition which is very oppressive, especially in the initial stages of cooperation, since examples of such cooperation did not exist on either side and since the best procedures remain yet to be discovered. At the same time, we should not fail to see that--mainly by the establishing of library-dedicated computer centers--certain restrictions in autonomy will develop and result in a salutary uniformity in library work processes. This development can be further enhanced by library-dedicated computer centers if they require a lively exchange of data among the various participants of a system. Such an exchange can lead to a considerable reduction in effort of a library in the area of capturing data and putting them in machine-readable form.

Personnel problems, organizational problems, and competency problems form a broad spectrum of consequences resulting from the introduction of electronic data processing in libraries. Some of the difficulties mentioned here are certainly of a basic nature and reveal that each improvement in organization has also its negative aspects which can serve as ammunition to the critics of utilization of EDP, even if it is apparent that difficulties in one area are cancelled out by advances in another. Other difficulties, however, reflect only the troubles caused by mutation, difficulties usually encountered when one has to get accustomed to new structures and new kinds of qualifications. At the present state of development, one cannot decide with certainty to which of these two classes the above-mentioned examples belong. The answers of the individual librarian will differ depending on their respective temperaments and personal experiences. Only the future development, which will be formed by a compromise between the hopes of the librarians and the hard realities, will yield a definite answer. (Translated by Fritz Veit, Chicago)

32. The Retrospective Conversion Project at the University of Utah Marriott Library*

by Yasuko Kao

Introduction

The University of Utah Marriott Library initiated retrospective conversion of its catalog records to machine readable form on the OCLC archival tape in August 1976. In view of increasing interest in the use of computer data bases in the conversion of the library's bibliographic files from manual to automated operations, it seems timely and appropriate to present the conversion techniques and strategies used at the Marriott Library and its state of progress as a guide and measurement for a growing number of libraries which are planning the conversion of their catalogs.

Background

In August, 1975, the University of Utah Marriott Library joined OCLC on-line shared cataloging and catalog card production. As the Library develops its plan for automation, it becomes increasingly apparent that the full benefits of the computer cannot be realized unless the majority of the library's bibliographic information is available in machine-readable form. OCLC on-line cataloging provides a source of current cataloging data to cover the library's current output. Although this may take care of present and future catalog records, the task of converting the catalog information produced in past years still must be faced.

One of the multi-functions of OCLC is to provide archival tape service to its member libraries. The OCLC computer keeps a separate machine-readable record of each individual library's on-line cataloging, the way the library inputs the catalog record. In order to prepare for the future automated alternative to the present card catalog, it was suggested that OCLC archival service should be utilized for the retrospective conversion of the Marriott Library's catalog records. The retrospective conversion of the Library of Congress classification shelflist of the Marriott Library was thus proposed to the University administration, and the special fund was allocated to implement this project in July 1976.

―――――――――――
*Reprinted by permission of the author and publisher from Utah Libraries, 22 (Spring 1979), p. 39-43.

Implementation Approach

Since 1960, several small and medium-sized libraries containing less than 250,000 titles have replaced their card catalogs with some computer-generated alternative, and work in these areas has been reported in the literature. There is little published literature, however, on replacements for the card catalog with computer-based systems intended to handle 250,000 or more titles.[1] Furthermore, no literature is available as to methodology, staff complement, cost analysis and statistics for the retrospective conversion of a large academic library.

In August 1976, of a total 575,400 classified titles in the Marriott Library, 415,500 titles were in the Library of Congress classification, 149,500 titles in Dewey classification, and some 6,400 titles in other classifications such as the Superintendent of Document classification. The task of converting such a large mass of cataloging information produced in past years seemed overwhelmingly formidable. Since the fund allocated for this project was for one CRT terminal and two full-time staff members, the selection of catalog records to be input, the procedure, workflow, and statistical records had to be carefully examined and developed so that the project could be carried out most effectively and economically. The project organization and its results are described in the following categories: selection of catalog records, methodology, and statistics.

Selection of Catalog Record for Conversion Project

The proposed conversion was the Library of Congress classification shelflist, which contained 415,500 titles in August 1976, of which 13,510 titles had been already input in archival tape through on-line cataloging. The University of Utah Library changed its classification from Dewey to that of the Library of Congress in 1967, and its past eleven years' holdings have been classified in the Library of Congress classification. The holdings processed prior to 1967 remained in Dewey classification with some exceptions for serials and multivolume sets which were reclassified from Dewey to the Library of Congress classification.

The materials excluded from the conversion project are nonbook materials such as audio-visual materials, sound recordings, maps, and art reproductions. Music scores, microforms, scripts and serials are also excluded for various reasons. Some formats mentioned above are currently input in OCLC through on-line cataloging of new materials. However, the retrospective conversion project will not input these materials at the present time because of limited manpower and funds.

METHODOLOGY

Staff Training

Two library assistants were hired at the onset of the project's implementation. The Head of Cataloging Division was involved in planning, developing organization, work flow, and staff training. The experience at the Marriott Library has demonstrated that staff members assigned the task of verifying the bibliographic records and of preparing catalog records for conversion to machine-readable form must be familiar with cataloging fundamentals. In assigning content designators or proofing, conversion personnel must have knowledge of the cataloging rules necessary to make the correct decision for machine identification of cataloging information. Because of the limited numbers of staff members involved, the training was conducted on-the-job. Tagging and coding, additional instruction on Library of Congress subject headings, and the Marriott Library name and series authority files were given on-the-job. After the initial training period was completed, the work for original records was thoroughly reviewed by a catalog librarian in order to assure their accuracy and completeness. The input of exact and edited records, as well as original records, has always been revised before being updated to ensure the accuracy of all the catalog records. Discussions to improve the working procedure have been frequently held. New ideas, experimented with and proven helpful, have been implemented.

Work Assignment

The work assignment for the terminal operator Library Assistant II[2] mainly consists of searching for catalog records in the OCLC on-line catalog, verifying the bibliographic record in the data base against the Marriott Library shelflist, and adding the Marriott Library holdings on exact matching records. She also handles the records requiring editing. The primary duties of the terminal operator Library Assistant IV are the preparation of the original records and the revising of exact and edited records. As indicated in the flow-chart, the exact, edited, and original records are all proofread and revised before being updated in archival tape. The Marriott Library subject and series authority files are frequently checked to maintain accuracy for current subject headings and series decisions. The shelflist cards are stamped OCLC when updated in OCLC archival tape.

Statistics

Statistics are kept in various categories of the operation to be used as the means of evaluating the project's progress. These statistics provided us the vital information as to the time spent for each activity, the bibliographical data available in OCLC, and the numbers of titles input and updated in archival tape. The kinds of activities and the numbers of titles handled for each category are shown in the following tables. [See page 270.]

FLOWCHART — RETROSPECTIVE CONVERSION PROJECT

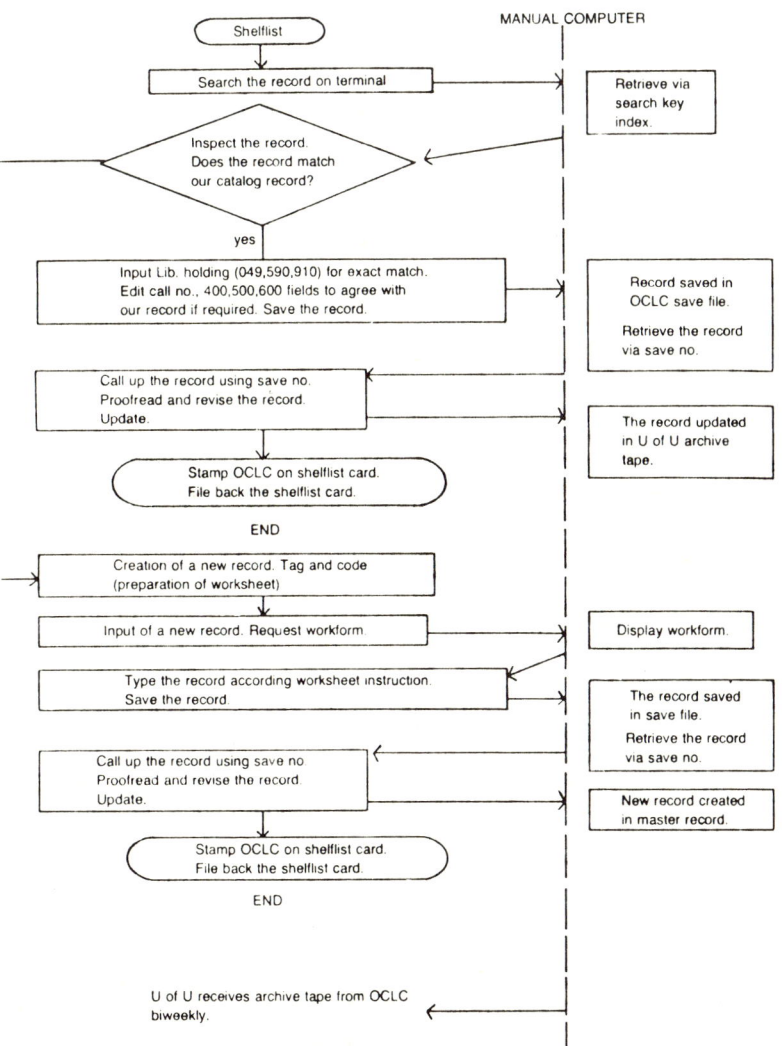

Table I. Bibliographic Searching on OCLC Data Base

Year	Month	Records found in OCLC	Records not found in OCLC
1976	Aug.-Dec.	4,306	3,233
1977	Jan.-Dec.	19,143	6,662
1978	Jan.-June*	17,790	7,687
	Total:	41,239(70%)	17,582(30%)

Total titles searched: 58,821

Table II. Input Statistics--Titles Updated

Year	Month	Exact record	Edited record	Original record
1976	Aug.-Dec.	2,710	1,418	1,184
1977	Jan.-Dec.	9,083	8,026	2,818
1978	Jan.-June*	6,072	11,586	2,289
	Total:	17,865	21,030	6,291

Total input: 45,186

Conversion Statistics as of June 30, 1978

Total LC titles in the Marriott Library excluding non-Roman and non-book materials	433,646
LC titles input through on-line cataloging	69,246
LC titles updated by Conversion Project	45,186
Total titles in archival tape	114,432

From the figures stated above, as of June 30, 1978, roughly 319,214 titles needed to be input in archival tape in order to complete the proposed conversion project. Based on past statistics, on the average, one person can input approximately 9,650 titles (original, edited and exact record averaged) per year, and it would take approximately 33.1 man-years to convert 319,214 titles.

According to the study made by the Library of Congress RECON Working Task Force, it was estimated that a staff complement of about 100 people could implement a conversion effort of 10,000 titles per week[3] which is equivalent to 5,200 titles per person per year. The literature also indicated that the production rates of the pilot project were significantly lower than was anticipated in the RECON feasibility study.[4] Although, the input of the Marriott Library catalog records consists of exact, edited, and original records as compared to the all original input of the Library of Congress, the Marriott Library staff members have performed very well for the conversion input. The problem mainly lies in the formidable task of inputting the huge holdings of over 400,000 titles with the limited facility and manpower.[5]

New Strategy

The retrospective conversion project of the Marriott Library made over 6,000 new bibliographic records available in the OCLC data base, and it also added the Marriott Library holdings on over 45,000 titles on OCLC records as of June 1978. These 45,000 catalog records in machine-readable form in archive tape will facilitate greater flexibility in manipulating data to create COM or on-line catalogs.

Meanwhile, as was anticipated for some time, the Library of Congress has announced its intention of closing its catalogs in 1981, and the Library of Congress plans to start on-line catalogs as well as to adapt AACR 2 on January 1, 1981. This Library of Congress decision has created a great impact on the future catalogs of all libraries. It is imperative for the Marriott Library to plan ahead and conduct an extensive study on the future automated catalogs in relation to the user's needs in the Marriott Library. Since the conversion of the whole LC shelflist of the Library will take a long time to complete, a new strategy would be to complete an independent segment of the Shelflist.

As of June 30, 1978, the classified and cataloged collection in the Science-Engineering Library of the Marriott Library was approximately 82,150 titles in the Library of Congress Classification, of which 19,972 titles were already input in archive tape through on-line cataloging and the retrospective conversion project. The Science-Engineering Library has a separate catalog and shelflist located in its Library. It was recommended and approved by the Library administration that the input of the Science-Engineering collection be given priority so that the converted records can be put into use upon its completion. Such a prototype COM catalog or on-line catalog will provide vital data as to user reaction, costs, and other unforseen information before we undertake the gigantic task of changing the Marriott Library's card catalogs to other automated alternatives.

Since this new strategy was implemented on July 1, 1978, the conversion project has made a remarkable progress. During the six months period between July 1-December 31, 1978, the statistics indicate a total input of 31,714 titles by 4.5 FTE conversion personnel. This high ratio of input is partly due to the increased finding rate of catalog records in OCLC data base (approximately 78%). The major factor is, however, the increased efficiency of very well-trained and experienced conversion personnel. Based on the dramatic increase in the number of title input during the past six months, we can project the completion of Science-Engineering catalog conversion by the end of June 1979. We are looking forward to seeing the archive tape being put into use for an automated catalog.

References

1. Kenneth John Bierman. "Automated Alternative to Card Catalogs. The Current State of Planning and Implementation." Journal of Library Automation 8:277-295 (December 1975).
2. Library Assistant I, II, III, IV are the four paraprofessional ranks at the Marriott Library.
3. In April, 1978, conversion personnel was increased to 4.25 FTE, and one more CRT terminal was added.
4. RECON Working Task Force, Conversion of Retrospective Catalog Records to Machine-Readable Form: A Study of the Feasibility of a National Bibliographic Service (Washington, D.C.: Library of Congress, 1969).
5. Avram, Henriette D., RECON Pilot Project (Washington, D.C.: Library of Congress, 1972).

33. Converting a Card Catalog to Microfiche*

by Phillip Watson

During a seminar on Computerised Cataloguing[1] held in November 1977, Footscray Institute of Technology Library announced that it was planning to microfilm its closed card catalogue into a microfiche format, as an interim measure pending the incorporation of these records into its COM catalogue. The proposal, initiated by Footscray's Chief Librarian, has generated a great deal of interest. This article has been prepared as a result of several enquiries, and is intended as a guide to others who may be considering a similar venture.

The card catalogue to be transferred to fiche consisted of 80,000 cards (about 30,000 titles) in three sequences--Author, Title and Subject catalogues--and represented titles in the collection up to December 1975, when the card catalogue was closed. Acquisitions since January 1976 have been processed using records retrieved from AMRS or by original cataloguing, and are listed in COM fiche catalogues which are cumulated every two months.

The purpose of converting the retrospective collection to fiche was to take advantage of the single format (fiche) for the whole collection, although there are now two distinct series--the Old Catalogue and the New Catalogue. The cost of converting these pre-1976 records into MARC format would have been neither possible in the short term with existing staff, nor economically justifiable.

An ad-hoc weeding programme had been in progress for some months. Superseded editions or unused multiple copies had been removed and discarded.

Methodology

The first stage of the conversion to fiche was to second a member of the cataloguing staff to the project. Her task was to ensure that the catalogue cards were filed correctly, and were in reasonable condition. Included in her brief were the following points:

---
*Reprinted by permission of the author and publisher from Australian Academic and Research Libraries, 9 (September 1978), p. 164-67.

(i) Cards should be typed on one side only. White cards are preferable to coloured cards for filming purposes.
(ii) Any open entries (e.g., for multi-volume sets) should be checked against the shelves, and entries closed.
(iii) Handwritten annotations should be removed and replaced, if necessary, with typewritten statements in the notes section of the entry.
(iv) Subject headings should be typed uniformly in upper case.
(v) All see reference cards should be checked.
(vi) Guide cards should be removed immediately prior to filming.

This operation took about eight weeks.

Twelve catalogue cards, in three columns of four cards each, could be filmed in each of the 208 frames available on each fiche.

An index was prepared by the library to the first entry on each frame of the Author sequence. This involved counting the cards by hand (identifying the first of the twelve cards) for each of 207 frames. The index which was derived was typed onto double A4 pages and inserted by the bureau--Latrobe Colourlab--into frame 208, the lower right-hand corner of the fiche, at the time of filming.

Eyeball headings were prepared by the library for each original fiche. The range (From ... To ...) to be covered by each fiche in the Author sequence was determined by the counting exercise described. For the other catalogue sequences, the cards were not counted but were allowed to run on to 208 frames. The range of each of these was checked when the fiche were returned to the library and a typed label was affixed to each one.

The cards were filmed at 48:1 reduction in row format, with a negative image on the final fiche. Filming took place during January 1978. Each sequence was filmed separately.

Calculating the Number of Original Fiche Required

The total number of cards to be filmed can be estimated by tightly compressing the cards in a catalogue drawer and adopting the standard of 125 cards to the inch.

The number of original fiche needed to store these records can be determined by using the following formulae:

Equation 1: $x = t \div (n \times f)$
(If no index frame is needed on the final frame of any fiche in a sequence).

Equation 2: $x = t \div (n \times (f-1))$
(If an index frame is needed on the final frame of all fiche in a sequence).

Where x represents the required number of original fiche
Where t represents the total number of cards in a sequence to be filmed
Where n represents the number of cards per frame
Where f represents the number of frames per fiche

If index frames are required in some sequences but not others, then the appropriate equation should be used for each sequence, and the results of all equations added together to determine the total number of original fiche required.

Costs

Our quotation was for:

Filming 80,000 cards onto 33 fiche at 48:1 reduction	$825
50 diazo copies of each fiche	264
Preparation costs	343
	$1432

The cost of producing an original microfiche was assessed on the basis of adding the microfilming costs and the preparation costs and dividing by the number of original fiche. In our case, $825 + $343, divided by 33, gave a unit cost of $35.40.

The production of our catalogue was the first time that Latrobe Colourlab had microfilmed catalogue cards into fiche format (it may have been the first time that any Australian bureau had done it), and the quotation that was given us seriously underestimated the amount of time needed for the job. Current quotations are based on a price closer to $50.40 per original fiche.

Fiche duplicates can vary in cost depending on the numbers produced. Ours cost 16 cents each.

Quotations on the microfilming of catalogue cards can be obtained from: Latrobe Colourlab Micropublishing Division, 95 Tope Street, South Melbourne, 3205, or McCarron Bird Micro Service Division, 594 Lonsdale Street, Melbourne, 3000.

Possible Future Refinements

It is the library's intention to convert progressively the records which were filmed to full MARC or MARC-compatible status over the next three years, removing the catalogue cards for each title converted. The reducing card-file, now housed in our Cataloguing Unit, will be re-microfilmed annually.

We have learnt a few lessons from our first microfilming venture and will endeavour to implement them next time.

(i) Positive image on the fiche rather than negative may produce a clearer image of the contents of the cards, which vary in quality depending on their age.
(ii) Column format rather than row format. COM fiche catalogues are read vertically and there is an inconsistency between our new COM catalogues and the microfilmed card catalogues which have frames arranged horizontally in rows. Some users and library staff find these different arrangements irritating.
(iii) Contrast striping behind the eyeball headings for all sequences, at the time of filming.

It is debatable whether the amount of time and effort needed to produce the Index to the frames on the Author Catalogue was worthwhile, as, in practice, most users seem to prefer random access rather than via the index. Copies of Footscray's complete monograph catalogue containing 47 fiche are available at the cost price of $8; samples of the microfilmed card catalogue can be supplied free of charge.

Footscray has recently taken over the compilation of the Union List of 16mm Films in CAE Libraries from Darling Downs Institute of Advanced Education. A microfiche edition, produced according to the techniques described, will be available shortly.

Reference

1. Computerised cataloguing without your own computer: proceedings of a seminar conducted by the Footscray Institute of Technology Library 23 November 1977. Footscray Institute of Technology, 1978.

34. Freezing the Library of Congress Catalogs*

The Library of Congress is continuing to refine its plans for freezing its catalogs in January 1981. The following document replaces and updates all statements previously published in the Library of Congress Information Bulletin.

I. Assumptions and Definitions

The basic assumptions are
   (A) The Library of Congress will freeze its catalogs on Friday, January 2, 1981 (Day 1);
   (B) new, temporary card catalogs will be started that can be discarded when the automated system is ready; and
   (C) the Library of Congress will abandon its policy of superimposition and implement the Anglo-American Cataloguing Rules, second edition, on Day 1.
   Since the terms will be used frequently, it will be helpful to define the catalogs.
   (A) Old Catalog. The existing card catalog through 1980. The singular form is an abstract concept. Physically, the catalog comprises a number of separate files--the Official Catalog (the largest, containing the authority records); the Main, or Public Catalog; the catalogs for law, maps, and music; and other specialized catalogs that to some extent contain bibliographic information not to be found even in the Official Catalog. The two general catalogs will be closed; the others may not.

   (1) Until a full freeze of the Old Catalog occurs (three to five years after 1980), a partial freeze will be in effect. During this period, activity in the Old Catalog will be severely limited, not because corrections are undesirable theoretically but rather because resources will be limited. Those activities that will be performed are
      (a) corrections of errors in main entry headings grossly affecting the filing position and call numbers affecting retrieval of the item;
      (b) filing of all cards for works cataloged before 1981;
      (c) withdrawals for recataloging of cards with access points incorrectly assigned originally (this is to be done only in very rare cases);

---
*Reprinted by permission of the editor from Library of Congress Information Bulletin, 39 (Feb. 22, 1980), p. 61-64.

(d) addition of notes to cards for serials continued or superseded by other serials; and
(e) withdrawals of cards for items newly acquired by the Library but represented by cards produced primarily during the cooperative cataloging program.

(B) New Catalog. The machine-readable bibliographic file comprising all pre-1981 MARC data bases and all records created from Day 1 except possibly certain nonroman script records.

(C) Add-on Catalog. The new card catalog of records created from Day 1 and older records withdrawn from the Old Catalog (see IA1c-e above) for recataloging. The Add-on Catalog will be a dictionary catalog arranged by Filing Arrangement in the Library of Congress Catalogs (Rather rules).

On Day 1 the Add-on Official Catalog will contain only name authority cards for those headings for which the AACR 2 or AACR 2-compatible decision has been made.

As post-1980 cataloging is done, additions to the Add-on Official Catalog will consist of

(1) references generated from name authority records included on Day 1 as the headings are needed in new cataloging and after the forms of the references have been reviewed and revised as necessary to fit into the structure of the post-1980 catalog;
(2) name authority cards and references for pre-1981 headings (taken and revised from the Old Official Catalog) needed in new cataloging;
(3) name authority cards and references for name headings new to the Library;
(4) subject authority cards and references for subject headings new to the Library or not included in the automated subject heading file;
(5) bibliographic records for items cataloged post-1980 (the MARC records may be produced on colored stock for later withdrawal);
(6) bibliographic records for items withdrawn from the Old Catalog and recataloged (the MARC records may be produced on colored stock for later withdrawal);
(7) temporary name authority cards;
(8) series treatment cards and references; and
(9) Official Catalog memoranda, form cards, and so forth.

On Day 1 the Add-on Public Catalog will probably contain no cards. As post-1980 cataloging is done, cards will be filed for

(1) name references, including linking references, as generated for new cataloging;
(2) subject references for subject headings new to the Library (microfiche or printed editions of the subject headings file will probably be used as reference to subject headings created before 1981);

Freezing the Library of Congress Catalogs 279

(3) bibliographic records for items cataloged post-1980 (the MARC records may be produced on colored stock for later withdrawal);
(4) bibliographic records for items withdrawn from the Old Catalog and recataloged (the MARC records may be produced on colored stock for later withdrawal);
(5) treatment explanations for untraced series; and
(6) references for traced series.

II. Automated System

For the purposes of cataloging, the only integrated use of the automated system will be at the precataloging stages for searching and the creation of an in-process record.

The expansion of the automated process information file (APIF) to cover all materials going into the cataloging system appears totally dependent upon the availability of terminals and printers in the Madison Building. The assumption is that if only limited terminals are available in the Madison Building, the terminals installed would be used for APIF (including shelflisting update) instead of for another stage in the system.

III. Nonroman Scripts

(A) The Library has decided not to adopt the romanization tables recommended by the International Organization for Standardization. The usefulness and validity of these tables, especially in the context of the machine-manipulation of bibliographic data, have been questioned. Therefore, adoption does not seem worthwhile at this time.
(B) The Library is still considering the possibility of a change from the Wade-Giles to the Pinyin system for the romanization of Chinese.
(C) The Library has reviewed changes to the romanization tables for the languages of South Asia recommended by a committee at the School of Oriental and African Studies (SOAS), London; however, no agreements have yet been made with SOAS as to which changes might be made. If changes are made, they are not anticipated to be major.
(D) The Burmese romanization table is the only table that has been identified as needing extensive revision. The revision is being done primarily by the Committee of Research Materials on Southeast Asia.
(E) The Library will input to machine-readable form and produce copy in romanization for all nonroman scripts except Arabic, Chinese, Hebrew, Japanese, Korean, Persian, and Yiddish.

IV. Descriptive Cataloging System

Beginning on Day 1, descriptive catalogers will implement AACR 2 exclusively for new cataloging. The New Catalog, however, will contain around 1.5 million records, a number of which will have headings that are not valid under AACR 2 or are not AACR 2-compatible, the incorrect choice of main entry, and/or incorrect bibliographic description. In terms of updating existing MARC bibliographic records, the following policies will be followed:

(A) Bibliographic description. Records will not be revised to bring this feature into conformity with AACR 2.

(B) Choice of entry. Records will in general not be revised. The choice of entry will be reconsidered only for those items withdrawn from the Old Catalog for recataloging as noted in IA above, for new analytics of an existing monographic series; and for serials for which a CONSER record for authentication is in accord with AACR 2. Although it would be desirable to revise existing MARC records in other cases for choice of entry (for example, editions, related works, existing analytics of monographic series, serials), the Library's resources will be too restricted both to maintain a reasonable level of current cataloging and to revise existing records.

(C) Form of heading. Records will be revised to reflect the AACR 2 form of heading unless the heading has been designated in the authority file as an AACR 2-compatible heading. Some of these revisions will be done by program, others on a project basis through the on-line update system.

NAME AUTHORITY FILES

The Library is currently inputting to machine-readable form all its newly established name authority records and is phasing in the conversion of its retrospective records. The Library is currently providing the AACR 2 form of heading when this form differs from the currently established form. The addition of AACR 2 forms of heading has several advantages, namely,

(A) a considerable part of the intellectual work involved in revising the headings will have been done before 1981;

(B) the information will be made available in microfiche and tape form to other libraries before January 1981 and a selection will be published in issues of the Cataloging Service Bulletin;

(C) a computer program is to be written to modify the authority data base to replace the current heading with the designated AACR 2 form; and

(D) computer programs may be written to allow a considerable portion of the revision of the bibliographic data bases by machine.

V. Subject Cataloging System

The Library will no longer wait until 1981 to make changes in topical subject headings. Instead, changes will be made on a continuing basis. Some changes that involve currently voluminous files (for example, European War, 1914-1918) will not be made until 1981. Changes in subject headings as a result of the provisions of AACR 2 (for example, placing qualifiers to geographic names within parentheses) will not be implemented until 1981.

Freezing the Library of Congress Catalogs 281

VI. LC Classification and Shelflisting Systems

(A) The Library of Congress classification schedules will continue to be revised on a regular basis as new cataloging indicates the necessity to add new numbers or revise older numbers. The Library of Congress has decided to defer a decision on closing the shelflist until after 1981. A major factor in deferring the decision was the impact of a change in shelflisting procedures on the classification schedules.

(B) In dealing with changes in forms of heading, if the name of a person or corporate body is printed in the classification schedules, a decision will be made on a case-by-case basis whether (1) to alter the printed caption and/or print a reference from the new form or (2) to create a new number(s) to match the revised form of heading. Solution one is more likely.

(C) When names of jurisdictions are not printed in the classification schedules but the schedules provide for arrangement by place (country, state, city, etc.), A-Z, in 1981 the latest name of the place rather than an earlier name will be used as the basis of the arrangement (for example, .Zx, Zambia, rather than .R4, Rhodesia, Northern). When there is no change of name as above but only a change in form of heading (for example, Paris to Paris (France); Jackson, Miss., to Jackson (Miss.); Birmingham, Eng., to Birmingham (West Midlands, England)), an attempt will be made to continue to use the same cutter number if the shelflister is able to identify the places as the same.

(D) Most editions of works will fall together as long as there has not been a change in the choice of main entry heading or an entry element change in the form of heading.

(E) An attempt will be made to keep literary works by a single person together, regardless of the number of names under which the person may be found in the alphabetic catalog.

(F) In dealing with serials,

(1) if a serial title changes with no change in numbering, the cuttering will continue unchanged;

(2) if the subject matter of a serial changes (in addition to the title changing), the classification number will be changed.

(3) if a serial title changes and there is no numbering but there are dates, the serials catalogers will send a note to the subject catalogers to indicate that it is the same publication and that the cutter numbers should not change; generally, serials catalogers will have evidence for the decision; and

(4) if the connection between two serials cataloged separately is not discovered until after the cataloging is completed, the Library will not go back and recutter them under the same number.

(G) In dealing with cutter numbers for persons an attempt will be made to continue existing numbers if the two forms of name can be identified as the same person (for example, Moore, Robert Lowell, 1919- and Moore, R. L. (Robert Lowell), 1919-).

(H) When cuttering is done for the subject of a work and the subject is a person or corporate body (other than a jurisdiction), an attempt will be made to continue existing numbers.

VII. Serials Check-in System

The Library of Congress is considering how to handle the Serial Record check-in file after 1980. The following options have been discussed:

(A) revise the headings in the Serial Record to AACR 2 form of heading as they come up;

(B) refile the entire Serial Record by title; or

(C) freeze the existing Serial Record and begin a new check-in file arranged by title ("unique serial title"); the new file would contain all serials to be added after 1980 and the serials in the automated system moved from the frozen Serial Record.

VIII. Links

The question of links between the catalogs is no longer considered a problem for the Library of Congress for the following reasons.

(A) The effort to add the AACR 2 forms of heading to the automated name authority records will provide the means for generating the links for the Public Catalogs.

(B) After 1980, Library of Congress catalogers will need to continue searching in the Old Catalog for at least a couple of years. This will allow the appropriate link to be added to the file as newly encountered retrospective name headings are converted to machine-readable form after 1980.

For other libraries the basis for these links will be found in the distribution of name authority data noted above.

IX. Maintenance and Disposition of the Old Catalog

The Library of Congress has identified several options for the Old Catalog: full freeze (filing the arrearages of cards and correcting the filing in one of the two principal catalogs in preparation for filming; no other changes would be made); partial freeze (continuing to file the arrearages of cards, correcting the filing in one of the two principal catalogs in preparation for filming, and continuing to record locational information and to correct egregious errors); shrinking freeze (removal of all MARC cards from the Old Catalog on a project basis).

The Library has decided on the partial freeze at least until such time as the filing arrearages have been added to the catalog. At that point a full freeze would be instituted, resulting in no further activity in the Old Catalog other than possibly correcting some filing errors and filming one of the principal catalogs, probably the Old Public Catalog.

Bibliography

Alternatives for Future Library Catalogs: A Cost Model. Washington, D.C.: Association of Research Libraries, 1980.
Association of Research Libraries. Retrospective Conversion. Washington, D.C.: Association of Research Libraries, 1980.
Axelrod, C. W. "Economic Evaluation of Information Storage and Retrieval Systems," Information Processing and Management, 13 (1977), 117-124.
Blackburn, Robert H. Management Experience with COM Catalogues in a Large Academic Library. Toronto, Ont.: 1977.
Butler, Bret, Aveney, Brian and Scholz, William. "Conversion of Manual Catalogs to Collection Data Bases," Library Technology Reports, 14 (March-April 1978), 109-206.
Clinic on Library Applications of Data Processing, 15th, University of Illinois at Urbana-Champaign, 1978. Problems and Failures in Library Automation. Urbana-Champaign: University of Illinois, Graduate School of Library Science, 1979.
Dailey, Kazuko M. "Financial Considerations Involved in Closing the Catalog," Alternative Catalog Newsletter, No. 6 (September 1978), 7-17.
Divilbiss, J. L., ed. The Economics of Library Automation. Papers Presented at the 1976 Clinic on Library Applications of Data Processing, April 25-28, 1976. Urbana-Champaign, Ill.: University of Illinois, Graduate School of Library Science, 1977.
Ferguson, Douglas. "Marketing Online Services in the University," Online, 1 (July 1977), 15-23.
Freezing Card Catalogs: A Program Sponsored by the Association of Research Libraries, May 5, 1978, Nashville, Tennessee. Washington, D.C.: Association of Research Libraries, 1978.
"Freezing the Library of Congress Catalog," Library of Congress Information Bulletin, 37 (March 3, 1978), 152-156.
"Freezing the Library of Congress Catalogs," Library of Congress Information Bulletin, 39 (February 22, 1980), 61-64.
Gallivan, Bernard. "COM Cost Comparison," VINE, 20 (February 1978), 29-30.
Gay, Ruth. "The Machine in the Library," American Scholar, 49 (Winter 1979-80), 66-77.
Gilham, Virginia, and Black, John B. Administrative and Bibliographic Uses of COM (Computer Output Microfilm) in an Academic Library. Paper Presented at the Ontario Universities Computing Conference, 7th. Waterloo, Ontario, Canada, June 2-4, 1976. ED 127 914.
Gorman, M. "Freezing the Catalog: Catalog Use Committee,

RASD" (ALA Conference, 1978 Midwinter), American Libraries, 9 (March 1978), 162.

Gorsch, Audrey N. Current and Retrospective Sources of Machine Readable Monograph Cataloging Records: A Study of Their Potential Cost and Utility in Automated System Development at the University of Minnesota. Minneapolis, MN: University of Minnesota Libraries, March, 1975. ED 107 280.

Horner, William C. "Use and Economics of Computer-Generated Microfiche Catalogs," North Carolina Libraries, 33 (Winter 1975), 31-33.

Hudson, Alice C. "Conversion to Automated Cataloging at the Map Division, NYPL," Special Libraries, 67 (February 1976), 97-101.

Information Systems Consultants, Inc. The Future of the Catalog. Background Paper for the Development of Cost Models for Alternatives to the Card Catalog. Information Systems Consultants, Inc.; Prepared for King Research, Inc. Boston: Information Systems Consultants, Inc., 1979.

Introduction to Data Management for Library Automation. 1st ed. White Plains, N.Y.: IBM Corporation, 1976.

Kao, Yasuko. "The Retrospective Conversion Project at the University of Utah Marriott Library," Utah Libraries, 22 (Spring 1979), 39-43.

Kazlauskas, Edward John. "Library Automation in California: A Current View," LASIE, 6 (January-February 1976), 21-28.

Krikelas, James. "Thinking About Automation? Consider These Factors in Making a Decision," Wisconsin Library Bulletin, 73 (May-June 1977), 98-100.

"LC to Freeze Card Catalog," Library of Congress Information Bulletin, 36 (November 4, 1977), 743-746.

"LC to Freeze Catalog in January of 1980," Library Journal, 103 (February 1, 1978), 305.

"Latest News on the Great Konversion," VINE, 31 (1979), 50-57.

Malinconico, S. Michael. "The Display Medium and the Price of the Message," Library Journal, 101 (October 15, 1976), 2144-2149.

Mayhew, Lewis B. Computerized Networks Among Libraries and Universities: An Administrators Overview. ERIC Clearinghouse on Information Resources, Stanford Center for Research and Development in Teaching, School of Education, Stanford University, November 1975.

Miller, G. D. and Ireland, C. "Maximizing the Cost-Effectiveness of a Computer-Based Catalog Support System," Journal of Library Automation, 10 (March 1977), 53-67.

Montague, Eleanor. "Automation and the Library Administrator," Journal of Library Automation, 11 (December 1978), 313-323.

Nelson, M. G. "Farewell to an Old But Estranged Friend [Card Catalog]," Wilson Library Bulletin, 54 (November 1979), 148.

"On-Line Catalog Conversion Commercially Available," Journal of Library Automation, 11 (June 1978), 171-172.

Pflug, Günter. "The Effects of Automation on Library Administration," IFLA Journal, 1 (1975), 267-275.

Pierce, A. R. and Taylor, J. K. "Model for Cost Comparison of

Automated Cataloging Systems," Journal of Library Automation, 11 (March 1978), 6-23.

Pizer, Irwin H. "Automation: Planning to Implementation: The Problems en Route," Bulletin of the Medical Library Association, 64 (January 1976), 1-4.

Reid, M. T. "LITA Offers Guidance on Catalog Closing," American Libraries, 10 (January 1979), 6.

Rosenfeld, H. E. "LC Delays Freezing Its Catalog Till 1981," Wilson Library Bulletin, 53 (September 1978), 18-19.

Rosenthal, Joseph A. "Planning for the Catalogs: A Managerial Perspective," Journal of Library Automation, 11 (September 1978), 192-205.

Spigai, Frances G., Grams, Theodore W., and Kawabata, Julie, eds. Information Roundup: Proceedings of the 4th ASIS Mid-Year Meeting, Portland, Oregon, May 15-17, 1975. Washington, D. C.: American Society for Information Science, 1975.

A Study of Conversion of the University of California at Berkeley Library Catalog to Machine Readable Form, With Options and Cost Estimates. Berkeley: University of California General Library, 1975.

Watson, Phillip. "Converting a Card Catalogue to Microfiche," Australian Academic and Research Libraries, 9 (September 1978), 164-167.

Wheelbarger, Johnny J. The Effectiveness of a Computerized Library Network in Meeting the Performance Expectations of the Members in the Administration of Academic Libraries. Ph.D. dissertation. George Peabody College, 1977. ED 143 370.

PART IV. CASE STUDIES

The need for a decision on the future of the card catalog has only recently become imperative in the library world. The adoption of AACR 2 along with the advancement in computer use in libraries has made it necessary to consider that future. In addition, card catalogs in many libraries are expanding too fast and providing space has become a problem. A corollary concern is the fact that the cards themselves are beginning to wear due to excessive use.

There are many factors involved in making the decision on the future of a library's card catalog, but two questions are particularly important: first, what form of bibliographic access can the library use to best serve its patron? And second, how can this service be performed in the most economical manner?

Although some libraries have already made the decision to close their card catalogs and use another form of bibliographic access, many are just now trying to make this decision. One approach to decision making is to study what other libraries have done and to examine their decision-making process.

Some Libraries Have Studied the Problem

Several libraries (such as the University of California at Berkeley and the Cornell University Library) have for several years had task forces studying their card catalogs and charged with making recommendations for their future. Although these are both relatively large libraries, some of the same plans can be adapted to a smaller library.

The fact that the Library of Congress plans to freeze its catalog will have a major influence on a number of libraries. That does not, however, necessarily mean that libraries will have to freeze their catalogs also. It does give libraries a starting point in the decision-making process. There have been several articles in the LC Information Bulletin on the steps the Library of Congress is taking, and these can be used as guidelines for other libraries. In addition, there are several libraries that have already found it advisable to close their card catalogs and convert to a machine-assisted form of bibliographic access. And there are also some who have set a date for closing their card catalogs and are now in the process of preparing for this activity.

Certain libraries may choose to integrate their present card catalogs with an automated system. This too takes planning in order to be most efficient and economical while still providing the maximum service to the user. An integrated catalog may take the form of interfiling cards which have been produced by means of an on-line system, using AACR 2, into the present card catalog. This could cause problems due to the fact that some headings under AACR 2 will be different from those using other cataloging rules.

Cases Offer Direction/Answers

In order to get a better idea of how a number of libraries have dealt with the change in form of bibliographic access, several articles are included here on this topic. These libraries report not only on how they have handled this change, but also give several suggestions on the ways their procedures can be improved.

For example, in "Computer-Produced Book Catalogue for New Brunswick Public Library System," Hall presents the planning procedures of the Library System when it replaced the manual catalog with a computer-produced book catalog. A step-by-step account is given including the type of equipment used.

Schwarz, in "Computer Output Microfilm, Stout Uses a New Library Tool," traces the steps in the development of a COM catalog at the University of Wisconsin-Stout Library. He also describes the advantages this library found in the COM catalog, as well as some of the library's plans for the future.

In "COM Comes to the Chicago Public Library," O'Brien describes the steps taken by the Chicago Public Library in converting its card catalog to a COM catalog. A brief history of the program is given along with the objectives of this project. A 14-step conversion process is discussed and the author mentions the two types of COM catalogs that the library planned to produce. Library procedures that are now in operation since converting to the COM catalog are presented.

As another example, in "RMIT COM Catalogue Study Results," Morrison discusses the results of a study of COM catalogs at the Royal Melbourne Institute of Technology Central Library. Three options were examined: printed book catalog produced by photocomposition from magnetic tape, then offset printing plus supplement; printed book catalog with a COM film supplement; and a complete COM catalog. The study was made over a period of three months and examined such factors as use studies, retrieval time, accuracy, attitudes, preferences, plus a cost comparison for the three options.

Aveney and Ghikas, in "600 Users Meet the COM Catalog," summarize a study at the Los Angeles County Public Library System on how the users feel about a COM catalog. The two-part study included the impact of a COM catalog from an internal management perspective and the users' views on the new equipment and system. Although the authors mentioned a number of negative comments by those surveyed on the COM catalog, still the end result was that patrons preferred the COM catalog to either the book or the card catalog.

Finally, in "COM Catalog vs. Card Catalog: The Experience of the University of Oregon Law Library," Hyatt explains the procedures employed at that Library in changing from the traditional card catalog to the Blackwell/North America (B/NA) computer output microfiche (COM) catalog. A brief overview of the B/NA system is also given. Several reasons are discussed for not using the Library of Congress copy available for law materials as well as some alternatives for relying on data bases other than B/NA. In addition, a brief description is given of the various services of B/NA and an interesting cost comparison.

35. Computer-Produced Book Catalogue
for New Brunswick Public Library System*

by Agnez Hall

General Information

In November of 1975 the New Brunswick Library Service started the discussion to examine the concept of a computer-produced book catalogue to replace the manual Union Catalogue and the manual production of complete sets of library cards for every book catalogued. In October, 1976, the production by computer of the first book catalogue became a reality.

This project was possible because of the structure of the New Brunswick Public Library System.

The New Brunswick Public Library System operates under the Province's Libraries Act, and under the authority of the Minister of Youth, Recreation and Cultural Resources. The New Brunswick Library Service is responsible for the administration of the Libraries Act. This Libraries Act divides the province among five regional systems. Each Region has an administrative headquarters to carry out the administrative tasks, and from which to distribute materials among the public libraries and one or more bookmobiles within their region boundaries. These regional systems are funded entirely by the Province. In New Brunswick, 99% of all public libraries operate inside the New Brunswick Library system.

New Brunswick Library Service already provides support services, e.g. centralized cataloguing and classification, to the Library Regions in New Brunswick.

The success of this program demands some adaptation and concession from the library regions. The basic concession was that the decision of the New Brunswick Library Service on cataloguing matters would be accepted by all the participating libraries.

During the preparatory period a coding manual was developed and distributed to heads of library regions. A coding form was prepared according to data processing specifications. When the com-

---
*Reprinted by permission of the author and publisher from APLA Bulletin, 41 (1977), p. 33-35. Also appears in Canadian Association on Information Science Proceedings (1977), p. 102-16, and in the Canadian Literary Science Society's Journal, No. 1 (1977), p. 54-59.

puter program and the complementary processing equipment and forms were ready, a starting date was set up. From that date on, new books only received by each region will appear in the computer-produced book catalogue.

The production of a computer-produced book catalogue showing all the retrospective holdings of the five regional libraries was rejected for the moment, because of time and cost involved. At the present time New Brunswick Library Service Union Catalogue contains approximately half a million titles. The data preparation is considered a major project by itself.

Input data

For each document to be entered there are six different records which all have the same general layout. Besides the standard information--author, title, imprint, subject and classification number--each document indicates type of documentation, i.e. one of two language codes for each document and one of two readership level codes for each document; a reference number that must be unique for each document (Record Zero) and finally one of 6 location codes for each document. (Record 4.)

Input procedure

The input system is a batch-data entry.

Data are printed on OCR (optical character reader) forms and are sent on a three weeks schedule.

Each document to be entered on the computer masterfile must be coded on coding forms prior to transfer on OCR form. This input method was chosen from several others available because NBLS prefers to control the complete data preparation and have the original OCR forms returned for internal double-checking with the masterfile.

Hardware

These OCR forms are then read by an IBM 3886 model 6 Optical Character Reader (OCR machine). The IBM selectric typewriters with typing element OCRA--FONT are needed to prepare the input document on OCR forms. This IBM 3886 is a stand alone reader with magnetic tape output (EBCDIC format, 9 track, 1600 bytes per inch (1 bpi)). The model is off line. The data printed on the magnetic tape are then transferred to the New Brunswick Government Computer which operates a UNIVAC 1100.

Output

There are four different output reports produced by the computer:

an edit updating list, a master file, a book catalogue and an author supplement. The computer print-out is all done in upper-case letters. In every report, the first entry is printed at the first indention and the succeeding lines of the second indention. For the book catalogue, the printing is done on a special paper using carbon paper. The second copy is used for reproduction. The reason for this is the lack of uniformity in the printed impression. All these four reports have date, paging, and the name of the report printed at the top of each page.

Edit Updating List

The first report is an "edit updating list" sorted by reference number. This report lists only the last documents or last "batch" of OCR forms submitted to the computer. The entries are printed exactly the same way the OCR machine had read the data, with errors from various sources. This report is intended for an internal use or checking document and is used by the NBLS staff only. Provision had been made in the program to show every transaction done by the computer when it interfiles new input data. Specific codes like "no type 4 record," "invalid type 5 record," "bad reference number," etc. are printed to identify the errors in the input data. These printed indications facilitate the corrections.

Masterfile

The second report is a masterfile sorted by author of the complete data presently in the computer memory relating to this programme. This masterfile is produced every three weeks and is continuously cumulated. Each document entry contains complete information typed on the OCR form: language, level, reference number, location plus the standard information. This catalogue format is a 8 1/2 x 14 inch paper stock using a four column presentation. For readability, the author entry is printed at the first indention and the succeeding lines at the second indention. All the printing is done at six lines per inch. The resulting volume is bound on the short edge.

Since the beginning of our programme on October 15, 1976, till June 17, 1977, 14,082 titles were catalogued and classified. The masterfile is up to 573 pages in the last printing. New Brunswick Library Service was cataloguing and classifying an average of 15,000 titles on a yearly basis. The alphabetization disregards the language of the printed document.

Book Catalogue

The frequency of printing the book catalogue is scheduled to appear every three weeks but for one region only, so 15 weeks is the maximum time allowed between a complete rotation for the five Library regions. This schedule was chosen because of the cost factor. In practice it works this way: every three weeks one region receives a complete cumulated book catalogue and the other four regions receive an author supplement list, e.g., books catalogued and classified during the last three weeks period for individual regions. This book catalogue is also continuously cumulated.

The book catalogue is produced in four separate divisions: English adult, English juvenile, French adult and French juvenile. Each division has three sections; author, title and subject, and the alphabetization is done independently. The author list includes the complete cataloguing entry. The title list shows: title, author, and DDC number. The subject list gives: subject, author, title and DDC number.

The cataloguing and classification are done in the language of the book, i.e. English or French.

The catalogue format is a 8 1/2" x 11" paper stock using a two column presentation. The printing is done at six lines per inch and with an average of 56 lines per page. The resulting volume is bound on the long edge.

Author supplement

The fourth report is an "author supplement list" produced by location and listing only documents catalogued and classified during the last three week period. This list is not cumulative. Supplement means an addition to the Book Catalogue. Every three weeks four Library regions receive this "author supplement" while the other one has a cumulated Book Catalogue.

The "author supplement list" format is a 8 1/2 x 14 inch paper stock using a four column presentation. The layout and the computer printing do not differ from the masterfile.

Reproduction

In order to produce the required master copy for catalogue production the following alternatives were investigated: photocomposition, printer simulation, video, stencils, computer printout. The first four methods have no representatives in New Brunswick. For the standard of quality required and the significant cost difference among the alternatives it was decided to use computer printout to produce the master copy.

From the master copy NBLS staff reproduce on offset press the number of copies requested by each Library Region. These book catalogues are then bound according to Region specifications on a Gestetner velo bind 292,101. Each region designs and provides their own book catalogue cover.

Cost

Since our programme is still under various changes, trying to establish costs could be an unfair indication of future costs and a futile exercise. Nevertheless, data processing charges for computer time and printing alone are predetermined costs with limited variations. The charges for the various hardware equipment are the following:

NAME	COST
OCR (Optical scanning)	$40/hour
Computer use	$105/hour
Printing	$0.55/page
Programmer	$20/hour

Conclusion

The impact of a book catalogue in a regional library system is enormous. The smallest branch has immediate knowledge of the total collection of their region. The loans or circulation inside the region could be "busted up". Surveys had not been conducted to assess the response of the public of this new concept of listing all new acquisition but criticisms were minimized.

Our immediate priorities are: the improvement of this existing program, the standardization of some of the subject headings, the expansion of the "see reference," the inclusion in the program of the current periodicals collection, and the retrieval of bibliographies by subject. As for long range priorities many interesting projects are presently at the preliminary planning stage, specially the inclusion in a book catalogue form of the total public libraries collection in New Brunswick.

New Brunswick Library Service is confident that this provincial network was the right step for the public library system.

36. Computer Output Microfilm*

by Philip Schwarz

During the late 1960s Stout, like many other libraries, began developing a variety of machine-readable data bases. In the ensuing years the number and size of these data bases have continued to grow.

The library completed conversion of its shelf list to machine readable form early in 1973. This was by far the largest data base consisting of over 50 million characters. It soon became evident that the cost in terms of computer time, paper and distribution for generating reports from a data base of this size would be prohibitive. In an effort to reduce costs, a truncated version was made, titled "The Public Catalog," consisting of one line per title and including the author, title, call number, publication date and collection code; it ran to over 2000 pages. It was our intention to run the report in title, author and call number sequence, but even this truncated report ran to over 6000 pages. It became obvious that a report of this size could not be economically produced and distributed in print form.

At this point the library began investigating the medium of computer-output-microfilm (COM). COM in very simple terms involves the recording of output from computers directly on microfilm rather than on paper. COM can be produced in a variety of forms; 4x6 microfiche, 16mm and 35mm roll film. It can also be produced at a variety of reduction ratios. The most common reduction ratio and format seems to be 42x microfiche. The library's examination of the potential of COM identified the following advantages:
    1. The programming required for converting from paper printout to COM is relatively simple requiring only a few hours.
    2. The savings in time required to produce a COM tape as opposed to a paper printout is generally in the 75-80 percent range.
    3. The cost of the original copies of the report are approximately 50 percent less than for the same report on paper.
    4. The savings on duplicate copies are even more dramatic. One microfiche, 207 pages at 42x, can be duplicated for about 10 cents.
    5. The resulting reports occupy approximately 2 percent of the space occupied by the same print report. The 6000-page public catalog described above can easily be carried around in a pocket.

---

*Reprinted by permission of the author and publisher from Wisconsin Library Bulletin, 72 (May/June 1976), p. 125-26, 130.

6. Access time is considerably reduced because of the ease of handling and scanning large amounts of data.
7. Distribution is considerably easier and considerably less costly if reports are to be mailed. For example, microfiche--1449 pages at 42x--can easily be mailed in a business envelope for 13 cents.
8. Turn-around time for COM reports is considerably reduced when compared to printing.

COM is not without its limitations.
1. Reports that "must" be annotated are not good candidates for COM production.
2. The necessity for reading equipment can be an important factor with the current budget constraints, although this factor can be easily offset by savings in production.
3. User resistance to microfilms can be a problem that has to be overcome.

The advantages of COM clearly outweighed its disadvantages when applied to Stout's problems. In the spring of 1973 a program was started to convert a number of our computer reports to COM. The library decided to use 42x microfiche as the medium. This reduction was chosen because it would allow 207 as opposed to 98 pages per fiche at 24x. A higher reduction ratio would allow an even greater savings. However, the library found that 42x could be read on standard microfiche readers available for checkout and in other locations on campus.

All reports would be produced on 4x6 microfiche as opposed to roll film. Admittedly roll film offers a convenience factor for in-house use, particularly with new readers capable of handling 500-foot rolls of film. It allows the library to place the catalog in a reader and requires no handling on the part of the patron. This, however, was balanced against several other factors. First, the library had the capability of duplicating microfiche. This would allow us to run one master set of COM fiche and provide duplicates of all or part of the catalog on a demand basis. Second, excellent microfiche readers were available with dual lenses, capable of handling 24x and 42x microfiche. These could be used for our large collection of standard microfiche as well as COM reports. These readers are considerably less expensive than the film readers capable of handling 500-foot rolls.

The library is currently generating the following reports on COM:
1. The public catalog set
2. Periodical holdings
3. A film catalog
4. A UW-system videotape catalog
5. A cumulated index to Wisconsin public documents.

Conversion of additional reports from a paper format to COM is currently under consideration.

Concurrently with the conversion of library reports to COM the library staff has been working closely with other university offices to identify other potential uses of COM. The rationale is that the more uses found for COM the more incentive there will be to purchase additional microfiche readers. This will in turn expand the number of reader stations available on campus for library uses. This program has been very successful. The business office, institutional research, and the registrar are all producing and distributing reports on COM. As a result of these activities the business office, student services and all of the academic schools have purchased microfiche readers.

A proposal to provide every department with readers is under study. Under a Higher Education Act Title VI-B grant, written in conjunction with student housing, every residence hall has been equipped with a microfiche reader and a copy of each of the COM catalogs produced by the library. Copies of all COM catalogs have been distributed to each Academic School. Index stations have also been provided throughout the library. Each station consists of a dual lens microfiche reader and copies of all library COM catalogs.

Conclusion

There is little doubt that COM has proved to be a powerful tool for the production and distribution of library information at relatively low cost. It has been very well received at Stout and every indication points to increasing use throughout the University.

37. COM Comes to the Chicago Public Library*

by Patrick M. O'Brien

In February of 1974 a major change took place at The Chicago Public Library. The library changed classification systems from Dewey Decimal to Library of Congress and began to process much of our own material through the Ohio College Library Center (OCLC). From that time we have continued to build bibliographic records in machine-readable form and have also written into our jobber bid specifications the stipulation that the bibliographic records for materials processed must also be available to us in machine-readable form.

With all of these records being produced for us, we were still maintaining card catalogs. The machine records were not being utilized for any public service purposes nor were they being used to any great extent for technical processes purposes. This double bibliographic record keeping prompted us to begin exploring possibilities for the future.

To get to that future we should examine a bit the recent past. In developing its potential as a system, The Chicago Public Library has been guided by the recommendations of several studies, including the computerization of the acquisition, recording, cataloging, and shelf preparation of books and serials, and that computer technology be used for bibliographic control to facilitate internal and external library cooperation.

In the spring of 1975, a task force appointed to examine intralibrary and interlibrary loan problems expressed the urgent need for a union catalog (we have never had a union catalog) for the library to expedite the locating and loaning of its materials. It further stated that the catalog should be in computer output microform for ease of distribution and updating. The Five-Year Plan of The Chicago Public Library 1976-1980, and the revised five-year plan for 1977-1981, both stressed the need for a useable record for listing all library materials owned by us with locations. Each progressive study or report has emphasized the need to achieve bibliographic control over our systemwide holdings. Even the Martin report of ten years ago, Library Response to Urban Change, recommended the use of MARC records to speed processing and attain bibliographic control.

―――――――――
*Reprinted by permission of the author and publisher from Illinois Libraries, 60 (April 1978), p. 397-402.

Collection development has emphasized The Chicago Public Library's function as a major reference facility as well as its role as an educational resource for adults and children and as a source for recreational print and non-print materials. Cataloging policy and practice has been primarily in support of the reference function of the library. Our catalog records are complete entries which include tracings, notes, see, and see also references, etc.

Over the years separate, unconsolidated catalogs and shelflists have been developed for the Central Library, Cultural Center, regional libraries, and branch libraries. Most shelflist information contained only partial bibliographic data and location information. Main entry catalog cards are the only source containing full bibliographic data but no location information.

The first problem we had to grapple with when contemplating conversion of the catalog was to identify just what card catalogs (data bases) existed and what they contained that would be of use. The existing data bases were as follows:

1. Central Library card catalog--a nonunion dictionary catalog representing some 500,000 titles, all held or once held in the Central Library.
2. Five Central Library subject division catalogs--all titles listed in the Central Library card catalog, plus additional holdings as classified government documents, some foreign titles, pamphlets, and the like.
3. Cultural Center, regional and branch library card catalogs--80 catalogs listing complete holdings of that unit including both unique titles and duplicate titles held elsewhere in the system.
4. Special Collections card catalogs--dictionary catalogs of the Special Collections Department and the Vivian Harsh Collection.
5. Central Library shelflist.
6. Six Central Library subject division shelflists--only shelflists containing complete foreign title holdings.
7. Branch and regional library union shelflist--prior to 1974 a main entry holdings list of all branches in shelflist order.
8. Cultural Center shelflists--holdings of Popular Library and children's collection.

Two additional data bases thought to be of use were also identified:

1. Name Authority file (500,000 entries)--card file listing of the forms of name of authors, editors, etc., used as headings in the card catalog.
2. Subject Authority file (130,000 entries)--a card file listing of subject headings and references used in the card catalog in addition to the Library of Congress list.

With discrete shelflists, some containing dead records, it was difficult to determine exactly how many titles were actually held by us. The overlapping between the Central Library and the branches was also unknown but after some sampling we were able to estimate systemwide holdings of approximately 600,000 titles with 10 percent or 60,000 of those held uniquely in the branches. The distribution of volumes between the Central Library and branches was known and if proportionate to the volume/title ratio, meant that the Central file consisted of 540,000 titles and the branch file consisted of 253,000 titles. We add approximately 25,000 titles yearly.

With the above identified, we decided to set forth the following objectives. To:

1. Eliminate the separate catalogs by developing a single, complete, and comprehensive machine-readable data base.
2. Improve user access through frequent production and wide distribution of the complete holdings of The Chicago Public Library System. This also includes distribution throughout the state and elsewhere.
3. Provide the means to improve the quality of the catalog and reduce the cost of catalog maintenance.

With these objectives in mind, we prepared a dummy conversion program that would give us a computer output union catalog for use in all public service and some technical service units of the library. We also studied existing machine-readable records and examined the by-products produced by various library systems.

Briefly, the original conversion process was delineated in the following steps:

1. The Central Library, Cultural Center, and all branch library shelflists would be microfilmed at their physical location.
2. From these films bibliographic data consisting of a minimum of title, author, call number, publication date, Central Library division, Cultural Center, and/or Special Collections codes, and LC card order number, where available, would be keyed to computer-processable form.
3. This keyed data would be run against the MARC bibliographic data and other machine-readable catalog files available to pull the full bibliographic data.
4. Matching titles would form the initial CPL machine-readable data base that would retain our call number and other unique keyed data. (It should be clarified here that we made the conscious decision to accept the bibliographic records available as they matched from other bases as our record. We contemplated no revisions or editing at time of conversion or later.)
5. Proof lists of the records retrieved would be produced for side-by-side comparison with the retrieved record to determine if the records were for the same title.
6. We would review list and correct any mismatches or duplications through OCR (Optical Character Recognition) methods.
7. Titles not found on the data bases would be arranged in main

entry sequence containing all data originally keyed.
8. We would retrieve the actual main entry from our catalogs for microfilming since the main entry is the only full bibliographic record we have.
9. All these entries would be fully keyboarded to add to the other records.
10. The same process would be repeated for the branch shelflists.
11. These short keyboarded entries would be run against our newly created record. If a match occurred, the branch location would be added to all records for the title and, if necessary, the branch call number which in many instances would be different from the Central Library's call number.
12. Branch titles not found would then be run against the same data bases to pull full bibliographic information.
13. These would be added to the data base with locations.
14. Steps 7, 8 and 9 would then be repeated for the branches.

At this point, conversion would be complete and The Chicago Public Library would possess in machine-readable form all bibliographic records with locations for any materials we had ever processed.

Originally we expected to produce two types of computer output catalogs for our data. Type A would be a full entry catalog, and Type B would be a short entry catalog.

Type A catalog:

1. Fully cumulated catalog including all 600,000 title records.
2. Divided into two sections containing separate author or main entry, and title and subject section or added entry.
3. All elements of main entry containing descriptive cataloging including all notes, full tracings displayed along with codes for all locations holding title. 600,000 records.
4. Title entry as short title, author, publication date, and Central Library division codes, and call number. 600,000 records.
5. Subject or added entry same as title entry under single subject headings. 1,200,000 records.

It was anticipated that the above would fit on two microfilm viewers, one handling the main entries and the other handling the title and subject entries.

Type B catalog:

1. Same general arrangement, scope, and organization as Type A.
2. Main entry would be abbreviated to short title, author, publication date, Central division codes, branch location codes, and call numbers associated with each. 600,000 records.
3. Title and subject entries would have same bibliographic data as main entry, including location codes. 1,800,000 records.

One option that we added to our final specifications and which we have elected to exercise was the ability to produce a juvenile title catalog. This would provide a catalog which would be discrete but following the adult main entry and added entry catalogs. This would still provide for the complete catalog, adult and juvenile, to be contained on two microfilm viewers. We may also elect to produce a separate juvenile catalog with the main entries, title, and subject entries all contained in one viewer.

An Authority Term listing would be produced when the data conversion was complete. This would give us an "as-used" listing of all terms and names in the catalog. It would be in term and name sequence and would give us a frequency of occurrence of each entry. This listing would allow us to edit and change forms of name and subject headings as warranted.

We determined that it would be cost effective to cumulate the master catalog for distribution on a quarterly basis. In the interim, a cumulative microfiche catalog supplement would be published on a weekly basis. This would be produced from the tapes supplied by the book jobber to the COM vendor and our own archival OCLC tapes. Each public service unit of the library using the COM catalog would also have a microfiche viewer for this weekly supplement. The supplement would tell them the status of materials as being "on order," "received but not in circulation" or "in circulation." In addition, each entry would list title, author, publisher, in-print date, call number, LC card order number, CPL Bibliographic Access Number, and location symbols. It was envisioned that this tool would be used by reference desk librarians when a user did not find a title in the COM catalog that he or she felt should be there.

The Bibliographic Access Number, or BAN, mentioned above, is simply an eight digit sequential check number. This control number goes on all records for an individual title and allows us to pull all records for that title by issuing a delete command using only the one number.

As mentioned earlier, all of our processing now is done (recorded in MARC II format) by our book jobber or is done through OCLC. Any original cataloging, or cataloging produced elsewhere, is added to our OCLC record. Theoretically, all classified material processing is captured on a machine-readable record that becomes our source for the weekly microfiche cumulation, and that, in turn, is integrated to the whole COM record on a quarterly basis.

The bid specifications were issued, and the contract for conversion was awarded to Brodart, Incorporated, of Williamsport, Pennsylvania, on the basis of performance and lowest bid in August 1977. The total cost through conversion completion was $291,464.30 with a not-to-exceed cost of $310,215.63. This included the first issue of the COM catalog. The specifications also called for one quarterly update, and the cost for that was $57,900.00 with a not-to-exceed cost of $63,690.00. This represents a per title conversion cost of approximately $0.50.

A separate bid for readers was recently let and the ROM III came in with the low bid. Our original distribution called for 186 (372 readers) complete catalogs for the Central Library, Cultural Center, and branch libraries. We have since revised those estimates because of anticipated queuing problems. We will probably add another 170 readers and issue more copies of the added entry (title and subject) sections than main entries based on the way people actually use catalogs; that is, the subject approach as opposed to particular item.

One other change has been made by mutual agreement since the original conversion plan. This had to do with the microfilming of each branch library's shelflist. After extensive sampling, it was determined that the Branch Union Shelflist, plus the Central, Cultural Center, and Woodson Regional's shelflists captures over 96 percent of the titles held by The Chicago Public Library. The flow charts illustrated in Appendix A illustrate this change.

From the product derived from these lists the vendor will be able to produce an individual branch's shelflist as reflected in the Branch Union Shelflist on microfiche. Armed with this microfiche shelflist of let's say, the Lake View Branch, an editing crew will go to that branch and check the actual card shelflist against it. They will also have with them the COM catalog representing 96 percent of our titles and a sequential BAN number list printed in OCR type. As they check the branch card shelflist, they will delete what appears on the microfiche, but not in it, by scratching out the attendant BAN number on the sheet. If a title appears in the card shelflist, but not on the microfiche, they will check the COM catalog as the title would be likely to be held elsewhere in the system. When the title is found they can add it to the microfiche record simply by checking its BAN number on the sequential chart. Any title not found in either the COM catalog or the microfiche shelflist will have its main entry pulled for searching on other data bases or for being originally keyboarded. As indicated, we expect this to happen with less than 4 percent of our titles.

The entire process, as envisioned by Brodart's George Steinbach, is attached as Appendix A.

APPENDIX A

Chicago Public Library Conversion Procedure

Shelflist records from each of the Central Subject Division, Woodson Regional Library, Cultural Center, and Special Collections (V. Harsh) will be microfilmed in simplex mode (front of card only). Simplex mode was chosen because no relevant data appears on the reverse of these records. The shelflist records resident in the Dewey-Classed

Branch Union Catalog and the LC-Classed Adult Nonfiction Catalog will be microfilmed in duplex mode (front and back).

As microfilmed, the source records will be returned in sequence to the appropriate locations. This process will assure minimal disruption of internal activities requiring use of the shelflists.

From each of the microfilmed records the following data will be captured through a key-boarding operation:

Central Subj., Div., Spcl. Coll., Cultural Center, Woodson: Short Author, Short Title, Call Number, LCCN, Publication Date, Source Catalog Symbol, and Shelflist Drawer Number.
LC Adult, DC Branch Union-(OE the L.C. Adult records, only agency designated records will be keyed): Short Author, Short Title, Call Number, LCCN, Date of Publication, Source Catalog Symbol, Shelflist Drawer Number.

Note

For the purpose of establishing an internal/external record control, each record of each drawer of each source will be automatically assigned a sequential number. This number will be carried as an integral field of each record. (Hereafter, the LC, and DC classed branch shelflist records will be referred to as "Branch" records; all others as "Central.")

Once in machine-readable form, central records will be consolidated to eliminate duplicates, then indexed by LCCN and Search key. Branch records will be identically indexed to produce a manageable search argument. Branch records will be matched to the central records and where a match occurs the records will be combined, with Branch data being appended to the Central record. Since original record sources are essentially the same for both Branch and Central records, the exposure to mismatches is quite minimal. Due to processing logic and index construction, however, multiple record selections and combinations will be experienced. For this reason a manual editing routine is required. This edit will be the first task performed by CPL staff. Successful matches will be out-filed and printed in drawer sequence within central division source catalog symbol. Staff members will edit the lists by examination and comparison of the Branch short entry request and the multiple records selected through the Branch argument. Once edited, Brodart will recombine files and eliminate incorrect multiple selections.

Using the same search argument, all combined, central and branch only titles will be used to search the OCLC archival and Tech-Serv files inhand, MARC, LA, and UC data bases. Unique selections, unsuccessful requests, and the short entry request resulting in multiple selections will be out-filed and processed to produce a union, divided catalog in two alphabets: Author/Title, and Subject.

The catalog, in microform, will be distributed throughout the system, providing system-wide patron access, and a measurement of catalog organization and distribution utility.

Records successfully matched and extracted from the named bibliographic data bases will be sorted by Branch only, and Central titles. Central titles will be further sorted by descending order of Branch symbol occurrence. The sorted files will be utilized to generate proof listings; dividing the listings into four (4) groups--i. e.; agency-only multiple extracts, agency-only unique extracts, central multiple extracts, and central unique extracts. The lists will be distributed as follows:

1. Multiple Extracts
    a. Agency-only to CPL Central cataloging
    b. Central to source subject divisions
2. Unique Extracts to central cataloging

Editing of the multiple entries is expected to be a rapid process since in the majority of cases the appropriate record will be present. For those few records where the editing of multiple extracts does not yield a satisfactory entry, such records will be treated as mismatches, discussed later. Multiple extract editing will be performed by comparing the selected record with the request.

Unique extract editing will require both more time and skill due to an increased likelihood of incorrect, or 'mismatches.' The process of comparing the short bibliographic request with the selected record should be augmented by comparison of the selected record to the appropriate shelflist entry in cases wherein the selected record is questionable. In order to gauge the magnitude and impact on editing of 'mismatched' record selections, a sample of the selections will be taken at random and thoroughly edited. This process will give measurable understanding of the actual need for rigorous editing and its relationship to cost.

For those unique and duplicate records found to be total 'mismatches,' continued processing will follow the procedure to be employed for unsuccessful extract requests, or 'non-matches.'

Such records ('non-matches') will be first processed to sort central from agency-only titles. Central titles will be further sorted by their source Subject Division Catalog. Similarly, agency-only titles will be further sorted by descending order of Branch symbol occurrence. Machine-sorted titles will be printed; the resulting lists merged with those titles found to be mismatches from the unique and multiple extract lists, and distributed to the appropriate source catalog division or branch.

Using the lists, CPL staff will pull the main entry cards from either the branch public catalog, or the Central Division Public catalog (not PCC). Brodart will microfilm these cards, encode the bibliographic and control data, and keyboard the records in their entirety. The machine-readable files will then be merged with the CPL master file to produce a newly updated master in machine-readable form.

This updated master will be sorted in its entirety by Branch Agency symbol and within each symbol by the shelflist arrangement of each Branch Agency. The file will be formatted to display the full main entry, and will be printed in microfiche form for distribution to each Branch Agency.

Each Branch Agency will edit the listing by comparing their individual shelflist records with the microfiche shelflist. Omitted files will be indicated by searching the full microfilm catalog and reloaded appropriate holding information and variant call numbers. Other more common corrections will be the notation of withdrawals and variant call numbers. These errors will be likewise recorded, sent to Central Cataloging for OCR typing and ultimate processing by Brodart to produce a complete and accurate master file.

38. RMIT COM Catalogue Study Results*

by Elizabeth Stecher Morrison

A research study of catalogue provision in libraries of colleges of advanced education was funded under the Research and Development Program of the Commission on Advanced Education and undertaken at the Royal Melbourne Institute of Technology Central Library in 1974.[1] It had as its central aim the investigation of suitable forms of computer output for catalogues of CAE libraries.

Standards of Catalogue Provision

Two assumptions underlie the study:
(1) That minimum standards of catalogue provision for the libraries of colleges of advanced education are: (a) currency--the catalogue must be up-to-date; (b) completeness--records of the works listed must be accessible by author(s), title(s), series, subject(s) in accordance with accepted (AACR) practice; (c) convenience--the catalogue must be provided near the collection or, in the case of closed access, its service point; and (d) accessibility--the catalogue must be physically accessible and usable.
(2) That use of computers in providing catalogues (whether in-house, bureau service, or as part of a co-operative scheme) should be considered if this provides a cost-effective means of meeting the above standards.

Catalogues in CAE Libraries

Single-campus colleges which have a centralized library service may be able to meet the above standards of catalogue provision. Others--and returns from a questionnaire sent out in September 1974 to the (then) eighty-one CAE libraries indicated that approximately half of these libraries would not fit in this category--would need to provide at least more than one copy of all or part of their catalogues. In some of the colleges resources were scattered through departments; in others, there were separately maintained special collections (often 'curriculum materials'); and then there were dispersed services ranging from small branches to major divisions.

---

*Reprinted by permission of the author and publisher from The Australian Library Journal, 24 (Oct./Nov. 1975), p. 384-89.

It was taken as a further assumption that full replication of card catalogues is sufficiently costly of labour, materials and space to warrant consideration of alternative physical forms of catalogue, notwithstanding the possible use of computers to print out cards in pre-sorted batches.

Impetus to consideration of alternative forms of catalogue was also provided by the fact that numbers of college libraries indicated serious interest in computerization of catalogue production. In some instances this is related to imminent institutional mergers which will inevitably result in the need to amalgamate and then duplicate collection records (Ballarat Institute of Advanced Education with the State College of Victoria at Ballarat is a case in point). In others it is part of the growing interest in large scale co-operative and centralized cataloguing schemes. Planning for computer-assisted catalogue production entails the specification of output form, and a number of options are readily available.

Computer Outputs Examined

Three options were experimentally investigated in the RMIT study:
(1) Printed book catalogue produced by photocomposition from magnetic tape, then offset printing, together with a supplement in the form of pages of computer printout in a looseleaf binder.
(2) Printed book catalogue, as above, together with a supplement in the form of COM (computer-output-microform) film. [2]
(3) Complete catalogue on COM film.

Option 1 is the way in which catalogues have been provided at RMIT for the past few years. Use of COM (Options 2 and 3) was new.

The study took the form of providing these alternatives over a period of three months in the RMIT Central Library and observing catalogue use, measuring performance, and eliciting attitudes of library users. The library is on two levels within a multi-storey building. There is a catalogue consultation area on each floor where normally several sets of the printed book catalogue plus one or two copies of the printout supplement are provided (RMIT has had computer-produced catalogues since 1967). During the period of the tests, the usual book plus printout combination was continued on the upper level, while COM film was introduced in the lower level consultation area, first together with and as a supplement to the book catalogue, and later as the only form of catalogue.

The experimental design, taking in the phases studied before and after the actual three months trial may be represented as:

Phase	Dates (1974)	Floor 1 Catalogues	Floor 2 Catalogues
Before	13 May-12 June	Option 1	Option 1
1	13 June-10 July	Option 2	Option 1
2	11 July-7 Aug.	Option 3	Option 1
3	8 Aug.-4 Sept.	Option 2	Option 1
After	5 Sept.-30 Sept.	Option 1	Option 1

Option 1 was provided as: Book catalogue, four sets each in four viewers; Printout supplement, two sets each in two binders.

Option 2 was provided as: Book catalogue, as above; Microfilm supplement, four sets each in two cassettes; four viewers.

Option 3 was provided as: Microfilm catalogues; four sets each in five cassettes; four viewers.

Options 2 and 3 were not seen as dissimilar alternatives but rather as two levels of the independent variable-microform catalogues.

Measurements and Evaluation

During the experimental period, the microfilm catalogues were obviously heavily used and, in association with the viewing equipment provided, were usable and durable with no significant technical hitches. Data on their properties, their use and the views of library users were systematically collected over three to five months, using a variety of techniques.

Tests of retrieval time and accuracy carried out under controlled conditions with a sample group of catalogue users yielded evidence that microfilm catalogues as provided took longer to search than full print catalogues, although participants in the tests were unaware of this. Evidence from general questionnaires confirmed that the longer search time was usually not recognized and in any case was not regarded as a draw-back. Accuracy was not significantly different.

Controlled observations of library traffic and catalogue use indicated considerably increased use of catalogues in both areas during the phase of the trials when complete COM catalogues were provided (Phase 2). Analysis of questionnaire data revealed that the percentage of library users consulting catalogues remained constant but that these users were undertaking more searches. From results of the retrieval time tests it would be assumed that searches were also taking longer. The increased catalogue use of the lower level, combined with the limitations of access occasioned by the provision of only four viewing stations, gave rise to a considerable amount of queueing, and to some displacement of catalogue users to the Floor 2 area. Many users commented in questionnaire returns on the access limitations and recommended more viewers be provided.

Preferences

Information about attitudes and preferences for catalogue provision was sought through a number of questionnaires: detailed ones to small sample groups and special groups of users (library staff, teaching staff) and general ones distributed on a large scale to all library users on selected days. Results indicate acceptance of some form of microfilm, as the following table shows:

Questionnaires	Preferred Options Percentages (approximate)			
	(Book+ Printout)	(Book+ Microfilm)	(Microfilm only)	No Opinion
To Users (Phase 2)	8% (93)	55% (662)	25% (308)	12% (141)
To Users (After)	18% (237)	23% (316)	40% (540)	19% (254)
To Teaching Staff (Tertiary)	24% (35)	22% (32)	44% (64)	10% (14)
To Teaching Staff (Technical)	38% (9)	22% (5)	34% (8)	6% (2)
To Library Staff	4% (2)	37% (18)	53% (26)	6% (3)
To Test Group (Intensive Familiarization)	18% (5)	36% (10)	46% (13)	(0)

A stringent analysis of comments and opinions supplied, particularly by respondents preferring Option 1, indicated no consensus concerning any noticeable drawbacks of microfilm for catalogue consultation, and also indicated that respondents not wanting change tended to be light or even non-catalogue users as compared with the norms established from data collected.

Catalogue Utilization

The technique to arrive at a measure of catalogue utilization--both for the whole library during each phase and for each consultation area during each phase--involved the simultaneous observation of catalogue use in the two areas, at instants of time randomly chosen, averaging out at intervals of thirty minutes apart and not closer than intervals of one minute over the whole period of the catalogue trials. On each occasion, in each area, the numbers of persons consulting particular catalogues and waiting (presumably) to consult were recorded.

Indices of use were obtained by coordinating numbers of users observed at particular times with the frequency of such observations. Frequencies were then expressed as percentages, and ranked, thus enabling comparisons of use between phases and between floors.

Tables showed use to be heaviest during the middle (total COM on Floor 1) phase with a markedly atypical pattern on Floor 1. Taking the presence of four persons at the Floor 1 catalogues in Phase 2 to indicate full utilization (because four viewers were provided), it was possible to examine the degree of full utilization, under-utilization, and queueing. A technique was devised for quantifying these states and also for obtaining a measure of the total demands on the catalogues and the degree of displacement occasioned by the limitations of access.

This provided a basis for calculation of the number of access points (or viewing stations) required in the RMIT Library situation to meet user needs without investing in equipment which would be under-utilized. [3]

Costs

Comparative costs of catalogue provision for the three options described above were estimated over the forthcoming 1976-78 triennium. Unit costs will vary in given situations, but the cost factors or components identified should have general application.

No attempt at a comparative costing of computer time for each option was made, although estimates of elapsed time extrapolated from sample studies, were projected, and showed that, in the RMIT situation, while slightly less time would be taken for Option 2 as compared with Option 1 (because the time to actually print out would be

	Timing Summary for Triennium 1976-78		
	Option 1	Option 2	Option 3
1976	61 hours	45 hours	119 hours
1977	65 hours	56 hours	132 hours
1978	68 hours	52 hours	150 hours
1976-1978	194 hours	153 hours	401 hours

saved--the print tape would be, instead, delivered to the COM service bureau), more than double machine time would be needed to provide monthly file updates and output tapes for complete COM catalogues instead of annual updates and monthly supplements.

Major cost components for output production were identified as: Book catalogue--Photocomposition (a), $2 per page master; Printing (b), quotes obtained on specified number of pages and fifty copies.

Printout--Paper (c), $55 per 1000 (four part) sheets.
COM Supplements--Original film (d), $27 per 1000 frames (pages); Negative copies (e), $4.51 per 100 feet.
COM Catalogues--Original film (f), as d; Negative copies (g), as e.
COM Viewers--Purchase (h), capital outlay $600 each; Maintenance (i), annual charge $50 per viewer.

Components were combined into formulae to cost the three options being compared for RMIT for the 1976-78 triennium.
(1) Book catalogue annually (fifty copies) and monthly printout supplements (four copies) (Option 1). Each year, cost equals (a plus b) plus c.
(2) Book catalogue every two years (fifty copies), and monthly microfilm supplements (Option 2 takes advantage of the fact that use of COM enables larger usable supplement files than does printout). Year 1, cost equals (a plus b) plus d plus n (e plus h plus i); Year 2 d plus n (e plus i); Year 3 (a plus b) plus d plus n (e plus i) where n equals eight.
(3) COM catalogues only, updated each month (Option 3); Year 1, cost equals f plus n (g plus h plus i); Years 2, 3 f plus n (g plus i) where n equals ten.

The actual costing was based on an estimated file size of 70,000 title records at the start of 1976, growing by 1000 titles each month for eleven months of the year. Costs arrived at using the above formulae and parameters and actual or quoted charges were:

	Option 1	Option 2	Option 3
	$	$	$
1976	15,448	20,492	12,792
1977	17,886	1,688	7,705
1978	20,070	20,314	8,617
1976-78	$53,404	$42,494	$29,114

These are gross comparisons and do not allow for the factor of cost of computer time referred to above.[4] They must be considered in conjunction with the known characteristics, advantages and disadvantages of the respective output forms.

A series of cost comparisons also undertaken to determine up to what number of copies COM is economic (taking into account a one-for-one COM viewer equipment cost) indicated that when more than twenty sets of the catalogue are required it begins to be cheaper to produce a book catalogue once a year rather than to invest in COM viewers and produce an updated COM catalogue monthly.

Conclusions

A conclusion of the research study is that COM can provide a cost-effective alternative to full print for computer-produced library catalogues but it is not claimed that it can or should supplant other alternatives. Optimum methods of catalogue provision have to be carefully planned on an informed, individual basis, with a delicate balancing of known costs and benefits. The RMIT study aimed to provide some guidelines for doing this.

References

1. Stecher, E. Catalogue provision in libraries of colleges of advanced education. (Royal Melbourne Institute of Technology, 1975).
2. 16 mm COM film, 24: 1 reduction, cine mode, code-line indexed, in twin-spool cassettes, with Memorex 1644 Autoviewer. Preliminary investigations and a pilot study indicated film to be more suited than fiche to the RMIT situation.
3. For RMIT this was calculated to be a minimum of six viewers on the figures provided, for dedicated public use. In fact it has been decided to purchase ten viewers in 1975 and a further three to five in 1976.
4. Comparative computer costs cannot be deduced from estimates of elapsed time (i.e. twice the elapsed time does not cost twice as much); the formulae for calculating computing costs vary from installation to installation, and take into account such factors as CPU time, allocation of disc and tape storage, and use of other peripheral devices.

39. 600 Users Meet the COM Catalog*

by Brian Aveney and Mary Fischer Ghikas

A pioneer in automation-aided access to its collections, Los Angeles County Public Library had moved through two stages of computer-assisted book catalogs before investigating the possible use of COM--which was thought to be less expensive overall.

The potential cost benefits of the COM catalog compared to the printed, cumulated catalog currently in use were quite easily calculated. The main problem was perceived to be in public acceptance and use patterns. Experience with the last generation of printed book catalogs suggested that the COM catalogs would bring forth even greater challenges in adapting to change.

Design and Equipment

The study was divided into two phases: 1) impact of the COM catalog from an internal management perspective, and 2) the user perspective on the new equipment and system.

Phase 1 sampled viewer use by day of the week, time of day, type of user, and queuing problems, and it reviewed equipment failure records. Autographics LCR 1100 and Information Design ROM 3 readers were used interchangeably, and researchers found no significant variation in reliability. Most of the data used in this phase was gathered by direct observation.

Phase 2 used an extensive questionnaire administered in patron interviews. The questionnaire combined specific and open-ended questions to determine patron response to the new COM catalogs and readers--as well as to existing library catalogs and related tools. A total of 602 interviews was conducted in late summer and fall 1977.

A sample of 18 test libraries and 10 control libraries was used for both phases of the study.

The User Perspective

In this summary, we look first at the more important factor, user

---
*Reprinted by permission of the authors from American Libraries, 10 (February 1979), p. 82-83.

acceptance, the sine qua non of COM.

Acceptance of the new COM catalogs was measured in a number of ways. In the very first month of installation, blank comment slips were filled out by 230 patrons in 14 of the 18 test sites. Some of these comments are discussed below.

Months later, during the formal patron survey, we asked those who had indicated use of the COM catalogs to evaluate them in two ways: with an overall reaction, and then a specific comparison with book and card catalogs.

The overall reaction to the COM catalogs was quite significant. An "adjusted" table in the full study report shows that 75.8 percent indicated they were favorable to the COM catalogs, and only 10.9 percent were unfavorable.

In the specific comparisons of COM use to book and card catalogs, the respondents continued to show much greater favorable response than unfavorable. The proportion of those responding with an indifferent or "same" reaction, however, increased relative to the more general question. The table summarizes these responses.

The question about waiting is closely related to allocation of COM readers. In general, the responses indicate that the application to reader allocation of an activity index formula (such as that given later, below) seems to result in less queuing problems on the machines than on existing book and card catalogs. Though the question tests patrons' subjective feelings rather than recording actual queuing, those feelings are perhaps more important than the facts of actual physical queuing.

In comparing COM to card catalogs on the matter of waiting, patrons are both more positive and more negative than when comparing COM to book. This may reflect a situation specific to LACoPL, where the card catalog is only a branch shelflist while the book/COM catalogs list the entire system's collection. (In general, respondents were comparing COM and book catalogs to the card catalogs they had worked with in other libraries.)

A number of patrons noted that pages cannot be torn from the COM catalog; this is an availability as well as security factor.

In terms of difficulty, patrons rate COM more favorably when compared to card than to book. Greater ease might be expected, since both COM and book catalogs display a large number of entries on one frame or page, whereas a card file only allows one entry to be seen at a time. Some portion of the negative responses may be merely indications of a learning curve situation. Among the open-ended responses (gathered the first month) were: "Took time to get used to." "The only drawback I can foresee might be the adjustment from using a book to a machine." "Frankly, I've become attached to the old catalogs." "I was a little confused at first, but think after I've tried it a few times it will prove faster."

The greatest negative response to the COM catalog came on the question of how much <u>time</u> it took to find what was being sought. Almost a quarter of the patrons found it took more time to use than a card catalog, and 21 percent found it more time-consuming than the book catalog. The size of LACoPL's catalog may account for some of these responses. One patron noted, "It takes too long to look up a book, especially when the machine is on letter A and your author's name begins with W." Some problems may relate to improper adjustment of the visible indexes on the COM readers. "The subject printer should be adjusted." "Index does not agree with what's shown on the viewer."

In spite of the increase in negative responses compared with other questions, <u>the positive responses were almost double the negative</u>. A substantial number of the patrons saw no difference.

Patron Comparisons of COM with Book and Card Catalogs

The question: How do you feel about using the microfilm machine compared to using the library's old book catalog, or card catalogs in other libraries:
- Getting to use the catalog (waiting for the machine?)
- How difficult was it to find what you wanted in the catalog?
- How much time it took you to find what you wanted in the catalog?
- How readable was the catalog information on the screen?

	Wait	Difficulty	Time	Readability
	(Percentages of those interviewed)			
Better than book catalog	47.8	44.8	55.7	57.6
Same as book catalog	37.1	36.6	23.3	26.4
Worse than book catalog	15.2	16.6	21.0	16.0
Better than card catalog	66.5	66.2	41.0	38.7
Same as card catalog	15.6	21.6	35.0	38.2
Worse than card catalog	17.9	12.3	23.0	23.0

As to <u>readability</u>, patrons seem overall to rank book better than card, and COM better than both. Interesting patterns emerge from the open-ended responses gathered at the outset. One patron remarked, "Not bad once I figured out how to focus it"--raising questions of how many negative responses were caused by machines out of focus.

Patrons both damned and praised the readability. Most negative responses seemed to relate to the glare caused by the backlighting of the microfilm shining directly on the eyes. Due to variations in library buildings, it was not always possible to situate the COM readers in the most advantageous setting.

Other negative responses may be related to problems a minority of people have in seeing objects in motion. "Slow speed is still a little too fast to read." "Makes some people dizzy." Some of these problems may be caused, or at least aggravated, by user unfamiliarity with machine operation, particularly with regard to focus.

The Internal Management Perspective

Among implications for management identified in Phase 1 of the study were factors which could affect decisions on the number of readers needed and their placement.

Data from the test libraries varied somewhat, but catalog use peaked in late afternoon and early evening in 17 of the 18 sites. About one-third of the test site libraries reported their peak in viewer use to be around 7 p.m.

Survey results show that 75 percent of those test sites open Sundays have most viewer use on that day. Of the libraries not open Sundays, half indicate Monday as the day of highest microcatalog use. Friday is lightest, followed by Thursday and Saturday.

The greatest use of the viewers was, as expected, by patrons. In all sites, 49% of observable use was by a single patron, 27% by multiple users, 11% by a patron assisted by a library staff member, and 15% by staff alone.

It was noted that the smaller libraries have a higher percentage of staff use of the microcatalogs, whereas higher patron use is indicated in the larger libraries. Of the libraries with four or more viewers available, three-fourths reported that over 75% of the observed microcatalog use was by patrons.

An increase of 9% in total catalog use activity was noted in the test libraries, compared with the control libraries. This increase is compatible with the experiences of other public libraries that have installed COM catalogs. Most seem to suggest general use of the catalog increased; one library has suggested a doubling of use. Since few libraries have been sampled as extensively and methodically as LACoPL, we might say that this study confirms the theory: that COM catalogs will increase patron use of the catalog by some undefined amount.

The question of how many COM viewers are needed is a critical one for any library considering a microfilm catalog. Too few viewers results in excessive queuing and consequent patron dissatisfaction. Too many viewers wastes scarce funds.

In order to place viewers in the test site libraries, a method of allocation based on some measures of library activity had to be developed. A measurement called the "Activity Index" was developed and tested as a part of this study. Given variation in use over time, allocation on the basis of these formulas seems to have struck an acceptable cost/benefit balance. The formula recommended in the study is:

$$Y = 41.64 + 10.1A + 0.87B + 3.82C + 1.01D$$

Where: Y = Activity index
A = Registration of patrons per year (in thousands)
B = Circulations per year (in thousands)
C = Number of square feet of floor space (in thousands)
D = Reference questions per year (in thousands)

The initial value in the formula (41.64) is an attempt to provide a "floor" for small libraries.

Based on the experiences at LACoPL, a reasonable minimum formula for COM viewer allocation based on activity indexes is:

Activity Index	Minimum Viewers
200 or less	2
201-400	4
401-600	6
601-800	8
800 or more	10

In Summary

Briefly, the major pragmatic conclusions which can be drawn from the discussion above and other aspects of the study are the following:

● The COM catalog is more acceptable to patrons than either its book or card alternative.
● The specialized viewing equipment used in the test posed no obstacles to patron use of the catalog (except for patrons wearing bifocals).
● The most significant factor in providing satisfactory patron service is having enough viewers available at a given site to eliminate waiting.
● Provision of information in COM form seems to increase general use of the catalog.
● There is no significant difference among types of user groups in reaction to the COM catalog, although juvenile users of the motorized COM viewers may add a dimension of play to catalog use.
● Staff training, proper installation and illumination, and adequate information about the catalog are as important as provision of the COM publication and the viewers.

40. COM Catalog vs. Card Catalog: The Experience
of the University of Oregon Law Library*

by Dennis Ray Hyatt

In January 1977 the University of Oregon Law Library began recataloging and classifying its entire collection, using the computer services of Blackwell/North America, Incorporated (B/NA). By September 1977 over ten thousand of the estimated twelve thousand titles to be recataloged had been keyed into the B/NA computer. In that month the Law Library discarded its public card catalog and replaced it with copies of a B/NA computer output microfiche (COM) catalog. Several copies of the COM catalog were placed in the Library and additional copies were sent to Law School faculty and surrounding county law libraries.

The University of Oregon Law Library is unique among academic libraries in its reliance upon a COM catalog as the sole indicator of its holdings. The COM catalog is optional output of the B/NA system and several economic and noneconomic factors were considered in the Law Library's decision to select this option in preference to a card catalog which is as easily produced by the B/NA system. Other law libraries investigating the possibility of using the services of Blackwell/North America need not reach the same decision regarding the COM catalog option to find B/NA services useful and competitive with other computer service operations. The experience of the University of Oregon Law Library may help in the evaluation of the COM catalog and the computer system producing it.

The Law Library subscribes to the Blackwell/North America Title Index, a COM catalog of all entries in the B/NA database. The database is composed of Library of Congress MARC records and records of original cataloging as submitted by subscribing libraries. Because B/NA billing procedure is a function of output, the cost of the B/NA Title Index is the only initial charge to a library using the B/NA system. The subscription price of the Title Index varies, the cost of production steadily increasing as the number of records increases. However, this is offset by a growing number of subscribing libraries to share the cost. The current annual subscription rate is approximately $700, which includes cumulative weekly supplementation to incorporate new entries and quarterly recumulations of the entire record file. Additional copies of the Title Index are avail-

---

*Reprinted by permission of the author and publisher from Law Library Journal, 71 (November 1978), p. 668-72.

able at a slightly reduced price of the first copy. Rather than purchase an additional copy of the Title Index, however, the University of Oregon Law Library retains its prior superseded Title Index to have a second copy only one week out of date compared to the most recent.

The Blackwell/North America Title Index is a title entry catalog of short-form records. Each entry shows the title, main entry, imprint and collation information. A B/NA identifier number and the source of the record, i.e., whether from a MARC record or original input from a particular library, is also shown. The Library of Congress Card Number and classification number, if assigned, are displayed.

The B/NA Title Index reveals two important aspects of the Blackwell/North America system. First, Blackwell/North America is not an online, interactive system. Access to the database occurs only at the company's computer center in Beaverton, Oregon. This aspect of the B/NA system is attractive to the Law Library because down time, access scheduling, terminal costs and key operator training are not the worries of the Law Library. Furthermore, the number of staff able to work simultaneously with the B/NA database is a function of available microfiche readers rather than available terminals. By limiting access, Blackwell/North America claims its database is subject to greater quality control. That this quality control extends beyond clerical accuracy in keypunching is not entirely clear. University of Oregon Law Library records have had exceptionally few keying errors but the library division of B/NA has returned cataloging copy as unacceptable only when formatting is incompatible with programming. A second important aspect of using the B/NA Title Index is the short-form record which does not display field information below the collation. Librarians are often as concerned with notes and tracings as with bibliographic information appearing below the collation. The B/NA Title Index compels the catalog librarian to select a record without seeing it in its entirety. For existing MARC records this may pose no serious drawback but there may be serious reservations in using an original record submitted by another library.

A library wishing to add a particular record to its local database from the B/NA Title Index need only send the B/NA identifier number to Blackwell/North America. Because no extensive keypunching is required, the cost of selecting an entry already in the B/NA database is relatively low--about one dollar. However, to alter existing records in the B/NA database or to input original cataloging increases the cost. Thus, the economic incentive of participating libraries is to find and use existing records whenever available. The cost of inputting original cataloging has been almost double the cost of using existing records.

For many titles in the University of Oregon Law Library an existing record in the B/NA database was not available. Few other libraries had yet submitted entries for most law materials and MARC records were limited for the most part to imprints after 1967. For more than ninety percent of the pre-1968 titles in the

Law Library, Library of Congress descriptive cataloging was found and submitted. About ten percent of the pre-1968 titles required original cataloging. For uniformity, Blackwell/North America requires work copy in 3 x 5 card format for keying. Accordingly, the first ready source of LC descriptive cataloging copy was the Law Library's existing shelflist, composed of forty percent LC cards. After reverifying holdings, the Law Library sent these shelflist cards directly to B/NA for keypunching. Other LC descriptive cataloging was found in familiar bibliographic tools, photocopied, mounted on 3 x 5 card stock and submitted.

For file integrity, Blackwell/North America has decided that any alteration of LC copy was to be considered original cataloging by the participating library. Subsequent users of the B/NA Title Index can thus be assured that a record showing LC descriptive cataloging as the source of input in no way differs from the LC card entry. The University of Oregon Law Library was faced with the necessity of altering many pre-1967 LC cards--specifically those which lack LC classification numbers and falling in the Class K schedules. Blackwell/North America treated the addition of a class number to LC descriptive cataloging as alteration of the LC card. Thus, the B/NA Title Index shows the source of these records as original cataloging of the inputting library and fields which might otherwise give a clue to the source of descriptive cataloging, i.e., LC card numbers are left blank. As a result, even though ninety percent of all University of Oregon Law Library descriptive cataloging has LC bibliographic sources, about fifty percent of all entries are shown as having been originally cataloged by the University of Oregon Law Library, the major difference being those records where a class number has been added.

There are several reasons LC copy has not been used by the Law Library even when available. For example:
1) LC copy with a dashed-on entry is incompatible with the B/NA (i.e., MARC) program. Where LC descriptive cataloging contains a dashed-on entry, original cataloging must be submitted to omit the dashed-on information or change the dashed-on information to a bibliographic note, or create a second original catalog entry for the dashed-on material.
2) The Law Library has cataloged periodicals by successive entry and found most LC descriptive cataloging for them unusable.
3) In some instances LC descriptive cataloging was not used because of the undesirable nature of the LC entry. Pacific Reporter, with its lengthy title statement, is a case in point.
4) The University of Oregon Law Library has, in fact, considered not using available MARC records where additional subject tracings might be desirable since with computer technology the economic considerations limiting each entry to three subject tracings are less imperative.
5) Occasionally, LC descriptive cataloging did have a class number attached that was not preferred; in particular, some materials in Classes H and J were thought better located in Class K.

6) MARC records lacking class numbers, which include those items expected to appear in the foreign law and general law schedules, are also treated as original cataloging when a class number is attached.

The Class K General Law Schedule was not available when the University of Oregon Law Library started its classification project. Therefore, the Law Library used a temporary call number (K340 plus Cutter) for entries considered destined for this class in order to maintain relative shelf arrangement of these materials with other parts of the collection. With the publication of the Class K General Law Schedule, the Law Library began reclassing these records by requesting alterations to the existing records. Blackwell/North America will make any alterations in a local database but because another library may have since requested one of the records that the University of Oregon Law Library submitted, Blackwell/North America is understandably hesitant to make alterations in its main database. As a result, despite its commitment to quality control, Blackwell/North America is still faced with the same problem encountered by other computer services--a satisfactory method of purging its database of erroneous or interim input.

Rather than using the B/NA Title Index, libraries new to the B/NA system might consider relying instead on the local database of a library already in the system. For example, a law library might consider using the University of Oregon Law Library COM catalog as a source of cataloging information. The COM catalog of a local database is accessible by main entry as well as by title and is not a short-form entry catalog. Full descriptive cataloging data can be evaluated before selecting a record. Furthermore, the chance that records of pre-1968 law materials have been submitted by a library other than the University of Oregon is still relatively small. As other law libraries produce COM catalogs of their local databases, they too become useful sources of cataloging information for new subscribers.

For a variety of reasons a library may find a record in the B/NA database unacceptable. In these instances the University of Oregon Law Library ordinarily submits a new record as original input and does not use a B/NA option called customer variation whereby small alterations to an existing record may be made for the local database only. This option costs less since it requires less keypunching than would an original entry. The advantage to B/NA of the customer variation option is the savings of storage capacity in its database. However, the customer variation approach has one main disadvantage: the local database COM catalog cannot be used as a source of cataloging information by other libraries since corresponding records in the B/NA database do not necessarily match.

Invoices accompany products as they are sent to the subscribing library, costs depending on product options selected. The billing of one dollar or two dollars per entry for the Law Library occurs with B/NA production of proof copy of catalog cards of each entry. Although libraries may elect to receive complete card sets at this output stage, the University of Oregon Law Library receives only two unit cards for each entry, one unit card serving as a main entry file control, the other serving as a shelf-list file control. The cards replace temporary slips in each file serving as the order control of outstanding input. In addition to cards, Blackwell/North America provides computer-generated self-adhesive spine labels and short-form entry labels for card pockets and circulation cards. By foregoing production of labels, subscribers can reduce their costs per record. The University of Oregon Law Library has now begun inhouse marking to avoid the book back-log caused by the four- to six-week turn-around time for original cataloging input and the wait for labels. As a result, costs have been reduced approximately 15 cents per record.

One reason for delaying the production of a card catalog for as long as practically possible during a reclassification project is the necessity of handfiling cards for entries once the catalog is produced. With a substantial portion of the collection recataloged, the University of Oregon Law Library had to decide whether to produce a card catalog or COM catalog for the public. At present the cost advantage appears to favor the COM catalog. A COM catalog is priced according to the number of entries manipulated in its production. Since there is no price differential for electing a dictionary catalog or split catalog, the Law Library chose a split author-title subject catalog to remain consistent with the University of Oregon Main Library catalog. Current discussion of the COM catalog format at the Law Library centers on whether the same supporting arguments for a card catalog format are applicable in the format decisions of a COM catalog. The first Law Library COM catalog was produced at seven cents per entry for the ten thousand records in the local database, for a total cost of $700. Additional copies of the catalog were produced for six dollars each. Each COM catalog station requires a reader to accommodate the 42x fiche and these set-up costs may affect the decision to have a COM catalog. The same catalog produced in hard copy was estimated by B/NA to cost approximately $3500 based on the estimated number of cards as well as the number of records. Computer format and type size results in more multicard sets for entries than found in LC-produced cards.

Maintenance costs of the two catalogs are more difficult to compare. The COM catalog is updated by cumulative supplements but the cumulation of manipulated entries in each supplementation causes the cost to grow progressively. For example, assuming a steady growth of new entries at two hundred per month, monthly supplementation and seven cents per manipulated entry, the first supplement manipulates two hundred entries for $14, the second cumulative supplement manipulates four hundred entries for $28, the third cumulative supplement manipulates six hundred entries for $42, and so forth. At some point it becomes desirable to recumulate the entire catalog and start supplementation over and the recumulated catalog costs seven cents per entry to produce. There are obvious cost control methods to be considered by the individual library in this scheme. Supplements can be cumulated less often. In the example above, if the cumulation period is changed from once per month to once every two months, the costs of supplementation are reduced over a year from $1092 to $588. Also, recumulations can be less frequent and from an economic standpoint should be less frequent, as the catalog grows and new records constitute a smaller percentage of total records to be manipulated.

Aside from the costs of card sets, maintenance of a card catalog includes the staff costs of filing and revising. These costs may be difficult to measure, but the University of Oregon Law Library estimated that file upkeep would initially amount to $4,000 annually and would increase as the size of the catalog increased. In 1976 the Main Library of the University of Oregon used the costs of technical service staff in maintaining the card catalog as a major argument for using the B/NA system. As a result of discontinuing the subject catalog alone, the Library now has three fewer technical services clerical staff devoted to catalog maintenance. Discontinuance of a subject catalog may be especially desirable because Blackwell/North America offers automatic changes in subject tracings in COM catalog output with its subject authority file. The Main Library is presently considering the discontinuance of its main entry and title filings as well, although this may not occur until 1981 with the closing of the Library of Congress catalog.

Noneconomic considerations cause greater reservations in relying on a COM catalog, although user reaction at the University of Oregon has not yet proven to be one of them. Multiple locations of COM catalogs on each of the three floors of the Law Library and in the faculty library have given quicker access to holdings than a centrally located card catalog could. Other libraries may also be surprised at user acceptance of microfiche when advantages such as multiple locations are discovered. It is the technical service limitations of COM catalogs that pose the stronger noneconomic drawbacks. These limitations all center on problems of the quick and efficient change of status of a catalog entry. For example, titles withdrawn from the collection cannot have the entry withdrawn from the COM catalog until the next cumulation which, if the record is located in a recumulated catalog rather than the current supplement, could mean a year or more. Books whose location change with some frequency, such as class reserve items in academic libraries, cannot have the location status changed with sufficient speed using the COM catalog. In fact, monthly supplementation of a COM catalog may be undesirably slow for some libraries to reflect current acquisitions. At present the Law Library prepares acquisition lists to supplement the COM catalog, with no attempt to maintain a public record of items on order.

The University of Oregon Law Library has seen little feasibility in a COM catalog replacing a hard copy shelflist for maintaining such information as numbers of copies, accession numbers and records of withdrawals. A hard copy shelflist, however, only points to a notion that is sometimes overlooked in weighing the merits of a COM catalog and card catalog, namely, the two are not mutually exclusive options. It is entirely possible for the University of Oregon Law Library to decide to have COM catalogs for off-site use and rely upon the traditional card catalog for on-site use. And even if a hard copy catalog is produced, it may rather be in the form of a book catalog in multiple copies supplemented with pocketparts.

That the University of Oregon has elected the COM catalog option of the B/NA system is not nearly as significant as the fact that a computer system has been used which offers manipulation of records in the local database. With careful monitoring of input, the B/NA system allows for manipulation through controls not contemplated by a card catalog. Subsets within the library identifier field allow the subscribing library to indicate whether a particular record is a treatise, serial, microform or other publishing format. For example, it is possible to generate a subset of entries which have been designated as serials into a serials holdings list. Blackwell/ North America also provides a field for each library to assign its own entry identifier number for each record in its local database. In this field, the Law Library assigned sequential numbers to keep track of the number of entries submitted, exactly the same information provided with production of the first COM catalog since billing is based on the number of entries manipulated. Carefully monitored input would allow subsets of any kind to be controlled by the entry identifier. For example, one identifier sequence could be used for current serials, while another could be used for closed serial entries. Or, an identifier sequence could be used for nonserial continuations. The University of Oregon Law Library now uses local entry identifiers to keep track of entries which required complete original descriptive cataloging. Subset identification by the entry identifier is limited only by the creativity of the library.

The willingness of Blackwell/North America to create programs and work with individual libraries is a valuable asset in working with the B/NA system. When the Law Library desired computer-produced multiple spine labels for large multivolume sets, a simple program for production of multiple labels was written in twenty-four hours. It had not occurred to B/NA to produce more than one spine label per entry. On request multiple spine labels are now produced for five cents each on a program separate from the bibliographic program. These sorts of computer uses are mundane when compared to the as-yet-unmentioned potentials a database with manipulation and COM capabilities holds for the future of libraries. Field searching is certainly possible but instead of Blackwell/North America becoming an online information retrieval system, tapes of the local database may be made available for local computers of smaller capacity. The B/NA program can merge and manipulate the local databases of any combination of subscribing libraries. Klamath County and Lane County Law Libraries in Oregon, also entering the B/NA system, can produce union catalogs with the University of Oregon Law Library to show the legal research resources available in middle and southern Oregon. Attorneys, legislators and other libraries will find these COM catalogs available to them for free or for the minimal costs of their reproduction. As other libraries enter the B/NA system such catalogs foreshadow a future of shared acquisitions, greater cooperative lending, joint storage facilities and other considerations of networking, as well as shared cataloging information.

Blackwell/North America is not resting on its current services and products. Already there is some discussion of satellite communication links between Blackwell/North America and the British Library Automated Information Service (BLAISE), an online interactive system with four million UK MARC records in its database. Blackwell/North America access to BLAISE may encourage B/NA to become an interactive, online service for subscribing libraries. Even if it does not, the Blackwell/North America computer system has thus far proven satisfactory for the bibliographic control purposes of the University of Oregon Law Library and brings the promise of the future somewhat closer to fulfillment.

Bibliography

Aveney, Brian and Ghikas, Mary Fischer. "600 Users Meet the COM Catalog," American Libraries, 10 (February 1979), 82-83.
Baker, Alfred W., Boots, Frederick, and Pultz, Donald. Automation at the Fairfax County Virginia Library System. Tempe, Ariz.: LARC Association, 1975.
Blackburn, Robert H. Management Experience with COM Catalogues in a Large Academic Library. Toronto: 1977.
_____. "Two Years With a Closed Catalog," Journal of Academic Librarianship, 4 (January 1979), 424-429.
Bright, Franklyn F. "New Catalog for UW--Madison: Work of the Steering Committee on Bibliographic Control," Wisconsin Library Bulletin, 75 (May-June 1979), 129-130, 132.
Christoffersson, John G. "Automation at the University of Georgia Libraries," Journal of Library Automation, 21 (March 1979), 22-39.
Cox, Carolyn M. and Juergens, Bonnie. Microform Catalogs: A Viable Alternative for Texas Libraries. Dallas, TX: AMIGOS Bibliographic Council, 1977.
"Fairfax County Public Library: COMCAT (Computer Output Microfilm Catalog) Is Coming!" Virginia Librarian, 21 (December 1975), 15-16.
"First Card-To-Micro Catalog Claimed by Harford, MD.," Library Journal, 101 (May 15, 1976), 1164.
Hall, Agnez. "Computer-Produced Book Catalogues for New Brunswick Public Library System," APLA Bulletin, 41 (1977), 33-35.
Harbord, H. "Computer Catalogue at the Dartmouth Regional Library," APLA Bulletin, 41 (1977), 31-32.
Hewitt, Joe A. "Planning for the Adoption of AACR-2 at the University of North Carolina-Chapel Hill," North Carolina Libraries, 37 (Summer 1979), 5-14.
Hill, J. and Brown, N. A. "COM Catalogues at the University of Guelph Library," Microform Review, 7 (July 1978), 213-216.
Hodgkinson, L. "Computerisation in the Lancashire Library," Program, 9 (October 1975), 184-197.
Horny, Karen L. "NOTIS-3 (Northwestern On-Line Total Integrated System): Technical Service Application," Library Resources and Technical Services, 22 (Fall 1978), 361-367.
Hyatt, Dennis Ray. "COM Catalog vs. Card Catalog: The Experience of the University of Oregon Law Library," Law Library Journal, 71 (November 1978), 668-672.
Kao, Yasuko. "The Retrospective Conversion Project at the University of Utah Marriott Library," Utah Libraries, 22 (Spring 1979), 39-43.

Kloepper, D. "Nebraska Union Catalog on COM? Not Enough!" Nebraska Library Association Quarterly, 9 (Spring 1978), 17-18.
Kopischke, J. L. "Community & Technical Colleges Get COM Catalog," Nebraska Library Association Quarterly, 8 (Winter 1977), 4.
Kuhner, D. A. "Sprague Library Adopts Microfiche Catalog," Sci-Tech News, 29 (July 1975), 84.
"L. A. County PL Establishes a Series of Firsts by Converting to a COM Catalog," Advanced Technology/Libraries, 6 (September 1977), 2-3.
"LA Public Library Moves to COM," Journal of Library Automation, 10 (December 1977), 377.
Le Croissette, J. C. "Microfilm Catalogs in a British Public Library System," Microform Review, 4 (April 1975), 104-107.
Leide, John. Development of Automated Systems at Columbia University Libraries. Tempe, Ariz.: LARC Association, 1975.
"Los Angeles & Cook Co. Switch to COM," Library Journal, 103 (January 1, 1978), 10.
"Michigan Public Libraries Converting to COM: Lower Costs a Major Factor," Advanced Technology/Libraries, 5 (January 1976), 1-2.
Michigan State University Libraries. Cataloging Coordinating Committee. "Closing the Card Catalogs in the Michigan State University Libraries: A Discussion Paper," Alternative Catalog Newsletter, No. 7 (October 1978), 1-32.
"Microfilmed Catalog Slated for Baltimore Co.," Library Journal, 100 (May 1, 1975), 802.
Moore, Sharon. "AACR2's Impact on Southampton University's Catalogue, An Analysis," VINE, 31 (November 1979), 19-25.
Morrison, Elizabeth Stecher. "RMIT COM Catalogue Study Results," Australian Library Journal, 24 (October-November 1975), 384-389.
North, John. "Card Catalog to COM," Library Journal, 102 (October 15, 1977), 2132-2134.
O'Brien, P. M. "COM Comes to the Chicago Public Library," Illinois Librarian, 60 (April 1978), 397-402.
Rogers, J. A. "From Cards to COM in St. Louis County," Unabashed Librarian, No. 25 (1977), 27-29.
Schwarz, Philip J. COM: Decisions and Applications in a Small University Library. Stout, WI: University of Wisconsin November 1976. ED 135 391.
"Southampton University Library Changes Over From COM Film to COM Fiche Catalogues," Program, 11 (July 1977), 115-116.
"University of Toronto Announces the Availability of Machine-Readable Catalog Records," Journal of Library Automation, 10 (March 1977), 87-88.
"University of Birmingham: Microfiche Trial," VINE, No. 20 (February 1978), 14-17.
"University of Toronto Closes Public Card Catalog and Initiates COM Catalog," Journal of Library Automation, 10 (March 1977), 85.
Wintour, B. J. C. and McDowell, B. "Automation at the New University of Ulster," Program, 10 (April 1976), 60-74.

INDEX

AACR 10, 15, 57, 60
AACR-2 1-5, 7-11, 14-15, 33, 35-36, 38-39, 59, 60-62, 64, 69, 71-73, 76-77, 81, 90-93, 221, 227-228, 239, 277-280, 288
ALA see American Library Association
Access 21
Access points 2, 222-223
American Library Association 7, 9-10, 14
Anglo-American Cataloging Rules see AACR
Anglo-American Cataloguing Rules, Second edition see AACR-2
Association of Research Libraries 7-8, 10
Association of Research Libraries' Management Review and Analysis Program see MRAP
Audit trials 187-188
Author/title catalog 44
Authority control 13-15, 40, 52-53, 57, 64, 109-110, 120, 211, 228-229
Authority file 3, 15, 39, 92, 212, 280
Authority record 15
Automated circulation system 216-217

B/NA 148-155, 320-327
BALLOTS 116, 203, 225, 229
BIBNET 117-118
Bidding, competitive 249
Blackwell North America, Inc. see B/NA
Book catalog 2, 4, 46, 68, 99-100, 109-110, 119-122, 126-127, 209-210, 224, 228, 291-295, 309-310
  Cost 127, 224, 295, 312-313
  Preparation 291-295
  Use study 312-319
Branch library catalogs 292-294, 304-307
Budget 217-218

CARDS 48
CARDSET 122-123
CIP 48, 69, 122, 130
COM catalog 2, 4, 10-13, 22-23, 25, 40, 46, 52, 56, 60-61, 63-64, 68, 100, 122-124, 128, 134-135, 140-153, 155-171, 175-188, 209-213, 223-224, 228, 273-276, 296-311, 315-327
  Cost 123, 176-177, 184-185, 223-224, 275, 303-304, 312-313, 320-321, 324-325
  Use 123, 170, 211, 310, 312

Use study 155-171, 315-319
Preparation 273-276
Supplements 162-167, 169, 312
CRT Terminals 115-117, 133, 179
 Cost 133
Call Number Query System 208, 210
Canadian Association of Research Libraries 7
Card Catalog 1-2, 8, 17-18, 30-34, 37, 42-43, 51-52, 141, 155-171, 320-327
 Use study 312-319
Cathode Ray Tube terminals see CRT terminals
Closing the card catalog 3-4, 7-8, 22, 34, 36, 38-39, 45-48, 59, 60-61, 70-75, 84-89, 205-206, 209, 277
 Cost 61-62, 219-227
College Bibliocentre 141-142
Collocating function 77-78
Computer facilities (library-dedicated) 263-264
Computer facilities (non-library-dedicated) 215-216, 259, 263-264
Computer-Output-Microfilm see COM
Conversion 2, 4, 25, 52, 68, 99, 120-121, 196-198, 204, 221-222, 229-230, 266-276, 300-307
 Cost 4, 197-198, 220-222, 275, 303-304
 Staff 268, 270, 273
 Statistics 268, 270
Conversion, Cooperative 4, 221
Conversion by commercial vendors 68, 204, 221
Cost 8, 21, 52, 61-62, 68, 79, 133-134, 136, 147, 176-177, 183-185, 206, 245, 253
Cost effectiveness 53, 61, 68, 133, 204-205, 222
Council on Library Resources 14
Cross reference 3, 23, 69, 81, 120

"Day 1" 7, 15, 25, 61, 65, 277-279
Delay in catalog closing/freezing 7-16
Departmentation 260-261
Desuperimposition 8, 10, 14-15, 33, 45, 59, 75, 77, 79
Deterioration 37, 44, 287
Dictionary catalog 44, 278, 324

Editing 15, 142-145, 293, 306

Farmington Plan 130
Filing 1-3, 10, 22, 36-38, 43-45, 81, 120, 136, 142, 210, 221, 277-278, 282
Freezing the card catalog 1, 3-4, 7-10, 15, 46, 67-68, 155, 198, 277-282

INCOLSA 88
ISBD 56-57, 91

Index 333

ISBN 211
Impact studies 11
Incompatibility rate 59, 62-63, 69
Index/register file 15
Institutional commitment 196, 213-214
Interlibrary loan 12, 100, 252-253, 299
International Standard Bibliographic Description see ISBD
International Standard Bibliographic Number see ISBN
International standardization 9

Juvenile title catalog 303

Key-word indexing 32

Library Catalog Reader (LCR) 500 124
Library of Congress 1, 3-5, 7-8, 10-11, 13-14, 30-31, 33-36, 38, 45-48, 52-53, 58-59, 69, 271
   Add-on Catalog 278-279
   Classification 281
   New Catalog 278-280
   Old Catalog 277, 282
   Shelflisting 281
Library of Congress card service 48-49, 69
Line-printer produced catalog cards 118-119, 134-135
Linking 3, 14, 23, 36, 38, 61, 63, 70, 82, 236, 282

MARC 9, 11, 12, 35, 45, 47-48, 57, 59, 62, 68-69, 109, 122, 128, 148, 222, 229, 239, 244, 246, 251, 275, 278, 303, 320-322
MRAP 206, 250
Machine readable (LC) cataloging see MARC
Management decisions 197, 238-240, 242-265
Menu 16
Microform frame layout 152-153, 175, 274, 297
Microform readers 11-12, 123-124, 128, 135, 150, 152, 158-159, 298, 304
   Cost 12, 135, 177
   Ease of use 100, 149, 158-159, 162, 169, 210, 310-312, 316-318
   Frequency of use 159-164, 310-312, 316-319
   Location 158-159, 176
Music cataloging 40

Name authority file see Authority file
National Cataloging Distribution Center 53
Non-book materials 267
Non-Roman alphabet 33, 40, 208, 222, 236, 279
Nonprint media 53-54, 222

OCLC 2-3, 12, 14, 45, 52, 58, 60, 68-69, 84-86, 88, 100, 109-110, 115-118, 133, 203, 221, 225, 229, 266, 299, 303
OCR 292-293, 301
Ohio College Library Center see OCLC
On-line catalog 4, 10, 25, 39, 46, 68, 84-86, 100, 115-124, 128-129, 133, 136, 179-188, 210, 224-225, 228, 253
   Cost 133, 136, 183-184, 224-225
   Retrieval and output speed 180-182
   System design 179-180
On-line catalog systems 2, 12-13, 115-117
Optical character reader (recognition) see OCR

Personnel 198, 217, 257-260
Physical condition of catalogs/cards 32, 37, 44, 68
Planning 3-5, 19, 26-27, 35, 39, 42, 202-204, 206-213, 227-254

ROM III Reader 123-124, 304, 315
Real time 185
Retrospective conversion see Conversion

Search key 16
Search time 32
"See also" 36, 49, 70
Serials 3, 74-83, 175-178, 208, 235-236, 281, 326
Serials check-in 85, 282
Special purpose catalogs 56
Split files 60, 63, 76, 170, 324
Staff involvement 4, 92, 237, 250-251
Staffing considerations 70, 250-251, 257-259
Standardization 12, 75, 108-110
Subject access 14, 32-33, 84-85, 105-106, 152, 221
Subject headings 13, 33, 52, 62, 69, 105-108, 142, 278, 280
Superimposition 7, 16, 35-36, 39, 45-46, 60, 69
Systems development 13, 248

Tree 16

UTLAS 141, 229-230
Union List of Serials (ULS) 76
University of Toronto Library Automation System see UTLAS
Update of information 176, 182
User edication to machine assisted catalog 24-25, 40, 85
User needs 2-3, 19-20, 78, 106
User studies 10, 19-20, 105-106, 130, 149-152, 156-171, 206, 238, 311-312, 316-318

VDU (Visual Display Unit) 133

Work flow 261-263

LIBRARY OF DAVIDSON COLLEGE